A Network of Objects

Other VNR Communications Books . . . .

- EDI Guide: A Step by Step Approach. *By Edward Cannon*
- NetView: IBM's Network Management Product. *By Alfred Charley*
- Doing Business on the Internet. *By Mary J. Cronin*
- Routing in Today's Internetworks. *By Mark Dickie*
- EDI: A Total Management Guide, 2nd Edition. *By Margaret A. Emmelhainz, Ph.D*
- Digital Signal Processing in Communications. *By Marvin E. Frerking*
- Broadband Networking. *By Lawrence Gasman*
- Data Communications Test and Troubleshooting, 2nd Edition. *By Gilbert Held*
- Mastering PC Communications Software. *By Gilbert Held*
- Working With NetWare: For Network Supervisors and Users. *By Gilbert Held*
- The Complete Cyberspace Reference and Directory. *By Gilbert Held*
- Low-Cost E-Mail With UUCP: Integrating Unix, DOS, Windows and Mac. *By Thomas Wm. Madron*
- Analyzing DECNET/OSI Phase V. *By Carl Malamud*
- Analyzing Novell Networks. *By Carl Malamud*
- Analyzing Sun Networks. *By Carl Malamud*
- The Handbook of International Connectivity Standards. *Edited by Gary R. McClain*
- Networking NT: Using Windows NT in the Corporate LAN Environment. *By Christopher Monro*
- The Illustrated Network Book: A Graphic Guide to Understanding Computer Networks. *By Matthew G. Naugle*
- Making Telecommuting Happen: A Guide for Telemanagers and Telecommuters. *By Jack M. Nilles*
- JPEG Still Image Data Compression Standard. *By William B. Pennebaker and Joan L. Mitchell*
- X.500 Directory Services: Technology and Deployment. *By Sara Radicati*
- SNA: IBM'S Systems Network Architecture. *By Stephen J. Randesi and Donald H. Czubek*
- Using Wireless Communications in Business. *By Andrew M. Seybold*
- Network Topology Optimization. *By Roshan Lal Sharma*
- Communications Standard Dictionary, 2nd Edition. *By Martin H. Weik, DSc.*

Thomas C. Tsai

A Network of Objects

How to Lower Your Computing Costs and Improve Your Applications Delivery

VNR

VAN NOSTRAND REINHOLD
I(T)P A Division of International Thomson Publishing Inc.

New York • Albany • Bonn • Boston • Detroit • London • Madrid • Melbourne
Mexico City • Paris • San Francisco • Singapore • Tokyo • Toronto

Copyright © 1995 by Van Nostrand Reinhold
I(T)P™ A division of International Thomson Publishing Inc.
      The ITP logo is a trademark under license

Printed in the United States of America
For more information, contact:

Van Nostrand Reinhold
115 Fith Avenue
New York, NY 10003

International Thomson Publishing GmbH
Königswinterer Strasse 418
53227 Bonn
Germany

International Thomson Publishing Europe
Berkshire House 168-173
High Holborn
London WCIV 7AA
England

International Thomson Publishing Asia
221 Henderson Road #05-10
Henderson Building
Singapore 0315

Thomas Nelson Australia
102 Dodds Street
South Melbourne, 3205
Victoria, Australia

International Thomson Publishing Japan
Hirakawacho Kyowa Building, 3F
2-2-1 Hirakawacho
Chiyoda-ku, 102 Tokyo
Japan

Nelson Canada
1120 Birchmount Road
Scarborough, Ontario
Canada M1K 5G4

International Thomson Editores
Campos Eliseos 385, Piso 7
Col. Polanco
11560 Mexico D.F. Mexico

1 2 3 4 5 6 7 8 9 10 QEBFF 1 00 99 98 97 96 95 94

Library of Congress Cataloging-in-Publication Data
Tsai, T. C. (Thomas C.),   1949–
    A network of objects / Thomas C. Tsai.
       p.   cm.
    Includes bibliographical references and index.
    ISBN 0-442-01933-5
    1. Client/server computing.   2. Management information systems.
3. Object-oriented programming (Computer science)   4. Computer
networks.   I. Title
QA76.9.C55T75   1994
004'.36—dc20   94-31519
                                                          CIP

This book would not have been possible without the generous support and the sacrifices of many hours of family time by my wife, Peggy and my son, Michael to whom this book is dedicated.

TRADEMARKS

TABLE OF CONTENTS

PREFACE

This book is written for information systems (IS) professionals who are contemplating transforming their organization's host-based computing platform to a client server computing platform.

Computer platform transformation, unlike individual application development, involves everything from an organization's business strategy to the wiring in the office building. Success depends upon a good understanding of many diverse technologies by those who participate in it.

To make informed decisions about client server technology, IS professionals must acquire a certain level of technology and technical knowledge. Today's IS professionals have seen a rapid succession of technologies and products come and go, and many vendor alliances form and dissolve. IS professsionals today face a constant barrage of widely divergent views on client server technology from their colleagues and suppliers. Indeed, confusion permeates the field.

However, few good and impartial reference materials exist that synthesize the "big picture" in a manner that can help IS professionals to ask the right questions and to formulate the right strategies for their organization. This book is intended to serve this function. The thrust of this book is neither product-specific nor technically intensive. It does, however, use many existing commercial products as examples.

Transformation to a client server computing platform should never be done as an exercise in installing new hardware and software. Cost reduction alone will not justify client server. The proper way to install a client server platform is to include it as part of an organization-wide re-engineering effort.

The intelligent use of information can help management and workers to spot weaknesses in the system and opportunities for better system use. Managing a modern business enterprise without making good use of available information resources and technologies is like flying a Boeing 747 without using its instrument panel. It is feasible but highly inefficient.

In the world of commerce, competitive advantages do not last long. Not long ago we all had to stand in line in a bank to cash our checks. Today, no one can imagine getting into retail banking without automatic teller machines, or running an airline without an online reservation system.

In the past, technology was developed to meet needs. Now technology is inventing applications. The challenge for management is to make strategic use of information as a continuous mode of operation in their organization, not as a one-time exercise.

This book examines the forces behind the client server technology. It also shows how today's barriers to data access, data integration, data presentation, and data analysis can be overcome by a client server computing infrastructure that is based on the twin technologies of network computing and object-oriented programming.

On their own, neither network computing nor object-oriented programming offers significant benefits. However, when they work together, these two technologies provide an integration platform for "legacy" applications, data warehouse applications, and client server applications.

Network computing allows programs residing in different computers to work together to produce useful results. Network computing breaks down the barriers in data access and it enables application tasks to run on the computer hardware and software that are best suited to those tasks. It simplifies addition of new applications and prolongs the lives of existing ones.

The net benefits of network computing are lower computing costs, improved application delivery, easier data accesses, tighter data integration, friendlier user interfaces, and more effective use of information resources.

Object-oriented programming treats data and programs as inseparable components. Information presented through software objects is easier to understand. An object-oriented approach to building applications is like building houses with pre-built or slightly modified parts: it promotes the reuse of program code and hence, lowers the cost of application development.

In this book, we take a highly granular view of objects. An object can be an entire application or merely a single code fragment. Object technology offers a second generation model for the client server, to which objects can make requests as clients make requests to servers, and as servers make requests to other clients. A network of objects, in which objects communicate by sending and responding to requests, provides the best price performance for your application needs.

Network computing and object-oriented programming are two very profound and fast-changing subjects. A book of this size and intent cannot give these two subjects full and updated treatment. This book tries to present the basic concepts of the two technologies: How each works. What to look for when implementing them in an organization. How to make them work for a particular situation. The book assumes that readers are familiar with the products and practices of the data processing industry in North America.

Chapter One examines the driving forces behind network computing, object-oriented programming, and client server architecture. It explains the four barriers to strategic use of information resources by business enterprises of today: data access, data integration, data presentation, and data analysis.

Chapter Two is about a network computing model on which client server applications run. The Open System Interconnection (OSI) Reference Model is used as the benchmark for comparison of functions of various commercial products.

Chapter Three is about object-oriented programming. In this chapter, the concepts of objects, object-oriented programming languages, and object-oriented database management systems are reviewed. Brief descriptions of the C++ programming language and Microsoft's Visual Basic are used to illustrate the power of object-oriented programming.

Chapter Four deals with the real world implementation of the bottom four layers of the OSI Reference Model, known in this book as the "network transport environment." The key components of each layer and the respective commercial products are reviewed. Specifically, TCP/IP is used to explain the working of a typical transport protocol.

Chapter Five deals with the real world implementation of the top three layers of the OSI Reference Model, which are identified in this book as the "network operating system" to denote its functional similarities with a host operating system. HP's Network Computing System (NCS) is chosen for in-depth review because of its textbook-like architecture.

Chapter Six is about IBM's System Network Architecture (SNA). Since this book is about changing the computing platform, a good understanding of the largest installed network computing base is necessary. Special emphasis is placed on IBM's network computing strategy regarding Advanced Program-to-Program Communication (APPC) and Advanced Peer-to-Peer Network (APPN).

Chapter Seven reviews the critical application servers in a client server environment. These include the database server, the transaction server, the electronic mail server, the directory server, and the object server. In particular, the relational database server is reviewed in greater detail for its key role in client server application.

Chapter Eight suggests an eight-step planning and implementation process to transform a host-based computing environment to a client server network computing environment. It shows the importance of a strategic blueprint for an information architecture. It shows how network computing and object-orientation can solve today's problems of data integration, data access, data presentation, and data analysis.

1

The Winds of Change

INTRODUCTION

Why network computing and object oriented programming now? One has to look both backward and forward in time to find the answer. By looking back, one can find what makes these two long-known technical concepts acceptable now but not before. By looking forward, one sees the business benefits that point to the inevitable future growth of the information processing industry.

1.1   GLOBAL DIGITIZATION

The mass production of microprocessors has started a revolution in the 1980s that is still changing the course of human civilization. The impact of the microprocessor will be no less than that of the printing press, gun powder, the compass, and the steam engine.

The ability to transfer vast amounts of repetitive activities of human reasoning and information processing to microprocessors has freed humans to make things and perform activities that were unimaginable a few decades ago.

Software, like the steam engine of the Industrial Revolution, is now the driving force behind our economy: manufacturing, farming, financial services, medical services, biotechnology, the entertainment industry, education methods, aerospace, and the sciences. Today most household products use some form of microprocessor technology for their creation or operation.

This global "digitization" of almost everything also means that we now have

1

much better communication networks for applications, and linked with places, that were unimaginable a few years ago. Indeed, our world has become a global village in which everyone is a neighbor.

1.1.1 The Software Dilemma

Although computers are increasingly called upon to help solve real-world problems, software products are still difficult to develop and to use. Software development, even of modest complexity, requires highly-trained professionals. For end users, most business applications are tedious to learn and difficult to use. Many end users work with computers because they are forced to, not because they want to.

The traditional host-based computing platforms and procedural programming methods have proven to be incapable of satisfying users' needs for friendlier systems and the system professionals' needs for higher productivity. Network computing and object-oriented programming are the two technologies that can be used to overcome many of the cost and productivity barriers. These technologies are made possible by microprocessors, without which both network computing and object-oriented programming would have been too expensive to implement.

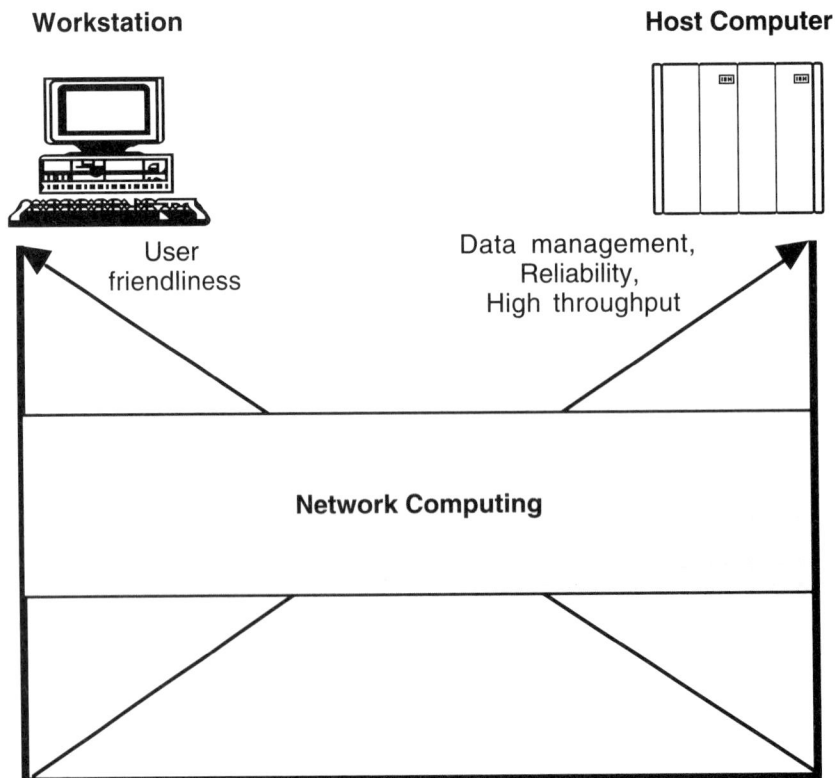

Workstation

Host Computer

User
friendliness

Data management,
Reliability,
High throughput

Network Computing

Figure 1–1. Network computing brings together the strong points of host computers and workstations

1.1.1.1 Client Server Computing

On its own, a microprocessor-based workstation is capable of providing more intuitive ways to present information to users. This type of workstation is incapable of storing and managing large amounts of data, however. On the other hand, in a host computer, because of its immense input / output capability, much larger "unit" of work can be executed more efficiently.

Through network computing, the strong points of both technologies can be brought together to give users a friendly interface and access to powerful functions and to the vast amount of data available on host computers. This new infrastructure, as illustrated in Figure 1–1, is known as client server computing, to which this book is dedicated.

1.1.1.2 Upstarts vs. Establishment

The widely available and affordable microprocessors have ended the hegemony enjoyed by a small number of mainframe and mini computer manufacturers throughout 1970s and 1980s. Smaller, yet often more innovative upstarts in the late 1980s—such as Intel, MIPS, Microsoft, Borland, Novell, Sequent, Sun Microsystems, and Apple—produced hardware and software products that have turned the market into a red-hot competitive arena for new applications and new customers.

Without exception, network computing, object-oriented programming, and client server architecture are the center pieces around which new products are designed. The broader selection of hardware and software has also changed the relationship between the traditional systems professionals and their users. Powerful workstations and servers connected by local area networks costing thousands of dollars instead of mainframes costing millions are within the budget of the smaller user departments. Many previous "dumb" users are now quite adept in producing professional-looking reports and querying databases with a deluge of end user tools.

Microprocessor technology has indeed "liberated" end users from their total dependence upon the IS department. On the other hand, it has also pushed IS professionals to find faster and better ways to deliver applications to the end users.

1.2 THE GLOBAL ECONOMY

Today some 3 billion people from the third world are joining the world economy. Over the next ten years, they will want to be manufacturers. The results will be the biggest global reallocation of industrial products. The way that the poor countries have to pull themselves up is by exploiting competitive advantages like cheap labor.

A complacent attitude toward information resources could be tolerated in the 1950s and 60s when the United States had a commanding lead in all manufacturing sectors. Now, the rest of the world has caught up. The competition for customers will get more intense.

Advanced countries such as the United States and Canada have no choice but to work harder in developing new industries ranging from raising cattle to building space shuttles. Resources of all kinds including capital, labor, and information are necessary to maximize business performance.

Much of these economic readjustments are driven by and depend upon the innovative uses of information technology and information resources.

1.3   STRATEGIC USES OF INFORMATION

An enterprise's information resources features two strategic aspects. The first is the information flow. The second is the information itself.

1.3.1   The Information Flow

In turn the strategic use of information flow has two aspects. The first is within an enterprise. The second is with outside business partners.

1.3.1.1   The Internal Flow

All commercial activities depend upon the exchange of information. Such exchanges are referred to as business processes. They range from a customer placing an order and getting a receipt to a research engineer passing on his drawings to the production department. These activities are typically repetitive. Computing technology has already been used to automate a significant portion of them, such as:

- Issuing paychecks
- Taking customer orders
- Measuring the temperature of a boiler
- Controlling robotics welding machines
- Designing buildings and machines
- Controlling the flight path of an aircraft

The last quarter century of computer automation has occurred within "islands" of business processes: accounting, process control, marketing, payroll, and so on. These islands are made up of applications running on mainframes and mini computers.

Typically these applications do not "talk" to each other. Exchanges between them are carried out at manual speed and on paper. In fact, many people argued that much of the white collar work force within a large organization is consumed in performing some form of communication tasks between these islands, which typically are categorized as administrative activities. Computer technology had not yet advanced far enough to bridge these islands.

Today, availability of faster networks and computers allows development of a new breed of applications to bridge these islands and to enable some form of enterprise wide automation. This higher level of automation knocks down the barriers between these islands. It reduces or eliminates much of the administrative activities that add no value to the final goods or services delivered to the customers.

Like the automation of the previous era, business processes must be adjusted accordingly. This adjustment is commonly known as the **Business Processes Re-Engineering (BPR)**.

BPR is the main instrument by which much of the downsizing of the white collar worker group in the 1990s is enacted.

Traditional Top-Down Hierarchical Organization

An Information-Enabled Organization

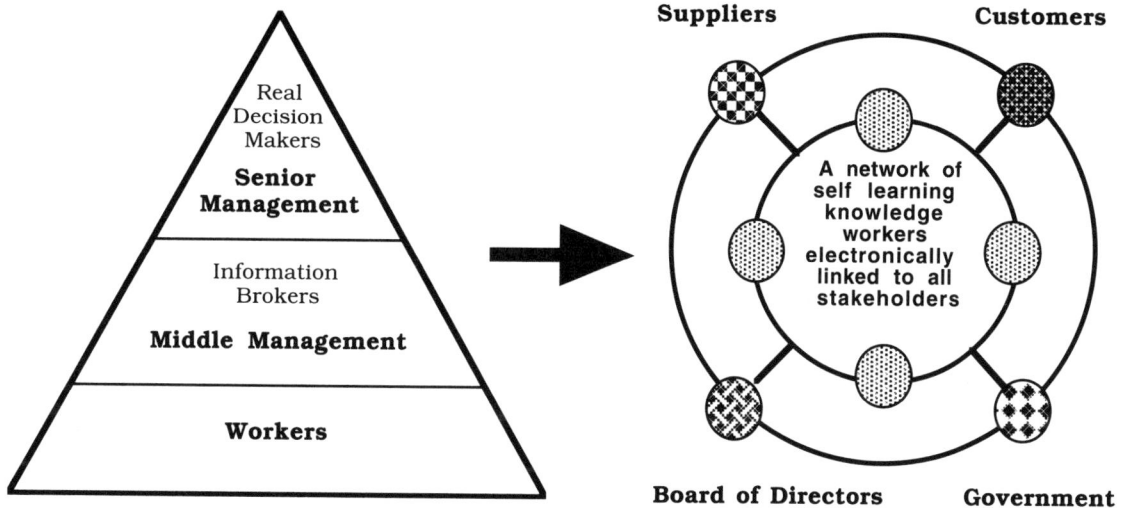

Figure 1–2. New Paradigm in business organizations

The Management Revolution

The main casualties of business processes re-engineering themselves have not been the "worker" but the so called "middle" management. The "downsizing" that is happening in large companies in the 1990s is changing the traditional management style.

As shown in Figure 1–2, senior managers can no longer depend upon the much thinned out middle managers—"information brokers"—to generate summaries and analysis. They must be given direct accesses to all relevant and accurate data. The hierarchical organization of the past has given way to a structure which consists of a network of knowledge and workers who are empowered by today's information technology.

Computer automation has moved from the sales counters and shop floors to the executive suites. For commercial enterprises, this automation of a higher order, the decision support level, is the point at which network computing and object-oriented programming technologies will have the highest impact.

1.3.1.2 The External Flow

With client server technology, the flow of information does not have to be restricted to the inside of an enterprise. Network computing enables electronic information flow to suppliers, customers, government agencies, and business partners. Wise use of the flow of information has created a number of commercial success stories, and certainly many more will come.

A major retailer in the U.S. linked its computer systems with its top 200 suppliers to provide warehouse and sales information online in return for faster, more frequent deliveries. Suppliers can now forecast demands for their products, while retailers strengthen their supply network, reduce inventory, and improve product availability.

Other successful examples include the frequently-cited American Airline's Saber seat reservation system through which thousands of travel agents across the globe are tied to the same data base. All of a sudden, the system is not only for reserving tickets on an airplane. It becomes the hub of all activities involved in traveling—hotels, limousines, cruises, and so forth. In fact, it is now a more "valuable" asset to the company than its fleet of aircraft!

In April 1994, Ford Motor Company announced that it plans to spend 100 million U.S. dollars to install digital satellite communication dishes at 6500 dealer sites in North America. Ford did not say exactly what those are for, but certainly Ford is not about to compete with AT&T at the dealers' sites!

To survive and to thrive in the global economy, one must aggressively go after problems with technology solutions.

1.3.2 The Information Itself

Although business records are generated by computer applications instead of by hand, the records themselves often meet the same fate of their paper counterparts. They are viewed by many as paperwork, a necessary "evil" in doing business.

Typically, we are so focused on the daily tasks that we tend to overlook what have been recorded until something has gone "wrong." Records that are stored on reels of magnetic tapes are mostly collecting dusts in the vaults. This often leaves some unanswered questions:

- How does senior management know their company does not have a "cancer" that is threatening its competitive position or survival although individual business lines appear to be doing OK?
- What are the hidden costs of the unintegrated application islands? How much time do middle managers and planners spend gathering information and analyzing it?

- What is the impact on sales volume if the merchandise is placed in the front rather than the back of a supermarket?
- What are the missed opportunities of not being able to spot a trend sooner than one's competitors?

Most managers do NOT have answers to these simple questions. Their decision-making relies on a combination of experience and intuition instead of on accurate information. This is not to say that experience and intuition are unimportant. The issue, however, is that managers could have made better use of information resources to augment their experiences and intuitions to make better business decisions.

Management cannot answer those questions partly because their information resources, which are distributed in individual application systems, are hard to access, often the information is not accurate, is not subject to easy analysis, and is difficult to read. They do not have a computing platform that ties together all their information resources.

Competing in today's market is tough enough. Making decisions without the full confidence that the project is based upon the best available information is something that you should and can avoid.

Knowing the data is no guarantee that a business will become more profitable. It means that the users have a solid foundation based on the strategic use of the information resources is now possible. Without such knowledge, managers would have to rely solely on intuition and experience in making business decisions.

The situation is like flying an old DC-3 instead of a Boeing 747. The on-board computer on a Boeing 747 gives a pilot better control over the aircraft and without this control, flying in difficult weather conditions could be dangerous, if not outright impossible.

1.3.3 Technology Seeks Solutions

In the 1990s, dis-inflationary economy has been caused by technology changes and globalization of trade. The new game is to learn what customers are willing to pay for a product, then reverse engineer the corporate process to hit that target. Instead of price being based on a company's cost, price now drives the cost. Speed, flexibility, and innovations are the keys to success.

Strategic use of information resources will enable a business enterprise to improve the productivity of their knowledge workers, to see patterns in their business more readily, to base decisions on real information, to integrate the various, diverse activities of the enterprise, to improve market analysis, to run their operation more efficiently, to provide better customer service, and ultimately to gain competitive advantage.

Looking at the strategic value of information requires a paradigm shift in thinking by management. One does not simply look at an invoice as a piece of paper that must be produced with accuracy every month. It is a resource like any other resource such as capital and labor. For instance:

- Why not show the trend of customer's purchases on the invoice?
- Why is the buying habits of one region so different from the others?
- Why must the invoice be sent via the post office?
- How about electronic fund transfers?

1.4   THE FOUR BARRIERS

What has been preventing businesses from embracing information resources in a more strategic way?

Four major barriers are inherent in today's host-based computing platforms. These barriers prevent users from making full use of their information resources. They are:

Data access
- inability to access information from various sources easily

Data integration
- lack of confidence in the quality of the information coming from various sources

Data presentation
- information cannot be easily presented in its "natural" state

Data analysis
- information cannot be easily analyzed in a dynamic manner

On their own, these applications are critical to the survival of the businesses they serve. However, the computing platforms on which they run are very difficult to integrate with one another. This disjointedness often means sub-optimal utilization of the available resources. In a competitive global economy, it could mean life and death of an enterprise.

These barriers are all interrelated. That is to say, the barrier to better data presentation cannot be solved without solving the problem of data access. Similarly, the barrier to better data access cannot be tackled without thinking about the impact on data integration.

The goal of an object-oriented and network based computing platform is to overcome these four barriers so that information technology and resources can be used to their maximum potential.

1.4.1   Data Access

Data access refers to the ability of a user to access the information he or she needs to do his or her job. The issue is not getting at the information. If we try hard enough, we can always get them. The issue is the ease with which information can be obtained.

Ease of access is important because users are not inclined to depend upon diffi-

cult-to-access information resources in decision-making. Today's information resources for commercial activities are so well hidden that management hardly see
any value for them. Imagine if the Boeing 747 cockpit computer were hard to
use, pilots would have continued to fly on manual.

A major goal for a network computing platform is to provide a user access to ANY
INFORMATION, at ANY TIME, and from ANY WHERE. This brings us to the
topic of application and technology islands found in many large organizations.

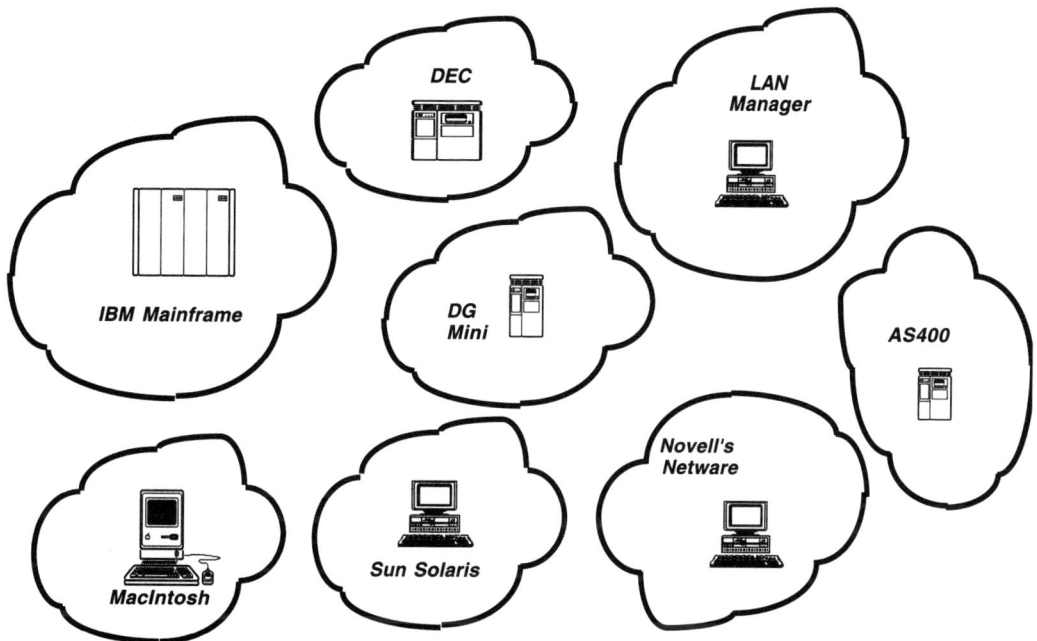

Figure 1–3. Application and technology islands

Figure 1–3 shows a typical situation in a large organization where incompatible
technology islands exist.

Today's host based platforms are designed to be proprietary and exclusive:
they can only communicate with its own kind. Different platforms cannot be easily connected because they have incompatible hardware and software.

Each island was brought to automate certain repetitive commercial processes.
Each application manages its own data and shares them with others either in the
form of paper reports or electronic file transfers. These islands work well for the
automation of realtime and routine, operational functions. If they did not, they
would not have survived their daily intensive usage.

Examples of successful application island abound. Plant operation staff like
their process control system. Marketing people are happy with their state-

of-the-art order processing system. Human Resources people are content with their batch payroll system. The Distribution Department is ecstatic about its new LAN-based inventory control system. The Engineering Department is making good use of the linear programming package in its departmental mini-computer. The invoicing system works well in producing monthly bills on time. The list goes on.

While application and technology islands serve the needs of individual departments, they are not as useful to the planning and corporate management staff who coordinate activities between divisions to achieve the corporate objectives. As shown in Figure 1–4, paper reports and manual efforts are the main access methods to information from the application islands. They face a data access problem.

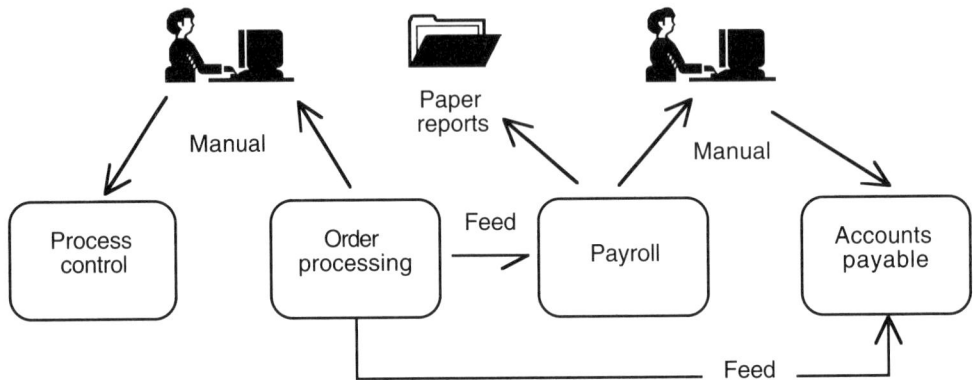

Figure 1–4. Application islands and their methods of integration

A main design goal of network computing is to enable a user to access all existing applications from a single point—the workstation in the user's office or from home. Easy access to the existing applications from a single point is important, as is the fact that platform must also allow easy addition of new application islands.

1.4.2   Data Integration

Making data available to users is one thing; organizing data in a manner that is useful to the organization is another. The goal of data integration is to enable users to get at relevant and accurate information.

Once again, data integration is typically NOT a serious problem in a line organization, where users cannot afford to have any data problem that would slow down their daily business. If the payroll system did not pay a person on time, that person would have screamed. If the invoicing system keeps on overbilling a person, he or she also would have screamed! On the other hand, corporate managers, planners, and coordinators have been given irreconcilable data from their line organizations.

An example is the "customer's address." One would expect that same customer name should have the same address for all systems, yet they are all different. For a marketing manager, the customer address means the address of the customer's purchasing manager. To the invoicing clerk, the customer address means the address of the customer's accounts payable department. To the warehouse person, the customer address means the customer's retail outlets. So if a clerk asks for the customer address for the same customer but from three different applications, the clerk will get three different answers and might then conclude erroneously that he or she is dealing with three different customers!

Data Modeling

To bring about data integration, system professionals have been turning to a new type of system development methods known variously as "information engineering," "software engineering," and "enterprise information planning."

A common goal in these methodologies is to generate an organization-wide data model or information architecture. The data model defines things and activities that must be carried out to achieve the goals and objectives of the organization as set out by senior management. This concept is reviewed in more detail in Chapter Eight: A Network of Objects.

Data modeling is an object-oriented approach to model "things" used in business transactions. The term entity describes a "thing." Examples of "things" are customers, customer orders, products, warehouses, and so on. The relationship between entities is documented in an entity-relationship diagram, which specifies how an entity can be updated, changed, or destroyed.

This is similar to the definition of an object. An object possesses both functions and properties (data). This will be discussed in more detail in Chapter Three: The Object Oriented Model.

The important point here is that both network computing and object-oriented programming will play an important role in ensuring an integrated and accessible data environment.

1.4.3 Data Presentation

Aside from accessible and accurate data, another barrier that must be overcome is the manner in which data is presented to users. We all live in a multi-media environment. We are surrounded by sounds, images, smells, and sensations. Although we use computers to simulate real life processes, our interactions with computers, that is the "user interface," have been based on one form of simple image: text and numbers.

Describing a circle is best through an image of a circle instead of an equation or rows of numbers. Describing a music score is best through sound instead of some notations on the computer screen. Describing the sales trend is best though a chart instead of rows of numbers on a report. Describing the impact of a meteor strike on a planet is best described through motion images (video) instead of rows of calculated numbers.

Therefore the issue with data representation is ability to present data in its "natural" state, the one that a human would have experienced with his eyes, ears, fingers, and (even) nose. This is what is known as "virtual reality."

In engineering design applications, data presented in the form of images and animation are already the norm. Object-oriented programming has been a key enabling technology for this phenomena.

Commercial data processing has quite a different story. Commercial data has always been presented in two dimensional paper and text. Until the so-called Graphical User Interface, (GUI), commercial data have suffered the syndrome of dullness to a degree that information resources are mostly overlooked as an electronic form of paperwork.

The GUI, with its array of new data presentation techniques such as charts, graphs, point and click, hyper-access, and drilldown, brings "alive" the commercial data.

Traditional programming languages were designed to solve problems using text and numbers as their principal data types. They translate things and activities into text and numbers. On the other hand, object-oriented programming languages are more powerful in dealing with complex multi-media data structure. Object-oriented programming will be discussed in more detail in Chapter Three.

1.4.4 Data Analysis

The last of the four barriers is the barrier to data analysis. Data analysis means how best to analyze data that will help a user to make business decisions. Here, we are talking about a new class of applications in the commercial world known as modeling or simulation.

Computerized simulators have been available to train pilots, drivers, golfers, surgeons, and others. Why not put a CEO at the helm of a simulator of his or her business? Can the simulator be used to try out new operational ideas, and to ask what-ifs?

A business simulator is an invaluable tool for the decisionmakers. The simulator will not make any decision, however—it can if if requested to do so. It helps those who will make decisions. In the commercial world, however, modeling the dynamic performance of an organization is slowly being recognized as an important tool for competing in the global economy. A good simulator must be able to present data in a more human-like fashion. Information resources, when properly managed, should represent a virtual state of the business enterprise. They will help management and workers to identify and correct weakness in their operations and indicate new opportunities.

Here again, object-oriented programming and network computing will be the most cost-effective platform for this type of applications by far.

We will devote a section in Chapter Eight: A Network of Objects to the discussion of this type of application.

2

The Network Computing Model

INTRODUCTION

The Open System Interconnection (OSI) Reference Model sets out the functional characteristics of the seven communication layers required for two application programs to exchange messages and achieve useful results.

Network computing, like any emerging technology, is full of confusing terms, hype, and jargon. The OSI Reference Model provides a standard against which all commercial products and can be compared.

This chapter introduces the basic concept of network computing using the OSI Reference Model. Examples in non-computer and computer communication are used to explain the OSI seven layers of protocols, and issues surrounding standards and terminology are discussed.

2.1 BASIC COMMUNICATION CONCEPTS

Seven layers of protocol are necessary to effect program-to-program communication on a network. The greatest advantage of having a layered architecture is to allow separation of duties among layers so that changes in one layer will not affect the others. This plug-and-play architecture ensures that the technology growth of each layer develops at its own pace, without having to hinder—or be hindered by—the overall development of the network.

The choice of seven layers is based on experience, intuition, common sense, and above all, a consensus among major players in the data processing industry.

The concept and specifications of the OSI seven layers are researched, sponsored, established, and documented by the International Organization for Standardization (ISO) OSI Reference Model. The hierarchy of these layers are:

- Application
- Presentation
- Session
- Transport
- Network
- Datalink
- Physical

OSI Standards vs. Reference Model

The OSI Standards and the OSI Reference Model are two distinct documents. The former are technical specifications for hardware and software products; the latter is a functional specification of the seven layers.

Significant OSI standards, especially those at the top three layers, are still evolving. Most commercial network products today do not comply with the OSI Reference Model, even though they perform similar functions. Nevertheless, the Model continues to be the best "yardstick" for comparing commercial network products and for understanding their function within the bigger picture of network computing.

2.1.1 The OSI Reference Model

A non-computer and a computer example are given below. These illustrate the OSI Reference Model's seven layer protocols.

2.1.1.1 A Non-Computer Example

Three factories are located in a high rise industrial building in New York City: a shoe factory, a garment factory, and a watch factory. Like all manufacturing concerns, these factories exchange documents with their trading partners: orders, invoices, specifications, and so forth.

In this example, readers should keep in mind that the factory building represents a computer, the three factories represent three separate applications inside the computer, and the correspondence between the manager and client represents a conversation session in a computer application.

The names of the OSI's seven layers of communication protocol also appear here for later reference even though their meaning may not be clear at present.

The communication begins with the manager of the shoe factory dictating a letter on his Dictaphone. The letter is a response to a Japanese client request. She gives her Dictaphone tape to her first secretary.

Application Layer

The first secretary types up the letter in draft form. She then gives the letter to the second secretary.

Presentation layer

The second secretary translates the content of the manager's letter to the language of the recipient, in this case, Japanese. This secretary's responsibility is to present the message to the outside world so that each correspondent can communicate in his or her own language, similar to the way diplomats communicate in a UN meeting. After he finishes, he passes the translated copy to the third secretary.

Session Layer

The third secretary types the translated copy in the company standard correspondence format, he assigns a reference number to the correspondence, makes a copy of the letter, records the mailing date in the record book, and puts the letter in an addressed envelope. These steps are followed so that the letter can be re-sent if the delivery system fails for any reason. The third secretary then puts the envelope in the out box of the Shoe Factory.

The third secretary has a number of choices on the delivery method: the letter could be sent by fax, by courier, or by electronic mail. The choice depends upon the rules that have been set up for the job. For example, one rule may say that all letters marked URGENT must be sent by fax. In this example, we chose the traditional postal service.

Transport Layer

The building messenger collects letters from the out boxes of the three factories in the building. The messenger's job is to deliver the mail to the nearby post office. The messenger does not know the content of the letters; he or she only recognizes the factory names on the envelopes.

Network Layer

In the post office, a postal clerk decides the route the letter must take to arrive in Tokyo. He or she has been given some guidelines on routing letters; perhaps all registered mail to Japan must go through San Francisco. Another instruction may require all registered mail not to go through more than three intermediate stops.

The postal clerk may decide that this letter will be sent to Japan via Chicago, Denver, San Francisco, and then on to Tokyo. The post office is not interested in the content of the letter, or in the out boxes of the factories. As long as the letter has a correct address and postage, the post office will deliver it.

Data Link Layer

Now the postal clerk can put the manager's letter in a postal bag destined to go to Chicago. A postal worker loads the bag onto a postal truck that is heading out to Kennedy Airport. Another set of rules governs the behavior of the traffic between New York and Chicago. One rule may say that the transfer between airports must be within 3 hours. Another rule may require that all registered mail must re-register after each intermediate stop.

Physical Layer

Trucks, planes, and trains deliver the postal bag to Chicago.

The Reverse Steps

Ultimately, the shoe factory manager's letter arrives at the Tokyo central post office. The letter goes through many stops before it arrives at the building where the client office is located.

Like its counterpart in New York, the messenger in that building will hand the manager's letter to the recipient's secretary. Like their counterparts in New York, the Japanese secretaries will ensure acknowledgment, translation, privacy protocols, etc. are observed before handing the letter to the Japanese recipient.

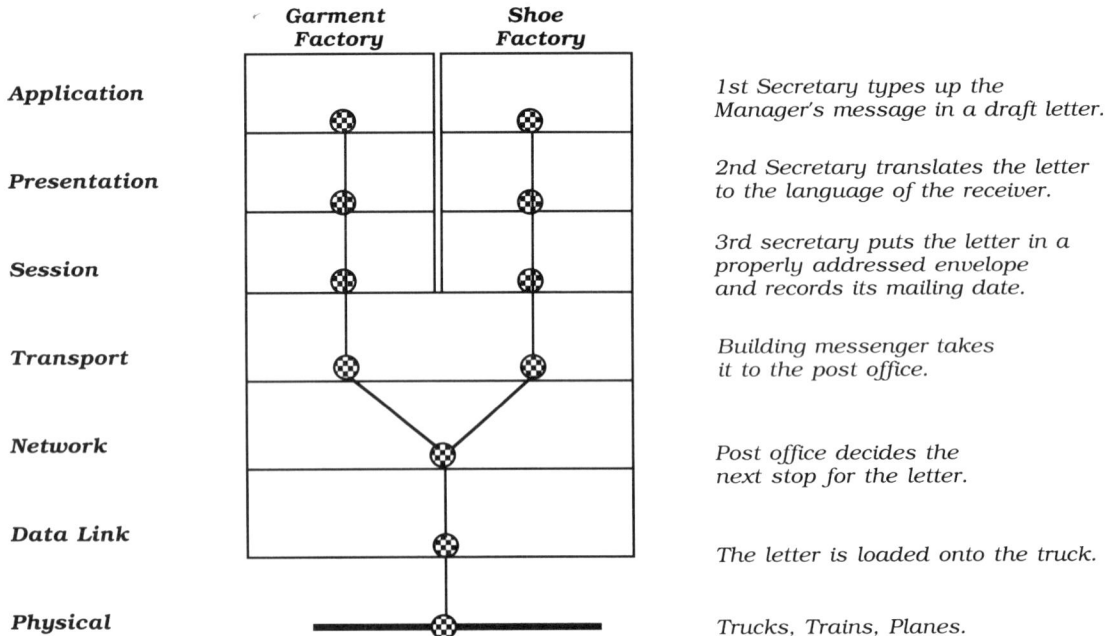

Figure 2–1. Seven layers equivalent of the non-computer example

Summary

Figure 2–1 represents the OSI seven layer equivalent of the non-computer communication process described above.

In Figure 2–1 notice that:

- the top three layers deal with the content of a message, and
- the bottom four layers deal with the delivery of the message.

The actions taken by the top three layers depend upon the content of the message while the steps taken by the bottom four layers are independent of the message itself. This is an important dividing line of the seven layers. Most commercial network products are divided into these upper and lower environments.

In this book, the upper environment, represented by the top three layers of the OSI Reference Model, is called the **network operating system**. The lower environment, represented by the bottom four layers of the OSI Reference Model, is called the **network transport environment**. These environments will be explained in detail in Chapters Four, Five, and Six.

2.1.1.2 A Computer Example

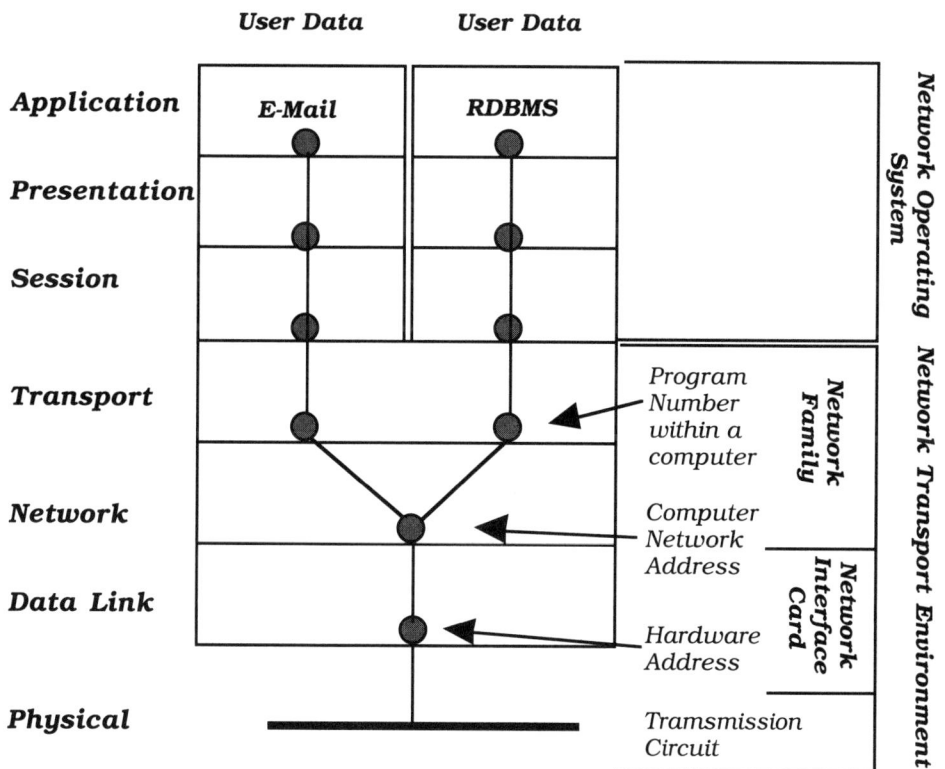

Figure 2–2. A networked computer with two application services

Figure 2–2 shows the seven-layer software architecture within a computer that has two application servers: the electronic mail server and the relational data base server.

A computer has its own network address the way a building has its street address. The servers are two different programs. Each has its own network program identifier or program number like an office has its room number within a building.

This section follows the steps necessary to send a message generated by a computer program, say the electronic mail server, through the protocol layers on its way to the receiving program, a client program.

Application Layer

A user prepares a letter in the form of a text file on a word processor. The user program then passes this text file to the E-mail server which is responsible for putting all necessary control and address information on top of the message so that its counterpart, the E-mail server in the receiving computer, will know what to do with it.

Presentation Layer

When the E-mail server finishes its work, it passes the user message down to the presentation layer. In this simple case, the presentation layer is responsible for translating the message into a format acceptable to the receiving application in the destination computer.

For example, if the sending computer is a workstation, most likely the text file is in ASCII characters. If the receiving program is in an IBM mainframe, then at the least, the presentation layer must convert the contents of the text file to the EBCDIC character code.

The principal function of the presentation layer is to shield the local applications from the differences of computer environments. This will allow the local application to access data and to execute functions as though they were residing in the same computer. Because of this layer, network applications become independent of computer platforms and networks. We will have more a detailed discussion of this layer in Chapter Four: Network Operating System.

Session Layer

Upon receipt of the message from the presentation layer, the session layer establishes a virtual communication circuit to the receiver if one has not been started. If one already exists, the session layer takes a copy of the message before handing it over to the transport layer. This is done so that, in the event of transport layer failure, a re-send can be carried out on the transport layer recovery.

Transport Layer

The main function of the transport layer is to obey the order from the session layer to start, maintain, and terminate a virtual communication circuit for the server and the client program. From this layer down, the **network transport system** delivers all types of application messages that are passed down from the session layer. The network transport system does not care if the application message is E-mail, process control, or order processing.

To deliver a message, the transport layer needs to know the address of the computer as well as the identification of the program within that computer. The combined information is generally known as the socket address.

The word socket is analogous to a telephone jack in your house. Each jack has a telephone number (socket address) associated with it. By connecting a telephone (session layer) to the jack, a user can dial to establish a connection with another telephone number.

Network Layer

The network layer decides the route for a message to take to arrive at the destination computer. If the destination computer is within a local area, then the network layer simply passes the message to the data link layer below and lets the data link handle the delivery.

Before it does that, however, the network layer must translate the computer address into the hardware address that is imprinted on the network interface cards of the sending and the receiving computers.

The socket address is strictly a software abstraction, not recognizable by electronic hardware on the network interface cards. The hardware address must also be known to allow physical delivery of the message.

On the other hand, if the destination computer is not in the neighborhood, then the network layer plans the route to get there. One method is to send the message to a router on the network, which then forwards it to another router on another network until the destination computer is located or determined to be unreachable.

Data Link Layer

The data link layer is partly implemented as software and partly as hardware. The hardware part is located in the network interface card of a computer. The data link layer is responsible for loading the message onto the network physical transmission facility and for monitoring the network traffic for messages destined for the data link layer.

Physical Layer

Last but not least, a physical path must be present for the message in the envelope to travel to the receiving computer. Such physical path is provided by various types of transmission circuits.

2.1.1.3 A Comparison

This table compares the main functions of each of the seven layers with the non-computer example in previous section.

Layers	Non-Computer Example	Program to Program
Application	The first secretary types a draft of the message from the manager.	Performs the function as instructed by the user program. The end result is a message to be sent to a receiver.
Presentation	The second secretary translates the draft to the receiver's native language.	Makes the message to appear to the receiver as though it was sent within its own computer.
Session	The third secretary puts the translated letter into an addressed envelope, records the mailing date and assigns a reference number for later referral.	On behalf of the application, arranges a communication circuit to deliver the message.
Transport	The building messenger picks up the envelopes from all companies in the building, and takes them to the post office.	Provides the virtual circuit to deliver the message to the correct program in the receiving computer
Network	The post office plans the delivery route for the letter from New York City to Tokyo.	Plans the route by which the message must take to arrive at the destination computer.
Data Link	Put the letter in the postal bag that is to be sent to the next immediate stop: New York City to Chicago, Chicago to Denver	Controls the physical layer facilities to deliver the message from one computer to another computer on the same network segment.
Physical	airplanes, trucks, trains, etc.	wires, transmission circuits

2.1.2 Moving Through the Layers

Network computing means the exchange of messages by two programs to achieve useful results. In this section, we will review the fundamentals of how the seven layers handle user messages.

2.1.2.1 Data Packets

All messages consist of data packets, a seriesof 1s and 0s that are eventually transmitted through the physical layer of the network. Each communication layer has its own design of data packets. The size and the design can only be interpreted by the equivalent layer in the receiving computer.

A user message may consist of many data packets. Typically, networking software program of each layer "chops up" a user message into data packets and stores them in a virtual envelope before passing them onto the next layer.

Figure 2–3 shows typical design of a data packet. More detailed discussion on data packet can be found in Chapter Four: Network Transport Environment.

Sender Addr	Receiver Addr	Control Information	User Message	Error Control Bits

Figure 2–3. Typical data packet design

An envelope is made up of the header and the trailer information added to the message data packet. The header is composed of addressing and control information. The trailer contains control information to ensure that the transmission is error free.

In a sending computer, the next layer will treat the header and the trailer information as though they were part of the original user message. The new envelope will enclose them.

2.1.2.2 Virtual Envelopes

Under the OSI Reference Model, a server or a user program message must pass through six layers of communication software before it arrives at its destination.

In the sending computer, the passing of a message from one layer to another involves:

- putting the message in a virtual envelope,
- putting the name and address of the sender and receiver of the message onto the envelope,
- indicating instructions for the receiver on the envelope,
- handing the envelope to the next layer,
- repeating the process until the original message is enclosed in the data link layer envelope,
- sending the complete package using physical layer.

In the receiving computer, the passing of the message from one layer to the next involves:

- opening an envelope to expose an inner envelope,
- executing the instruction on the inner envelope,
- passing the inner envelope to the next layer,
- repeating until the original message contained in the innermost envelope is given to the receiver.

2.1.2.3 Segmentation, Sequencing, and Reassembling

Very often, the transport or the network layer finds a message too long to be transmitted at one time. When that happens, the message will be segmented into smaller packets. Each segmented packet will be assigned a sequence number so that when the segmented packets arrive at the equivalent layer of the receiving computer, they can be reassembled to the original message.

2.1.2.4 Virtual Circuits

A principal function of a network is to establish a virtual communication circuit between two programs in two different computers connected by a physical network. In the OSI Reference Model, the bottom four layers (Transport, Network, Data Link, and Physical) are responsible to establish a virtual communication circuit for the two programs. The top three layers (Application, Presentation, and Session) in a computer always work in tandem as one program that uses the virtual circuit to communicate with its counter part in another computer.

2.1.2.5 Network Families

In any communication system, a key component is its addressing scheme. For example, in postal services, we have street names, lot numbers, and postal codes. In telephone communication, we have country code, routing code, area code, and phone numbers. Similarly, in program-to-program communication, a system must be used to pinpoint the programs on a network.

As shown in Figure 2–4, to uniquely identify a program on the network, a minimum of three addresses are required:

- Transport address,
- Network address, and
- Data link address.

A transport address is to identify a program within a computer. The network address is to identify a computer on a network. Both transport address and network address are software addresses. Together, they form a **network family.**

Many network families are in use in the commercial world. Each has its own way to identify a program on their networks. They are not compatible with one another. Although they do not talk to one another, they can co-exist with one another in a computer. It is possible that the same program in a computer may assume different names under different network families.

For example, a program identified as TOM in TCP/IP might be called DICK in

	Sender	Receiver

Application		
Presentation		
Session		
Transport	ID_TRA_Send	ID_TRA_RECV
Network	ID_NET_Send	ID_NET_RECV
Data Link	ID_DLK_Send	ID_DLK_RECV
Physical		

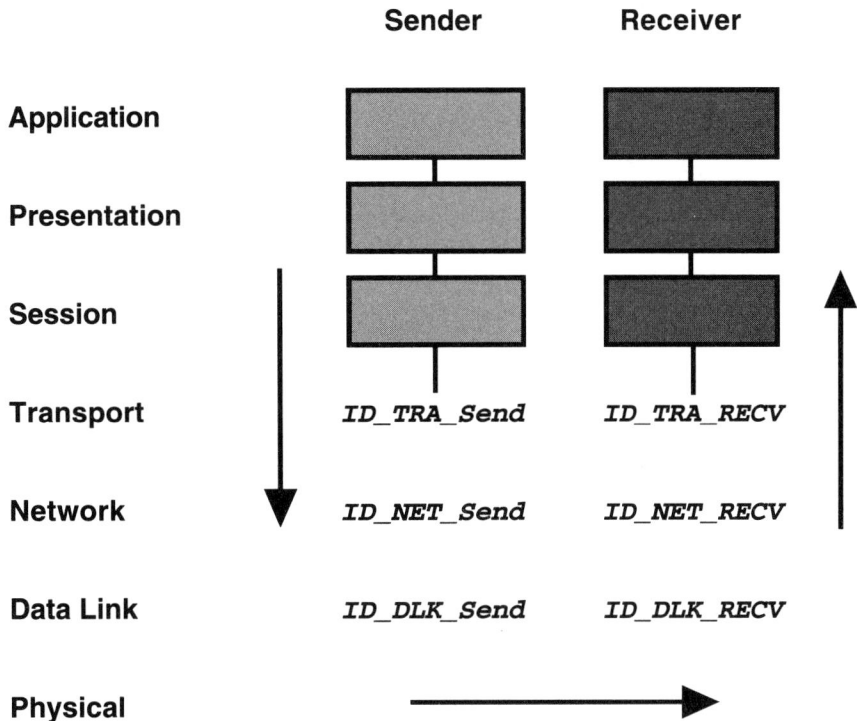

Figure 2–4. Three addresses are required to identify a program on the network: Datalink address, Network address, and Transport address

AppleTalk. TCP/IP and AppleTalk are different network families. On the other hand, the data link address is a hardware address at the physical layer. It is the address imprinted on a network interface card. It has a one-to-one correspondence with a software network address.

When multiple network families share the same network interface card in a computer, the network layer address of each network family has a one-to-one relationship with the data link (hardware) address.

This is discussed in more detail in Section 4.2.6: Logical Link Control Sublayer of Chapter Four: Network Transport Environment.

2.1.2.6 *Server Operations*

In the past, network computing was all about program-to-program communication. But the OSI Reference Model has taken network computing to a higher level.

Having a scheme to identify programs on the network is important, and equally important is being able to identify operations within a program. When a program wants to talk to another program on the network, it must also specify the topic of discussion to its communication partner.

Narrowing the conversation to specific topics between two parties is a fundamental characteristic of today's network application. In this type of computer application, useful results are produced by a pair of programs on a network known as "client" and "server," which are discussed next.

2.2   TERMS USED IN THIS BOOK

The OSI Reference Model uses very clear terms to denote each layer. However, today's commercial products use proprietary designs that are functionally equivalent to some combinations of the OSI layers. And for marketing reasons, different terms are used by users, consultants, and manufacturers to describe equivalent OSI functions.

For clarity and consistency, we now define four key terms used in this book. They are:

- Network computing environment
- Network operating system
- Network transport environment, and
- Client server architecture

2.2.1   Network Computing Environment

The network computing environment is a physical and logical infrastructure designed to enable different parts of an application to execute in different but networked computers. Two main structures exist within a network computing environment: **the network transport environment**, and **the network operating system**.

This division reflects today's commercial products, and the software standards development. In general, the network transport environment is better defined than the network operating system.

2.2.1.1   Network Transport Environment

The bottom structure, approximated by the bottom four layers of the OSI Reference Model, deals with the mechanics of message delivery from one program to another. It does not care about the message content.

In this book, these bottom four layers are collectively known as the "network transport environment," which is discussed in detail in Chapter Four.

2.2.1.2   Network Operating System

The top structure, approximated by the top three layers of the OSI Reference Model, interacts directly with user programs. The user programs depend upon this structure to control the message flow (the session services), to translate the message syntax between each other (the presentation services), and to access system services (application services) such as filing, directory, and communication.

In this book, this top structure is called the "network operating system" to denote its functional similarities to host based operating systems. Like operating systems, a network operating system provides the necessary inter-program communication facility between programs running on networked computers instead of between programs inside the same computer.

The network operating system is discussed in detail in Chapter Five.

2.2.1.3 Network and CPU Hardware

The relationship between hardware and software is more complex in a network computing environment than it is for a single computer. For each computer on the network, its operation is still completely controlled by its native operating system.

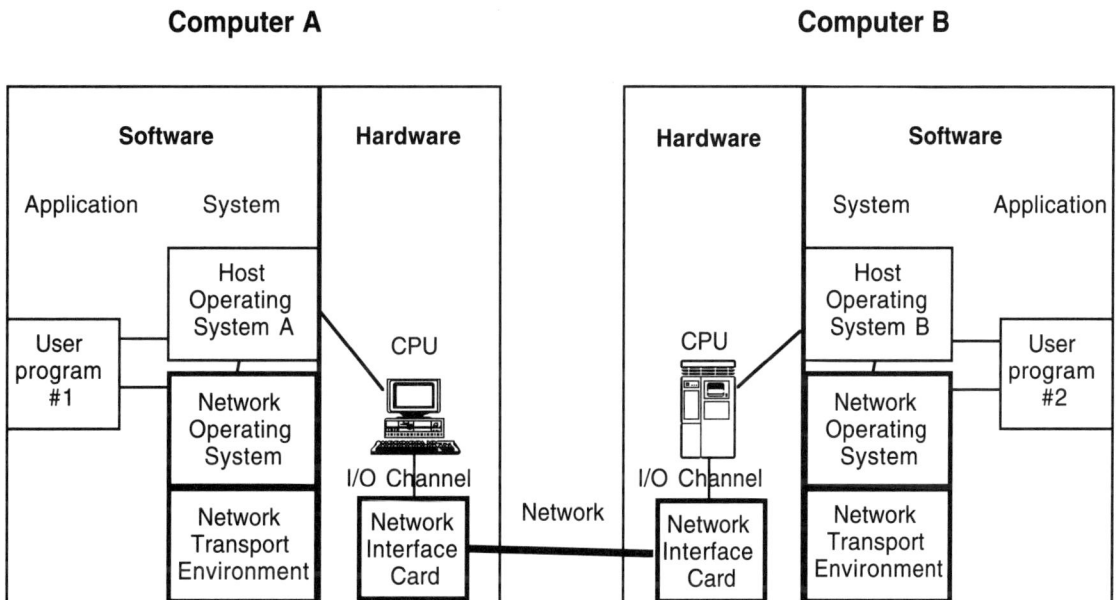

Figure 2–5. Relationship between network and CPU hardware and software

An application executing under these various native operating systems controls the traffic between itself and other computers on the network. This application has its parts distributed in all the native operating systems in computers connected to the network. The totality of these application parts forms the network operating system.

Figure 2–5 shows the relationship among:

- CPU hardware
- CPU I/O Channel

- Network Interface Cards
- CPU Operating System
- Network Operating System
- Network Transport Environment
- User applications

As shown in Figure 2–5, a network computing environment is a software and hardware (the network interface card) environment. It runs under the host operating system software just like any other computer applications. All input and output to and from the computer are carried out through the operating system I/O drivers.

The program that operates the network interface is the **Media Access Control** (MAC) sublayer of the data link layer driver. MAC does not directly act on the network interface card. It uses the host computer operating system I/O routine to do that.

2.2.2 Client Server

The term client server means different things to different people and circumstances. No hard and fast rules have been established to determine what is a client program and what is a server program. In the end, the definition of client server must be interpreted as a matter of balance.

A **unit of work** is split between two components to maximize its price performance. How and where the split should occur is situation-specific. When two programs communicate with each other, one tends to take on the role of a requester of services, and the other is a provider of those services.

The term "client" identifies the requester and the term "server" identifies the provider. A client is the requester of information while a server is a supplier of information. Listed below is more of a description to differentiate between clients and servers.

- A client is the requester of services (e.g. printing, file transferring); a server is the provider of the services.
- Client programs are consumers of resources; servers are the providers of resources.
- Client programs are initiators of the communication session with the servers.

Server interface

Servers stand by to serve. A server makes its available operations known through a server interface. Each client request must specify the server operation it wants. For example, a client request must contain the following:

1. Name of the server (e.g., SQL_Server_1)
2. Specific server function (operation) to be invoked (e.g., Update)
3. Parameters of or input data to the server function (e.g., Column names)

The name of the server, or the server identification, will be translated by the session layer protocol to the appropriate program identification on the network. Such program identification is different for different network families. Nonetheless, the point here is that for a client server network application, identification of an operation within a server is required in addition to the server itself.

Neither the client nor the server needs to do anything unless some event takes place. The relationship between client and server is event-driven, a characteristic quite different from traditional procedural programming by which events happen when a program runs.

The client server architecture is natural to network computing because it divides an application into different tasks each of which can be resident in a computer best suited for its execution. This division of labor makes sense because of the availability of increasingly powerful microprocessors, low cost massive storage devices, and high speed local data networks.

Client Server Within a Host Computer

The term "client server" implies that clients and servers are resident in different computers on a network. However, this does not necessarily need to be the case. A client and a server can exist in the same computer.

For example, in an IBM mainframe environment, a COBOL program uses Data Language (DL/1) calls to invoke the services of the database manager Information Management System (IMS). IMS understands these calls and responds accordingly. In this case, the client program is the COBOL program. IMS is the server.

Client server computing can also take place within a workstation environment such as Microsoft's Windows. The Windows facility known as Dynamic Data Exchange (DDE) lets two Windows applications to dynamically exchange message. For example, the Annual Sales figure in a word processor document is tied to the value of a cell in a spread sheet application. Whenever the value in the spreadsheet changes, the value in the word processor document also changes.

2.3   OSI LAYERS AND COMMERCIAL PRODUCTS

A brief summary of the seven layers is presented here as a prologue to their more detailed reviews in Chapters Four, Five, and Six. Examples of commercial network products and how they fit within the OSI Reference Model are also included for topical interests.

Figure 2–6 is an overview of the six layers of network software in two computers. The computer on the left has two server programs: an electronic mail server and a relational database server. The computer on the right has two client programs: a database reporting program and a word processor.

Other terms shown on the diagram will be explained in the following sections.

Figure 2-6 layout:

Server Computer   **Client Computer**

	User Mail Boxes	User Data Tables		E-Mail Composer	SQL Front End Report Pgm	
Application	E-Mail	RDBMS		E-Mail Exported Server Interface	RDBMS Exported Server Interface	*Network Operating System*
Presentation	Server Interface	Server Interface				
Session	Server Protocol	Server Protocol		Server Protocol	Server Protocol	
Transport	● ●	Program Number within a computer	● ●	*Network Family*	*Network Transport Environment*
Network	●	Computer Network Address	●		
Data Link	●	Hardware Address	●		
Physical	━━━━	Transmission Circuit	━━━━		

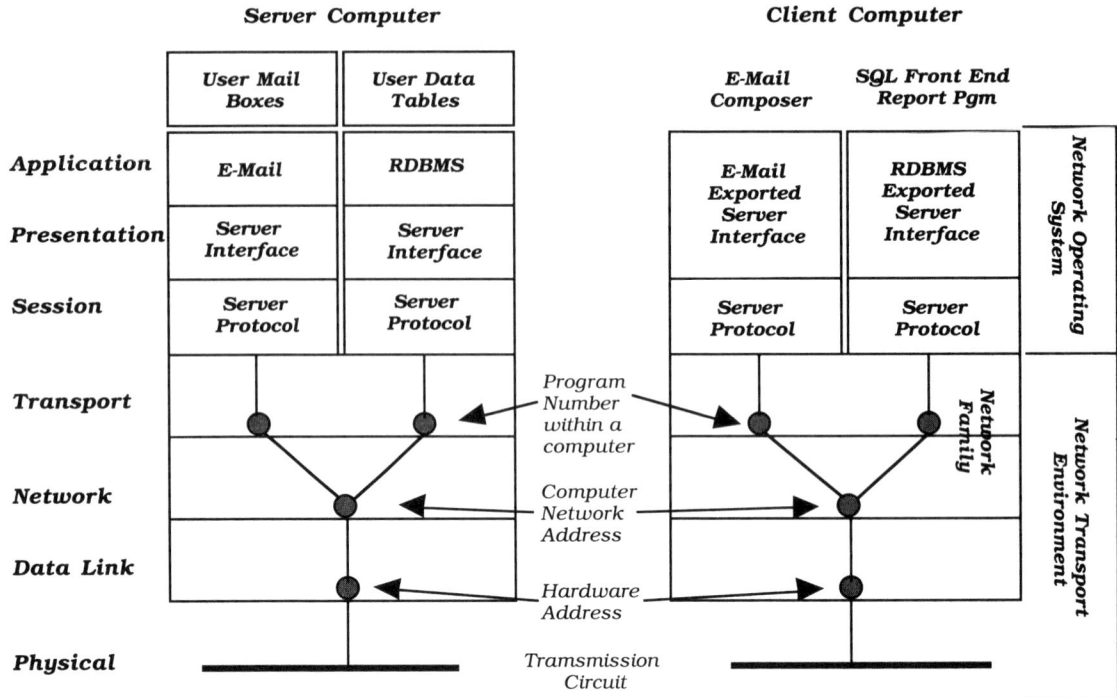

Figure 2–6. Two networked computers with two client server pairs

2.3.1 Application Layer

The application layer is responsible for providing various services to client programs. Server is the term used to describe the providers of these services. The two general types of server functions are: common and specific.

2.3.1.1 Common vs. User Servers

Common server functions refer to those that are shared by all applications on the network. For example, the filing function is a common function while the accounts payable is a user application function. Similarly, the directory server is a common function while the order entry is an application server.

Other common function servers include the printer management system, database management system, communication management system, catalogue management system, and the electronic messaging system.

Client programs make service requests to a server. The server responds by returning the results of the request to the client program.

Commercial products that approximate the functions of the Application layer:

- TCP/IP file transfer protocol (FTP)
- Sun Microsystems' Network File Services

- Novell's Netware File Server and Print Server
- Microsoft's LAN Manager File Server, SQL server
- Netware Loadable Modules: RDBMS
- X400 electronic mail system
- X.500 Directory services
- IBM mainframe data servers: DB2, IMS
- IBM mainframe "file server": VSAM

2.3.2 Presentation Layer

Services provided by a server must be advertised to the outside world so that others can make use of them. The principal function of the presentation layer is to present a server's services in the form of a server interface so that other clients can make use of those services as though the functions were available in their own computer. This produces a "local feeling" effect for the application programmers.

2.3.2.1 Server Interface

In a host-based application system, the user interface is a set of "dumb" terminal panels (on-line screens) through which a user can invoke various types of server services such as update, delete, and browse. The functions of the presentation layer in a network computing environment is identical to the above.

All server interfaces must have a pre-defined format and content of the data that it will accept and that it will return. Each application has its own server interface.

For example, in IBM's 3270 environment, the server interface is limited to the one-screen-at-a-time capability of 3270. All application functions, be it common or user specific, must abide by the interface format.

The server interface is a program module rather than a set of "dumb" terminal panels. Instead of a human operator interacting with a dumb terminal, a client program invokes the programming interface (APIs) of the server interface.

In network computing, a server interface may be completely devoid of any physical format such as a 3270 screen or a VT100 screen. For example, the X.400 electronic mail server has many programming interfaces in the form of direct function calls from within a client program. Each function call has a predetermined format and content requirement for its service.

Another example can be found in the server interface of a relational database server. This interface consists of pre-defined inputs parameters (table names, selection criteria, . . .) with specific formats (8 character names, floating point numbers, . . . etc.) for a pre-compiled SQL program. The output of the SQL program will always be presented as rows and columns of tabular data to the calling program.

On the server interface or the application screens, all the available functions or operations are presented to the outside world. Users or client programs can only invoke functions that are listed or accessible through the declared server interface.

2.3.2.2 Server Interface Exported

There are two parts to any server interface in network computing. One part of the server interface resides in the server computer. Another part of the server interface resides in the client computers. These two parts are known by many names including stubs, middleware, and APIs.

A server interface is "exported to" or "placed in" the client workstation or computer. The exported server interface is the server's representative in the user's workstation. Client programs "talk" to its APIs as though the "real" server was running locally.

Users' requests will be automatically and transparently sent to the destination server by the built-in capability of the exported server interface and the server protocol. Server protocol is the session layer protocol which we will discuss next.

2.3.2.3 The "Local" Feeling

Besides listing of functions of a server, presentation layer is also responsible to translate messages between the communicating programs so that each would "feel" as though it was dealing with another program inside its own computer. A common example is text data. It is represented by the EBCDIC code in IBM mainframes but by ASCII in the non-mainframe environments.

Commercial products that approximate the functions of the Presentation layer:

- Sun Microsystems' External Data Representation, XDR
- HP-Apollo's Network Data Representation, NDR
- Abstract Syntax Notation ASN.1 or ISO 8825
- Application server and client stubs

2.3.3 Session Layer

Messages generated by the server and by the client program must be transmitted over a communication circuit. **The session layer is responsible for starting up, maintaining, and monitoring this type of circuit on behalf of the application layer.** The session layer will also resend undelivered messages until the number of retries has exceeded the preset limit. The session layer is dependent upon its lower layers—transport, network, data link, and physical layers for the establishment and maintenance of the circuit.

The session layer function is like the operator in the old days of telephone operations. When the boss said, "Give me the Chairman," the operator would set up the circuit before handing the headset to the boss. The operator was responsible to the boss. In turn, the telephone company was responsible to the operator.

2.3.3.1 Server Protocol

In this book, the session layer communication protocol is called the server protocol to reflect the fact that it is serving a specific application layer server and to differentiate its role from that of the transport layer below it. The server depends on the server protocol, and no one else, to handle its communication needs.

A server protocol may use multiple transport layer protocols, just as the third secretary in the last example may choose to send the letter by fax, post, or courier. The important point is that as far as the manager is concerned, the responsibility of the third secretary is to ensure that the correct recipient receives the letter. How the letter is transmitted does not matter to the sender.

2.3.3.2   *The Top Three Layers*

Session layer is under direct command of an application server. The program modules of the application server, the server interface, and the server protocols must run in tandem and not in parallel in a computer. A one-to-one-to-one relationship always exists among these components.

For general purposes, "talking" to the server protocol means "talking" to the server. The three are viewed as one program by the network transport environment (Transport layer and below).

This is an important concept to remember, and one to which we will return many times in this book.

Commercial products that approximate the functions of the Session layer:

- IBM Logical unit type 6.2 APPC
- Microsoft's Named Pipes
- Microsoft's Dynamic Data Exchange
- IBM's Net BIOS
- Netware Core Protocol
- Network libraries, RPC Runtime libraries

2.3.4   Transport Layer

The transport layer is responsible for the maintenance of a virtual communication circuit between two programs on a network.

In order for the transport layer to accomplish its goal, it must have an addressing scheme that allows it to pinpoint the identity of a program on the network. Since multiple programs may be active in one computer, delivering a message to the destination computer is not sufficient. The transport layer must know the identification of the receiving program of that computer.

Two addresses are required for complete identification of a network program: the address of the computer on the network, and the address of the program inside the computer. The combination of the two addresses is known as the "socket address" or "network family." For two programs to communicate with one another, they must adopt the same socket addressing scheme.

2.3.4.1 Session vs. Transport

Confusion often arises in the roles of the session layer and the transport layer. The session layer is quite similar to the transport layer in terms of its main task: to deliver upper layer messages from one computer to another computer. There are, however, two major differences:

The first is that the session layer protocol is application-specific whereas the transport protocol is not. The transport layer is equivalent to two telephone sets that provide the end-to-end connection for two parties. The telephones do not control or care about the conversation.

The session layer, on the other hand, is responsible for the manner by which the server and client must communicate. For example: Is "Hello" a proper greeting? Who should speak first? What should be done when the telephone connection is cut off?

What is proper for a U.S. family may not be proper for a Swiss family. Yet the telephone system will not be able to distinguish the difference.

The second difference is that session layer is a higher layer. As a result, session layer can straddle multiple transport protocols on its lower side while maintaining the same interfaces on its upper side.

The session layer can be used to shield the upper layer of a multiple transport environment. In doing so, any changes in the transport environment will not affect the presentation layer, application layer, and user application software. This is a very important feature of session layer.

Commercial products that approximate the functions of the Transport layer:

- IBM's SNA transmission control modules
- TCP/IP's TCP Transmission Control Protocol
- ISO TP4
- Novell's SPX / IPX
- Apple's AppleTalk
- DEC's DecNet

2.3.5 Network Layer

The main function of the network layer is to plan the route a message must take to go from one computer to another. The network layer is a computer-to-computer protocol as opposed to the program-to-program transport protocol. The network layer is a lower layer because the message must arrive at the right computer before it can be delivered to the right program.

2.3.5.1 Address Translation

The socket address imprinted on the transport envelope contains two addresses: the destination computer address and the receiver program address (the identification inside the destination computer).

The computer address is a software address of the network family invented by the network designer. It must be translated into the hardware address recognizable by the network interface cards.

The network layer function is to translate the network family address to the hardware address of the destination computer. The network layer keeps a table that contains the hardware addresses of all reachable computers and its equivalent network family addresses. This table is periodically and automatically updated by the network layer software.

2.3.5.2 Message Routing

Based on the destination address, the network layer decides the path a message must take to reach its destination. Any message that cannot be delivered directly within the immediate local network is forwarded to a designated computer known as the router.

The addresses of other computers and other routers on the network are kept inside the router. The router will forward the message to the destination computer or to another router until the destination computer is found or determined to be non-reachable.

Commercial products that approximate the functions of the Network layer:

- IBM's SNA Path Control software
- TCP/IP's Internet Protocol (IP)
- CCITT X.25
- Frame Relay

2.3.6 Data Link Layer

A message that arrives at the data link layer will be transmitted to either the destination computer, if it is in the immediate network (as is the case in local area network), or to the immediate router computer, if the destination computer cannot be found on the local area network.

The data link layer protocol is implemented partly on the network interface card and partly on the software drivers.

Commercial products that approximate the functions of the Data Link layer:

- Institute of Electrical and Electronic Engineers, IEEE's 802.2 Logical Link Control
- IEEE's 802.4 token bus, IEEE 802.5 Token Ring, IEEE 802.3 Ethernet
- IBM's Synchronous Data Link Control SDLC
- ISO's High Level Data Link Control, HDLC
- CCITT X.25's Link Access Protocol (LAP)
- Apple's Local Talk
- Asynchronous Transfer Mode (ATM)
- Fiber Data Distributed Interfaces (FDDI)

2.3.7 Physical Layer

The physical layer provides the physical media through which computer signals travel between two computers.

It specifies the standard for the physical media (wiring, microwaves, fiber optics), data transmission devices (serial ports, modems, communication controllers), and associated control signals (starts/stops, error handling) between two or more computers.

Commercial products that approximate the functions of the Physical layer :

- The voltage level, the wiring, fiber optics, EIA-232C
- Analog and digital transmission circuits T1, T2, . . . etc.
- Integrated Services Digital Network (ISDN)

2.4   ISSUES ON STANDARDS

Broadly speaking, the two types of standards are: official standards and industry standards.

Official Standards

Official standards are adopted through public standard bodies such as the International Organization for Standardization (ISO), the American National Institute of Standards (ANSI), the Consultative Committee for International Telecommunication and telephone (CCITT), and so on.

Examples of official standards are ISO's Open System Interconnection (OSI) seven layer communication reference model, ASCII character and control sets, and SQL database language.

Industry Standards

Industry standards are established through common usage. Some products become standards because they are first to market, acquire a large market share, or excel on merit.

Examples are IBM's System Network Architecture, DOS for personal computers, TCP/IP for network protocol, HP Laserjet printers, DBASE for PCs, and so on.

2.4.1   Standards Organizations

Standards organizations come in many flavors. Some are international, while others are national. Most international standards in reality are adaptation of many existing widely used national, industry, and de facto standards.

2.4.1.1   ISO

In 1977, the International Organization for Standardization (ISO), whose membership is composed of many national standard bodies such as the American National Standards Institute (ANSI), decided to establish international data communication standards. Its objective is to enable computer programs all over the world to exchange messages with one another like the global telephone network does for people.

The standards will be expressed in terms of the seven layers of the Open System Interconnect (OSI) Reference Model. Details of this model are still evolving and incomplete, indicating the tremendous challenge in bringing international consensus to a fast-changing technological arena. The ISO International Standard 7498 is the original document of the OSI reference model.

Today, almost all computer system manufacturers pledge to evolve their products to the future OSI standards. They know their network products must compete in a global market. The speed of OSI adoption, however, will depend on customer demand and leadership from the major users, the computer system manufacturers, the telecommunication services providers, and the governments of advanced industrial countries.

The Europeans and the Japanese appear to be more inclined to proceed rapidly with the OSI standards than the North Americans. The Europeans and Japanese have been dealing in a heterogeneous computer market for a long time. Due to historical, geographical, and cultural reasons, their market tends to be more segmented, which encourages multiple suppliers. On the other hand, the North American market, still the largest computer market in the world, has traditionally been quite homogeneous, and largely based on economy of scale. Also, the general acceptance by user communities and major manufacturers of the TCP / IP protocol has lessened the urgency for a multi-vendor network transport standards.

2.4.1.2   CCITT

ISO is not the only international standard setting body on data communication. It collaborates very closely with another international standard organization whose original mandate was in international voice and telegraph communication.

International Telegraph and Telephone Consultative Committee (CCITT) is based in Geneva, Switzerland. CCITT is one of three technical divisions of the International Telecommunications Union (ITU), which derives its authority from a United Nations treaty.

CCITT has developed a set of standards for data communication that is described in a series of recommendations with names such as X.25 for packet switching, X400 for electronic mail, X500 for directory services, etc.

The OSI reference model is now also documented in the CCITT X.200 series of recommendations. The ISO and CCITT versions of the OSI reference model are essentially the same.

2.4.1.3   IEEE

Institute of Electrical and Electronic Engineers, a U.S.-based electronic engineering society, introduced the local area communication standards which are now part of OSI: IEEE 802.2 for logical data link control, IEEE 802.3 for Ethernet, IEEE 802.4 for token bus, and IEEE 802.5 for Token Ring. We will discuss these in more detail in Chapter Four: Network Transport Environment.

2.4.1.4   Manufacturers and Users

Several independent groups of manufacturers and users have been formed to speed up the process of developing and adopting OSI. They all share the same interest in the standards which will affect a manufacturer's product plan, as well as users buying preferences.

Examples are the U.S.-based Corporations for Open Systems (COS), the Europe-based Standards Promotion for Open Systems (SPAG), the Japan-based Promote Open System Institute (POSI), and the U.S.-based users' group, Manufacturing Automation Protocol and Technical and Office Protocol MAP/TOP.

2.4.2   Open Systems

Over the years, individual companies have implemented proprietary ways of data communication best suited to their own business goals. As different brands of computers are being used within business organizations, users are finding that the cost of electronic message exchanges at the application level is unbearably high. This leads to a strong user movement to demand establishment of a common protocol for computing equipment for easy and cost effective application integration. From this movement comes the concept of open system.

What is an open system? An open system is a vendor-independent computing environment having commonly available products that have been designed and implemented in agreement with accepted standards. The perceived benefits of an open system are availability, scalability, portability, and interoperability.

Availability means that the computing products should be available from a wide variety of manufacturers so that customers are less likely to be bound to a single supplier.

Scalability refers to the ability of customers to choose the right size computer to fit their needs without having to worry about outgrowing a certain platform, as in having to redesign the application when it moves from the minicomputer platform to the mainframe platform.

Portability means software can be easily transferred from one computing platform to another without expensive modification. For example, programming languages such as FORTRAN, COBOL, C, and SQL have established standards. Applications based on these languages have greater portability.

Interoperability means that different makes of computers can communicate with one another easily at the application level: Two programs can talk to one another to produce useful results. It means more than the early days when computer communication meant simply transferring a file from one machine to another.

2.4.2.1   Open Software Foundation (OSF)

Of all the standard setting efforts on network computing, one stands out to embrace the ideals of an open system. It calls itself the Open Software Foundation—OSF. This initiative has little to do with the OSI Standards activities other than the fact that they acknowledge one another's existence.

The OSF has the support of major vendors and users such as IBM, DEC, HP, General Motors, the U.S. Government, and others. The OSF has more than 300 members and 200 employees in locations around the world. The OSF is a non-profit research and development organization whose stated goal is "to provide a software solution that enables computers from multiple vendors to work together in a true open systems computing environment."

The objective of OSF is to select a set of existing interoperable products and to sponsor new components that will fill any gaps in them. OSF calls this system the Distributed Computing Environment (DCE).

The OSF will pick and choose network computing technologies from current commercial products. This approach gives OSF a fast track to establish a workable open system, instead of "vaporware."

One of the critical selection points for DCE was platform and operating environment independence. To illustrate how OSF works, in 1992 the following technologies were selected:

- Network Computing System (NCS) 2.0 from HP/Apollo with Digital enhancements for the RPC mechanism
- Andrew File System (AFS) 4.0 from Transarc for a distributed file system
- Support for diskless workstations from Transarc and HP
- Kerberos, with HP extensions for authorization
- LAN Manager for UNIX (LM/X) from Microsoft, and PC-NFS from Sun for PC integration
- DECdns from Digital with DIR-X from Siemens for X.500 directory service

These products will be available from the participating companies (IBM, DEC, HP) as an OSF Remote Procedure Call, an OSF Distributed Naming Service, an OSF Distributed Time Service, an OSF Threads Service, an OSF Distributed File System, an OSF Distributed Security Service, and an OSF Personal Computer Integration Service.

A cautionary note for users is called for here: Associations among high-tech partners are often like war games, where partnership is not built on technical elegance but is largely dependent upon survival and market share—the bottom line. This leads us to the next section on users' real choices.

2.4.3 Users' Real Choices

Standards for network computing, especially the top three layers, are far from being well-established. The stakes are high. Setting standards becomes a concern not only for individual companies, but also for the national political agenda. Many people perceive that standards will affect a nation's competitiveness.

Perhaps the only truth about standards is that there is no standard for standards. What is "standard" in a centrally-managed organization would be viewed as too inflexible in a decentralized management structure. Conversely, what is "standard" in decentralized organizations would be viewed as out of control by some. Thus, the argument for or against standards is often quite meaningless unless the argument is considered according to the "standard" of individual or organizational practices.

Many people argue that standards are the key to solving the problem of interconnecting disparate computing platforms. Theoretically they are right. Practically, most users lack the patience to wait. The process of developing standards can be very slow and highly uncertain.

Standards must keep pace with, if not keep ahead of, the technology to which they apply. Establishing standards that technology could not support, or standards that fall far behind the capability of available technology is pointless.

No absolute rules have been established for choosing the right technology for any given situation. The best approach is to focus on your business and productivity needs. Technology must fit your business strategy, not the other way around. If a standard does not exist or is still primitive, but a good product or a de facto standard is available, it would be wise not to wait for the former. Choose the latter.

Building a pure OSI compliant product is not yet practical. One must also be reminded that OSI as it is proposed now is monolithic—it cannot work with any existing, commercially-available network architecture. Most users will not throw out their investment in favor of something similar. Any product architecture that does not deal with the installed base and user preferences will not be successful.

It is also risky to acquire technology based solely on promised future standards unless it is very clear that the future will arrive tomorrow. Like friendship among nations, vendor alliances come and go. Witness the 1992 rift between IBM and Microsoft, the desktop industry is now in an intense war on market share. Microsoft's LAN Manager, initially fervently backed by IBM and DEC to be the industry's LAN standard, has failed to attain a significant share of the microcomputer network operating system market, which remains dominated by Novell Inc.'s Netware.

Another example is the initial difficulty encountered by IBM's OS/2 in gaining market share from Microsoft's DOS. Ultimately, products that make profit for the manufacturers will be the ones that have market support and penetration. Time and again, the profitable products prove to be the ones that last. The lesson learned is that computer technology is changing so fast that the market is beyond the control of any single vendor. Technology democracy has finally arrived!

Companies should select products based on their fit to the company's business strategy and their capacity to get the job done, and on its market support.

3

The Object-Oriented Model

INTRODUCTION

Objects are software modules that contain programs and data. No external agent can directly modify the data without going through the object's own programs. This phenomena of "data encapsulation" helps to hide the structural complexity of the encapsulated data, thereby enabling developers to concentrate on the use of information rather than the mechanics of getting at them.

Software objects can be easily re-used by others through a technique known as inheritance and hierarchy. An object is always part of an hierarchy of other objects. The simplest object is at the top of the hierarchy and the more complex ones at the bottom. All programs and data of higher layer objects are inherited by the lower layer objects. Each object on its own is simple. When an object inherits all the programs and data of objects above it in a hierarchy, it becomes very useful. In an object-oriented application, building such a hierarchy of objects is an incremental effort. Code is written only for additional functions, and the programmer uses as much as possible of what is already written—that's programming productivity!

An object-oriented application's ability of dynamic binding, commonly known as polymorphism, enables a single command to elicit different responses from different objects in the same hierarchy. An example is a single command: rotate 90 degrees, instead of three different commands, will invoke three different programs for a circle, a rectangle, and a picture. This apparent "intelligent" behavior is more like human behavior and, hence it makes the user interface of an object-oriented application inherently more friendly than the traditional ones.

It also means programming productivity because separate interfaces (e.g. command menu items) for different objects are not needed in an object-oriented application.

3.1 BASIC CONCEPTS

3.1.1 Object Definition

An object possesses both form and functions. The form is an object's inherent properties. Functions are an object's responses to external events. The responses are dependent upon the values of the inherent properties of the object.

- OBJECT_X possesses inherent properties (P1, P2, P3, ... PN) where P1, P2, ... PN are inherent properties expressed in known data types such as integers, floating point numbers, text characters, dates, logical operators.
- OBJECT_X possesses the ability to respond to specific requests. The response is a function of the inherent properties at the time of the request.
- A request to execute FUNCTION_A, is made to OBJECT_X.
- Response = Function_A. OBJECT_ X

An object is an entity that contains both program and data as inseparable components. Access to an object's data must done through objects own functions. An object-oriented application consists of software objects "talking" to one another to produce useful work.

3.1.1.1 Object Examples

Customer as an Object

A customer is an object. Its inherent properties are name, address, sex, age, and total purchases. Its responses to requests such as "show sales tax rate" and "show discount rate" are determined by interactions of its attributes such as address, age, and total purchases.

- A customer object CUSTOMER_JOHN_DOE, and an associated function known as SHOW_DISCOUNT_RATE
- The external request: A clerk wants to know the sales tax rate for Mr. John Doe
- The response from the object CUSTOMER_JOHN_DOE,
  = SHOW_DISCOUNT_RATE.CUSTOMER_JOHN_DOE (address, age, total purchases)
  = John Doe's discount rate

Customer's Order as an Object

A customer's order is an object. Its inherent properties are product name, product quantity, delivery date, and customer number. Its behavior in responding to requests from an external agent such as "show product quantity" and "show total product by customer" are determined by the interactions of its attributes.

- A customer orders object ORDER_123, and an associated function known as TOTAL_SALE.
- The external request: Another program wants to find out the total sale represented by that order, so it sends a request, TOTAL_SALE, to the object ORDER_123.
- The response from the object ORDER_123:
  = TOTAL_SALE.ORDER_123 (product_name, sale_by_product, customer_name)
  = Numeric value of the total sales to the customer.

An Integer as an Object

An integer is an object. Its properties consist of observable attributes such as "another integer will result when two integers are added" that are well-known to mathematicians. Its behaviors in responding to requests such as "show square root" and "add itself" are determined by interactions of its internal properties.

- An integer object, TWO, and an associated function known as SQUARE_ROOT.
- The external request: Another program wants to find out the square root of two, so it sends a request, SQUARE_ROOT to the object TWO.
- The response from the object TWO:
  = SQUARE_ROOT. TWO (inherent properties)
  = Numeric value of 1.1412

3.1.2 Object Classes and Instances

Objects that possess IDENTICAL inherent properties are known as instances of an object class. Each instance adopts a set of unique values of the object's inherent properties.

All instances of the same class will have the same ability in responding to external requests. In other words, they share the same functions.

3.1.2.1 Object Classes Examples

An Automobile Object Class

An object class can be CHEVY. Three of the inherent properties of the class might be air conditioning, color, engine size. The first property, air conditioning, can be expressed by the logical data types of "yes" or "no." The second property, color, can be expressed by the character string data type with a length of six characters, such as red or yellow. The third property, engine size, can be expressed by the numeric data type with two places after decimal, such as 385.50 or 758.00.

An instance of the object class may be DAD's_CHEVY. It possess a unique set of values for its properties such as:

- no air conditioning
- color red
- engine size 124.60

Other instances may be JOHN's_CHEVY, MARY's_CHEVY, and so on. An associated function for this object class CHEVY might be PRICE. The request response model can be expressed generically as:

- PRICE.CHEVY (air conditioning, color, engine_size)

When an external agent, either another program or a person, wants to know the price of MARY's car, it sends a request, PRICE, to the object MARY's_CHEVY, which will return the price of her Chevy.

A Customer Object Class

An object class can be CUSTOMER. Three of its inherent properties might be name, birthday, sex. The first property, name, can be expressed by the character string data type with a length of 36. The second property, birthday, can be expressed by the date data type with format of dd/mm/yyyy. The third property, sex, can be expressed by the string data types with a length of one character (either M or F).

An instance of the object class may be CUSTOMER_JOHN_DOE. It possess a unique set of values for its properties such as:

- Name: John Doe
- Birthday: 14/02/1930
- Sex: M

An associated function for this object class CUSTOMER might be AGE. The request response model can be expressed generically as:

- AGE.CUSTOMER (name, birthday, sex)

When an external agent, either another program or a person, wants to know the age of John Doe, it sends a request, AGE, to the object CUSTOMER_JOHN_DOE, which will return the age of John Doe.

3.2   THE OBJECT-ORIENTED APPROACH

Users often question the value of using the object-oriented approach to their application development. In fact, some user surveys indicate that only a small minority (less than 15%) of application development today uses the object-oriented approach.

3.2.1   New Breed of Applications

This is not be a reflection of the effectiveness of object-oriented technology. Its slow acceptance is due to a general lack of knowledge of the subject and the methodology. More importantly, the success of object-oriented technology will probably not be found in displacing or improving the existing types of applications. Its success will be found in newer types of applications.

These newer types of applications, such as multi-media applications and document imaging, have not been economically feasible in the past because the technology was not ready. However, the fact that they do not exist does not mean that they are not needed.

When Henry Ford first introduced the horseless carriages quite a few prominent people expressed serious doubts about the automobile's viability. More recent examples are microwave ovens, automatic teller machines, and home videos.

Intense global competition will force companies to adopt some form of object-oriented approach in their application development. They have few other options.

3.2.1.1   *Better Emulation of Reality*

Real life objects and processes possess both properties and functions simultaneously rather than separately. Therefore even at a conceptual level, a software object is a better emulation of reality than the traditional separation of program and data.

In traditional programming approach, program and data are brought together or matched using additional programmed logic.

For example, when a programmer wants to access a data file, he or she must know if the file is a text file or a graphic file. If it is a text file, he or she would need to count spaces and character positions to put in the proper program logic. The program must match the data. If the file is a graphic file, the programmer would be required again to write special graphic code to match his data.

In an object-oriented world, the text or the graphic file itself is an object. The object not only contains the "data", a manifestation of one or more of its internal properties, the object also contains the built-in programmed logic known as functions or procedure to open the file. This programmed logic knows the minute details of everything that is required to open this file. Only one programmer needs to worry about this.

Anyone else who uses the same function does not have to carry out the additional task of matching the program logic with the data. In an object-oriented world, every file must belong to a certain class in which this function will be a part. The program needs only to send the message open to the object, and the file will be made available to the program. In a purely object-oriented world, data cannot be accessed directly. The user always requests someone else to do it on his or her behalf.

This may seem no big deal. But its subtlety belies its importance. This is indeed the importance of object-oriented programming. All data belongs to certain class objects. All functions that can manipulate the data are part of the object.

If this object-oriented approach is applied to all aspects of an application, it will have a significant impact on the programmer's productivity. By adopting an object-oriented approach to application development, duplication in data handling and programming efforts are minimized.

The inherent modular nature of objects will force better emulation of real life commercial and physical processes. These points will be more apparent when we discuss the three fundamental characteristics of the object-oriented approach (data encapsulation, hierarchy and inheritance, and polymorphism) in the next section of this chapter.

Traditional Structured Approach

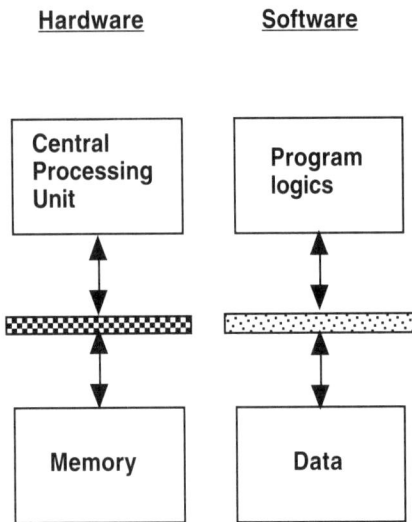

Object-Oriented Approach

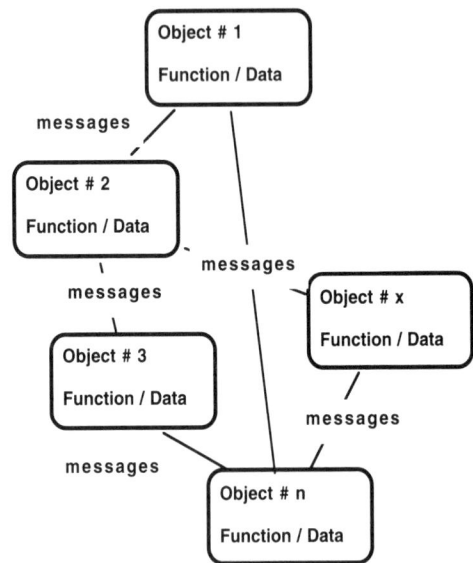

Hardware   Software

Central Processing Unit

Program logics

Memory

Data

Object # 1
Function / Data

messages

Object # 2
Function / Data

messages

messages

Object # x
Function / Data

Object # 3
Function / Data

messages

messages

Object # n
Function / Data

Architecture

Architecture

Von Neuman machine:

Separation of 'CPU' and 'memory'

Programming languages:

Abstraction of hardware architecture
Separation of 'function' and 'data'

Hardware:

Parallel and cooperative processors

Modelling methodology:

No separation of function and data
Each object an 'intelligent' entity
Interactions through messaging

Figure 3–1. Traditional Sequence vs. Object-Oriented Event Driven

3.2.1.2 Event vs. Sequence Driven

Traditional program execution is determined by a central sequence of logic. It has a start and an end. The program starts, data is brought in as required by the program, the program executes, and then the program stops. This paradigm applies to both traditional batch systems and many on-line systems.

When an object-oriented application is launched, all the objects within the application are first initialized and then made available to respond to messages from other objects or from outside events such as a keyboard or a mouse action. These objects remain active until they are terminated by the program or the program itself is terminated.

3.2.1.3 Distributed vs. Centralized

Unlike traditional programming, data and programs are distributed among individual objects. An object owns its data, which can only be accessed by invoking pre-declared functions or procedures. In effect, objects in an object-oriented application are like a team of baseball players who take up their positions in the playing field and are ready to respond to an event-driven situation.

An object can be thought of as a self-contained "specialist" performing its tasks. It has its own data and the ability to perform certain actions on that data. To use an object, a message to it to perform a particular function. That object may in turn send messages to other objects, requesting that they perform specialized services using their own data.

In this way, we can envision an object-based system as a community of specialists cooperating to perform many complex functions, where each specialist is responsible for maintaining its own information. If this division of labor is accurate and communication among the specialists is good, the community can accomplish complex tasks quickly and efficiently.

3.2.1.4 OOPL vs. Traditional

In traditional programming languages, the programmer follows the following steps:

- write the program logic statements
- compile the program statements to obtain the executable code
- prepare the data
- submit the program and matching data for execution
- obtain the results of the execution

In an object-oriented programming language, the programmer would follow these steps:

- declare various object classes by specifying their inherent properties and functions names
- write the program logic for each declared function
- compile the object class declarations and program statements of associated functions

- populate each class with instance objects by supplying sets of values for their inherent properties.
- start the main program by initializing the required object classes
- the execution sequence will be determined by the interactions of the declared objects
- the program terminates only when the object decides to do so

3.2.2 Object Granularity

As shown in Figure 3–2 below, the degree of object-orientation has progressed from batch programming environment, online application environment, client server environment, and the object-oriented programming languages.

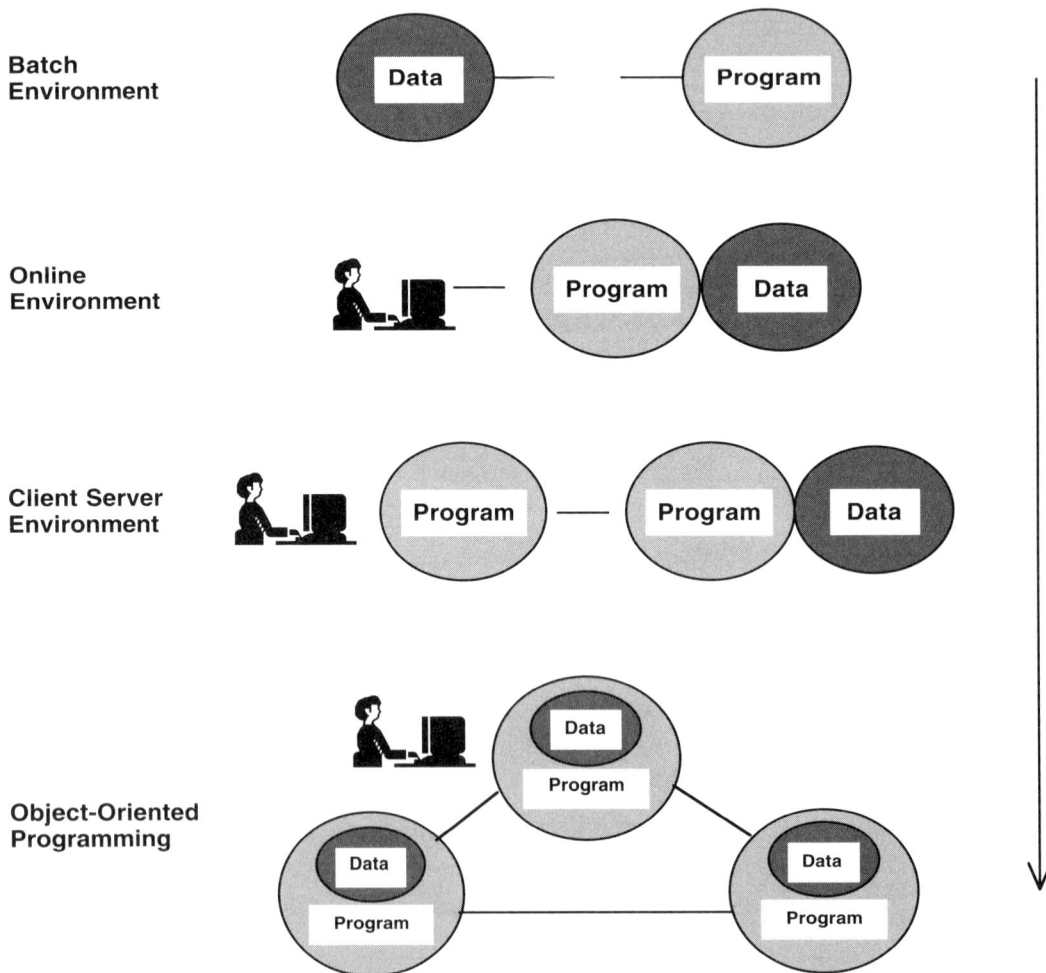

Figure 3–2. Definition of an object can be granular

In the batch environment, separation of program and data is 100%. An operator is required to bring them together to produce useful result.

In the online environment, an operator does not have direct access to the data. He or she does everything through a programmed interface. The data manipulation ability of a program is at the record and the data table levels and not at the data elements level. From the operator's point of view, however, the data is encapsulated by a program. The operator's ability to manipulate the data is limited to the operations offered by the user interface.

In a client server environment, two programs are talking to one another instead of to an operator's physical keyboard. Typically the programs are operating on data records or data tables rather than on individual data elements.

In the object-oriented environment, data encapsulation is complete in that it takes place at a data element level. For example, in a pure object-oriented programming language such as SmallTalk, every integer is treated as an object.

3.3   OBJECT-ORIENTED PROGRAMMING

In this section, we will discuss the three features that differentiate object-oriented programming from traditional programming: encapsulation, inheritance, and polymorphism. Throughout, the focus of this discussion will not be on technical details, which one can obtain by going through appropriate manuals and books suggested in the Reference Section. Rather, the focus will be on understanding the essential features of the two programming types to appreciate the productivity potentials of each.

The discussion will be followed by a brief review of the two popular object-oriented programming languages/environments: AT&T's C++ and Microsoft's Visual Basic.

3.3.1   Encapsulation

Data encapsulation is the key difference between the traditional and the object-oriented programming approach. In the traditional approach, program and data are separated.

As shown in Figure 3–3, an external agent is required to match the program and the data to produce the desired result. This is most evident in the batch program environment in which a user must ensure the deck of data following the program is separated by the last job card.

It is also the responsibility of the programmer to ensure that the format of the data is EXACTLY what the program calls for in order for the program properly. There can be no missing commas, and no extra spaces!

3.3.1.1   Encapsulation and Productivity

Data encapsulation enhances productivity in application development when it is properly understood and utilized. By removing the need to deal with data structure of an object, encapsulation allows analysis and design to be done in a modular manner, thereby freeing the developers to concentrate on the big picture of his or her application.

Building software applications with objects is like building houses with slightly modified ready-made parts such as doors, counter sinks, plumbing parts, and so forth. One does not need to know how a door is manufactured to install a door!

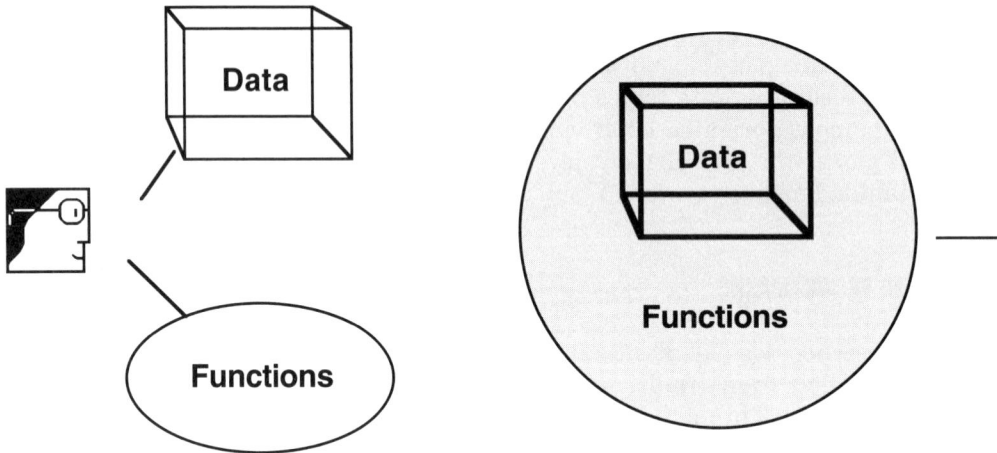

A user is responsible to
match the data to the
functions

A user deals only with
functions, which shield the data
formats from the users

Figure 3–3. An object-oriented approach—Data Encapsulation

3.3.1.2 Encapsulation Examples

The automobile object

In one of the previous examples, the PRICE function for the CHEVY objects would have been a "subroutine" in the traditional programming approach with a generic call syntax as follow:

```
PRICE = PRICE (air_conditioning, color, engine_size)
```

Here, a user has to supply the values of the parameters each time a price is to be calculated. The subroutine does not know nor care whether it is calculating the price for Mary's car or John's car. The programmer must know exactly what are the required data types and the format for each parameter in order for the subroutine PRICE to execute properly.

In the object-oriented approach, the programmer who wants to know the price of MARY's_CHEVY needs only to ask the object MARY's_CHEVY for the price. The object MARY's_CHEVY has within it the values of its inherent properties as well as the subroutine that calculates the price based on the values of the inherent properties.

An object possesses data, which are a set of values of the object's inherent properties. An object also possesses various functions or subroutines that know the minute details of the data within it.

If a person wants to know something about an object (such as the price of Mary's Chevy), and if this something can be obtained from a pre-declared function (such as PRICE), then he gets the price by simply sending a message (the request for price) to the target object. This call can be symbolized by:

```
PRICE . MARY's_CHEVY
```

The target object will respond by providing the price of Mary's Chevy without the programmer needing to know anything about the inherent properties of the object.

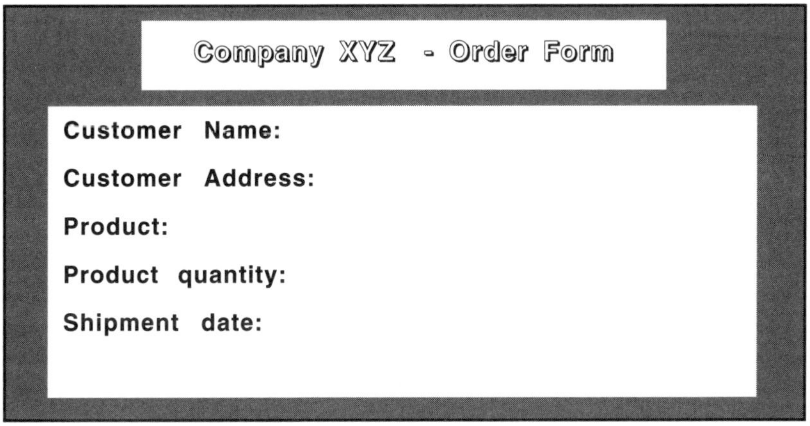

> **Company XYZ - Order Form**
>
> **Customer Name:**
>
> **Customer Address:**
>
> **Product:**
>
> **Product quantity:**
>
> **Shipment date:**

Function1 = get_customer (product)
returns all customers who order that product

Function2 = get_product (product, date)
returns the total quantity of product to be shipped before date

Figure 3–4. Customer Order Object

The Customer Order Object

Figure 3–4 shows a typical paper based customer order. It can be simulated by a software object. The attributes of the objects are:

```
the customer name      datatype - text
the customer address   datatype - text
the ordered product    datatype - text
```

```
the ordered quantity    datatype - integers
the shipment date       datatype - date
```

The functions defined for the object could be the ones shown in the diagram. There are many instances of the object. In the real world, each paper copy of the customer order is an instance of the customer order object.

With this customer order object, all information needs involving customer order attributes must interact with the object's declared functions. For example, another object known as "warehouse" may need to know the total quantity of a product that requires shipment by a certain date. Warehouse obtains its answer by sending a request to the customer object and asking for function2.

The Document Object

A popular class of objects is the document class. All documents share common properties: size of the paper, orientation of the page, text fonts, paragraphs, tables, graphics, and many others. They also exhibit common behaviors to messages from the computer keyboard, mouse action, or another screen object. The message can be: to format a paragraph, to paginate the document, to generate a table of contents, to print the document, and others.

In an object-oriented environment, the word processor is in effect a class object from which many instance objects are derived. The word processor itself (the class object) comes complete with all the default properties and behaviors of a document. Derived documents (the instance objects) contain only those information that is different from the default properties and behaviors.

For example, the default property of the word processor (class object) for page layout is portrait, whereas for a particular document, the page layout is landscape. The default text font is "Courier" whereas for a particular document the default is "Helvetica." The default body is "empty" whereas for a particular document it is the content of a letter to the customers, and so on. The default behavior of the word processor (class object) contains all the necessary commands to compose a document. These behaviors become part of every document (instance objects).

3.3.1.3 Encapsulated Object Classes

The class object contains the default properties and functions of all the objects in that class. The instance objects contain specific properties that are different from those of the class object. Properties are valued based on each instance that the object possesses different values of these properties. The instance objects always have the same functions as the class object.

In the real world implementation of an object class and its instance objects, it may seem that we are back to the separation of data and program, because the class object and the instance objects are stored on the disk as separate files.

This is done to save disk storage space to avoid the need to physically attach the program code of a class object to each instance object. Instead, object-oriented environments, such as Microsoft's Windows and Apple's Macintosh, will allow a virtual implementation of object class and object instances as one seamless object.

For example, when you click on your Microsoft's Word document, the Windows environment or the Macintosh environment will automatically "know" to launch the program code of the word processor "Word," the class object.

Contrast this with a non-object-oriented environment word processor such as IBM's DisplayWriter 3: the user has to first launch the program, and the user takes on the responsibility to select and to open the correct document and document type. In this case, an external agent is required to match the data and program because a DisplayWriter 3 document is pure data and is not an object.

3.3.2   Inheritance and Hierarchy

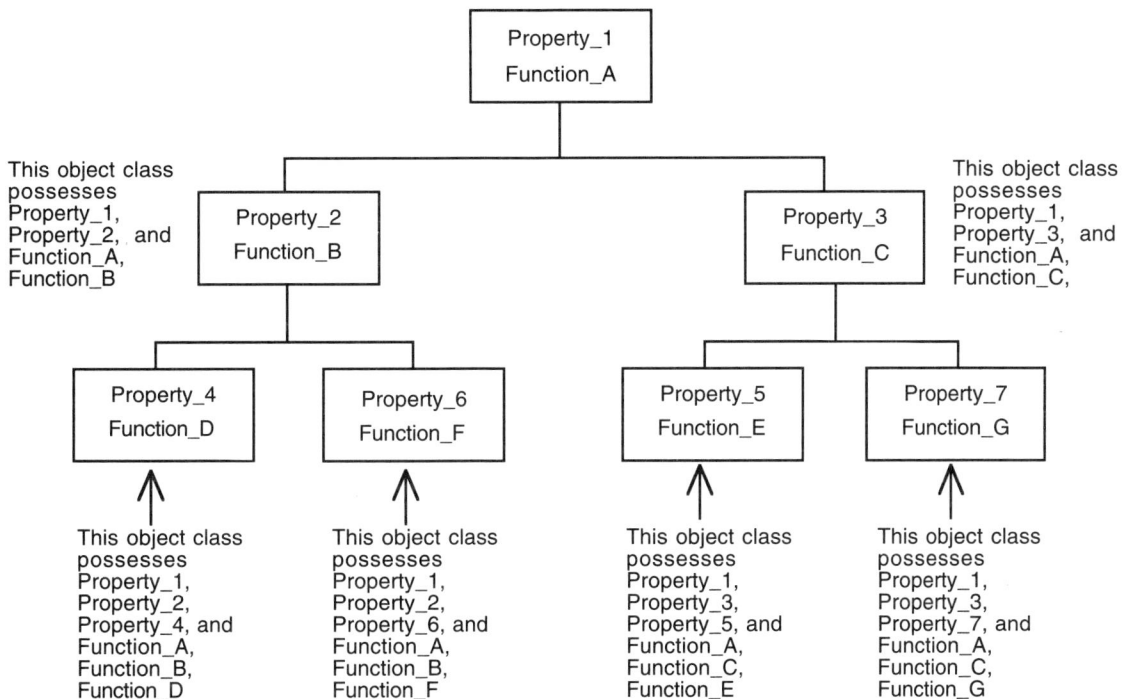

Figure 3–5. Object hierarchy and inheritance

Another productive way to use a software object is to relate it to other objects in a hierarchy. The main reason for doing this is sharing of program code and data. Figure 3–5 shows a hierarchy of objects.

3.3.2.1   Data and Process

All applications are made up of data and processes. In old applications, applications are completely separated as data and programs. Recently, with the arrival of database management systems, application design has been focusing on the data design, in particular, the relationship between the data elements.

These relationships are static and are modeled in a hierarchical parent-child manner, or in a tabular manner. A database management system is responsible for storing and managing these relationships on behalf of the application.

What has been missing is the process model is still implemented as application program logic separated from the database management system. The object-oriented approach could provide a means to integrate the data and process model.

3.3.2.2   Object Inheritance

In analyzing the attributes of various objects of an application, the common or shared attributes are identified. These attributes should be tabulated in a hierarchy with the most common ones, usually the simplest ones, at the top.

The principle of inheritance says that the lower hierarchy objects will assume all the attributes of the entities above them. As mentioned above, this type of data analysis is not new. In traditional programming, the purpose of this analysis is to share data and to ensure data integrity.

In the object-oriented approach, not only data is shared, but the program codes are also inherited up the hierarchy! This is a major difference between traditional and object-oriented applications.

In a hierarchy, the more generalized object classes are at the top with the more specialized classes lower in the hierarchy. The lower classes are known as the derived classes. The one class above is always known as the parent class. Thus, behind an object are generations of knowledge accumulation. This makes an object-oriented system act like a living entity.

3.3.2.3   Inheritance and Productivity

The main benefit for a hierarchy is to eliminate duplication of efforts in writing code for different object classes. The developers need only to write those properties and functions that are additional to the object class above it. If, after creating the derived classes, a programmer makes changes to the properties or behaviors of the parent class, the changes are automatically inherited by the derived classes.

Inheritance lowers the cost and decreases the complexity of software development. It makes incremental design and problem solving possible. Many call this process prototyping. Instead of modifying existing software code, new classes can be created from a set of baseline classes. If the environment supports the dynamic linkages (bindings), the software changes can be dynamically re-configured without the need for a global recompile. This topic will be revisited in the review of the C++ programming language.

In object-oriented programming, common attributes and behaviors of objects are defined and developed only once. When sub-categories of an object type calls for variations in attributes and behaviors, shared attributes and behavior may be overridden. The programmer refines the object types by addressing the exceptions of how an object type is different from other objects. Therefore, an object is as flexible as the imagination of a programmer.

3.3.2.4 Inheritance Examples

A Payroll Application

In a traditional system, a database designer defines a relation for Employee, and a relation for Student. He or she writes the program code for the functions of "income tax," "insurance," and "pay" for the Employee relation. He or she also writes the program code for the functions of "income tax," "insurance," and "Grade Point Average" for the Student relation. Thus, the application programmer writes six programs.

In an object-oriented system, using the inheritance property, Employees and Students are Persons. They have something in common and something unique. Let us introduce an object class: Person, which has attributes of Name and Age. After that, the functions of "income tax" and "insurance" for the Person Object can be written.

Next, Employee Objects are declared as derived class of Persons, who inherit Persons' attributes and functions and have a special property called Salary and a special function called Pay.

Traditional approach: Six programs

Object-oriented approach: Four programs

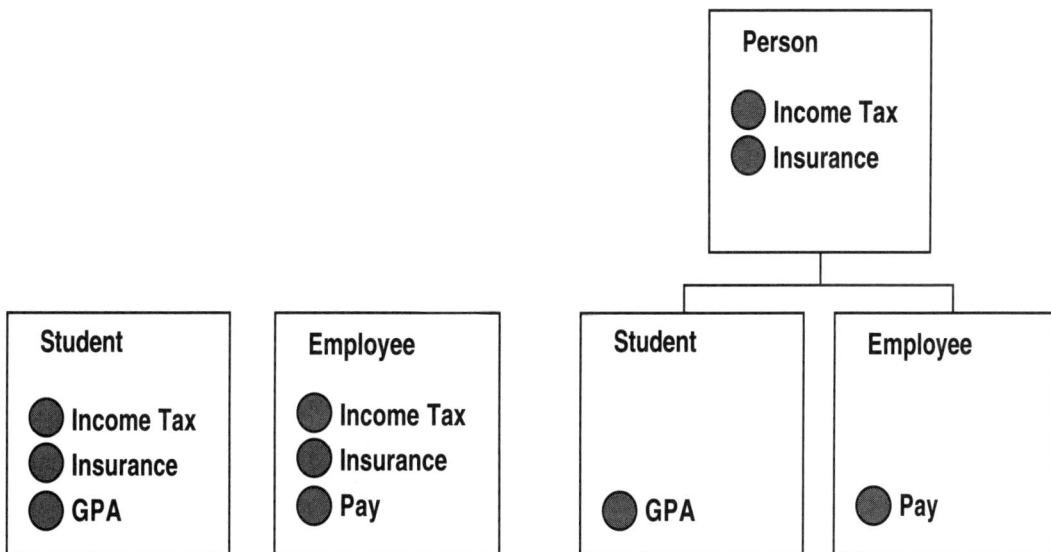

Figure 3–6. Object-oriented vs. traditional application development methods

Similarly, Student Objects are declared as a derived class of Person, with a specific subject_grades properties and a function called Grade Point Average. By seeking out the common attributes, and arranging them in a hierarchy, a better structured and more concise description of the scheme is obtained. And only four programs (instead of six) are needed!

Figure 3–6 illustrates the difference between the two approaches.

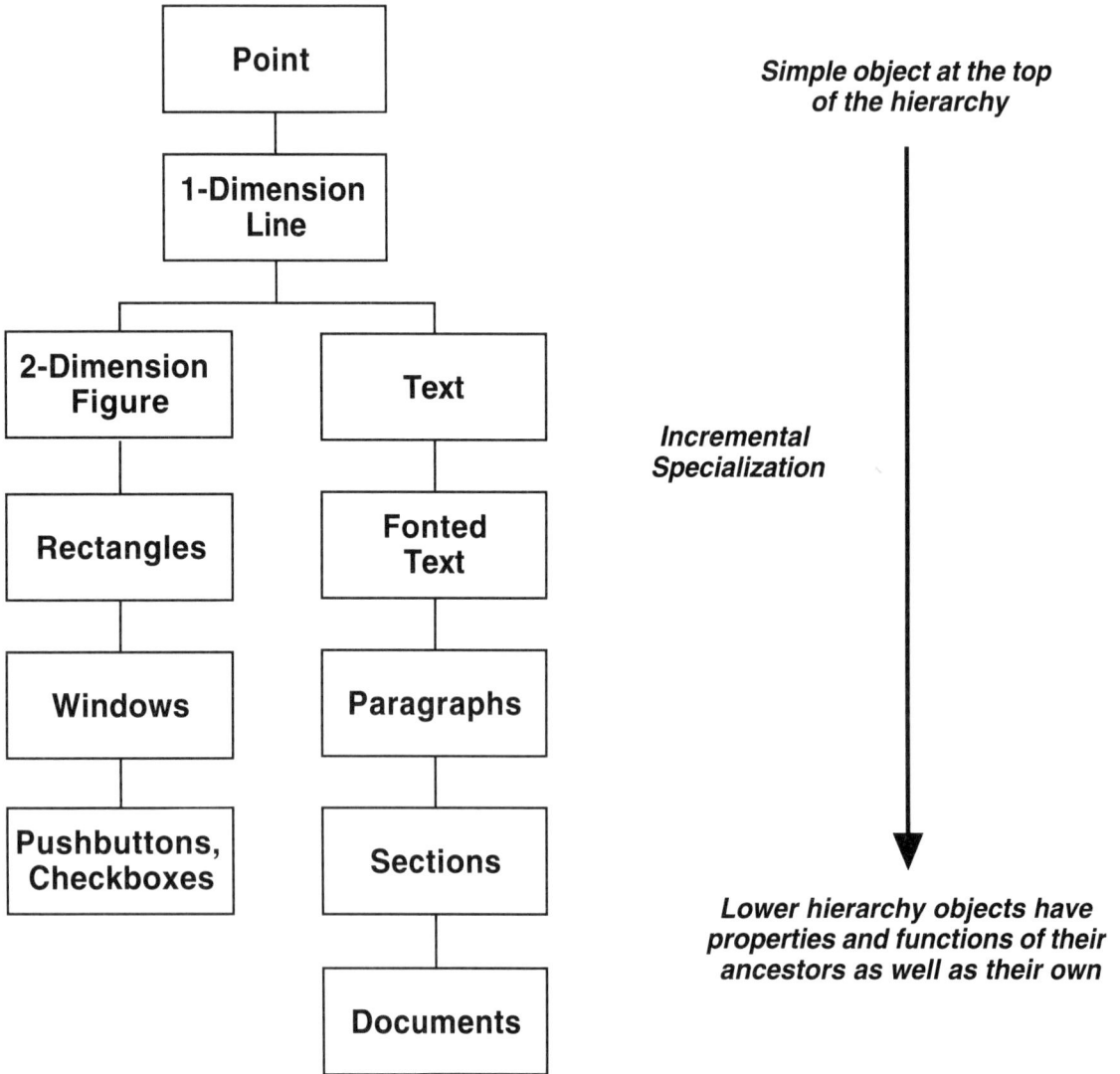

Figure 3–7. An example of Hierarchy and Inheritance

In Microsoft Windows screen objects, we can trace them through a hierarchy of object classes. The top of the hierarchy is a point object class on the screen. It is followed by a rectangle object class, which in turn is followed by a rectangle with all the properties of an application window: menu bar, scroll bar, sizing, color, and others. The window is followed by different buttons and boxes: the OK button, the Cancel button, the Check boxes, the List boxes, and many others.

Every object on the screen always contains the properties and the functions of the point object class, the "root object," if there is such a term. For example, rectangle objects always have points coordinates to denote its length and width. Any window object includes a rectangle object. Any button object includes a window object.

3.3.3 Polymorphism

Polymorphism refers to the ability to use the same function name for object classes in an hierarchy even though vastly different functions are executed.

For example, in a graphics application, the object hierarchy consists of simpler objects at the top and more complex objects at the bottom. A user wants to rotate a number of objects on the screen by 90 degrees.

It is obvious that different objects on the screen will require different programs to perform the rotation: rotating a letter "A" is quite different from rotating a hexagon. The fact that a user needs only to issue one command to rotate and does not have to issue two separate commands (say: rotate_text, and rotate_polygon) is a phenomena known as polymorphism, unique to object-oriented programming.

3.3.3.1 *Dynamic or Late Binding*

To use the same function name throughout a hierarchy of objects, the object-oriented application cannot bind function names to programs at compile time.

For example, the function rotate_90 for the text object class or for the polygon class is not bound to the executable code during their respective compilation because function names (i.e. rotate_90) must be translated into program addresses at runtime (i.e. rotate_text_90, and rotate_90_polygon). This delayed translation is called **late binding** or **dynamic binding,** another characteristic of object oriented programming.

Why is this ability of sharing the same function name in an object hierarchy so important for programmer's productivity? There are a couple of reasons.

3.3.3.2 *Programmer Productivity*

Firstly, a programmer does not have to add another "button" on the screen, a saving in terms of user interface programming. He or she will simply put the new object in the same hierarchy with other objects that use the same function name.

This may not look like a significant property initially. However, when you look at the user interface of your current applications, you will notice that there are many generic functions (print, display, open, close, save, delete, duplicate, copy) that apply to different object classes (text, multi-media, and graphics).

While each object class still requires a different set of programs to enact these generic functions, with polymorphism the interface to each does not need to be re-written, which is a great time saver.

3.3.3.3 Better Data Presentation

Polymorphism gives a real life look and feel to object-oriented applications. An important indication of intelligence in living things is in their ability to generalize ideas, activities, and things in their environment. Psychologists call this ability "abstraction." This capability of communicating ideas at a higher abstraction level is something that computers have tried to emulate without much success despite years of research on artificial intelligence.

For example, we understand the word "draw" to mean putting a figure of some kind onto something so that other people can see. This statement does not sound vague to a human, but it is too vague for a computer to understand. Draw is an action, a function, or a procedure that means different actions under different circumstances. Drawing a circle is different from drawing a line. Drawing an object on paper is different from drawing it on a computer screen. And so on.

The ability to use the same message for a similar operation on different object classes is consistent with the way humans relate to their environment. It is not natural to use different terminology for printing, deleting, editing, copying, and duplicating whether it is for text, pictures, sound, or video.

3.4   OBJECT-ORIENTED PROGRAMMING LANGUAGES

To assist in object-oriented application development, a number of object-oriented programming languages (OOPL) are available commercially. The more popular ones are SmallTalk and C++. SmallTalk was originated in Xerox. C++ was originated in AT&T's Bell Lab. While both are object-oriented, SmallTalk was conceived for applications in a single user environment. C++ has higher performance characteristic and is more suited for large, commercial applications.

3.4.1 The C++ Programming Language

C++ is a superset of C. It is a hybrid language in which the object-orientation can be exploited fully to produce a purely object-oriented application. Bell's commitment to make C++ compatible with the existing C makes it a strategic tool because of the millions of lines of production C code, libraries, and tools. It provides a tremendous incentive for a C programmer to learn C++.

Another big push on C++ is from the standards bodies. American National Standards Institute (ANSI) is standardizing C++. The C++ library comes in the form of header files with descriptions of the public interface of classes.

3.4.1.1 *Visual Programming Languages*

Not to be ignored, however, is a new breed of Microsoft's Windows-based object-oriented application development tools such as Aysmetrics Toolbook, Pilots Lightship, Microsoft's Visual Basic, Borland's ObjectVision, Powersoft's Power-Builder, White Water Group's Actor, and MDBS's Object 1.

These tools come with a set of pre-built Windows based screen objects (buttons, boxes, menu . . .), each of which has a set of default properties and procedures for keyboard and mouse inputs. Users build Windows-based applications by modifying these objects and by incorporating procedures using a high level script, 4GL, or Basics.

This category of products is also known as **visual programming.** It allows programmers to design interface to user applications in a "what you see is what you get—wysiwyg" manner, hence the term "visual." Because of these applications, programming in the Windows environment becomes a much more productive effort than writing C programs and making function calls to the Windows library.

The potential of these tools is not limited to PC applications. They can be used to develop more intuitive workstation front ends tapping into the vast number of existing mainframe character-oriented applications. In other words, they provide a face-lift for existing user interfaces.

We will discuss both types of object-oriented programming environments by choosing a typical product for each. For the first type, we choose C++ for its strategic importance. For the second type, we choose Microsoft's Visual Basic for its popularity among Windows application developers.

This discussion is meant to illustrate the fundamental power of object-oriented programming. The objective is not to teach object-oriented programming, for which readers can be better served by going through their technical manuals or the books in the Reference Section.

3.4.2 Borland's C++

In this section, we will use Borland's C++ to illustrate the working of an object-oriented programming language. This section assumes that the readers have some knowledge of C. Every effort is made to explain the content in a generic way for the non-C programmers.

The advantages of C++ over C are in the ability of C++ to define objects through the encapsulation facility, to create new class objects through the inheritance facility, and to allow a function to exhibit different responses through the polymorphism facility.

Encapsulation is achieved by a new data type known as a class. Objects of the same class share the same properties and behaviors.

Inheritance is achieved by a new process known as deriving class. A new class of objects can be created by deriving it from a parent. The derived class inherits all the properties and behaviors of its parent class plus its own additional properties and behaviors.

Polymorphism is achieved by using the new virtual function to override the behavior of a function of the same name and of the parent class.

Programmer's Productivity

The effectiveness of the inheritance and the polymorphism facilities is that programmers need only "include" the header file of the parent class in the derived class header file. They do not need to recompile or change any source code of the parent class. Existing parent class executable code is reusable immediately.

Both aspects are very significant to programmer's productivity. A programmer can compile a class and place it in an object library. Anyone can then take this library, and the header file for the class, extend the class by modifying it to suit the application. The following example expands this idea.

3.4.2.1 C++ Programs

This example shows how a C++ program can be created and executed. In C++ programming or in C programming, the program is contained in two types of file: the source file and the header file.

The source file contains the program logic. The header file contains the declarative statements on the data structure. Header file has no executable constructs. The source file and the header file are both needed for the compiler to produce the executable code.

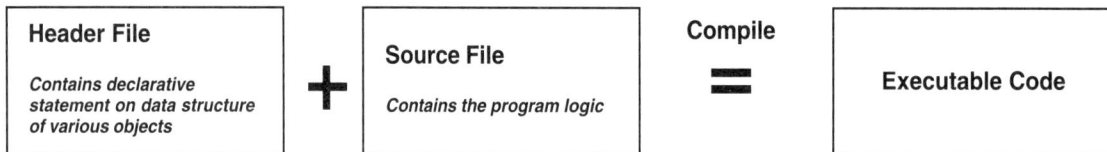

Figure 3-8. Header file and source file

The first thing a programmer should do is to create a header file in which he or she will define all the object classes required for his or her application. In the header file, he or she must include various header files from the standard system and user libraries. The class object definition should include all data types for class variables and class functions. Object classes are related in a hierarchy.

For class functions, only prototypes (not the function body) are included in the header file. In the source file, initialization functions (constructors) for object classes should be specified first. Class functions that were defined as prototypes in the header file should also be defined.

After the creation of the header file and the source file, the programmer can write the main program which tells the computer what to do after all the objects have been initialized. All are then fed to the C++ compiler, which produces the executable code. The C++ compiler creates the initialization code for each object, and the main program code.

When the program is launched, all objects will be initialized before the main program is executed. In an object-oriented application, most of the intelligence (data and program) resides among the initialized objects. Since objects are event driven, the significance of the main program is reduced when it is compared with the traditional approach.

If an analogy of this situation must be made, the objects are like the baseball players in the ball park. When the game starts, they all run out and take up their respective positions in the field (Objects initialized). The game starts when the umpire yells "Play ball!" (Main program starts). The rest is up to the players (the interacting objects).

3.4.2.2 Class Objects

In a C++ application, objects are declared in the header file.

```
class name {
      private: member1 member2 member3 . . . ;
      public: memberP1 memberP2 . . . ;
      constructor  ;
      destructor  ;
      overloaded operator functions;
         }
```

The "class" keyword followed by the name of the object is required. There are two compartments within an object. The private compartment and the public compartment. In the private compartment, all member objects or functions are available for access only by member or friend function of this class object. The private section must come before the public section in the declaration. In the public members section, all member objects or functions are available for general access.

The members are variable definitions (e.g., integer, character, void, ... data types), and function prototypes. Note that the function body is not in the header file; it is contained in the source file.

Two special functions in the public compartment are the Constructor and the Destructor functions. They control the creation, initialization, copying, and destruction of objects during program execution. C++ objects are never created during program compilation, they are created during the execution of the Constructor function at run time.

The constructor not only sets values for the members of the object, they can perform dynamic memory allocation, open files, and others. Constructors always have the same name as the class object. They have no return type, not even void.

The destructor is used to deallocate memory allocated by an object. The destructor function is invoked when the program execution leaves the scope of the object. A class cannot have more than one destructor, which cannot have any arguments or return type, not even void.

Besides the Constructor and the Destructor functions, there is another special function used in the creation of class object. It is the override operator function.

In C++ there are a number of built-in operator functions such as the assignment operator =, addition operator +, subtraction operator -, multiplication operator *, division operator /, and others. There are times, however, when programmers need new operator functions. For instance, the programmer may want to redefine the + operator to not only add numbers, but to combine strings as well.

When a programmer wants to add additional operator functions, he or she is said to be overloading the operator function. This facility allows the programmer to customize operator function for an object class that he is defining. Like any other function in C++, the overloaded function has types as well as function prototypes in the header file and the function body in the source file.

Create C++ Objects

During the program execution, once the class object is loaded and initialized, instance objects can be created by invoking the name of the class object and by supplying the correct private members for the instance. Creation of instance objects can be invoked by the main program, or other objects in the same application. In C++, the syntax to create instance objects is:

```
Class_Object_Name.Instance_Object_Name (private members)

Class_Object.Instance_Object (data)

e.g.   Purchase_order.Car0001 (Cadillac, 1992, $50000)

Purchase_order.Truck0001 (Jeep, 1990, $25000)

Customer.0000001 (John Smith, Manufacturing, United_States)

Customer.0010000 (Joe Kennedy, Electronics, Ireland)
```

Call C++ Function

After all the class objects and instance objects are initialized, the objects can be put to use. To use any function, one must associate that with an object. With this calling mechanism in place, the objects simply start making things happen by sending each other messages. The general calling syntax is:

```
Instance_Object_Name.Function (arguments)

object_name.function (message)

e.g.   Car0001.sales_tax (Virginia)

//sales tax for the car0001 sold in Virginia

0010000.sales_total (August, 1992)

// total purchase from Joe Kennedy in August, 1992
```

Example of Class Object

In a typical commercial transaction, a product is sold at a certain price for a certain quantity. Since there are many products, a class object for product can be created. Typically, a product has an identification number and price. The amount paid by the customer is equal to the price multiplied by the quantity.

The product object has an integer for the product identification number, and a floating number for the price. These data elements are kept in the private compartment of the object not accessible directly from outside. It can only be accessed through functions declared in the public compartment.

> Here is a simple class object known as product. The class object's data includes the product identification number, and the price for each product. It also has a very simple function which upon given the quantity sold for a particular product, it will calculate and print out the amount paid.

```
// Class declaration
class product
{
private:
int  id;
float price;
public:

//Constructor function
       product (int i, float p);

//Destructor function
       product (void);

//Member function
       void print_product (float quantity);}

// Class implementation
product::product (int i, float p)
       {
       id = i;  //set product ID = i
       price = p;  //set price = p
       }
void product::print_product (float quantity)
       {
       printf(" Product #%d: %s\n", id);
       printf("Quantity sold: %5.2f\n", qty);
       printf("Amount paid: 7.2f\n\n",qty*price); }
product::~product (void)
       {
```

```
            delete;
            }
```

// Let the 'game' be started

```
main ( )
{  product milk (100, 1.50)
        product juice (200, 1.25)
        product wine (500, 10.75)
        milk.print_product (45.00)
        juice.print_product (12.00)
        wine.print_product (8.00)
        return 0}
```

3.4.2.3 Inheritance

In C++ special facilities are provided for creating new classes from existing classes. To derive a class from a base class, the following syntax is needed:

```
class derived_class_name : parent_class_name
{additional members}
```

Derived Class Function

The new members can be either functions or data. In a derived class object, the parent class object's data and function are an integral part of the object. Derived class objects cannot have functions that have the same name as those in the parent class. This does not mean that this function cannot be done. The polymorphism feature of C++ is designed to enable this to happen. The next section on polymorphism will discuss this in greater detail.

In the last example, the Product Class object has two properties: the product identification number and the product unit price. However, products have groupings: Dairy products, Meat products, Beverage products, and so on. Each group by itself can be a class object derived from the product class object. We can have a Dairy_Product Class object. Products such as milk, cheese, butter are typical instance objects. The Dairy_Product Class object shares the same properties and functions of the parent Product Class object.

In the header file, the programmer creates the new class dairy_product by using the class keyword and by specifying the name of the parent class object. He or she then specifies the data types of the new members: product type, brand name, size, and tax. He or she also adds a new function called print which has only one argument: the quantity of the product sold.

In the source file, a programmer specifies the constructor function, the destructor function, and the new member function. C++ provides the ':' operator for constructor and destructor specification. In this case, the constructor function simply initializes the new members and pick up the existing value of the parent class.

In the new function, print, the programmer specifies the function to print the product ID, type, brand name, size, tax, and amount paid. The C++ compiler knows that the product ID and the product unit price is not available in this class and will go up one level to the parent object to fetch them.

In the main program, dairy_product instance objects are created by issuing the commands "class_object . instance_object (data)." Each instance object can be used to print the product ID, type, brand name, size, tax, and amount paid based on the quantity sold.

In reality, all the programmer has to do is to include the header file of the parent class in the new header file and then extend the parent class by adding new data and functions for the derived class object. The parent class object compiled code is immediately reusable. It does not have to be recompiled.

Example of Derived Class Function

```
// declare new object and its parent class
class dairy_product : product
{ private:
      char type [80];  //product type
      char brand_name [80];   //brand name
      char size [10];  //size
      float  tax;  //state tax

public:

//Constructor function for this class
      dairy_product
      (char*a, char *b, char *c, float x);

//Destructor function
      dairy_product (void);

// Member function 'print' has one argument
      void print (float quantity); }

// Class implementation
dairy_product:: dairy_product
(char *a, char *b, char *c, float x)
: product ( i, p);
      { strcpy (type, a);
        strcpy (brand_name, b);
        strcpy (size, c);
        tax = x;};

// Member function specification
void dairy_product::print (float quantity)
      {printf ("Product #  %d \ n", id);
      printf ("Type: %s \ n ", type);
      printf ("Brand name: %s \ n", brand_name)
```

```
      printf ("Size: %s \ n", size)
      printf ("Tax: %5.2f \ n", tax)
      printf ("Amount paid: $%7.2f\n\n", price *
      quantity * tax)}
```

// Destructor implementation
```
dairy_product::~dairy_product
(void){delete}
```

main ( )
```
{// Create dairy product instant objects
dairy_product milk
      ("milk", "Beatrice","1/2 Liter", "7%");
dairy_product cheese
      ("cheese", "Beatrice","1 Kg", "7%");
dairy_product butter
      ("butter", "Farmer's","1 lb", "7%");

// Print out product information:
      milk.print (45.00);
      cheese.print (20.00);
      butter.print (10.00);
      return 0 ;}
```

3.4.2.4 *Polymorphism*

The special facility that C++ uses to implement polymorphism is known as the virtual function. With polymorphism, the same function name can be used throughout a hierarchy of object classes, with each class exhibiting different behaviors and responses.

In a hierarchy of two-dimensional geometric objects, the Point Class is the obvious root class since all geometric objects are comprised of points. Hence, a Circle Class can be created from the Point Class, and a Cylinder Class can be created from the Circle Class.

The function to calculate the surface area of these geometric objects will yield different results even though the function name "AREA" is the same throughout the object hierarchy. With the C++'s virtual function facility, the programmer can implement a function that automatically readjusts itself for different object classes to calculate the correct surface areas. The function "AREA" is polymorphic.

Virtual Function

The virtual function implements a function by the function pointer. It takes on the behavior of whatever happens to be specified in location pointed to by the function pointer. This is generally known as **dynamic binding** or **late binding,** which takes place at run time, rather than during program compilation.

When the function pointer happens to be pointing at the circle object, the area will be calculated for the circle. If the function pointer is set to point to the cylinder, then the area for the cylinder will be calculated instead.

Once again, this is a very powerful programming productivity feature. If a programmer wants to include a new geometric object to an already highly stable and successful graphics application, he or she can use all the existing menu commands (e.g., rotate, print, stretch, . . .) for the new geometric object.

All he or she needs to do is to get the header file for the existing graphics application and add the new data and virtual function declarations to form a new header file. This new header file and his or her own source file are compiled to form the executable. As a result, the graphic application can now handle a new object type.

Notice the program has overridden the parent class functions (rotate, print, stretch, . . .) with his own functions by way of the virtual function facility. The programmer achieves this without modifying the source. The existing compiled code is immediately reusable without any recompilation. Without polymorphism, the programmer's users would still be using all the previous functions with the other geometric objects.

Example of Virtual Functions

```
        // Class declarations in the header file
class point
{
        float x,y; // A point
//Constructor function
        point (float xi, float yi);
//Destructor function
        ~point (void);
//Virtual function AREA
        virtual float AREA (void);
        };
//derive circle from point
        class circle : point
{
        float radius  // Add the radius circle
        (float r)  //Constructor function
        ~circle (void)  //Destructor function
        float AREA (void)  //Virtual function AREA
}

class cylinder : circle
{
        float height;  // Add the height
        cylinder (float ht);
        ~cylinder (void)
        float AREA (void)
```

```
}
// The source file
// Constructor functions implementation

point :: point
(float xi, float yi){ x = xi; y= yi;};

circle :: circle
( float r){ radius = r;};

cylinder :: cylinder
( float ht) { height = ht; }

// Virtual functions implementation
virtual float AREA (void) { return 0.0;}
float AREA (void)
{ return 3.14159 * radius * radius}
float AREA (void)
{ return 3.14159 * 4.0 * radius * height + 2 *
    circle :: AREA( ) }
// Destructor function definition

point ::~point (void){ delete}
circle ::~circle (void){ delete}
cylinder ::~cylinder (void){ delete}
```

main ( )
```
{
point center (0.00, 0.00)// value for the
  center
circle cross_section ( 10.00)// value for the
  radius
cylinder beer_can ( 20.00)// value for the
  height
point *pointer_to_virtual_function

//declare the pointer

pointer_to_virtual_function = &center

//assign pointer to the point

float center_area =
pointer_to_virtual_function -> AREA ( );
pointer_to_virtual_function = &cross_section;
```

```
//asgn pntr to circle
float cross_section_area =
pointer_to_virtual_function -> AREA ( );
pointer_to_virtual_function = &beer_can;

float beer_can_area =
pointer_to_virtual_function -> AREA ( );

printf ("Area for the center is : %5.2f\n",
  center_area);
printf ("Area for the cross section is : %5.2f\n" ,
  cross_section _area);
printf ("Area for the beer can is : %5.2f\n" ,
  beer_can_area);}};
```

3.4.3 Microsoft's Visual Basic

Microsoft's Visual Basic is one of many Windows-based application development products that came on the market in the early 1990's. Products such as Borland's Object Vision, Asymetric's ToolBook, MDBS's Object 1, PowerBuilder, and Pilot's LightShip come with their own high level programming language or scripts. In Apple's Macintosh, the HyperCard application is one example.

Applications generated by these tools are naturally based on the graphical user interface (GUI) objects such as windows, list boxes, drop boxes, command buttons, and text boxes. Their object-orientation is derived from the fact that actions are triggered by objects on the screen.

Windows objects have properties and can be programmed to respond to keyboard input, mouse actions, and dynamic data exchange requests. Tremendous potential offered by this type of tool is in the programmer's productivity and in providing a user friendly interface for host based or workstation-based applications.

By incorporating extended communication features, these type of workstation based applications can be made to access information from many host based applications. They provide a very cost effective way to downsize, to integrate, and to enhance many of the existing legacy application systems.

This type of easy-to-learn, high level programming language application development environment fits a market niche not quite intended to compute intensive and large data volume processing.

The latter is best handled by using the more powerful programming languages such as C++, where platform independence is required. Microsoft's Visual Basic is chosen for discussion because it is a good product, well documented, and priced competitively to gain wide acceptance by programmers.

3.4.3.1 Basic Concepts

Visual Basic is an object-oriented programming tool designed to help programmers develop Windows- or Presentation Manager-based applications. The Basic

Programming Language in Visual Basic is an outgrowth of the original Microsoft DOS-Basic. The old Basic code will run under Visual Basic with some modification. The big difference is in the user interface, and in the object orientation.

Visual Basic is in itself a Windows application. It is a programming tool designed with plenty of point-and-click type interfaces for programmers to build their applications. Visual Basic application is built with pre-built Windows objects: push buttons, selection boxes, text boxes, list boxes, scroll bars, menu bar, and so on.

Basic programs are incorporated to provide functions behind each object. These functions are invoked by external events such as keyboard inputs, mouse actions, or direct calls from other objects (DDE). The Windows operating system is responsible to capture or intercept these external events and pass them onto the appropriate objects of the Visual Basic application.

3.4.3.2   Form and Controls

A Visual Basic application always has a customized application window called the Form. Inside the Form are other Windows objects such as push buttons, scroll bars, list boxes, and text input boxes. They are called Controls. Each object in the application must be identifiable by an unique name. For example, the Close button for an application known as File Manager may be called FileManagerCloseButton.

3.4.3.3   Properties

All Window objects possess properties such as the size, the color, the font, and others. The syntax in Visual Basic to identify such property is : ObjectName.PropertyName. For example, to specify the text in the text box ABC, one can issue simple commands as follows: ABC.Text = "Please enter your name here". ABC.Text = str$ (amount) where ABC is the name of the object–the text box, and Text is one of the properties of the box–the text string.

3.4.3.4   Events

An event is a keyboard action, a mouse action, or a dynamic data exchange (DDE) activity. The reference to an event is: ObjectName.Event

3.4.3.5   User Functions

User actions could be keyboard inputs, mouse actions, or a timer event. For example, when a user clicks the button identified as OK, Visual Basic will invoke the execution of the object function OK_Click, if there is one. More generic representation of this event program would be: WindowObjectName_EventName.

After the function finishes executing, Visual Basic will wait for the next event.

3.4.3.6 Examples

The following are examples of Visual Basic programming. Readers who wish to go into more detail of Virtual Basic programming should obtain the Professional Edition of Visual Basic from Microsoft.

Examples of Windows Objects

Visual Basic has an extensive collection of Windows objects. It makes Windows-based application development a much easier job than writing C programs and making calls to Windows Dynamic Link Libraries.

Each Windows object is a class object having a set of default properties and behaviors. Modification of these default properties and behaviors to create new individualized applications, instead of re-writing from the ground up. This is the gist of object-oriented programming.

Objects	Description
Check box	A control object used to represent an option (on/off, true/false) that the user can set or clear by clicking.
Command button	A pushbutton for the user to carry out a command
Directory list box	A control object that displays a hierarchical list of directories. It is used by the user to select directories and paths at run time

Examples of Window Objects Properties

The following is a representation of properties that can be associated with a very simple object: the Check box.

Properties	Description
Backcolor, Forecolor, MousePointer, Visible	Appearance : Color of the check box
Caption	The text on the check box
Index, Ctlname	Control name and index for the check box

Examples of Window Object Functions

Besides properties, each object is endowed with a set of default functions to handle outside commands, messages, and requests. Note the syntax of all calls: The object is identified by name, and then the function name followed by the associated arguments. Note the same syntax as a C++ program. This is by no means a complete listing; however, the following are typical methods that are associated with an object: the "form."

Methods	Description
Point	Return the RGB color of the specified point on a form or picture box. Syntax: [object.]Point (x!, y!)
Print	Draw text on the 'form' Syntax: [object.]Print[expressionlist][{	, }]

Typical Keyboard, Mouse, and Windows Events

Triggering Action	Resulting Windows events an object may react to
User mouse operation	click, double_click, mouse_down, mouse_up, mouse _move

3.5 OBJECT-ORIENTED DBMS

In this section, we will discuss the merit of an OODBMS, its essential components, and how the RDBMS can be extended to satisfy some of the object oriented requirements.

An object is essentially a new data type (in addition to integers, characters, floating point numbers, and so on) from a database management system point of view. Unlike other data types, objects are not pure data. They contain programs. Therein lies the complexity of managing objects based on the traditional database management system ideas.

Currently, there is no agreed upon specification of what constitutes a true object-oriented database management system (OODBMS). Unlike the relational model backed up by a disciplined mathematical treatment on entity relationship, the OODBMS has no equivalent data model.

3.5.1 OODBMS vs. RDBMS

Data base managers manage pure data. They are, by definition, class objects because besides holding data, they also respond to requests from user programs. For example, to access IBM's Information Management System (IMS) databases, one has to use IBM's Data Language (DL/1). To access the DB2 or other relational type of databases, one has to use the Structured Query Language (SQL).

Each data table under a relational data base manager (RDBMS) is an instance object of the database class. Data managed by RDBMS are characterized by simple data structures. All access to data and relationships between tables is based on values. A data value is uniquely determined by the table name, the column name, and the unique identifier of the row (the primary key).

RDBMSs are for applications with simple data structure. For applications that use complex data types: objects, lists, arrays, and time series, RDBMS has failed. Complex data types are commonly found in engineering, geological, computer-aided design applications, and applications with time series data.

For example, product specifications for a jet engine, or an automobile exhaust system have more than 2000 object classes to describe how these parts are supposed to be put together. These 2000 objects correspond to at least 2000 tables!

Accessing a composite object like those above requires accessing hundreds of component objects. This is equivalent to joining many relational tables. This is so many that it exceeds the system limit for most RDBMSs. A task that is beyond the capability of today's RDBMS.

Chasing the object identification references available in most object-oriented programming language is inherently faster than even the best RDBMSs optimizer can do with joins.

Wants

What is needed is an objects base management system that will perform the tasks not normally found in a programming language such as C++. These are tasks a data base management system would perform: object management, object sharing, object persistence, object transaction management, recovery from hardware and software failures, versioning, distribution, security, and query mechanisms.

3.5.2 OODBMS Features

An OODBMS must be able to support all the three basic features of object orientation mentioned earlier: encapsulation, inheritance, and polymorphism.

3.5.2.1 Object Factory and Warehouse

An OODBMS should provide facility for the user and the user program to easily create new instance objects of an object class. The concept is one of object factory and object warehouse.

The object factory is responsible to manufacture instance objects and the object warehouse is there to store the instance objects of an object class. The object factory can create new objects by performing the new operation on the class, or by cloning some prototype object representative of the class. The user can manipulate the warehouse by applying operation on all elements of a class, using a simple interface such as a graphical browser.

There should also be a means to define new classes so that there is no distinction in usage between system-defined and user-defined classes. This type of feature is currently available in most RDBMSs, in which the new operation will create a new data record and new field definition will create a new record type.

3.5.2.2 Object Access Languages

Traditional data access languages such as DL/1 and SQL do not possess sophisticated computational functions such as trigonometric functions, string manipulation functions, or exponential functions.

Most database management system developers are of the opinion that the database manager's job is to manage the data. What one wants to do with the data (such as manipulation and calculation) should be left to the real programming languages such as COBOL or C, because it is felt that the same language cannot be optimal both for writing an application and for manipulating the data.

However, it is hard to apply the same philosophy to OODBMS. The reason: The data inside an object can only be meaningfully operated by the functions defined along with it. One can imagine the role of the OODBMS being that of a messenger. When a user program or another object needs access to an object under the OODBMS, it will make the request to the OODBMS. The OODBMS must check that the request for the object has the right "stuff" before it passes the request to the intended object.

There is no definitive outcome of this debate yet. Most likely both sides (the object-oriented programming language group and the database management group) will extend themselves respectively to some middle ground as demanded by the market. For example, a number of vendors are now talking about **SQL Plus,** which, as its name implies, will incorporate ability over and beyond the current SQL capability.

3.5.2.3 Object Transaction Management

Traditional database management system is designed to perform tasks measured by units of work known as transactions. By definition, transaction processing guarantees either that an entire transaction is completed and all resulting changes are reflected in the database or that the transaction is rolled back to a predetermined point without changing the database.

Transaction processing assures that all transactions are performed as a single unit of work—even in the presence of a hardware or general system failure. The importance of transaction processing can be seen by a typical banking application: transfer of fund from the saving account to the checking account.

```
BEGIN TRANSACTION XXX
DEBIT SAVINGS ACCOUNT $1000
CREDIT CHECKING ACCOUNT $1000
COMMIT TRANSACTION XXX
```

Both debit and credit steps, or neither, must be completed. If the account debit is reflected in the database but not the account credit, the bank will end up with a very unhappy customer!

Object-Oriented View

In the object-oriented world, what constitutes a transaction? This is a matter of some debate because objects contain functions as well as data. A unit of work is less well defined.

To illustrate the meaning of committed transaction in an object-oriented environment, let's turn to our favorite document objects. A user accesses his or her object through an OODBMS. He or she wishes to make some changes to the document and then store it back to the object database.

By definition this is a transaction. The transaction begins when the user opens the document, and ends when the user closes the document after modifying it. While the user was modifying the document, which may take hours or days, the changes will not be committed to the original object databases unless this action is either explicitly specified by the user (a "save" command in the middle of the work), or when the user closes the document.

Thus, the differences between the RDBMS and the OODBMS applications are in their transaction duration, and the function varieties. In RDBMS applications, the transactions are simple updates taking only milliseconds to complete, and with fast throughput. A bank customer would be rather upset if he or she had to wait for two hours to get a transfer done by the computer!

In OODBMS applications, a transaction takes much longer to complete. Also, unlike RDBMS applications where the program logic is independent of the database itself whereas in the OODBMS, the program logic is part of the object rendering it less control over the execution of the transaction.

Recovery from Failures

The OODBMS should offer the same level of service as the RDBMS, which guarantees the consistency and recoverability of databases. A transaction is not considered consummated until a commit command is issued. Thus it guarantees either that an entire transaction is completed and all resulting changes are reflected in the database or that the transaction is rolled back to a predetermined save point without changing the database.

For an OODBMS, it will have to provide facilities to log all the object activities for recovery from any type of failure. (For example, taking snapshots of the document while the user is modifying it.)

Whenever a request to modify the database is received, a copy of both old and new states of the database affected portions is recorded in the transaction log. These changes are always made to the log before they are made to the database itself.

Concurrency

Unlike the traditional RDBMS applications, the transaction throughput in an object-oriented application is much slower. Instead of hundreds of transactions per second typical of an on-line commercial application, an engineering transaction environment is characterized by a low transaction rate with a duration of hours, days, or weeks.

In OODBMS client server implementation, an object may be executing in the client computer for a very long time lasting for hours or even days. This will require locking or de-locking mechanisms different from that of a traditional RDBMS.

Furthermore, because the nature of an update is known through the function, there is additional information available for the system to use in determining concurrency mechanisms. A frequently-used approach for concurrency management is the creation of multiple versions of an object so that each user sees a consistent, but different, database.

3.5.3   OODBMS Commercial Products

A number of OODBMS systems are starting to appear on the market. The following is just a sample to provide readers with a sense of what is available, and it is not intended to get to the details of them. Readers can always contact the respective vendors to obtain more information.

3.5.3.1   HP's Open ODB

HP introduced its object-oriented database product known as the OpenODB in 1991. It has a relational database engine with a variety of interfaces that let users and application developers handle data in an object-oriented manner. Users store data in a relational format.

HPs OpenODB provides an object-oriented version of the SQL for either interactive or procedural use. Features supported include a true object-oriented paradigm with multiple inheritance, polymorphism and data encapsulation.

Application programming interfaces for C, C++ and Object SQL are provided. The program will run on HP's HP-UX UNIX and the OSF/Motif graphical interface.

3.5.3.2   Microsoft's OLE

Microsoft has produced an OODBMS dedicated to the compound document object class. This type of document can contain objects of audio, video, bit-mapped images, text, and graphics, commonly known as multi-media. Microsoft calls this the Object Linking and Embedding (OLE).

Application software such as spreadsheets, chart makers, draws, and word processors can be designed to comply with the OLE standard. Linking lets one document refer to another document that can also update it in real time. It is like the DDE. Embedding lets one application's document contain information created by a second application in the second application's native format. It is like clipboard clipping. All OLE applications share a common objects database, which takes care of the DDE problem of one application needing to know the details of another by establishing a protocol of standard topics and procedures with which the applications talk to each other.

For example, a document may contain text objects that were created by OLE word processor, data objects that were part of an OLE spreadsheet application, and bit-image objects created by Paintbrush.

The OLE database, which is an OODBMS will automatically handle the dynamic data exchange that must occur between the spread sheet data and the data object on the document. Any change in the data on the spreadsheet will be reflected immediately on the affected documents.

Similarly, when the image object on the document requires changes, OLE will automatically start up the embedded Paintbrush application with the image loaded inside it. When the change is done, the new image will appear on the document while the paintbrush program is made to retire. An OLE based file system is an object-oriented document management system, which keeps track of all registered objects.

For example, if a document has embedded graphs objects, text objects, paint objects, and so on, these objects can be sent or copied across a network or disk drives without losing any referenced objects and or applications within that document.

Today's file system manages files as unrelated entities. The object-oriented approach puts life into the content of each document (or what used to be called files).

3.5.4   OODBMS Summary

An object-oriented database management system can be built fundamentally in two ways: The first is endorsed by the object oriented programming language purists, while the second by the database management system advocates.

An OODBMS is just another object! In it, objects are the data. Access to the objects is constrained by the functions defined for each particular object. A few predefined functions are available as well (for example, functions to create or destroy an object). In other words, the essence of an OODBMS is the same as object-oriented programming. Access by any applications to the stored objects is via the functions defined for (or also known as the message handling facility of) an OODBMS.

Another way to manage the objects is to make use of the existing relational database managers such as DB2 and RDB. The relational tables are used to store the pointers that point to locations of the objects. Access to an object will be via standard SQL calls to a data elements which do not contain the object itself, but which do contain the location of the object.

A good example in extending the RDBMS to include object orientation can be found in products from Sybase, Ingres, and Interbase. They use a technique known as the stored procedure, which is part of the database. These procedures can be executed by name, or automatically when an update to the specific data element occurs. For instance, when an update to the unit price occurs, the procedure to calculate the sales tax will be automatically executed. This functionality could become the basis for encapsulation (in which all interaction with an object is done through predefined procedures).

Vendors supplying OODBMS sometimes start with an OOPL (such as C+ + or Smalltalk) and enhance the language to include DBMS features, while other vendors have taken a DBMS and extended it to include object-oriented characteristics. Depending upon the chosen starting point, developers end up with either a good OOPL that can also handle some DBMSs, or a good DBMS that can be defined and used from an essentially object-oriented perspective.

4

Network Transport Environment

INTRODUCTION

The network transport environment is represented by the four bottom layers—physical, data link, network, transport—of the OSI Reference Model. Its main function is to establish and maintain a virtual communication circuit for a program to exchange message with another program on the network.

This chapter is divided into four main parts. The first part is about the physical layer. The second is about the data link layer. The third part is about the network and the transport layers, and the fourth part is about heterogeneous network connections.

In the physical layer section, transmission circuits, wiring types, and wiring connectors are discussed.

The data link layer section is divided into the general characteristics of data link protocols, media access control sublayers, and logical link control sublayers. Examples discussed include IEEE LANs, FDDI, ATM, and the start-stop protocol.

In the network and transport layers section, TCP/IP is reviewed in detail because of its textbook feature. Other protocols include X.25, Frame relay, Novell's SPX/IPX, Microsoft's NetBEUI, and various types of "dial" access to the network.

Interconnecting devices such as repeaters, bridges, routers, and gateways are also reviewed in the section on heterogeneous connection.

4.1   THE PHYSICAL LAYER

The physical layer is responsible to provide a physical path through which computer electronic signals travel. This layer consists of various types of transmission circuits and their associated wiring, electronic controls, and connection devices.

In this section we will discuss the general characteristics of transmission circuits, wiring, wiring connectors, EIA-232C, and wide area transmission circuits.

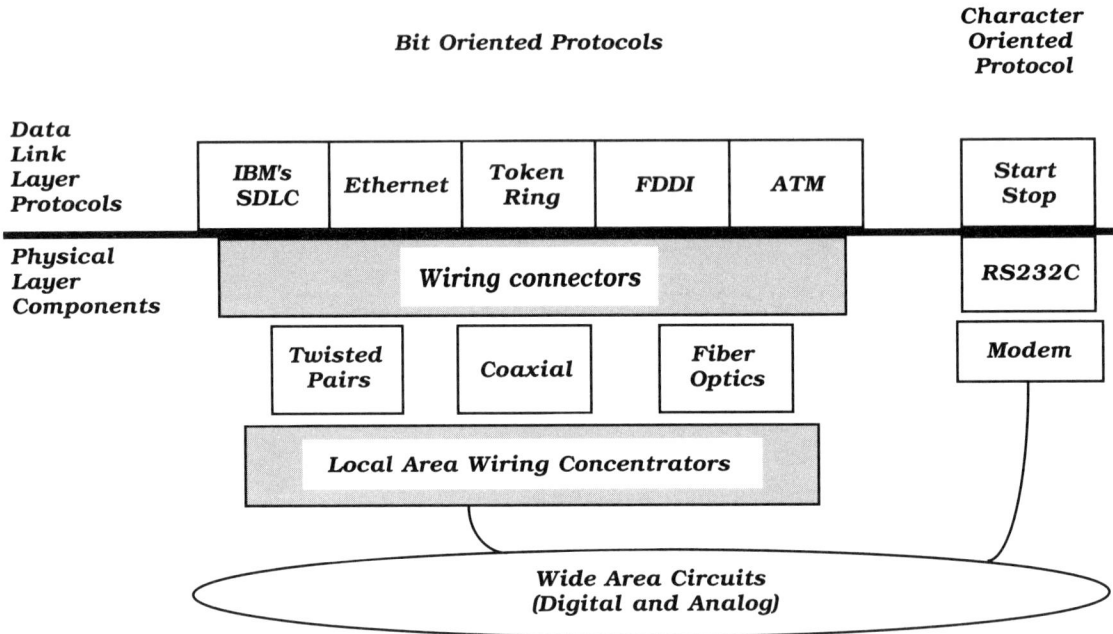

Figure 4–1. An overview of the physical and the data link layers' components

Certain data link layer components that have physical dimensions are often mistaken for part of the physical layer. Figure 4–1 shows the dividing line between them and the physical layer components. In Section 4.2 we will review the data link layer protocols shown in the diagram.

4.1.1   Transmission Circuits

Different types of transmission circuits can be classified in many ways. This section discusses the more common ways classifying transmission circuits. These include parallel vs. serial circuits, local area vs. wide area circuits, and analog vs. digital circuits.

4.1.1.1 Parallel vs. Serial Circuits

Before we go on to discuss various physical layer components, we need to explain the difference between parallel and serial transmissions since these terms tend to be used in computer-related discussions, even though they have little to do with network computing.

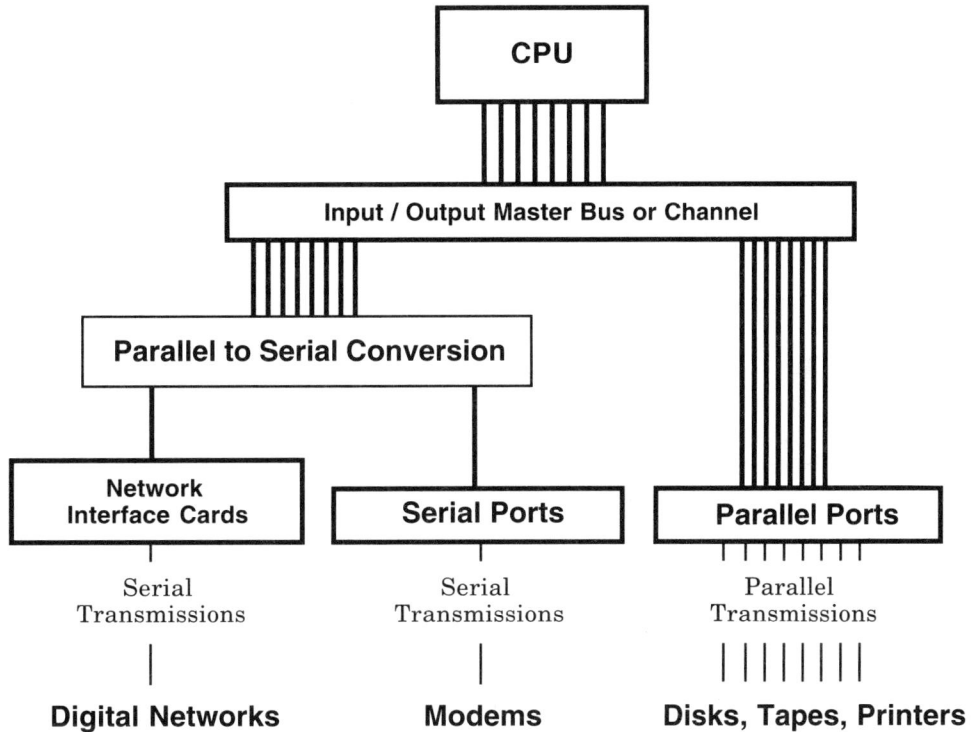

Figure 4–2. Serial vs. Parallel Transmissions with the CPU

Computers exchange data with the outside world in a parallel or in a serial manner. In parallel transmissions, 8 or 16 data bits (depending on the specific computer design) are sent simultaneously over 8 or 16 physical circuits. In contrast, a serial transmission sends one bit of information at a time through a single circuit.

Figure 4–2 shows that a computer has built-in communication hardware by which the internal CPU parallel data representations are converted to a series of 1's and 0's.

Communication between two computers on a network is always by serial transmission because it is much cheaper to send signals across single rather than multiple physical wires over long distances.

In this book, network communication always refers to serial transmission, NOT parallel transmission.

4.1.1.2 Local Area vs. Wide Area Circuits

From a wiring point of view, there are two types of transmission circuits: local area and wide area. Within a building or a complex of buildings, computing devices are connected by local area circuits. When transmission takes place between buildings, cities, and nations, wide area circuits are required.

The main difference between these two types of transmission circuits is in their electronics. For local area network, the electronic signals go from one computer to another computer directly, without the need for any intermediate booster.

For a wide area network that covers a large geographical distance, electronic signals must be bolstered by "repeaters" along the route in order to reach from one computer to another.

Another difference between a local area network and a wide area network is in their ownership. Typically, a local area network is paid for and administered by its owner. A wide area network is operated by telephone companies which already had the voice circuits in place before data communication become commonplace.

4.1.1.3 Analog vs. Digital Circuits

The two kinds of signal transmission are analog and digital. Analog circuits transmit signals of variable voltages such as human voices. Digital circuits carry signals that have only two voltage values: high and low (1's and 0's), which is the way one computer "talks" to another. Both analog and digital circuits transmit their signals serially.

In the early days of data communication, a device (known as the modulation and demodulation device, or modem for short) was invented to transmit digital signals using the analog telephone circuits. A modem simply turns the computer digital signals of 1's and 0's to a low and high pitch sound, which is then transmitted like voice. A major disadvantage of analog voice circuits (i.e. telephone lines) is their slow speed—less than 40,000 bits per second. The slow speed is due to the existence of "older" types of wiring and slow response control devices in the telephone network. Thanks to advances in micro electronics, however, the speed of a digital circuit is now approaching 1 terabit per second.

Today, all local area circuits are digital. Wide area circuits are still composed of a mix of analog and digital ones. The global trend, however, is to digitize all communication circuits by early next century. (See ISDN in the later part of this section.) In this book, all transmission circuits are assumed to be digital unless otherwise stated.

4.1.2 Local Area Circuits

To connect a computer to the network, you will need:

- a network interface card in the computer,
- a cable that connects the network interface card, depending on the data link protocol, to either a wiring hub where cables from other computers also end, or directly to another computer, and
- compatible connectors in both ends of the wire.

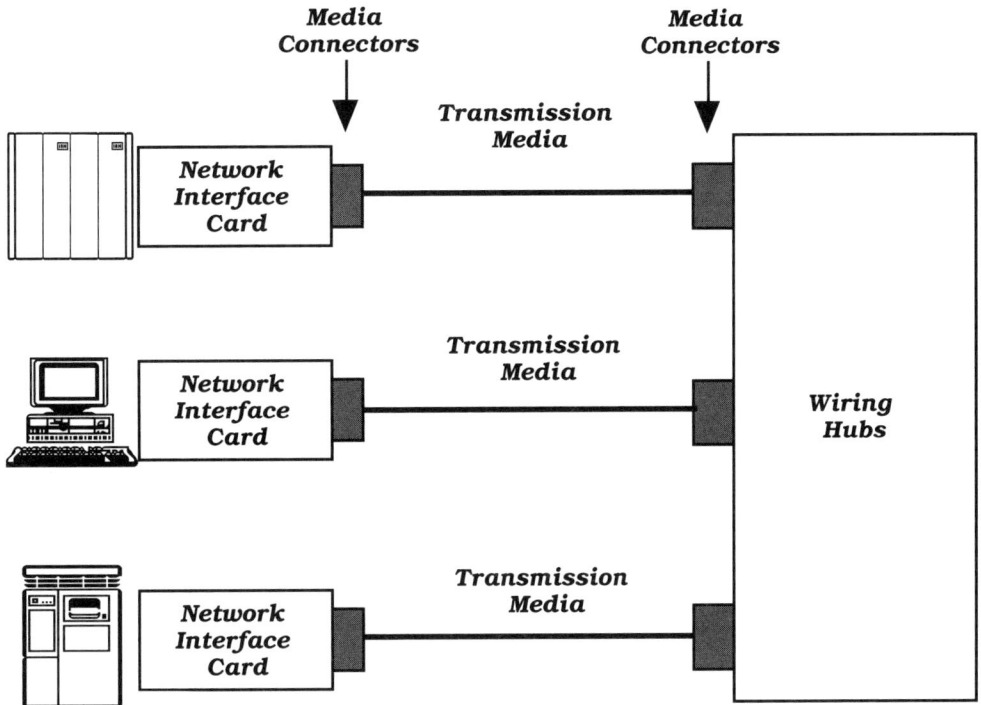

Figure 4–3. Physical layer components in a local area

This section reviews various types of transmission media, EIA-232C, and wiring hubs. The network interface card and the network wiring arrangement (topology) are data link layer components, which we review in Section 4.2.5.3.

4.1.2.1 Unshielded Twisted-Pairs

Unshielded twisted-pair wiring is identical to the conventional telephone wiring: a pair of twisted and insulated copper wires between 22 to 24 AWG (American Wire Gauge). The reason they are twisted is to avoid electronic capacitance build-up caused by straight parallel copper wires running over long distances.

In the early days, a twisted-pair could only handle low speed, digital transmissions of less than one million bits per second. Today, improved micro-electronic signal conditioning techniques can sustain transmission speeds of well over 10 million bits per second.

Twisted-pair cable is bundled in groups ranging from 4 to 3000 twisted-pairs. Most desktop twisted pair cable contains four twisted-pairs or total of eight copper wires—two pairs for data and two pairs for telephone (voice).

Because of its relative low cost and availability in most buildings, IEEE recommends twisted-pair cable as the standard wiring for the 10BaseT Ethernet data link layer protocol.

RJ11 and RJ45 Connectors

At the end of each unshielded twisted-pair, there must be a connector to which the computing devices can be easily plugged into and out of the network. Network connectors always come in two parts: the male and the female.

The connector for unshielded twisted pairs is the standard 8-pin RJ11 or RJ45 telephone jacks found in most buildings. RJ11, the smaller of the two, is used primarily for voice transmission. RJ45 is slightly wider, and it has a higher resistance to interference which is required by higher speed data transmission.

4.1.2.2 Shielded Twisted-Pairs

A shielded twisted-pair is bound in an external aluminum foil or woven-copper shield designed to reduce electrical noise interference. It has a slightly higher transmission speed. It is not as widely used as the unshielded pairs.

IBM Cabling System

IBM recommends shielded twisted-pairs for their Token Ring networks. Token Ring is a data link layer protocol. The IBM Cabling System provides two types of shielded twisted-pair cable. Type 1 cable consists of two separately shielded pairs of solid twisted wires. Type 2 cable consists of two pairs of shielded twisted-pair, and four unshielded twisted pair. Type 2 is meant to combine both voice and Token Ring wiring in one cable.

D-Shell Connectors

Because of the shielded twisted-pair requirement, IBM's Token Ring network requires the IBM cabling plan. In this plan, the connection at the Token Ring card of the computing device is known as a D-shell connector, which resembles, but bears no relation to, a 9-pin connector. On the other end, connection to IBM's Multi-station Access Unit (MAU), the Token Ring wiring hub, is made by another connector known as the Data Connector.

The maximum length of cable between the MAU and the wall plate is 150 feet, and the maximum length between the wall plate and the network adapter is 8 feet.

4.1.2.3 Coaxial Cables

A coaxial cable is composed of a copper conductor surrounded by insulator. An outer jacket of copper or aluminum acts as a conductor and it also protects the circuit from interference. This type of cable can be found in most home cable TV systems.

Coaxial cable supports much higher bandwidth—around 300 million bits per second, sufficient bandwidth to carry the cable TV signals to your home.

Two varieties of coaxial cable are: RG-62, and RG-58. RG-62 is used by IBM's 3270 network products. It is also used by the thin Ethernet designated as the IEEE 10Base2 standard.

BNC Connectors

For thin coaxial cables RG-58 or RG-62, the connector is the standard coaxial connector. It is similar to household cable television connectors. These connectors are called the BNC Connectors.

Balun

Balun stands for "balanced-unbalanced." It is an impedance matching device that connects a balanced line such as a twisted-pair line and an unbalanced line such as a coaxial cable. These baluns are quite common in buildings which have different wiring types.

An old building may be wired for telephones but not for IBM's 327x coaxial cables. With baluns, the telephone wires, which are twisted-pair can be used to connect IBM's communication controllers to the 327x terminals.

4.1.2.4 Fiber Cables

Fiber transmits computer information through a light beam rather than by an electrical signal. The transmission of the modulated light beam takes place over a thin strand of glass (fiber) surrounded by Teflon coating. It has almost an unlimited bandwidth. It can run for several kilometers without repeaters.

Today's fiber optics data communication is closely associated with a data link layer protocol known as the ANSI X3T9 FDDI (American National Standard Institute Fiber Distributed Data Interface). It has a bandwidth of 100 megabits per second. ANSI is also currently evaluating proposals to run FDDI on unshielded and shielded twisted pairs. FDDI is reviewed in Section 3.2.5.5.

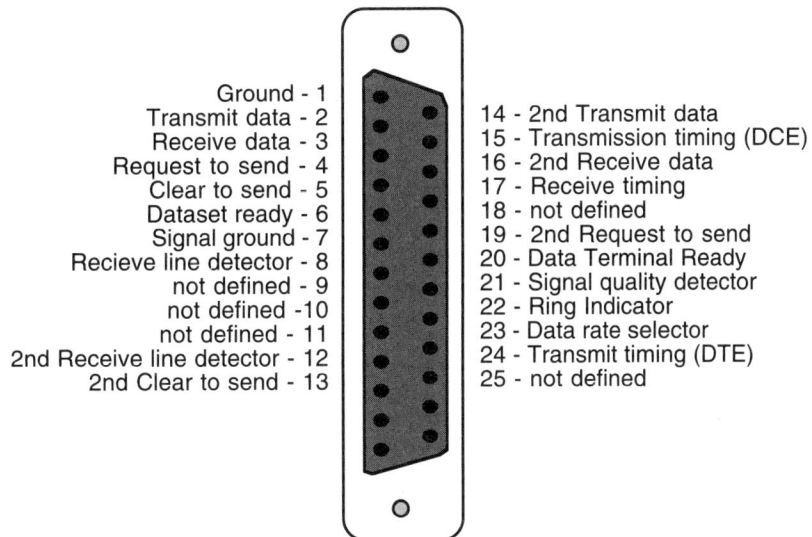

Ground - 1
Transmit data - 2
Receive data - 3
Request to send - 4
Clear to send - 5
Dataset ready - 6
Signal ground - 7
Recieve line detector - 8
not defined - 9
not defined -10
not defined - 11
2nd Receive line detector - 12
2nd Clear to send - 13

14 - 2nd Transmit data
15 - Transmission timing (DCE)
16 - 2nd Receive data
17 - Receive timing
18 - not defined
19 - 2nd Request to send
20 - Data Terminal Ready
21 - Signal quality detector
22 - Ring Indicator
23 - Data rate selector
24 - Transmit timing (DTE)
25 - not defined

Figure 4–4. RS232C cable connector

4.1.2.5   EIA-232C and Modems

In early days of data communication, long before the arrival of LAN data link protocols, a physical standard endorsed by the Electronic Industries Association of the United States was adopted by many computer manufacturers so that their computers can exchange messages with one another. The standard is known as EIA-232C as shown in Figure 4–4.

EIA-232C was designed for slow speed (< 40,000 bits per second), and short distance (< 50 feet) serial, point-to-point, and digital transmission. The limited distance of the EIA-232-C makes it useful only for local connections such as printers, terminals, and computers. EIA-232-C is also designed only for point-to-point data communication between two computers.

EIA-232C defines 25 circuits that can be used to connect two computing devices and describes the electrical characteristics of the signals carried over those circuits. Each circuit is assigned a specific function which can be divided into four groups: data, control, timing, and ground.

Note that only pin 2 and pin 3 are used to transmit and receive data, revealing its serial transmission nature, despite the 25 circuits (See Figure 4–5). The other circuits are for control signals.

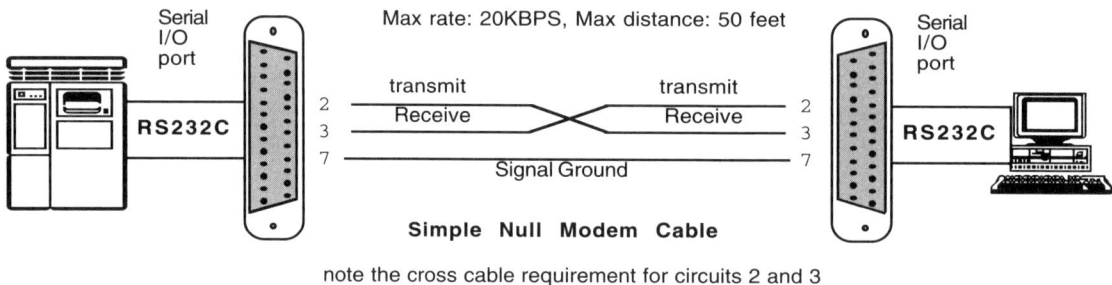

Figure 4–5. Direct RS-232C connection between two computing devices

Since all 25 circuits are seldom required, many variations of the EIA-232C are introduced to save on wiring and hardware costs. One such variation is the 9 pin EIA-232-C connector. Other implementations abound. For example, as few as three (i.e. 3 wires) of the 25 circuits can be used by two computing devices to communicate with each other while still conforming to the standard.

EIA-232C is a purely physical layer entity. It does not define functions of the layers on the higher levels. For example, EIA-232C does not specify how bits are to be grouped into characters. These are handled by software in the data link layer. See the Start-Stop protocol in the Data Link section of this chapter.

EIA-232C is now accepted by the ISO Consultative Committee International Telegraph and Telephone CCITT as the Data Terminal Equipment (DTE) standard Recommendation V.24 and V.28.

Modems

The point-to-point feature of EIA-232C restricts connection to two computers, making it a non-starter for computer networking where more than two computers must be able to communicate simultaneously.

In one particular situation, EIA-232C is quite useful, however. When a user needs access to information resources from his or her home or to call in when out of office, by using EIA-232C and the public telephone network, a computer can be accessed almost anywhere in the world—wherever there is a telephone line!

The EIA-232C standard, when used with modem and the telephone network, as shown in Figure 4–6, can extend data communication between two computers that are located thousands of miles apart.

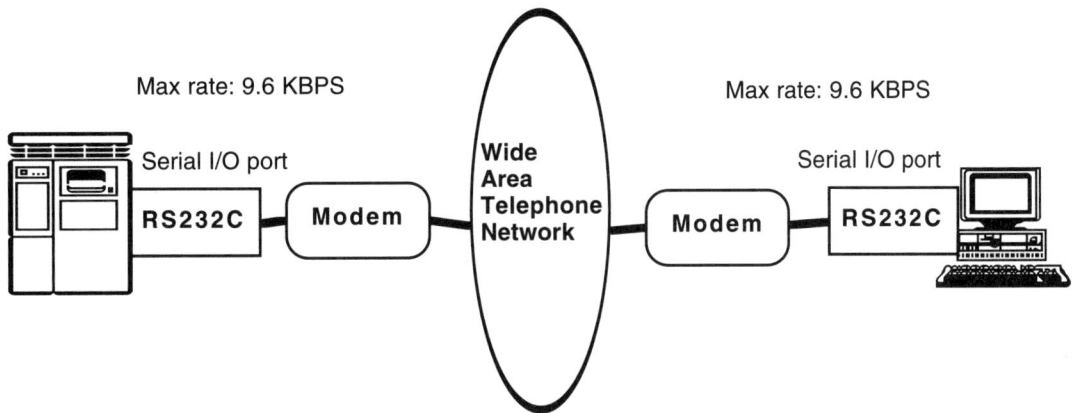

Figure 4–6. RS232C connection with modem

Modems are electronic devices that convert the digital ones and zeros from a computer to audible tones which are then transmitted as "voice" analog signals over standard telephone lines. Before the days of long distance digital circuits, this is the only way to transmit data to a wide area. Modems are designed specifically to interact with the EIA-232C circuits.

CCITT has published a number of standards for modems based on the speed and transmission modes. Some examples:

> Recommendation V.21: 300 bps duplex modem
> Recommendation V.22: 1200 bps duplex modem
> Recommendation V.29: 9600 bps for leased circuits

A more detailed discussion on remote access using modem can be found in Section 4.3.4 Dialed Access.

4.1.2.6 Smart Hubs

Wiring hubs range from simple wiring termination boards to a sophisticated, programmable computer. Wiring hubs are located in the same room as the floor's wiring closet. When a wiring hub is used to provide connections, it functions purely as a physical layer entity which is no different than a passive wiring board. Intelligent or "smart" hubs can do much more. The general construction of these hubs is similar to a micro or minicomputer, complete with its own hardware channel architecture and power supply. Most smart hubs have their own operating systems.

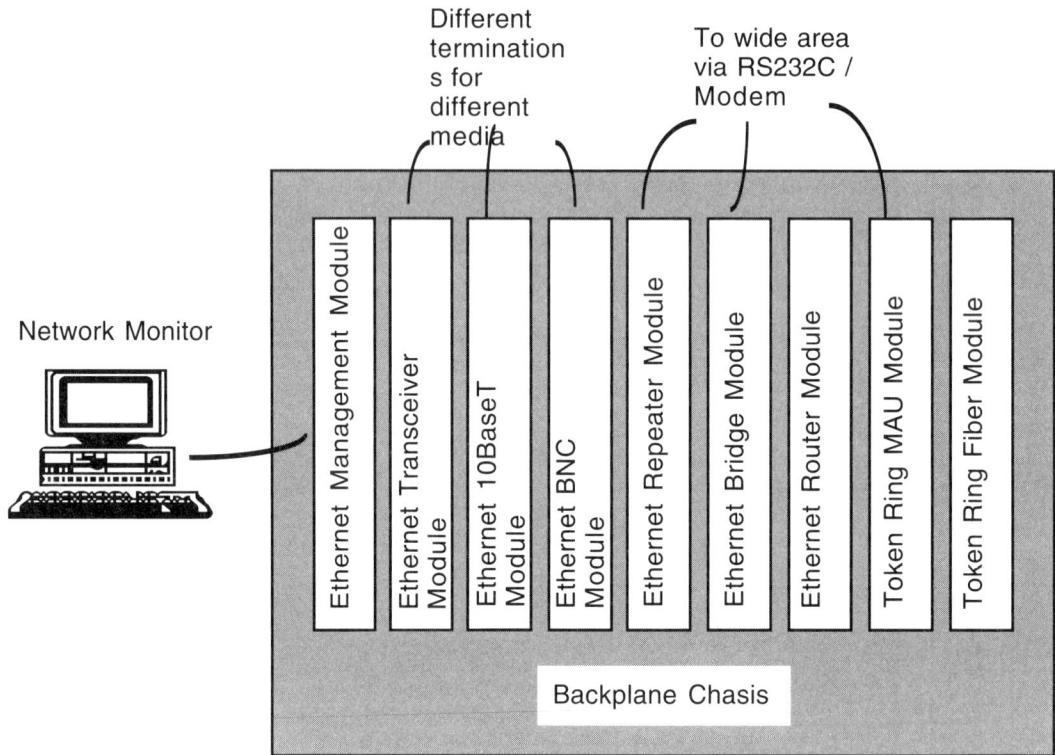

Figure 4–7. Intelligent wiring concentrator

These hubs are designed and programmed to accept multiple wiring types: twisted-pair, coaxial cables, and optical fiber. Wiring of different local area networks (Ethernet, Token Ring) can also end up in the same hub.

SNMP

At the physical layer, intelligent wiring hubs can be used to monitor network traffic. Many smart hubs are included with the popular Simple Network Management Protocol (SNMP) module, a hardware card inside the hub. The card contains electronics that monitor the network traffic. It collects traffic data continuously. The collected data can be sent to an SNMP compatible report program which typically runs on a PC.

As local area networks become the mission-critical infrastructure in large business organizations, problem resolution must be quick and precise. Without proper network monitoring, the traffic conditions of this wiring are unknown until the system breaks down.

This puts the hub in a unique position to play an important role in the integration of different LANs. Many hubs are now being programmed to function as a "bridge" and a "router," two key components in inter-connectivity. Since this is still a relatively new area, users are advised to check with the suppliers of this equipment for the latest advances.

4.1.3 Wide Area Circuits

Computing devices within a building (local area circuits) are always connected in accordance to specifications of the computer manufacturers. However, when signals must be sent outside of the building, telephone companies always have a claim to electronic traffic between buildings simply because they were there first with the telephone wires.

Figure 4–8 shows there are three types of wide area networks—dedicated non-switched network, packet switched public data network, and the circuit switched network.

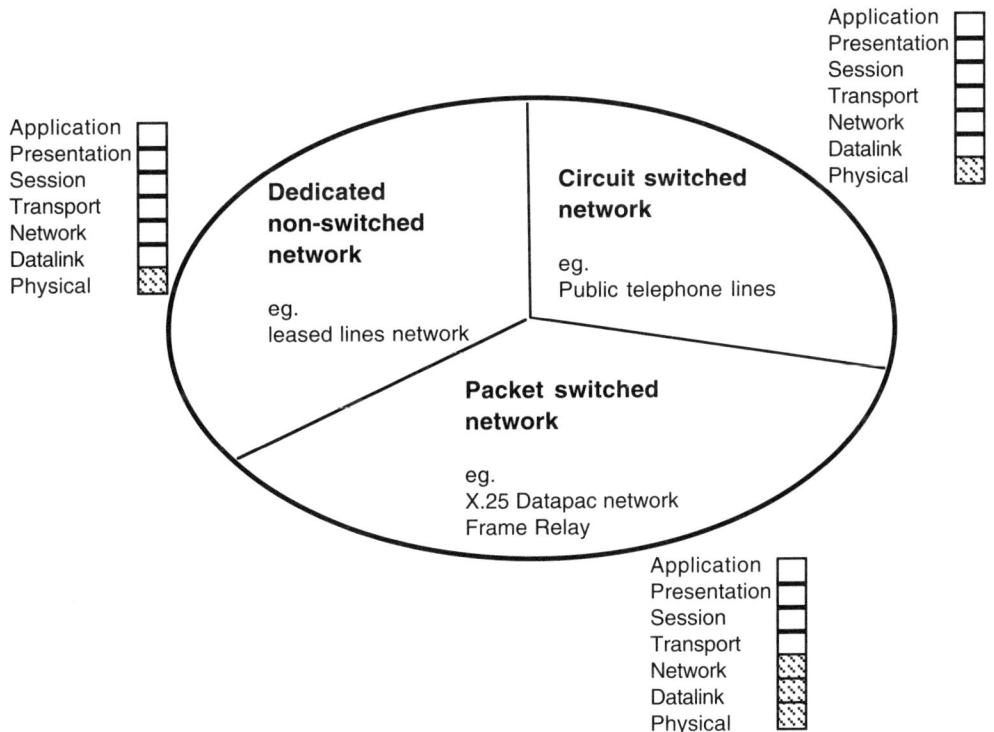

Figure 4–8. Types of wide area network

Dedicated switched and non-switched networks are physical layer components. They provide the copper wiring and the associated bandwidth that are external to the local area networks. They do not possess any switching capability based on the data packets floating through them.

On the other hand, packet switched networks and frame relay networks provide functions ranging from the physical layer to the network layer. For this reason, the packet switched network will not be discussed in this section but will be picked up in the Network Layer section later in this chapter.

4.1.3.1   Dedicated Non-Switched Networks

To meet the reliability and the speed requirement of data transmission, which cannot be satisfied by the old analog voice network, telephone companies had developed in the 1960s and 70s digital data circuits, commonly known as leased lines. These circuits carry the digital signals from the originating computer to the destination computer. Between two ends, the digital signals are reinforced through many electronic repeaters. These are purely physical layer entities.

From a user point of view, the circuit acts as though a strip of copper wire were connecting the two computers. The only thing users do not have control over is the speed of the circuits, which ranges from 56 thousands bits per second (KBPS) to multiples of 1.544 million bits per second (MBPS). Thus, the higher the speed, the higher the charge.

4.1.3.2   Circuit Switched Networks

In this type of network, users have the dedicated wire only for the duration of their "conversation." When the circuit is not being used, it can be "switched" to serve other users.

Circuit switched networks are dominated by the voice network, although many telephone companies are now offering switched digital circuits such as the switched 56KB circuits.

4.1.3.3   ISDN

One form of circuit switched network deserves special mention: Integrated Services Digital Network (ISDN). This is a new international standard for personal digital communication.

Each ISDN circuit has a bandwidth of 144,000 bits per second. Since the circuit is digital, it can carry voice, data, and video. Many industry experts predict that by year 2010, the world will be completely converted to ISDN. The major challenge now facing the telephone industry is to digitize the millions of household circuits. This project will require a vast capital investment, if only to replace the old analog switches located at street corners all over the country.

4.2   THE DATA LINK LAYER

In this section, we review three basic characteristics of communication protocols: transmission methods, encoding methods, and bandwidth sharing methods. We then review data link layer protocols including Ethernets, Token Rings, FDDI, ATM, and Start-Stop. IBM's SDLC will be discussed in Chapter Six.

A protocol is a set of rules agreed to by the sender and the receiver to allow meaningful exchange of messages between them. For example, if both person A and person B want to talk at the same time, speaks first? Protocols are rules that help resolve this and similar situations in program to program communications.

Protocols and their enforcement ensure that the messages will not be garbled, out of context, and meaningless. Protocols are as important as the message itself.

This chapter reviews the following protocol types:

- Protocols that control message transmissions
- Protocols that encode messages
- Protocols that enable computers to share the bandwidth of a transmission circuit

4.2.1   Transmission Methods

A program can send messages to another program in one of three ways.

The first way is for a program to secure a circuit so that it can talk to another program, like two persons talking over a telephone line. This method is known as the **connection-oriented** protocol.

The second is for a program to broadcast its message on the network and hope that someone "out there" is listening. This is generally referred to as the **connectionless protocol**.

The third is for a program to hire a third party whose job is solely to pass on the message to the correct receiver. This is known as the **store and forward agent**.

The transmission protocol dictates how a program can communicate to another program of the same layer. In a multi-layer protocol stack, each layer may assume different ways of transmission.

4.2.1.1   *Connection-Oriented Protocol*

Figure 4–9 shows how computers can be physically connected to form physical circuits as well as virtual circuits. Physical circuits exist only in the physical and data link layers. All other layers use virtual circuits.

Connection-oriented protocol requires a physical or a virtual circuit that remains committed to the communicating parties until their communication session is finished. It is a guaranteed delivery service because it always checks for acknowledgment of receipt of the sender message. If the circuit is malfunctioning, the program will try to resend for a number of times before it gives up. A telephone conversation between two persons is an example of connection-oriented mode of transmission.

**Non-shared physical circuit or virtual circuit
for the duration of a communication session**

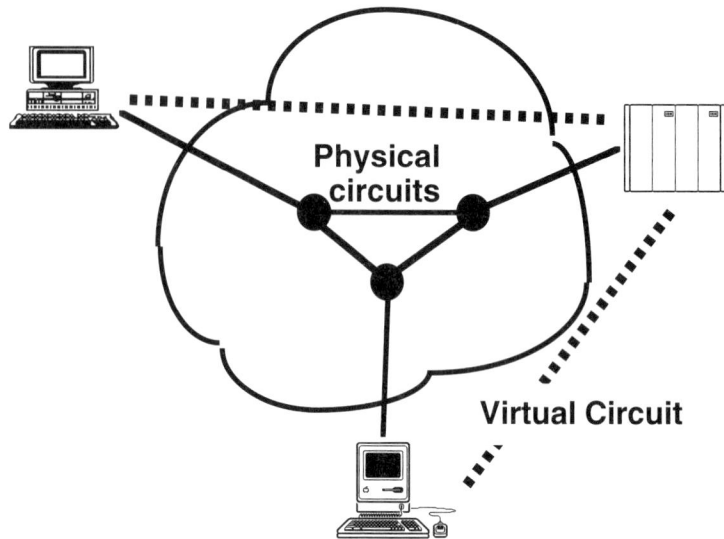

Figure 4–9. Connection-oriented protocol

A software circuit is known as a virtual circuit. It joins two programs together. One program sends messages to the other directly on a "first in first out" (FIFO) basis. The programs are "glued" to the virtual circuit for the duration of their conversation. The sender demands and waits for acknowledgment from the intended audience. It will take corrective action when such acknowledgment is not forthcoming.

Commercial implementation of virtual circuit can be found in Microsoft's Named Pipes, IBM's NetBIOS, Novell's SPX, TCP, and IBM's LU6.2, which are discussed in more detail in Chapter Five: Network Operating Systems.

4.2.1.2 Connectionless Protocol

"Best effort," "broadcast," or "datagram service" are terms used to describe the connectionless mode of transmission. For this type of transmission, the sender sends out a message onto a physical or virtual circuit with no guarantee of any response. The circuit is shared by other users who may also choose to do the same.

Responses to messages that are broadcast over a network must be initiated by the receivers. The sender program "broadcasts" its message to an audience without checking for acknowledgment from the audience. The sender does not know if its messages are properly received by the audience unless the audience makes some special effort to respond to the messages.

For example, members on an Ethernet LAN always broadcast their messages

Message broadcast to every member of the network

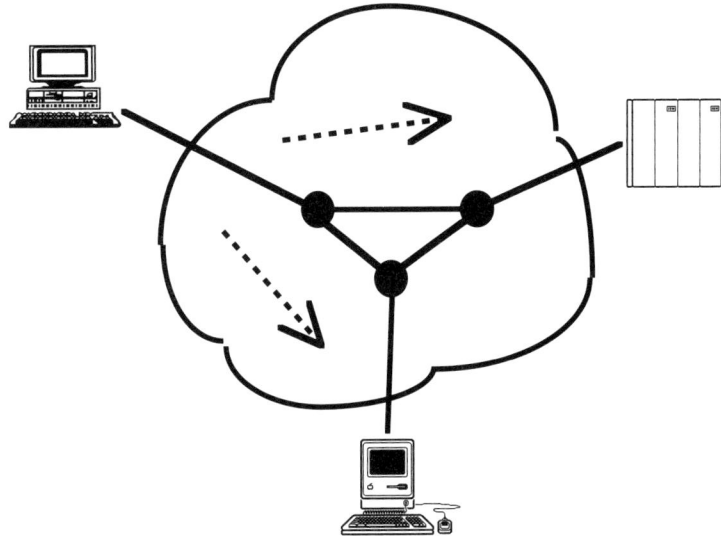

Figure 4–10. Connectionless protocol

on the physical wire so that anyone who chooses can receive them. Other examples of connectionless modes of message transmissions are movies, radio broadcasts, and time-of-day packets on a network.

4.2.1.3 Store-and-Forward Agent

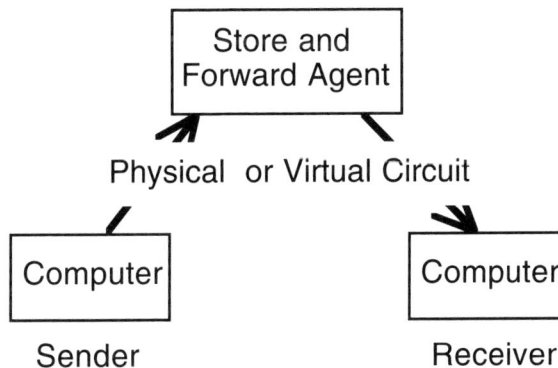

Figure 4–11. Store-and-Forward Agent

"Store-and-forward" message transmission involves an agent between the two communicating programs. Instead of sending the message directly to the audience (as in the case of broadcast), and to the receiver (as in the case of connection oriented transmission), the sender program sends its message to an agent with explicit instructions to forward it to a recipient.

Store-and-forward agents can be active inside a host operating system or as members of a computer network. The operating system software of the host computer or the network operating system provides a message agent to accept and to deliver messages among programs.

For example, in OS/2 Presentation Manager and in Microsoft's Windows, the message agent is known as Dynamic Data Exchange (DDE). Through DDE, two programs can communicate with one another within either Windows or the Presentation Manager.

In network computing, two computers separated by a wide area network must communicate via interconnecting devices such as routers and gateways, which are store-and-forward agents. Another example can be found in an electronic mail system where an "user agent" interacts with a "message transfer agent."

4.2.2   Encoding Methods

Information transmitted by a network is contained in units known as data packets. These data packets are a bunch of 1s and 0s sent out onto the physical transmission circuit in a serial fashion under control of a program.

How to interpret these 1s and 0s is another important function—the encoding function—for each layer. In a multi-layer protocol stack, each layer has its own data packet design because each layer performs a different function, and hence has a different transmission control requirement.

4.2.2.1   Data Link Layer Packets

Sender Addr	Receiver Addr	Control Information	User Message	Error Control Bits

Figure 4–12. Typical data packet design

The general design of data packets for all types of protocols and for all layers share the same fundamental structure. It contains, at a minimum, the following information:

sender's name or address	—header
receiver's name or address	—header
transmission control information	—header
transmission error control bit	—trailer
sender's message	—body

When broadcast on the network, data link layer packets will be automatically picked up by the network interface cards that match the destination hardware address. The term "packet switching" is used to describe this type of transmission action because the switching action is dependent upon the content of the data packet.

For example, each data link layer protocol has its own data packet design. Ethernet has its own design, as do Token Ring, FDDI, SDLC, and ATM. All data link layer protocols, except IBM's SDLC, have a specific limit on the size of their data packets.

If a user's message is longer than the maximum size, it would be the responsibility of the network layer protocol, not the data link layer protocol, to segment and to reassemble the message to fit the maximum size of a particular data link layer data packet. Any errors detected during or after the transmission will be detected by the error control bits. In some cases, resend actions will be taken to correct the error.

Only one data link layer protocol can be used in one physical segment of a network. Multiple data link protocols cannot physically exist in the same physical network segment.

4.2.2.2 Character- vs. Bit-Oriented Code

Data packets can be encoded by two basic methods. The first method uses a set of characters to represent user information as well as control information. The second method uses bit streams to accomplish the same thing.

Character-Oriented Code

Character-oriented data link protocols use sets of character code for data transmission as well as for control. The major code sets used in data processing are:

- The International Alphabets No. 5 is a 7-bit code that has been standardized by both the CCITT and by ISO 8859 code page. The common US ASCII (American Standard Code for Information Interchange) is a variation of this code.
- The EBCDIC code is an 8-bit code that was introduced by IBM whose dominance of data processing industry has made it a widely used code set.

A major shortcoming of the character-oriented data link protocols is that each manufacturer has a tendency to develop something slightly unique to its product line (e.g., use a special character to effect a special action for a specific printer), causing serious compatibility concerns to users interested in a multi-vendor environment.

The character oriented data link protocol is seldom used in modern protocols. It is primarily used in the point-to-point, "Start-stop" protocol for slow speed applications. IBM's binary synchronous transmission protocol (Bisync) is a character oriented synchronous protocol. It supports EBCDIC and ASCII as shown in Figure 4–13.

Start	Parity	7	6	5	4	3	2	1	Stop

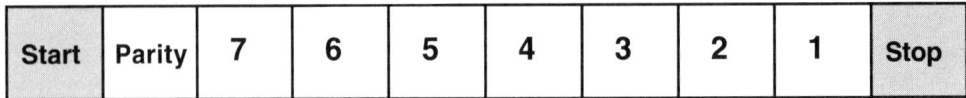

Asynchronous ASCII Code Frame

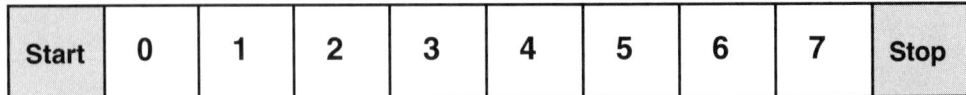

Start	0	1	2	3	4	5	6	7	Stop

Asychronous EBCDIC Code Frame

Figure 4–13. ASCII and EBCDIC code frames

Bit-Oriented Code

A bit-oriented protocol is independent of any code set. It is far more flexible than the character-oriented protocol. Data consists of bit streams and attaches no significance to the specific character set being used.

Without exception, all modern data link protocols are bit-oriented protocols. The major bit-oriented data link layer protocols are:

- Local area network protocols as specified in the IEEE 802.3 for Ethernet and IEEE 802.5 for Token Ring.
- High Level Data Link Control (HDLC), which was developed by the International Organization for Standardization (ISO) and is documented in ISO Standards 3309 and 4335.
- Link Access Protocol (LAP) and Link Access Protocol-Balanced (LAPB), which form the data link layer control for the CCITT X.25 packet switching network, commonly known as DataPac in North America. Both LAP and LAPB are compatible subsets of HDLC above.
- Synchronous Data Link Control (SDLC), IBM's SNA data link protocol. SDLC is a compatible subset of ISO's HDLC, and is similar to the LAP protocol of CCITT.

4.2.3 Bandwidth Sharing

Another important function of a data link protocol is to provide the rules for computers to share bandwidth on a physical circuit.

4.2.3.1 Bandwidth

Bandwidth is the capacity of a data circuit to move bits of data from one electronic device to another. It governs the speed at which a bit of information progresses through a transmission wire. The bandwidth of a digital circuit is determined by its electronic control devices, such as signal boosters, signal conditioners, and switch gears in the network.

No matter how fast a computer is capable of sending messages onto the network, messages can only be moved at the speed determined by these control devices. For example, an AT&T T1 digital circuit has a data rate of 1,544,000 bits per second over a twisted-pair of copper wires. It requires a signal repeater every 6000 feet. The repeater is designed to work at the speed of T1.

To illustrate the concept of bandwidth, let us say you were standing in a cross section of a 56 KB data circuit, you would have counted 56,000 1s and 0s passing by you in one second. If you did the same in an Ethernet circuit, you could have encountered 10,000,000 bits of information whisking by you every second!

Bandwidth Sharing

Bandwidth of a transmission circuit can be dedicated to a user or to be shared by a number of users. If the circuit is a dedicated one, a user should get the full speed for his or her data transfer. If the circuit is shared, then a user will have to share its bandwidth with others and will experience less than the full speed of the circuit.

Bandwidth is the only resource offered by a transmission circuit. Bandwidth is needed to carry the computer signal from one place to another. Because of geography, laying cables across hundreds and thousands of miles in cities and villages around the world is a very expensive, multi-billion dollar undertaking. To have a dedicated circuit for every conceivable combination and permutation of communication partners is an impossible task. The bandwidth of a circuit must be shared.

Over the years, highly sophisticated schemes and devices have been designed to share the bandwidth of a transmission circuit. Numerous Ph.D. theses have been written on bandwidth sharing methods. For the purpose of this discussion, we will review the two most basic concepts in bandwidth sharing: circuit switching and packet switching.

4.2.3.2 Circuit Switching

In circuit switching the bandwidth of a circuit is shared among users by a technique known as Time Division Multiplexing (TDM).

Time Division Multiplexing (TDM)

In TDM, the sharing is accomplished by slicing time. To illustrate how it works, imagine once again that you are standing in the cross section of a 10 MBPS transmission circuit, whose bandwidth is to be shared equally by ten users. For the first one tenth of a second, the bits that have passed by you have all come from User #1. For the second one tenth of a second, the bits that have gone past by you have all come from User #2. For the third one tenth of a second, the bits that have gone past by you have all come from User #3. And so forth.

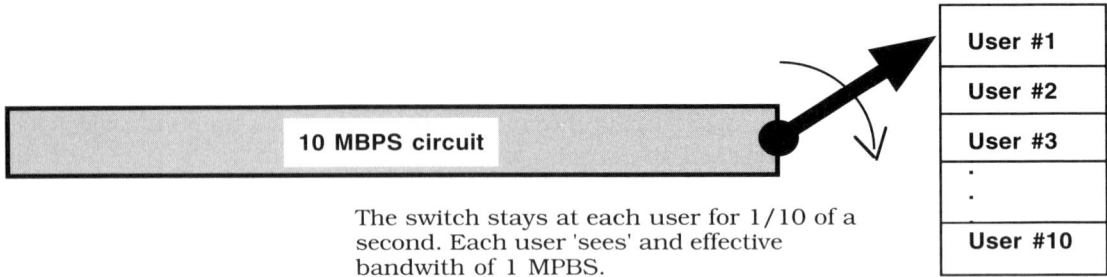

The switch stays at each user for 1/10 of a second. Each user 'sees' and effective bandwith of 1 MPBS.

Figure 4–14. Bandwidth sharing through circuit switching

The above transmission circuit has 10 sub-circuits or channels. Each user should feel as though he or she had a dedicated channel with a bandwidth of 1 MBPS. Users can use these bandwidths to carry any kind of information: voice, text, image, or video. The circuit itself does not scrutinize or care about the content of what it carries. From a user's point of view, using circuit switching is like using any other dedicated physical transmission circuit. The circuit itself does not care about the content of the data traveling through it; the circuit merely transmits the data.

The above is the simplest of all circuit switching schemes since the purpose here is to illustrate its basic principle. There are many "intelligent" multiplexors, such as ones that can change the time slices in a dynamic fashion to compensate for traffic patterns and hence improve response times to end users.

TDM is quite similar to time shared operating system software such as IBM's Time Sharing Option (TSO) on its mainframe computers. The difference is in the resources that are being shared by the users. In TDM, the resource is the bandwidth of a circuit. In TSO, the resource is the central processing unit of a computer.

4.2.3.3 Packet Switching

Another method to share the bandwidth of a transmission circuit is known as packet switching. The packet here refers to a unit of information—a data packet.

A typical data packet contains the following information:

- sender's address
- receiver's address
- control information
- user's message
- error correction controls

These data packets must contain both the user's information and the receiver's network address information. All users of the network must agree to the format beforehand. Data packets from one user can travel at the full speed of the circuit as long as no one else needs to use the same circuit.

For example, in a 10 MBPS circuit, one user may send out a 1,000-bit packet of information. It takes one ten thousandth (1/10,000) of a second for this circuit to broadcast the packet to the network. During this one ten thousandth of a second, no one can send anything on the circuit. Any user wanting to send something must wait until the first sender releases the circuit, or until the receiver acknowledges receipt of the data packet.

An advantage of this scheme is that it makes maximum use of the available bandwidth on the circuit when no one else needs it. However, if at the same time, other users want to send messages, the effective rate of transfer will be reduced because every user must wait its turn to take possession of the circuit.

For example, in Ethernet, which employs a form of packet switching, the sharing of bandwidth is effected through a data link protocol known as CSMA/CD (Carrier Sense Multiple Accesses / Collision Detection), which is reviewed in Section 3.2. Other examples of packet switching protocols are frame relay, CCITT X.25 or DataPac, and IBM's SDLC.

The difference between circuit switching and packet switching is that the former is "content insensitive" while the latter is "content sensitive." The fact that packet switching requires a pre-defined format and specific addressing scheme is an indication that extra control must be imposed by the data link and above layers for it to work properly. Packet switching networks are NEVER a physical layer entity.

4.2.4   Data Link Layer Protocols

Data link layer protocols consist of two sublayers: the media access control (MAC) sublayer and the link level control (LLC) sublayer. The MAC determines the data link protocol while the LLC layer is responsible for providing an interface to the network layer software to make use of the MAC layer. MAC sublayer is mostly implemented as firmware on the network interface cards while LLC sublayer consists of software drivers supplied by the network interface card manufacturers.

4.2.4.1   Essential Features

A data link layer protocol is responsible for delivering data packets between two computers which must be directly addressable to one another without the help of an intermediate store-and-forward agent. A store-and-forward agent can be a bridge, router, or gateway. Data link protocols deal with computers that are topologically adjacent to one another that is to say: in the same physical network segment.

A LAN is often extended to a wide area using repeaters or bridges. Under those circumstances, a computer on one side of the bridge is still capable of directly addressing another computer on the other side of the bridge as though the two were together locally. If a computer needs to send messages to another computer that is not on the same network segment, the network layer function is required.

Monolithic LANs

In North America, the greatest portion of the LAN market is dominated by two kinds of commercial LAN products. The first kind is known as monolithic LANs, and the second is known as multi-transport LANs. They are determined by the presence or absence of the link layer control sublayer.

In monolithic LANs, software vendors or the network interface card manufacturers supply software that covers functions from the session or transport layer down to the data link layer. This software has complete control over the network interface card (NIC). It disallows sharing the NIC with any other transport-network protocol . Examples of these monolithic drivers are earlier versions of Novell's IPX and Banyan's VINES.

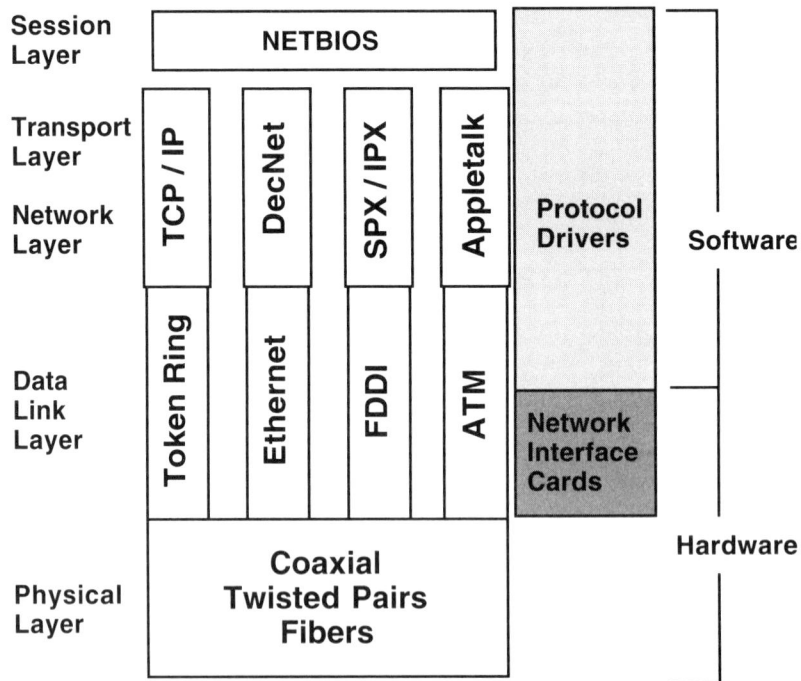

Figure 4–15. Monolithic LANs

Multiple-transport LANs

In multiple-transport LANs, the data link layer breaks into two sublayers. The upper sublayer, known as the Logical Link Control (LLC) sublayer, interacts with the MAC sublayer and the network layer.

The three main LLCs are IEEE 802.2, Novell's Open Datalink Interface (ODI), and Microsoft's Network Device Interface Specification (NDIS). The lower sublayer, known as the **Media Access Control (MAC)** sublayer, interacts with the physical transmission circuit.

Link Layer Control (LLC) Sublayer

This sublayer is "pure" software. It controls MAC layer of the network interface card. It is responsible for delivering user messages to the destination computer. It connects a media access method to work with multiple network transport protocols.

Media Access Control (MAC) Sublayer

The protocol of the MAC sublayer is implemented as the network interface cards, which are inserted into the input-output channel of a computer such as IBM's MicroChannel or the AT bus. The MAC sublayer has an unique hardware network address imprinted on it.

The MAC sublayer defines the maximum data packet size and data packet format. It provides all the appropriate electronic signals to send and to receive information from the physical media. It reacts automatically to abnormal conditions on the network.

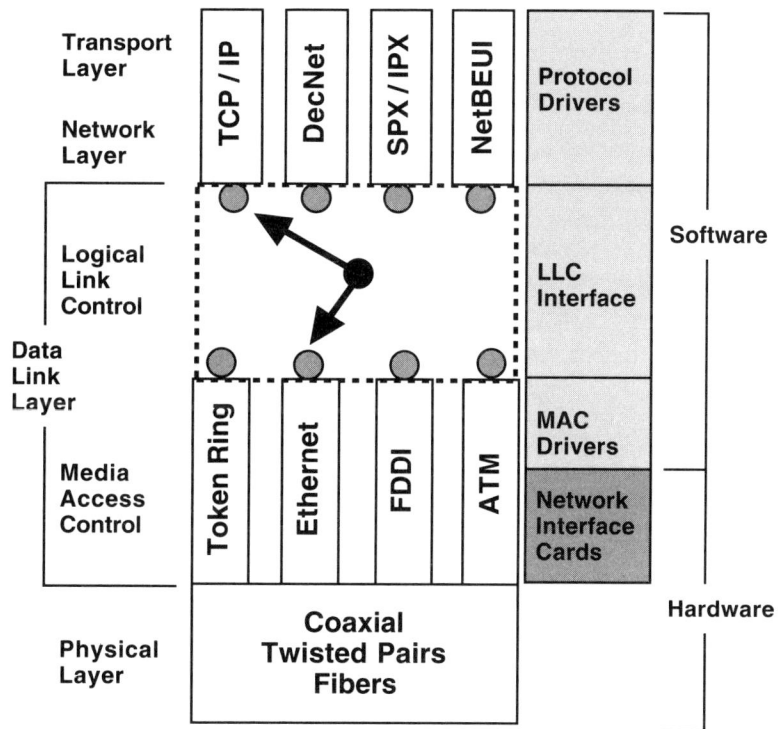

Figure 4–16. Data Link Layer and its relationship with the Network Layer and the Physical Layer

Usually the manufacturer of the network interface card provides a set of software modules, known as MAC drivers. These MAC Drivers provide the APIs for the network layer or link layer control sublayer.

Figure 4–16 shows the two sublayers and their relationship to their immediate physical and network layers respectively. It also shows the vital function played by the logical link control layer in interconnecting different network-transport protocols and different MAC protocols.

For the MAC sublayer, we will review the protocols of Ethernet, Token Ring, Fibber Distributed Data Interface or FDDI, and Asynchronous Transfer Mode or ATM.

Network Segment

In any physical network segment, only one data link protocol can exist even though there may be multiple network transport protocols. As such, a network segment can only have one bandwidth value. The more users share the same segment, the lower the bandwidth each user will receive. For example, over a segment of the twisted-pair wire, only one data link protocol can exist, say Ethernet.

Although multiple network transport protocols, say TCP/IP, and DecNet may use the same Ethernet card, the network transport data packets are enveloped inside the Ethernet packets, which are the only packets allowed in that physical network segment.

4.2.5 Media Access Control

4.2.5.1 *Network Interface Cards*

Network interface cards are electronic circuit boards designed to implement specific data link layer protocols. They are circuit boards inserted into the input-output channel of a computer. On the board, a media connector, such as a RJ45 (unshielded twisted-pair) or RG62 (coaxial), connects the physical network.

All MAC sublayer protocols are implemented in the Network Interface Cards (NIC). For Ethernet protocols, there are Ethernet cards. For Token Ring protocols, there are Token Ring cards. For Fiber Distributed Data Interface, FDDI protocol, there are FDDI cards. For Asynchronous Transfer Mode, there are ATM cards.

Each card carries a hardware address that is specific to a MAC protocol. This address is not recognizable by others and is used by a MAC sublayer to identify itself to the network.

Manufacturers of the network interface cards also provide a set of software modules known as the MAC Drivers which "talk" to the hardware on the card. MAC drivers provide the necessary application programming interface (APIs) for other programs, mainly the logical link control sublayer programs to exercise control over the protocol.

4.2.5.2 IEEE LAN Protocols

IEEE stands for Institute of Electrical and Electronics Engineers, which is based in the United States. The IEEE Committee 802 is a very large organization, with members from industry and universities interested in setting standards for data communication. IEEE LANs refer to those protocols conforming to the specifications of the Committee 802.

A number of subcommittees are formed specifically to set the local area network standards. Each subcommittee is given a decimal number for its designation. Each is responsible for setting the standard in a specific area of LAN. These standards are identified by the subcommittee number.

The work done by the various subcommittees of the 802 Committee of IEEE in the LAN has now been officially recognized by the International Standard Organization as part of the Open System Interconnect (OSI) standards. CCITT has done the same.

IEEE 802.2 : Logical Link Control		
Media Access Control **IEEE 802.3** **Ethernet** **1Base5:** Thick coax,1 Mbps **10Base2:** Thin coax, 10 Mbps **10BaseT:** Twisted pair,10 Mbps	Media Access Control **IEEE 802.4** **Token Bus** Shielded twisted pair,10 Mbps	Media Access Control **IEEE 802.5** **Token Ring** Shielded twisted pair,4 or 16 Mbps

Figure 4–17. IEEE Local Area Network Standards

4.2.5.3 IEEE 802.3 Ethernet

Ethernet is a MAC sublayer protocol developed by Xerox Corporation. IEEE has adopted it (with minor modifications) as their 802.3 Standard. Ethernet exists in at least 3 varieties. They all employ the same media access control technique, known as Carrier-sense Multi-access with collision detection or collision avoidance (CSMA/CD or CSMA/CA).

CSMA/CD

The CSMA/CD protocol requires all computing devices attached to the network to listen to the wire at all times. When a computing device needs to transmit data, it waits until the line is quiet and then transmits. This is known as "listen before transmit."

If two or more computing devices transmit at exactly the same time (which should not happen very often), a collision occurs. All the listening adapters should simultaneously detect such collision because of the higher electronic signaling level caused by the simultaneous transmission. Each adapter will then wait for a randomly-selected amount of time before listening and transmitting again.

CSMA/CA

The CSMA/CA protocol is same as the CD except that all computing devices implement an algorithm that helps to avoid collisions rather than to detect them when they occur, and then to re-transmit their data.

Connectionless Transmission

Computing devices on an Ethernet network transmit data in the form of datagram. Datagram is a connectionless mode of transmission. Each datagram contains the originator and the destination network addresses. The sender assumes that the receiver is somewhere on the network, is listening, and will voluntarily pick up the datagram. No attempt is made to ensure that the addressee does in fact receive the message. If such assurance is required, the network protocol in the higher layers must take steps to do so.

One advantage of the Ethernet protocol is that the failure of one computing device on the network will not cause the failure of the whole network. Overall, Ethernet is more forgiving than the Token Ring protocol described below.

Ethernet Data Packets

Even though Ethernet and IEEE 802.3 are very similar, they are not identical. The difference is in the use of one of the header fields, which contains a protocol-type number for Ethernet and the length of the data in the datagram for IEEE 802.3.

Preamble (8 bytes)	Destination (6 bytes)	Originator (6 bytes)	Type Field (2 bytes)	Data Field (46 to 1500 bytes)	CRC (4 bytes)

Preamble (8 bytes)	Destination (6 bytes)	Originator (6 bytes)	Data Length (2 bytes)	Data Field (46 to 1500 bytes)	CRC (4 bytes)

Figure 4–18. Comparison between Ethernet and IEEE 802.3

In practice, both datagram formats can coexist on the same wire or coaxial. This is done by using a protocol-type number (Type Field) greater than 1500 in the Ethernet datagram. However, different drivers must be used to handle each of these formats. The format of an Ethernet datagram is as follows:

Ethernet Bandwidth

Ethernet protocol calls for sharing the circuit bandwidth by all members on a network segment. Only one party can talk at any time in a network segment. The designed bandwidth of an IEEE 10BaseT segment is 10 MBPS. If only one computer is using that segment, it can send out information at a rate of 10 MBPS.

In reality, however, many users would share the segment. If there were 20 users in a segment and they all must speak, each must wait its turn. This method is a form of packet switching which we described earlier. A message from a user would have to be finished with multiple interruptions to let others get in. In a perfect sharing situation where each of 20 users had equal access, the effective bandwidth for each user would be about 0.5 MBPS. If we consider the overhead associated with the collision avoidance or detection, say 30%, then the net bandwidth of each Ethernet user would be about 0.3 MBPS!

Thus, users must be quite careful in sizing network segments. By having less users per segment, the effective bandwidth per user will be higher. This becomes critical during certain applications, such as image applications that require a high bandwidth to sustain a satisfactory response time.

Many new wiring hubs are programmable and are capable of varying the Ethernet segments to suit performance requirement. These techniques are known as switching hubs. They are becoming popular for performance tuning for high traffic segments.

4.2.5.4   IEEE 802.5 Token Ring

Token ring is a technology licensed through IBM. It uses the token passing protocol to transmit data on a ring network. Briefly, this is how it works:

A token travels around the ring in a pre-determined speed (4 MBPS or 16 MBPS). Any computing device on the ring wishing to transmit data must wait for the token to come by. When the token arrives, and it is not in use, the computing device can append the message to the token. It also changes the token status to "in use." The in-use (busy) token and its "cargo" then moves around the ring. When they reach the destination, the cargo is copied by the receiver. However, the in use token and its cargo continue to move on until they return to the originating station. There, the cargo is unloaded (erased), and the token status is reset to "free."

As long as the token is in use, other computing devices cannot send any message. With this scheme, only one computing device on the network can transmit at one time. This avoids collisions, which gives the Token Ring a distinct advantage over Ethernet.

With the Token Ring wiring hub, any breakdown of the token passing due to

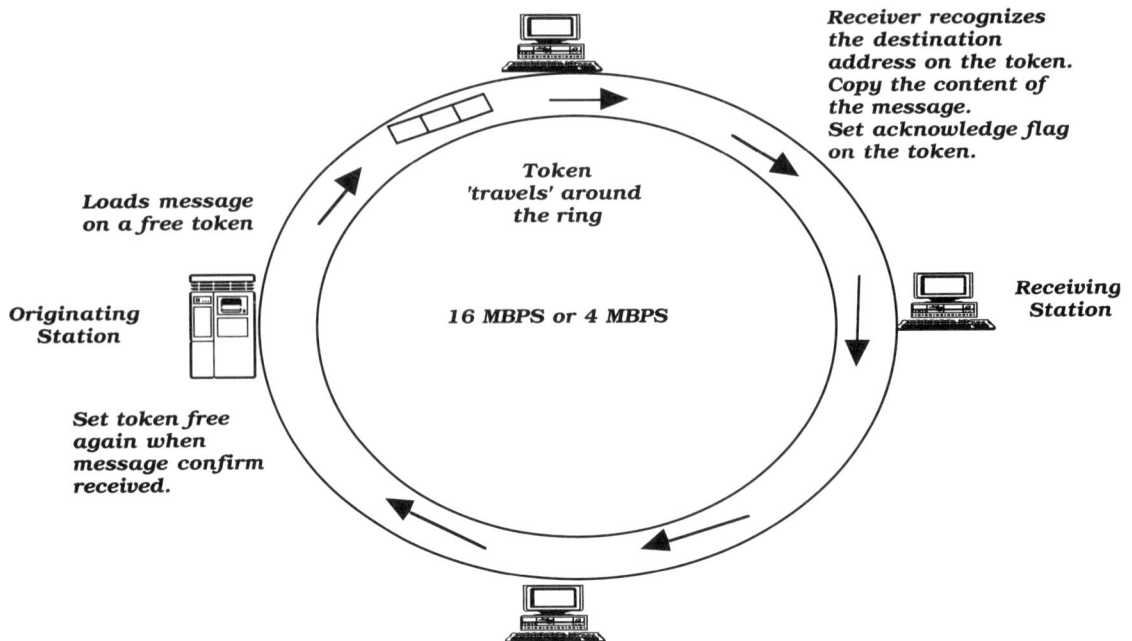

Figure 4–19. How Token Ring works

cabling problems between the adapter and the hub can be by-passed quickly by the relay action inside the MAU, which will be described in Section 4.2.7.4.

On the other hand, any malfunction inside any Token Ring adapter on the network can bring the whole network down, since the token must go through each adapter in each cycle through the ring. The token will thus be halted at the faulty adapter.

Even though this type of failure is not common, it is quite disastrous when it occurs. To amend this deficiency, some Token Ring manufacturers have designed their hubs to be capable of detecting and isolating adapter card failures to keep the token passing, and hence to keep the network alive.

Token Ring Bandwidth

The Token Ring protocol also calls for sharing of the circuit bandwidth by all members on a ring. Only one party can "talk" on that ring at any given point in time. The designed bandwidth of a Token Ring is at 4 or 16 MBPS. If only one computer were using that segment, it could send out information at a maximum rate of either 4 or 16 MBPS.

In reality, though, many would share the ring. If there were 8 users in a 16 MBPS segment and they all must speak, then each must wait for its turn. In a perfect sharing situation where each of the 8 users had equal access, the effective bandwidth for each user would be about 2 MBPS. By having fewer users per segment, the effective bandwidth per user would be higher.

Many new wiring hubs are programmable and are capable of varying the Token ring to suit performance requirement, the switching hub.

4.2.5.5 Fiber Distributed Data Interface (FDDI)

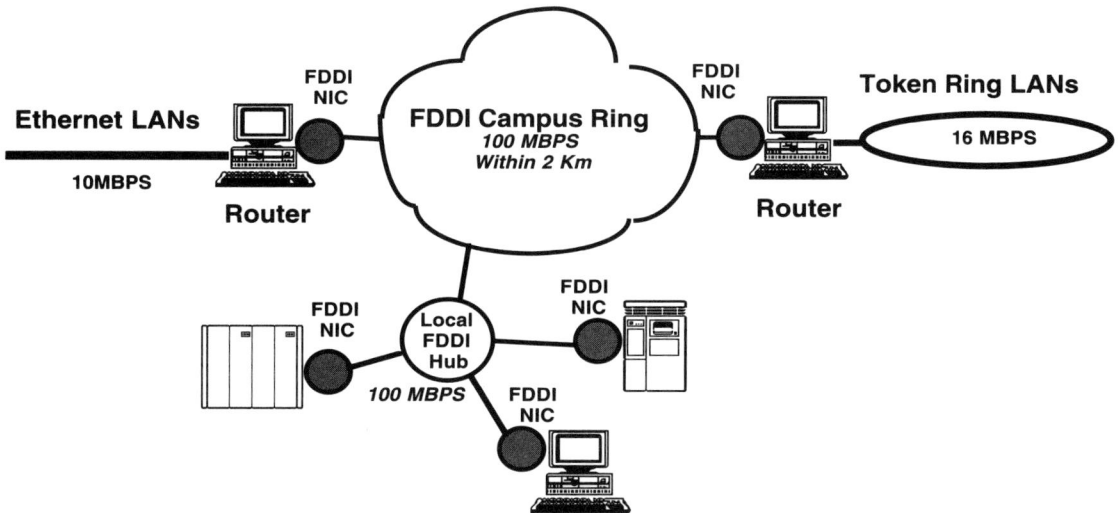

Figure 4–20. Desktop FDDI and Campus FDDI

FDDI is a data link protocol used primarily with optical fiber as the main physical layer component. The FDDI standard does include the Media Access Control layer, the physical layer, and the fiber optic physical media dependent layer. The FDDI data packet design is similar to that of Token Ring. The designed bandwidth is 100 MBPS, which is much faster than Ethernet and Token Ring and well suited for multimedia type of applications. FDDI can be deployed in two ways.

FDDI to the Desktop

The first way to deploy FDDI is to build a FDDI local area network using FDDI as the data link layer protocol. This is also known as FDDI to the desktop. Computers and workstations on this type of network are equipped with FDDI network interface cards. They should all be wired to a local FDDI hub.

The MAC drivers are supplied by the FDDI network interface card manufacturers. Network-Transport protocol drivers can be written to interface with these MAC drivers. With this approach, nothing is changed in the network transport area, nor is any change required of the user applications. The difference in the network response time will be order of magnitude, which will be better than either Ethernet or Token Ring.

FDDI for Campus Backbone

The second way to deploy FDDI is to build a FDDI campus-wide connection for all LANs in buildings in a campus or an office complex. Because of fiber optics, FDDI can go without any repeater for about two kilometers or 1.5 miles. Many users employ FDDI as their campus backbone to tie together LANs in different buildings.

To do this, an FDDI router is needed. This router is often implemented on a PC with two network interface cards in it. One NIC contains the FDDI data link layer protocol. The other NIC contains either Ethernet or Token Ring data link protocol. For a data packet to cross from one network segment to another, the FDDI router will first strip the header and the error control bits from the data packet before putting the user data (the network layer data packet) in its own FDDI packets. These FDDI packets will be traveling at 100 MBPS.

When the packets arrive at the other network segment, the router there will re-insert the appropriate header control and error control bits to form the new data packet conforming to the local data link layer data packet format. The network transport protocol software on the other side does not need to know that the message came through a router, as such "detour" did not happen.

A more detailed discussion on the functions of a router can be found in Section 4.4 on heterogeneous interconnection.

FDDI Recent Developments

At the end of 1992, FDDI had been installed at many sites, with a total in installations worth hundreds of millions of dollars. The technology has matured quite fast since its introduction in the mid-1980s. The cost of an FDDI network interface card for PC is about US$1300 and dropping fast. The cost of fiber, of course, is still a barrier to many organizations, but vendors are trying to improve network electronics so that FDDI can run over twisted-pair copper wires like IEEE's 10BaseT networks. Therefore, many people have predicted that for heavy traffic network segments, FDDI to the desktop is not an option but a must.

4.2.5.6 Asynchronous Transfer Mode (ATM)

No sooner has FDDI begun to take a foothold in network computing, than another new technology appears on the horizon that might have the ability to eclipse FDDI and other existing LAN data link protocols. The technology is known as Asynchronous Transfer Mode (ATM), a data link layer protocol that can handle both local and wide area network communication in a cost-effective manner.

ATM Basic Operation

ATM is a data link Media Access Control sublayer protocol. Unlike other data link protocols, ATM uses a combination of circuit switching and packet switching to let users share the bandwidth of a circuit.

ATM is not a "pure" circuit switching protocol as described earlier in Section 4.1.3.2. Time Division Multiplexing (TDM) technique is used to share the bandwidth by time slicing. In TDM, the bandwidth of a circuit is cut into a number of sub-circuits. The bandwidth of a sub-circuit is dedicated to a communicating pair even though the pair might be idling most of the time.

In ATM, the hub takes control of these idling sub-circuits instead of dedicating them to users. The ATM hub uses these circuits to carry any data packet that happens to appear on the network segment. Since these data packets appear with no forewarning, the word asynchronous is used to describe this type of action: Asynchronous Transfer Mode.

ATM sub-circuits are running either 155 million bits per second or 622 million bits per second. These speeds are orders of magnitude faster than Ethernet, Token Rings, and FDDI. They are aimed directly at the high resolution, multi-media applications such as video conferencing, high definition video, and the like.

Similar to FDDI, technology can be deployed in two basic ways: as a local area network data link layer protocol, or as a wide area network data link layer protocol.

ATM for Local Area Network

A local ATM network consists of an ATM hub. It is from this hub that the circuit bandwidth is controlled. The hub is a super fast circuit switching device. The hub's back plane has a bandwidth at the 1,000 million plus BPS range. Time Division Multiplexing technique is used to split the back plane bandwidth into 155 MBPS and 622 MBPS sub-circuits.

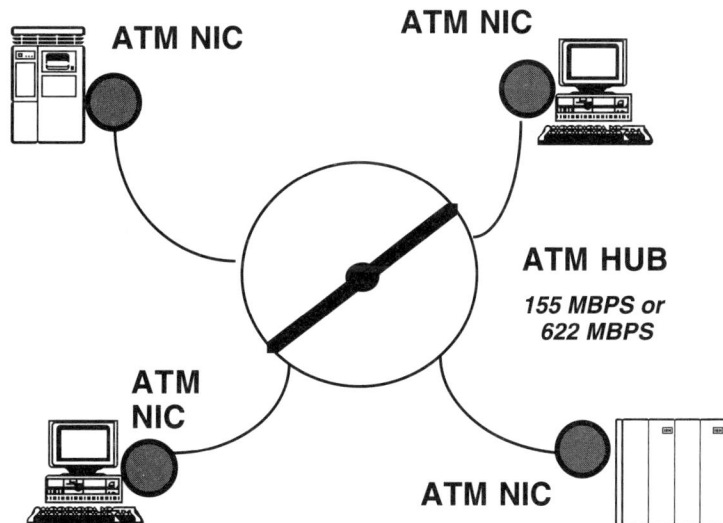

Figure 4–21. Local ATM network: An ATM Switch Hub—Any to Any Circuit Switching

Unlike other circuit switching techniques, which are insensitive to the content of the data packets, ATM demands its own packet design that contains, among other things, the hardware address of the recipient. This is why ATM is a data link layer entity rather than a physical layer entity.

The ATM hub will examine the address and will quickly dial an ATM circuit to the receiver. The circuit, at the full ATM speed of either 155 MBPS or 622 MBPS, will be dedicated to the user for the duration of the message transfer.

In addition to the ATM hub, each workstation and computer on the ATM network must be equipped with ATM network interface cards. The cost of an ATM interface card is still high but the target of US $1000 per ATM NIC workstation is achievable by 1994.

Anyone on the same ATM network segment should be able to "talk" to any one else. The connection topology is any-to-any. It is like our public telephone network except it has a much higher bandwidth for each user, and the switching is faster. If the number of users increases, a new hub can be added to avoid delays due to the overloading of an existing hub.

ATM for Wide Area

ATM can be used as a wide area data link layer protocol. Network segments of different kinds can be joined if they have the same network transport protocols. To do this, an ATM router is necessary. An ATM router is often implemented on a PC with two network interface cards in it. One NIC contains the ATM data link layer protocol, and the other NIC contains either the Ethernet or Token Ring data link protocol.

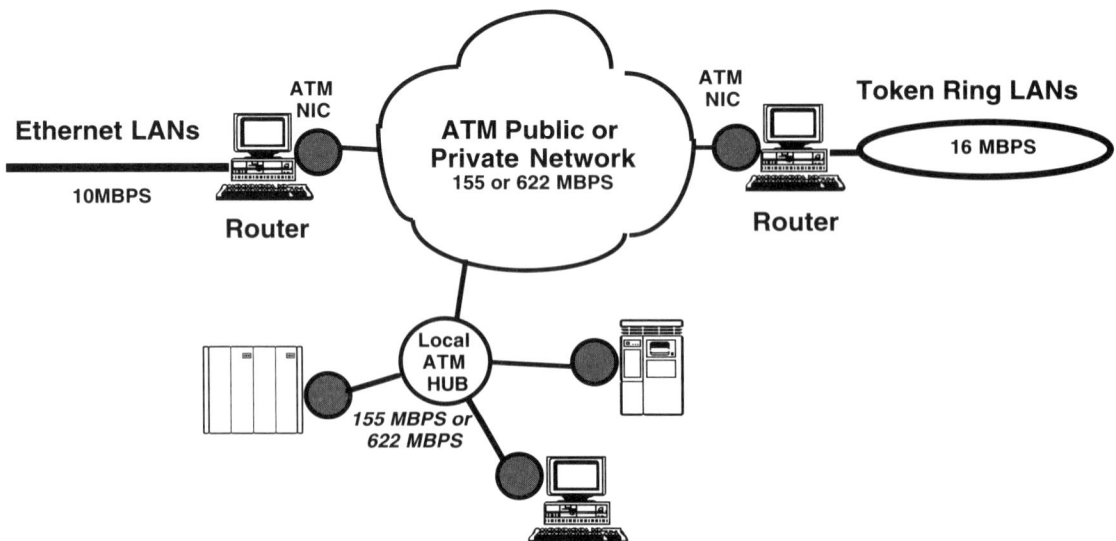

Figure 4–22. Local—Wide Area ATM Network: Any-to-Any Circuit Switching

For a data packet to cross from one network segment to another segment, the ATM router will first strip the header and the error control bits from the data packet before putting the user data (the network layer data packet) in its own ATM packets. These ATM packets will be traveling at 155 MBPS or 622 MBPS.

When the packets arrive at the other network segment, the router there will re-insert the appropriate header control and error control bits to form the new data packet conforming to the local data link layer data packet format. The network transport protocol software on the other side is not aware that the message came through a router.

A more detailed discussion on the functions of a router can be found in Section 4.4 on heterogeneous interconnection.

ATM Recent Developments

Much of the ATM specifications were developed by CCITT, the international telegraph and telephone standard-setting organization. Many ATM switches (hubs) have been available since 1991 for the telephone companies in their networks. Vendors are now testing user ATM products such as the ATM PC boards, ATM local hubs, local transmission media (mostly fiber, some testing on twisted-pairs), and others. By late 1994, ATM are expected to be widely available to the user communities.

4.2.5.7   *Start-Stop Protocol*

Start-stop protocol is not a recognized protocol. It is a common practice or programming method that makes use of the EIA-232C circuits. Individual user programs are responsible for controlling the message exchange between two communicating programs.

Start-Stop is a point-to-point and not any-point to any-point protocol. It depends on an outside agent, an application program or a human, to initiate and set up the circuit before the communication can take place.

Figure 4–23. Point-to-Point Link

Instead of adopting its own data packet design, the start-stop protocol depends upon the control character within the character set, as well as the individual application codes. For example, SOA is for start of addressing, EOA is for end of addressing, EOB is for end of block, EOT is for end of transmission, ACK for acknowledgment.

The start-stop protocol does not have the two sublayers like the local area network protocols do. Nor does it have a data link layer standard because each application will implement the protocol differently. The standard of EIA-232C is a physical layer standard.

The start-stop protocol is character oriented, asynchronous, and point-to-point. Because of the ready availability of telephone lines, RS232 with modem is used extensively for wide area network communication. The character code set most commonly used in Start-Stop is ASCII.

A typical exchange between two computers is as follows. You may notice its similarity with other data link layer protocols. The key difference is that the start-stop protocols are not standardized.

- The transmitting station places itself into transmit control mode and transmits an End of Addressing (EOA) command to the receiving station. (Note that there must be a physical connection established between the two computers prior to this. This can be achieved either via null modem or dialing modems.)
- The receiving station receives the EOA command and places itself into receive text mode.
- The transmitting station transmits the characters that make up a message one character at a time.
- The receiving station receives each character of the message and performs a parity check as it receives each character.
- The transmitting station goes into transmit control mode and transmits an End of Transmission (EOT) command, indicating the end of message.
- The receiving station receives the EOT command, performs the LRC error checking on the received message, and finds the message to have been received correctly.
- The receiving station then transmits an ACK command back to the transmitting station, places itself into a receive control mode, and waits for next control character from the transmitting station.

4.2.6   Logical Link Control

4.2.6.1   General Characteristics

Unlike the MAC sublayer, Logical Link control is 100% software. It "talks" with the APIs of the MAC software, as well as the network-transport layer software.

If the MAC sublayer is viewed as a truck that delivers, then the Logical Link Control (LLC) sublayer is the driver that controls the truck. The driver loads the truck with goods, and gives orders to the truck on destination address, and on what to do should an error occur in the delivery.

The network layer, which will be discussed in Section 4.3, passes to the LLC the segmented messages sized to fit the MAC sublayer. The LLC simply loads the messages onto the MAC sublayer, which in turn loads them onto the network wiring.

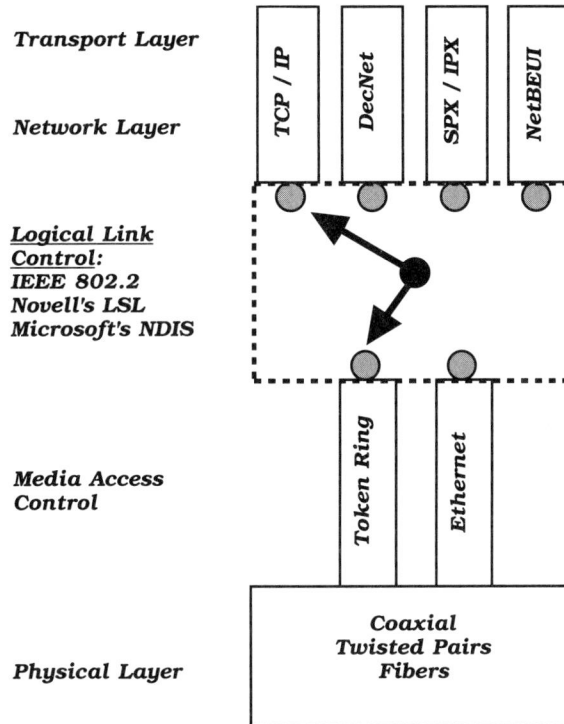

Figure 4–24. Multiple Transports LANs

The LLC sublayer, sandwiched between the network layer and the MAC sublayer, is a natural place to function as a switch for multiple network transport protocols and multiple MAC drivers.

The LLC sublayer is a software switch that allows two or more transport protocols to share the same Ethernet or Token Ring network interface card. For example, a client workstation can support two network transport protocols, say TCP/IP and DecNet, to enable its user to access two different applications at the same time.

Similarly, LLC can support a single network transport protocol over two types of network interface cards, say Ethernet and Token Ring, that are located in the same computer.

4.2.6.2 IEEE 802.2

The IEEE MAC standards on Ethernet, Token Ring, and Token Buses are almost universally accepted. The acceptance of the IEEE Logical Link Control, however, has yet to achieve the same recognition.

IEEE 802.2 uses a concept known as the Link Services Access Point (LSAP). Each service access point can support a network transport protocol. For example TCP/IP can be one such stack. Multiple SAPs mean that more than one protocol can share the same network card.

In practice, the 802.2 service access points have been defined to support IBM's SNA path control and TCP/IP, but not much else. The U.S. Government and IBM are two major supporters of the IEEE 802.2 Standards.

4.2.6.3 Novell's ODI

Novell's Open Datalink Interface (ODI), known as **Link Support Layer (LSL),** allows the MAC drivers and the network transport protocol stacks to work together independent of MAC sublayer and network transport protocol stack details. MAC sublayer can be Token Ring, Ethernet, or IBM's SDLC frames. Protocol stacks can be TCP/IP, IBM's 3270, NetBEUI, IPX, and others.

To make this work, both the MAC drivers and the protocol stacks must be written according to Novell's Open Datalink Interface (ODI) specifications. Novell certifies the MAC drivers and the protocol stacks from other vendors. With these ODI-compliant drivers and stacks, any ODI driver can communicate with any ODI protocols.

Under the ODI specifications, the ODI MAC driver does not interpret a packet, it merely passes the packet to the LSL. The protocol stacks, in turn are not required to know the frame type of a packet because LSL determines which packets are for which stacks. LSL acts like a switch, routing packets between the appropriate MAC drivers and protocol stacks.

This standardization removes the limitations on the number of protocol stacks and frame types a driver may support and minimizes processing overhead and space use at the protocol level. For example, the protocol stacks TCP/IP and the IPX can use the Token Ring adapter and or the Ethernet adapter at the same time. Any part of Novell's ODI (Open Datalink Interface) can be loaded and unloaded at will. A constant IPX connection to a Netware server and load TCP/IP can be maintained only when it is needed for a connection to a UNIX data server. One could also unload IPX layer first to make more room for the TCP/IP link and database client application.

4.2.6.4 Microsoft's NDIS

The Network Device Interface Specification (NDIS) was originally published by Microsoft and 3Com. It works only with those MAC drivers and network protocol drivers that are designed to be NDIS compliant. Like Novell, Microsoft will certify MAC drivers and the protocol stacks from their respective developers. NDIS, LSL, and IEEE 802.2 are functionally equivalent, but incompatible.

4.2.7 Network Topology

To form a network of computers, there must be some way by which each computer has a physical path to one another. Network topology describes the geometric arrangement by which computing devices are connected.

Which network topology to be used is determined by the data link layer protocol, even though the devices used in various network topologies are physical devices.

There are three basic topologies: ring, bus, and star. Only two are available commercially: the daisy chain or bus topology and the star or hub topology. No implementation of the pure ring topologyis commercially available.

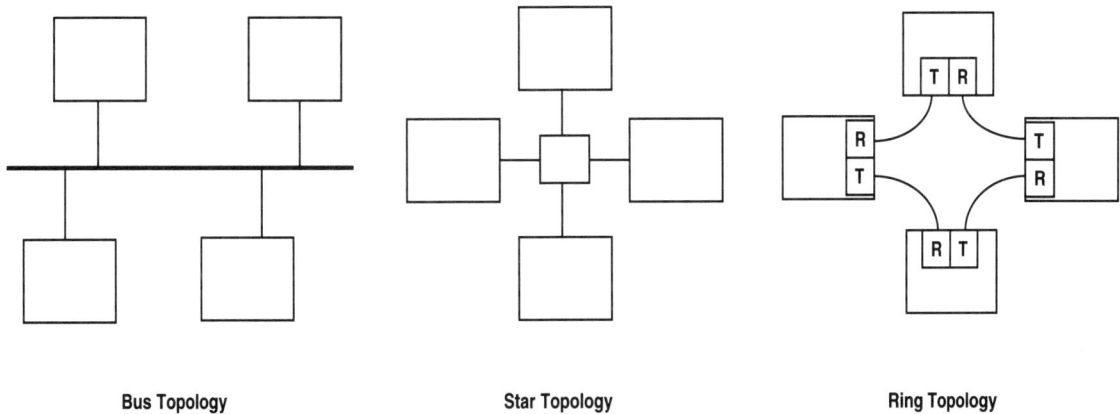

| Bus Topology | Star Topology | Ring Topology |

Figure 4–25. Wiring Topology

4.2.7.1 Bus Topology

In bus topology, the transmission media takes the shortest path from one computer to the next. Bus topology is principally associated with networks that use the data link layer protocol of thin and standard Ethernet. Bus topology has two advantages: It uses less cable, and it does not require room or power for a wiring hub.

A distinct disadvantage to bus topology is that it is not fault tolerant. If the cable breaks or has a bad connection at any point, the entire network fails. Troubleshooting and to isolating problems is also very difficult because a problem on one device can manifest itself on another device. For this reason, this type of topology is not as popular as it once was.

Thin Ethernet

Thin Ethernet uses a thin coaxial cable as the bus segment. According to the IEEE 802.3 rules, a thin Ethernet (IEEE 10Base2) segment must support 30 devices over a distance of 607 feet. Since most devices contain a built-in transceiver for thin coaxial cable, an external transceiver is not required. The transceiver monitors the cable for collisions. Devices are attached directly to the cable with the BNC T-Connector.

Thick Ethernet

For the standard (thick) Ethernet, IEEE 1Base5, coaxial cables are used to connect personal computers to mainframes and minicomputers. Each personal computer is attached to the cable segment with a transceiver and an **Attachment**

Unit Interface (AUI). Its distance is limited to 1,640 feet, and the number of attachments is limited to 100. The AUI cable may be up to 165 feet in length.

Thin Ethernet Coaxial cable: overall length 600 to 1000 feet

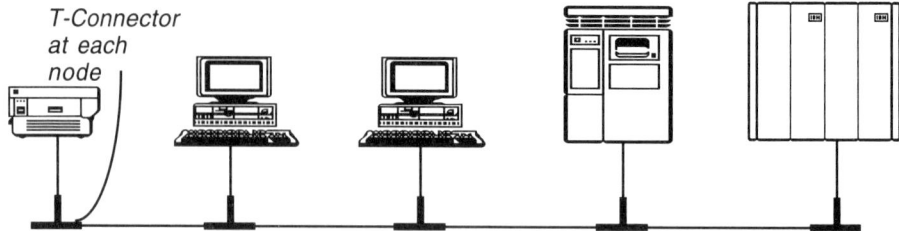

T-Connector at each node

Standard Ethernet Coaxial cable (Thick Cable): overall length 1500 feet

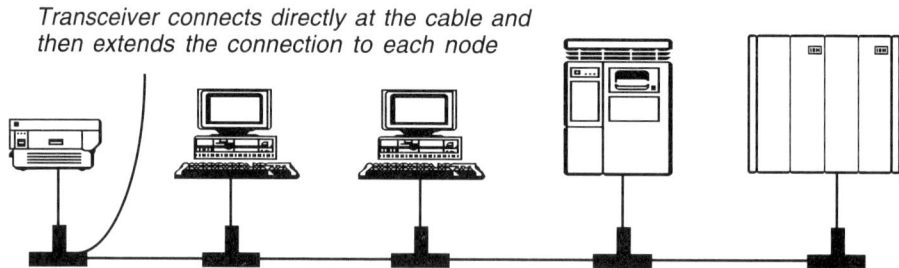

Transceiver connects directly at the cable and then extends the connection to each node

Figure 4–26. Bus or Daisy Chain Topology

4.2.7.2 Hub Topology

In a hub or star topology, all devices are connected through a central control point known as a hub. As mentioned earlier, the hub is a passive device. Many modern wiring hubs, however, do have built-in network traffic management intelligence capable of detecting network failure and taking corrective actions.

The advantage of hub topology is ease of fault detection. The disadvantage is that it requires more cable than other topologies require. Also it has a single point of failure.

An example of the star topology is IEEE 802.3 10BaseT Ethernet. It uses either the telephone wires (unshielded twisted-pair) available in most buildings, or optical fiber cables. For unshielded twisted-pairs, the computing devices are directly connected to the standard 8-pin telephone wall jacks (RJ11 or RJ45) through a short,

RJ-45: 8 pin telephone type of connector for twisted pair

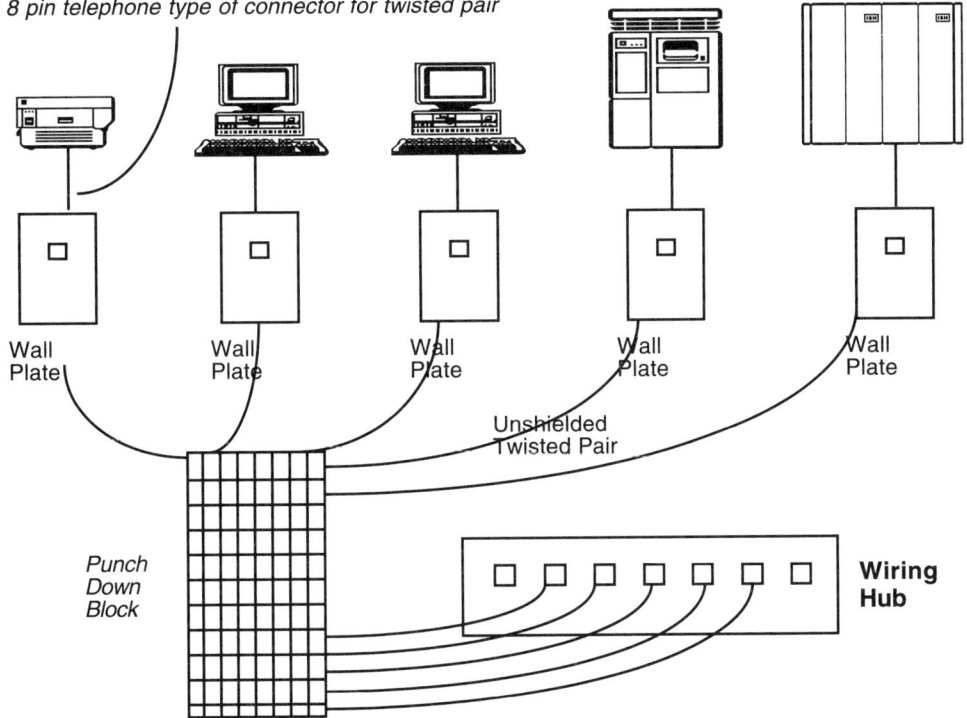

Figure 4–27. Star or Hub Topology for 10BaseT Ethernet

unshielded twisted-pair cable. From the wall plate, the unshielded twisted-pair will terminate at the traditional punchdown block at the wiring closet. A wiring hub is installed next to the punchdown block to accept connections from the computing devices. Jumper cables at the punchdown block provide the actual connections between the wiring hub and the computing devices.

4.2.7.3 Ring Topology

In a ring topology, each computing device is connected to the next one to form a closed loop. Each station has a transmitter and a receiver—called the transceiver. Data is transmitted in one direction around the ring. The advantage is in decreased distance sensitivity because each device regenerates the signals. The disadvantage is that a single failed device disables the whole ring.

No "pure" ring topology implementation exists in practice. The star-wired logical ring topology, like IBM's Token Ring multi-station access unit (MAU) described in the next paragraph, is the typical ring topology implementation.

4.2.7.4 Star-Ring Topology

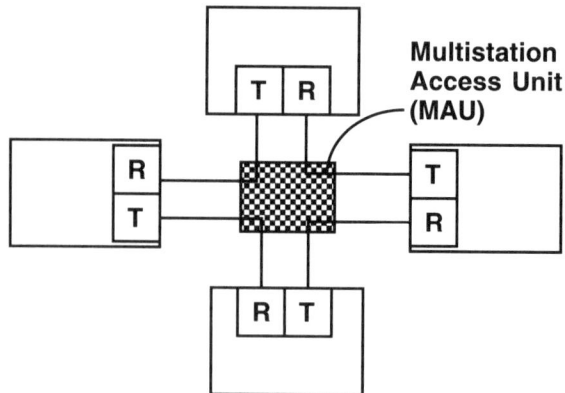

Figure 4–28. Star-wired logical ring topology

In IBM's Token Ring system, the MAU is an electro-mechanical relay. When a computing device tries to join the ring, it sends a signal to the hub relay, which upon activation and within several milliseconds will re-configure the ring by making the correct relay contacts inside the MAU.

When the same computing device drops because of system failure or is powered off, the relay will again configure the MAU to drop it from the network while keeping the connections of others intact. Token ring networks are the only networks on which one can hear an audible click wherever a computing device is activated within the ring.

4.3 THE NETWORK-TRANSPORT LAYERS

The combined network and transport layers form the "network family." In most commercial products, these two layers are bundled together. They provide the network addressing scheme to identify computers and programs of the same network family. This addressing scheme is totally independent of the hardware addresses of the media access sublayer of the data link layer protocols.

In this section, we review the Transmission Control Protocol/Inter-network Protocol (TCP/IP) because of its textbook-like features and its increasing importance in the information processing market. Many users suggest that TCP/IP should be adopted as the OSI standard.

Both Novell's ODI and Microsoft's NDIS in the link layer control sublayer of the data link layer are discussed in the previous section. In this section, we continue up the layers of the same product line and review Novell's Sequenced Packet Exchange/Inter Network Packet Exchange (SPX/IPX), and IBM/Microsoft's Network Basic Input Output System/NetBIOS Extended User Interface (NetBIOS/NetBEUI).

Two network-layer-only protocols are important in wide area networking.

They are responsible for delivering messages from one computer to another, but they depend upon an independent transport protocol to deliver the message to a receiving program within that computer. We will review two such protocols: CCITT X.25 and Frame Relay. CCITT X.25 public data network is widely available and is an OSI standard. Frame relay has the potential to replace X.25 as a higher speed alternative.

4.3.1 TCP/IP

The name TCP/IP represents two complementary protocols: the Transmission Control Protocol and the Internet Protocol. They are functionally equivalent to the transport layer and the network layer of the OSI Reference Model, respectively.

Since TCP/IP is strictly a software architecture, it is not tied to any hardware platform. TCP/IP can be implemented on all types of computers (mainframe, mini, and micro), and over all types of data link protocols. This makes TCP/IP an ideal tool to connect different computers.

4.3.1.1 Background

The initial objective for TCP/IP was indeed quite modest: to design a set of protocols to enable a myriad of different computers in the U.S. Defense Department to share terminals (remote log in), and to share disk (file transfer). To everyone's surprise, TCP/IP became so popular with the academic and the defense industry users that the U.S. Government adopted a policy that favors acquisition of computer systems that have the TCP/IP capability. This policy puts a lot of clout behind TCP/IP, since U.S. Government is the biggest user of computer systems in the world. For this reason, practically every computer manufacturer now supports TCP/IP.

TCP/IP (RFC)

TCP/IP is a public network protocol, and indeed it is a showcase in the democracy of technology. Decisions are made in the form of recommendations rather than edicts. Voluntary participation from all sectors of the data processing industry and academics are the norm. Implementation of any recommendation is completely up to the implementors, who are bound only by customer demand.

The mechanism for the evolution of the suite of TCP/IP protocols is the Request for Comment (RFC). On a continuous basis, many new protocols are being designed by researchers and developers. They put their ideas and designs in RFCs, which are collected, published, and managed by:

> Network Information Center,
> Stanford Research Institute International,
> 333 Ravenswood Avenue,
> Menlo Park, California 94025
> USA

All RFCs have designated implementation status, which are: required, elective, and experimental. The required status means that TCP/IP must implement. The elective status means TCP/IP may choose to implement. The experimental status means TCP/IP should not implement unless it is part of the experiment. In this way, compatibility among vendors of TCP/IP implementations will be guaranteed for a set of required functions.

TCP/IP got its biggest boost when University of California at Berkeley distributed it free of charge for the UNIX platform. From that point on, use of TCP/IP has been spreading rapidly among universities and research centers.

Anyone can write a TCP/IP implementation without getting a license or performing any other administrative procedures. As a result, the TCP/IP products are reasonably priced, since there is no royalty. TCP/IP is now implemented on many mainframe, mini, and micro computers including IBM's MVS, VM, OS/400, OS/2, Microsoft's DOS, NCR, Honeywell's, DEC's VMS, and others.

TCP/IP is without doubt the most common protocol for communications in the non-IBM environments. Even the large commercial enterprises that have been traditionally IBM SNA shops are beginning to implement TCP/IP as their secondary corporate backbone for data communication.

Internet

By 1980s, literally thousands of TCP/IP nodes sprang up. The largest one is the Internet that links together computers used by various U.S. Government agencies, universities, and research labs. Internet is composed of a number of large TCP/IP networks:

- ARPANET   for the US Defense Department
- NSFnet   for the National Science Foundation
- CSNET   for the Computer Science Network
- NERN   for the National Education and Research
- DRI   for the Defense Research Net

Network addresses on the Internet are assigned from a central authority: the Network Information Center at Stanford Research Institute in California.

Internet is one of thousands of TCP/IP networks. Many TCP/IP networks are not connected to the Internet at all. These are the growing private TCP/IP networks.

4.3.1.2 Basic Architecture

In this section, we discuss the TCP/IP architecture by reviewing its major components, its peer-to-peer structure at the network transport layers, and its client server structure at the application, presentation, and session layers.

TCP/IP Applications

Figure 4–29 shows the major TCP/IP components and their positions within the OSI Reference Model. The term TCP/IP means a suite of protocols associated with the transport layer protocol Transmission Control Protocol (TCP), and the network layer protocol Inter Network Protocol (IP). However, in most people's minds, TCP/IP means more than simply the transport and network layer functions. The TCP/IP-based application protocols such as the Network File Services (NFS), the File Transfer Protocol (FTP), and Telnet are responsible for TCP/IP's popularity.

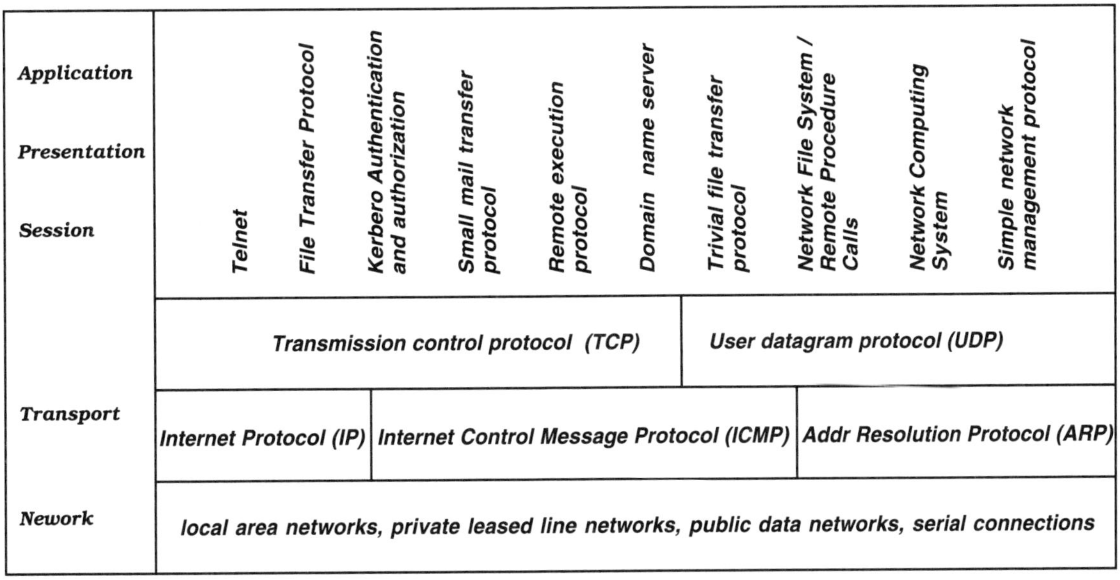

		Telnet	File Transfer Protocol	Kerbero Authentication and authorization	Small mail transfer protocol	Remote execution protocol	Domain name server	Trivial file transfer protocol	Network File System / Remote Procedure Calls	Network Computing System	Simple network management protocol
Application *Presentation* *Session*											
		Transmission control protocol (TCP)							**User datagram protocol (UDP)**		
Transport		**Internet Protocol (IP)**	**Internet Control Message Protocol (ICMP)**						**Addr Resolution Protocol (ARP)**		
Nework		**local area networks, private leased line networks, public data networks, serial connections**									

Figure 4–29. TCP/IP and its major application suites

Since TCP/IP was introduced before the OSI Reference Model, the term application protocol means protocols that cover the functional layers of application, presentation, and session. In this book, our intent is to describe the network and the transport layer protocols but not the application protocols of TCP/IP. Hence the term TCP/IP in this book means strictly the Transmission Control Protocol and the Internetwork Protocol.

Peer-to-Peer Nature

TCP/IP has its origin as a connection solution to a heterogeneous computer environment. Therefore, TCP/IP must be a peer-to-peer transport protocol because every computer manufacturer wants to be treated equally. There is no master in a TCP/IP network of computers. Every computer has equal network status. TCP/IP communication can be initiated by any one computer, whose listening can also be selective.

This approach is different from networks of hierarchical structure, a central master is controlling all network traffic. IBM's SNA, which we will review in Chapter Six, is an example of this.

Client-Server Nature

While the network transport layers of TCP/IP are structured as peer-to-peer, its application protocols are based on a client server model. TCP/IP applications are paired as clients and servers. For example, Telnet, a popular TCP/IP application, has a client component and a server component.

When a user uses a "foreign" computer to access his or her "home base" computer, the Telnet client must be running on the "foreign" computer, and the Telnet server must be executing on the "home base" computer. They are, in effect, two programs "talking" to one another over the network.

Individual computer manufacturers and software companies can take the Telnet, or any other TCP/IP application, specification contained in an RFC to implement client and or server programs for their own environments. These programs could be written in different programming languages (COBOL, Pascal, PL/1, C, . . . etc.), and under different operating systems and hardware (MVS, VMS, DOS, OS/2, UNIX). Since all programs are based on the same specification, the client server pairs should always work, regardless of hardware and software platforms. For example, a DOS FTP client should always be able to access an IBM MVS FTP server.

4.3.1.3   IP Addressing

In the next two sections, we review the network layer protocol of TCP/IP—the Internetwork Protocol (IP). They are followed by two more sections on the transport layer protocol of TCP/IP—the Transmission Control Protocol (TCP).

Figure 4–29 shows other complementary protocols in the network layer:

- Inter-network control message protocol (ICMP),
- Address resolution protocol (ARP), and
- Reverse address resolution protocol (RARP).

We briefly review them all in this section.

TCP/IP Dotted Decimal Form

The addressing scheme is an important element in any network protocol. Locating a computer on the network is like locating a building on a street. The computer must be assigned an address. In TCP/IP networks, each computer MUST have an Internetwork Address—the IP address.

The IP address is a 32-bit number. It is divided into two parts. The first part identifies the network address and the second part identifies the computer address within that network. This is analogous to a building address, composed of the name of the street (network address) and the street number (host address).

The 32-bit number can be represented by four 8-bit numbers. Since there can be 256 numbers (0 to 255) in an 8-bit representation, the IP address can be expressed as four separate decimal numbers separated by periods. This representation of IP address is known as dotted decimal form.

TCP/IP Network Classes

The two part IP address allows IP networks to be configured to suit various types of user organization. In the standard specification of TCP/IP, there are four classes of IP address: Class A, Class B, Class C, and Class D.

Class A address is designed for a network with a huge number of computers. Class C addresses are for networks with a small number of computers. Class B is somewhere in between. Class D addresses are for computers that receive broadcasts on the network.

```
Class A address = decimal NNN.HHH.HHH.HHH

where:

NNN = Network Addresses = decimal (0 to 127)

HHH = Host addresses = decimal (0 to 255)
```

In Class A, the highest bit is always zero, and bit number 1 to bit number 7 is the network address. Therefore, the network addresses for Class A IP addresses are from 0 to 127. Bits number 8 to number 32 are the computer addresses within a Class A network. For each Class A network, 2 to the power of 24 (16 million !) host computers are possible.

```
Class B address = decimal NNN.NNN.HHH.HHH where
```

NNN = Network Addresses = decimal (128 to 191). (0 to 255)

HHH = Host addresses = decimal (0 to 255)

In Class B, the highest bit is always one and the second highest zero. The next 14 bits are for the physical networks and 16 bits for hosts in each of those networks. For each Class B network, 2 to the power of 16 (about 65,000) host computers are possible.

Class C address = decimal NNN.NNN.NNN.HHH where

NNN = Network Addresses = decimal (192 to 224). (0 to 255).(0 to 255)

HHH = Host addresses = decimal (0 to 255)

In Class C, the highest three bits are always 110. The next 21 bits are for the physical networks and 8 bits are for hosts in each of those networks. For each Class C network, 2 to the power of 8 (about 256) host computers are possible.

```
Class D address = decimal NNN.XXX.XXX.XXX where

    NNN = Network Addresses = decimal (225 to 241)

    XXX = Don t cares

    In Class D, the highest four bits are always 1110. The rests
    are don t cares. This class is reserved for broadcasting to
    all hosts that have Class D addresses.
```

TCP/IP Subnets

The network address cannot be easily changed once it is assigned from a central administration to an organization. The organization may be a large business enterprise, a university, a government, or a research institute. But within an organization, many departments, divisions, and teams require separate administration of their own computer's network addresses.

While the main network address may be fixed, the host address space can be further subdivided into smaller networks. For example, a Class B network can have up to 65,000 hosts connected to it since it has a 16-bit address space. Many organizations have chosen to subdivide these 65,000 available host addresses by assigning the highest 6 bits (or 4 bits or 5 bits) as subnetworks within the bigger network. So, instead of having 65,000 hosts, an additional 64 (0 to 63) subnetworks are now located within the given Class B network. Since 10 bits still remain for hosts, 1,024 hosts are addressable on each subnet.

The bits that identify the subnets are specified by a bit mask. It is installation-specific and is not part of the standard TCP/IP specification.

4.3.1.4 IP Operation

Apart from assigning the network address, another important function of the IP protocol is to deliver to the destination computer information that has been passed down from the transport layer.

To do this, IP must have:

- its own data packet design,
- the capability to segment and to reassemble the information that it receives from the transport layer,
- the ability to find out the best route to deliver the message to a destination computer that is not in the same local area, and
- a host of other housekeeping activities.

IP packets

When IP receives a datagram from either the transport (TCP or the User Datagram Protocol, UDP) layer above, it will add a header to the TCP datagram to form the IP packet, a new datagram. The header contains instructions and descriptions of the data. For example, it indicates the version number of the IP protocol, the length of the header itself, the length of the data, the source IP address, the destination IP address, the protocol number to which IP should deliver the datagram, and the services required for this datagram (routine, priority, immediate, flash, critical, fragmentation control, network control, maximum travel time, throughput speed).

IP Segmentation

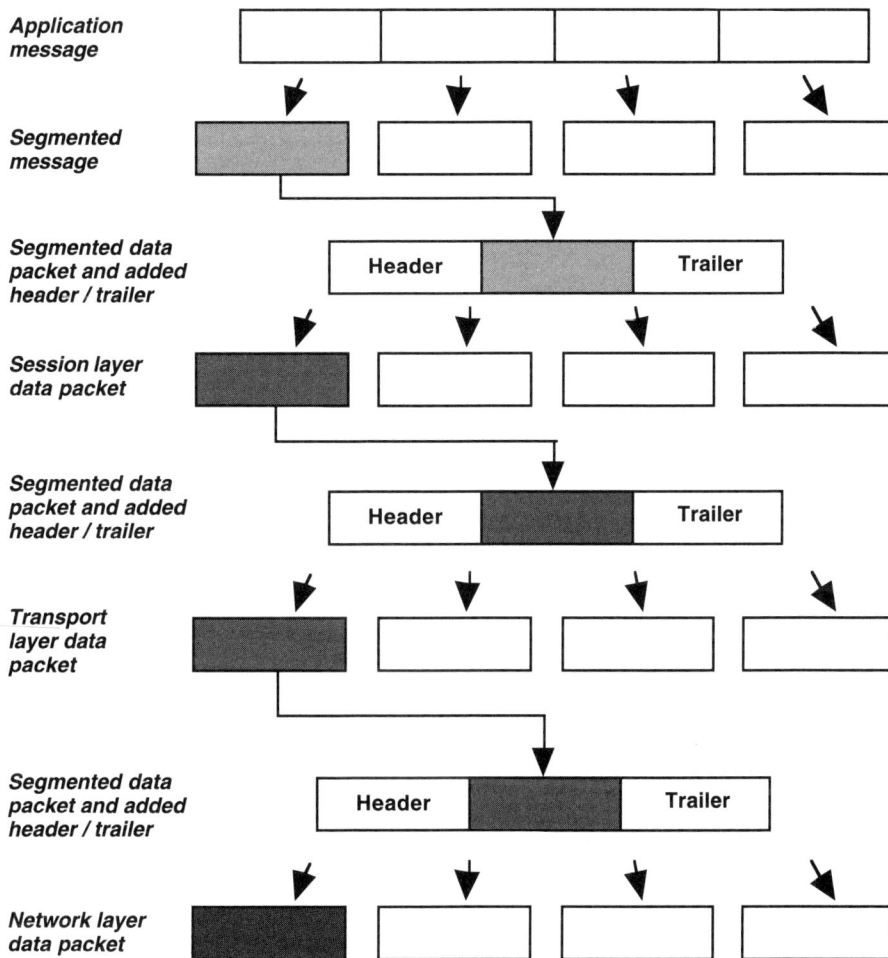

Figure 4–30. Segmentation of an application message to data packets through successive layers

The IP packet of the header and the datagram will be sent to the data link and the physical layers for transmission. However, physical networks always have a maximum frame size, called the maximum transmission unit (MTU) which will not allow a long IP datagram to be placed in one physical frame. These MTUs are different for Token Ring, Ethernet, SDLC, and X.25. For example, the MTU for Ethernet is 1500 bytes per frame.

Instead of limiting the IP packet length to some maximum size, IP can deal with segmentation and desegmentation of its own packets. This way, the IP does not have any maximum size. A scheme is designed to segment long IP datagram into smaller ones, and to reassemble them at the destination host.

The IP software splits the datagram into smaller parts. Each has a length that is a multiple of 8 bytes. The last data portion is padded with zero bytes up to a total length that is a multiple of 8. All data is placed in the datagram, the headers of which are copies of the original, with some modifications to account for the segmentation control. Each segmented datagram is forwarded as a normal IP datagram.

On the receiving side, when the segments arrive, before the timer expires, the data is copied into the buffer storage at the location indicated by the segment offset field. As soon as all segments have arrived, the complete original datagram is restored.

IP is a connectionless protocol. It simply passes the IP packets to the underlying layers. It adds no reliability, flow control, or error recovery to the underlying link and physical layers. Packets (datagrams) sent by IP may be lost, out of order, or even duplicated, but Internet Protocols will not handle these situations. The transmission control protocol in the transport layer takes care of that. IP is a connectionless protocol.

IP Direct and Indirect Routing

Routing is the process of deciding where to send a packet based on its destination address. Two kinds of routing are involved in communications within TCP/IP direct and indirect routing.

Direct routing is used when the source and destination computers are on the same network. The source computer IP program maps the destination address into a hardware address and sends packets to the destination computer. This mapping is normally performed through a translation table. If a match cannot be found, the address resolution protocol (ARP) will be invoked to determine this hardware address.

Indirect routing refers to sending IP packets from one TCP/IP network to another TCP/IP network. Here, the source computer IP program sends packets to a router on the same network using direct routing. From there, the packets are forwarded through intermediate routers, as required, until they arrive at the destination network. Direct routing is then used to forward the packets to the destination computer on that network.

IP Routing Algorithm

The IP routing mechanism only considers the IP network address. For every IP packet, the routing software within the sending computer will go through an iterating process to deliver it to the receiving computer. It treats every packet as unrelated to any other packet. Each computer keeps the routing table which contains mapping between the destination IP network address and the route to the next gateway.

Three types of mapping are possible. The direct routes are for the same physical network. The indirect routes are for networks reachable via one or more routers or gateways. The default route is for those networks that cannot be found in the routing table.

The process first checks the destination IP network address for direct route in the routing table. If positive, the packet will be sent directly to the host on the attached network. Otherwise, the destination address will be checked for indirect route.

If positive, the packet will be sent to the specified router or gateway on the network, from which it will be further checked for direct or indirect routes. Otherwise, the packet will be sent to the default network, if one is specified. If no default route is specified, the message "network unreachable" will be put out and the packet discarded.

IP packets get to the destination through the address resolution protocol (ARP), which is described later in this section.

IP Router

As mentioned above, if IP packets are sent to a network other than the one from which they originate, the packets must be first forwarded to a router. The complete IP address of this router should be in the routing table.

When a packet arrives at the router, it will go through the same routing algorithm as it used in the source computer. Thus, if the network address appears on the direct route, then the packet will be sent directly to the destination computer. If the network address appears as an indirect route, then the packet will be forwarded to another router listed in the routing table. This process can continue until a network address match is encountered.

In very large TCP/IP networks, such as the ARPANET and the Internet, comprehensive and complex gateways are maintained by a central authority. They provide reliable and authoritative routes for all possible Internet networks.

IP's Address Resolution Protocol (ARP)

ARP maps IP addresses and network hardware addresses. It automatically collects and distributes the information for mapping tables. It is an important element to bridge between the TCP/IP protocols and the underlying data link and physical layers. ARP is not directly available to users or applications. It is a program that comes as an integral part of any TCP/IP software package.

ARP is a program that interfaces directly with the logical link control or directly with the Media Access Control (MAC) drivers. ARP is essential because MAC drivers do not understand high level IP addresses. They only deal with low level hardware addresses.

If ARP finds the matching pair of hardware address and network address in its table, it gives the corresponding physical address back to the MAC driver, which sends the packet to the network with the correct hardware address.

When the address is not found in the ARP table, a broadcast is sent out by the ARP module on the network, with a special format called the ARP request. In this process, the datagram is discarded by ARP since it is assumed that a higher layer protocol will re-transmit the same datagram.

Now, if one of the computers on the network recognizes its own IP address in the request, it will send an ARP reply back to the requesting host. The reply will contain the physical hardware address of the host, and this address is put in the ARP table of the requesting host. All subsequent datagrams to this destination IP address can now be translated to a physical address, which is used by the device driver to send out the datagram on the network. If there were no machine on the network responding, ARP assumes that such network does not exist or is unreachable.

IP's Reverse Address Resolution Protocol (RARP)

This is an even more advanced implementation of the TCP/IP network. It enables a computer to find its own proper IP address on a network automatically. This is especially useful for the less intelligent computers such as the diskless workstations.

RARP requires one or more server hosts on a network to maintain a database of mapping between physical hardware addresses and IP addresses. These servers must be always active and are listening to the network for requests. To request its IP address, the requesting system broadcasts its physical hardware address. A server on the network responds to this request by providing the requesting system with its IP address.

IP's Internetwork Control Message Protocol (ICMP)

This protocol passes control messages between gateways, routers, and hosts. It provides feedback about problems in the communication environment. It does not reliably guarantee that an IP packet will be delivered.

It puts out messages in situations such as the following:

- when another computer checks to see if another computer is available (PING)
- when a packet cannot reach its destination
- when a gateway can direct a computer to send traffic on a shorter route
- when a computer requests netmask or a time stamp
- when the local buffer is full

Summary of IP

The Internetwork Protocol (IP) is a network layer protocol whose main objective is to deliver the transport layer packets. It is a connectionless protocol. It knows how to segment and assemble segmented messages. It determines the route by which its data packets have to travel to get to their destinations. It has an internal table that keeps track of the network addresses and their corresponding hardware addresses. Through ARP or RARP, the network and hardware address pairs are updated.

In the next two sections, we review the transport layer protocol of TCP/IP.

4.3.1.5 TCP Addressing

The transport layer is responsible for end-to-end data exchange between two programs on the network. In TCP/IP, there are two protocols specified for the transport layer. The first and most widely used one is known as the Transmission Control Protocol (TCP), and the second, and less commonly used one, is known as User Datagram Protocol (UDP).

TCP Port Numbers

TCP uses the term "port number" to identify a program in a networked computer, which may contain multiple active programs. A port number is represented by a 16-bit number. When a message arrives from the network to the computer, the transport layer's responsibility is to deliver it to the desired program within the computer.

Standard TCP/IP applications such as Telnet and FTP use the same port number on all computers. They are the well known ports. The well known ports occupy port numbers in the range 0 to 255. User developed applications should use port numbers above 255. Examples are:

Port number		Reserved for
5	RJE	Remote Job Entry
13	DAYTIME Time of	the day
21	FTP	File transfer
23	Telnet Terminal	emulation
42	Nameserver	Host name server
53	DOMAIN Domain	name server
103	X400	Electronic mail
111	SUNRPC	Sun RPC
137	NetBIOS_NS	NetBIOS Name Services
138	NetBIOS_DG	NetBIOS Datagram
139	NetBIOS_SS	NetBIOS Session Services

TCP Portmapper

Assignment of port numbers is not as simple as it appears. Applications inadvertently using the same port number are bound to occur. Having a central administrator to hand out port numbers every time someone writes a program is not practical.

One way to avoid this conflict is to write a program that allocates port numbers dynamically. In this scheme, instead of pre-assigning a port number, port numbers are assigned at the moment of connection. This assigned port number is then good for the duration of the communication session.

Within TCP/IP, the program known as a portmapper is responsible for dynamic assignment of port numbers within a computer.

4.3.1.6 TCP Operation

TCP is a connection-oriented protocol. When called upon to operate, it creates and maintains a virtual communication circuit for the two communicating programs. To understand how TCP operates, we must first examine the concept of socket interface.

TCP Socket Address

The port number and the IP address of the computer combined is known as a socket address, which uniquely identify a program on a network. It tells us what program on which computer.

The socket address points to a socket with which an application program can use to communicate with another program on the network. Two applications can communicate only after each application has been given a socket by the network operating system software. The nice thing about a socket is that it provides user applications with an API that hides the complexities of the bottom three layers of the OSI Reference Model.

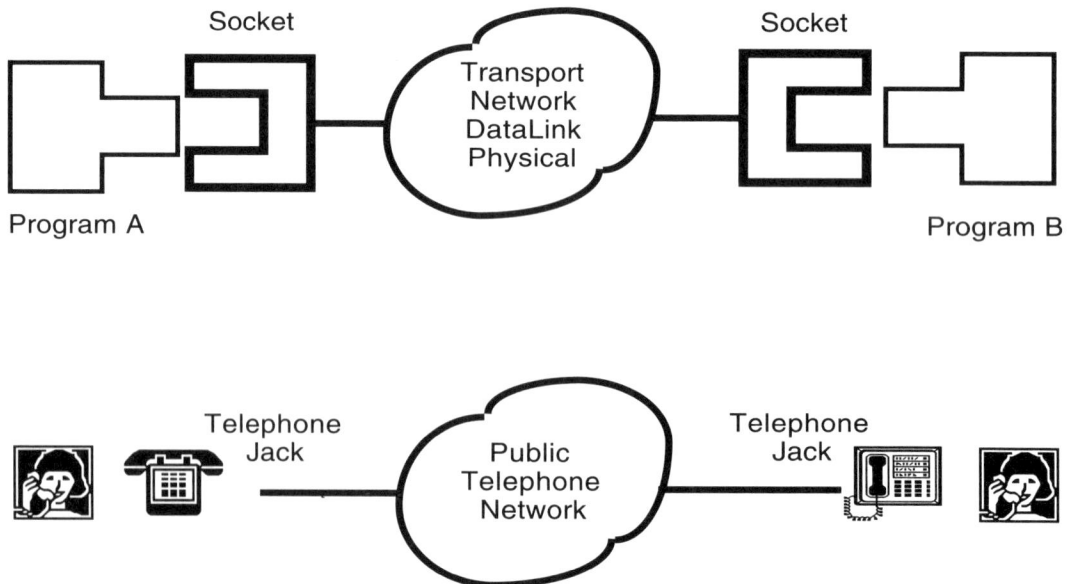

Figure 4–31. The Socket Concept

As shown in Figure 4–31, a socket is like a household telephone jack, which hides all the engineering complexities of a public telephone network—switches, wires, multiplexors, and so on.

An important point to remember is that what people do with the telephone (i.e. the content, the intent, and the protocol of the conversation) is completely up to the communicating parties.

The same principle applies in network computing, how the programs make use of the socket is completely up to the programs themselves. The socket only provides a path through which data expressed in 1s and 0s can be delivered to the other program. The programs themselves must decide their own communication protocols.

TCP Socket Types

In TCP, as in other protocols, there are three types of sockets: stream, datagram, and raw sockets.

A stream socket is a connection-oriented service. These sockets use the TCP as the transport layer protocol, very much like a virtual circuit connection.

The datagram socket is a connectionless service. These sockets use the UDP as the transport layer protocol.

The raw socket allows direct access to the lower layer protocols, such as the IP bypassing either the TCP and UDP transport layer protocols.

TCP Socket Programming

When an application program wants to communicate with another program on the network, it must first obtain a socket from TCP/IP. This process is done through a socket command API. When TCP/IP returns with a socket, the program identifies itself to the socket with its name and the socket address. This process is done through a bind command API.

From this point on, the program is registered on the network, and other programs on the network can access this program by connecting to this socket address. This binding process is similar to assigning a telephone number to a person. Once that is done, everyone on the network knows when they call this telephone number, they will be talking to this person.

If the program is a server, it must indicate its readiness to accept connections from clients. It can do this by issuing the listen command API. This puts the server on the network and enables it to accept connection requests from clients.

If the program is a client, then it can initiate a connection by issuing the connect commands API. In this command, the client must indicate the socket address of the server. When a server accepts a connection request from a client, it issues an accept command and returns a local connection name. This local connection name identifies the connection between a client and a server.

After the issuance of the accept commands, the server should be able to accept new connections. After a connection is established between the client and server, there are four calls available for data transfer:

```
send,
receive,
send_to, and
receive_from.
```

The send and the receive can only be used after the connection is made between the client and the server. The 'send_to' and the 'receive_from' can be used without a connection. Usually they are used when the socket is based on the UDP protocol, a connectionless datagram transmission.

TCP Data Packets

Depending upon the environment, TCP may be receiving user messages directly from a network application, or in the form of session layer data packets. The session layer is the layer above the transport layer. The session layer is responsible for monitoring and controlling the delivery of the application message. The session layer uses and supervises the transport and below layers for such delivery. Chapter Five: Network Operating System will review various session layer protocols such as OSF's DCS, Named Pipe, and NetBIOS.

TCP data packet is similar to other data packet design. It consists of a header, a user message, and a trailer. The header contains addressing and flow control information, and the trailer contains error control information. In the middle is the user message. The following are included for topical interest.

- The source port, a 16-bit number uniquely identifying the program at the source computer.
- The destination port, another 16-bit number uniquely identifying the program at the destination computer.
- The sequence number of the first data byte in this data packet. This is the number used by the receiving TCP to put the data packets arrived in the proper sequence. Note that this is an activity not carried out by the IP protocol below, whose connectionless characteristics have no flow control, error corrections, or sequencing. It is here, at the TCP layer, that these activities are carried out.
- The acknowledgment number is the value of the next sequence number that the receiver is expecting to receive. This is obviously needed for flow control, and sequencing.
- Other control indicators:
- RST—reset the connection
- SYN— synchronize the sequence number
- FIN—no more data from sender
- checksum field is used to ensure data integrity. It is the 1 complement of the sum of the IP header, the TCP header, and the TCP data.

TCP Flow Control

TCP also has certain advanced flow control features, which make it a very efficient transmission protocol. TCP assigns a sequence number to each byte transmitted and expects a positive acknowledgment from the receiving TCP. If the acknowledgment is not received within a certain time-out limit, the data is retransmitted.

The receiving TCP uses the sequence numbers to rearrange the data packets when they arrive out of order and to eliminate duplicate data packets. The receiving TCP, when returning the acknowledgment to the sender, also indicates to the sender the number of bytes it can receive beyond the last received TCP data packet without causing overrun and overflow in its internal buffers. This is sent in the acknowledgment in the form of the highest sequence number it can receive without problems.

This control mechanism is often known as "windowing" (see below). It ensures reliable transmission and better throughput. The reliability and flow control mechanism described above requires that TCPs initialize and maintain certain status information for each data stream.

The combination of this status, including sockets, sequence numbers, and window sizes is called a "virtual circuit." Each connection is uniquely identified by the pair of sockets used by the sending and receiving programs.

TCP Windowing

TCP has incorporated the principle of windowing to allow much faster throughput. Instead of waiting for an acknowledgment from the receiver on the receipt of every byte before sending the next one, the sender is allowed to keep on sending bytes, up to a certain number (the window size), without waiting for the acknowledgment.

When the acknowledgment comes back for the first byte, the window slides to exclude that byte. Thus the transmission continues while the next acknowledgment may come at any time. The window stops sliding only if there is a retransmission of a particular byte is necessary, due to time out or otherwise. Once the byte is retransmitted and received, the window can start again.

4.3.1.7 Summary of TCP

TCP/IP forms a network family. It provides all necessary addressing schemes to pinpoint a program on a network. Its socket APIs allow two user programs to exchange messages very much like the telephone outlets allowing two people to talk to each other.

TCP/IP based applications are structured along the client server model. The client program takes the initiative of contacting the server program to request specific services. With the socket APIs, a client program must first obtain a socket. It then establishes a connection with the server program. When its request is fulfilled, it terminates the connection. This model of communication is similar to telephone communication. First, the client must find a telephone outlet. It dials its partner. They exchange messages. Then they terminate the connection.

Again, the steps of this model of communication are: initiation, communication, and termination. Similar steps are used for all network families.

Communications within a network family is exclusive. An FTP client server pair designed to use TCP sockets will not work in another network family such as Novell's SPX/IPX.

In the next chapter on network operating systems, we review session layer protocols that allow multiple network families to be active at the same time. Applications written to this particular session protocol (e.g. NetBIOS, Named Pipe) are able to work over different network families.

4.3.2 Other Protocols

TCP/IP is not the only protocol available, there are others. Notable among them are IBM's APPN, IBM's SNA, Novell's SPX/IPX, Microsoft-IBM's NetBIOS/Net-BEUI, DEC's DecNet, and Apple's AppleTalk.

In this section, we review briefly the first two for topical interests. Readers should be able to obtain technical information on various transport network protocols from their respective suppliers.

4.3.2.1 Novell's SPX/IPX

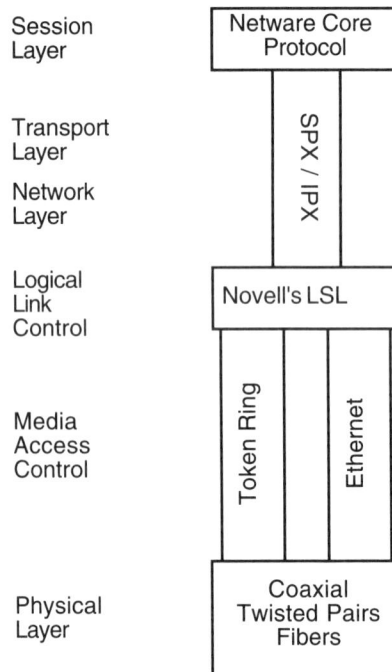

Figure 4–32. Novell's SPX/IPX

The network/transport protocol used by Netware is known as the Internetwork Packet Exchange (IPX) and Sequenced Packet Exchange (SPX). IPX is a connectionless protocol and SPX, which sits on top of IPX is a connection oriented protocol. If an analogy must be made, TCP is roughly equivalent to SPX. IP is roughly equivalent to IPX.

Internetwork Packet Exchange, IPX

The structure of IPX packet is identical to that of a Xerox XNS (Xerox Networking Standard) packet. The IPX packet has a 30-byte header and up to 546 bytes of data. The header has the following structure:

Source address = 12 bytes or 96 bits	4 bytes are for the network family address (32 bits)
	6 bytes are for the hardware network interface board address (48 bits)
	2 bytes are for the socket address for program (16 bits)
Destination address = 12 bytes or 96 bits	Same as above.
Packet type= identifies the type of service required by the packet:	4 = IPX 5 = SPX 16-31 = Experiment protocol 117 = Netware control protocol 120 = NetBIOS named packet
Transport control	Netware Internetwork bridges use this to monitor the number of bridges or routers that a packet has crossed.
Data length =	Length of the data.
Checksum =	Error correction code.

IPX has 32 bits to address a computer on the network. It has a theoretical capacity to accommodate 2 to the power of 32 computers or 4.3 billion, which is the same as TCP/IP. However, IPX is not as sophisticated because it does not have the addressing scheme for different network classes, dotted decimal representation, and subnets of TCP/IP.

The destination address is the hardware address on the network interface card. The address can be 48 bits long.

Within a computer, IPX can address up to 65,536 programs. It is equivalent to the socket address of TCP/IP.

Sequenced Packet eXchange, SPX

While IPX is a datagram or connectionless service, SPX is a connection-oriented protocol. An SPX connection is a virtual circuit. The SPX packet header consists of an IPX header (30 bytes) and seven additional fields. They are:

Connection control	Controls the bi-directional flow of data across an SPX connection.
Data stream type	Indicates the type of data in the packet. For example, value of 0X00 to 0XFD are defined by the client and ignored by SPX. Value of 0XFE indicates an end of connection packet.
Source connection ID	An ID assigned to the SPX connection by the source and the destination computers.
Destination connection ID	Same as above.
Sequence number	Keeps a count of packets exchanged in one direction on the connection. Each side keeps its own count.
Acknowledge number	Indicates the next packet that an SPX connection expects to receive.
Allocation number	Indicates the number of outstanding receive buffers available for a given SPX connection. It is used by SPX to implement flow control for the connection.

Assigning computer network addresses and program socket addresses is performed by various Netware modules in the client workstation, and the Netware server core program. The Netware server is not required to keep a record of the computer addresses of every computer on the network. It only records those computer or workstation addresses that are logged on to the server so that it can exchange messages with those workstations.

A client workstation on the network initiates the logon to the server by sending IPX packets containing its hardware address and other information (e.g. user name, password) about itself. The Netware server then picks up the request, if the user is a legitimate one, and if the maximum number of licensed users has not been exceeded.

4.3.2.2 NetBIOS / NetBEUI

Network Basic Input Output Subsystem (NetBIOS) was originally designed as an application programming interface to work with the network interface cards for PCs designed by IBM and Sytek during the early 1980s.

The intent then was to provide PC application developers a network programming interface so that their application can make use of other network resources through the network interface cards manufactured by IBM and Sytek. NetBIOS formerly was resident on a ROM in the network interface card manufactured by IBM/Sytek. As the LAN market exploded, such monolithic approach was not acceptable.

When IBM and Microsoft were cooperating on the development of LAN Manager, Microsoft decided to remove the network transport layer code from the NetBIOS programming interface and to create the code as loadable software so that other varieties of network interface cards and network protocol stacks could also be used in building networks.

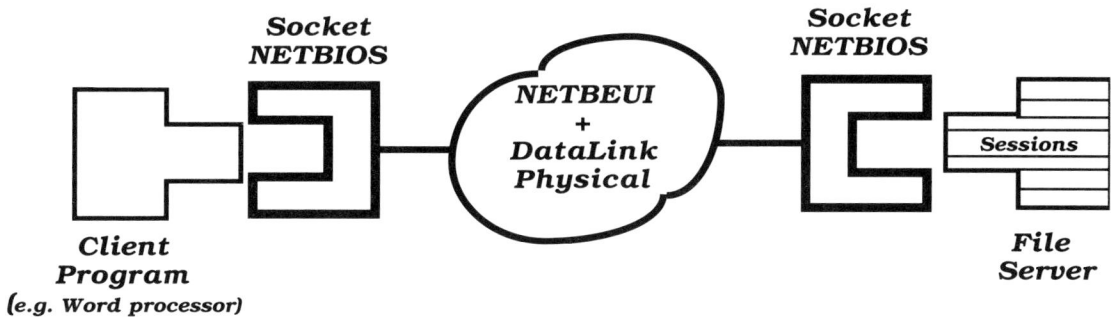

Figure 4–33. NETBIOS/NETBEUI

Microsoft calls the now separated network protocol underneath NetBIOS as the NetBIOS Extended User Interface or NetBEUI. With that, NetBIOS can also be used by other network transport protocols using NDIS, the logical link layer protocol discussed in Section 4.2.4.1.

Like many things IBM did in those days, the market was drawn toward adopting NetBIOS as a standard interface for network application development by the power of IBM. As a result, many applications, such as terminal emulators, word processors, spreadsheets, and SQL front ends, have been written to work with the NetBIOS interface.

NetBIOS as a Session Layer Protocol

Many network vendors, such as Novell and others that provide network products, recognize the importance of NetBIOS. They came up with NetBIOS emulators to work with their own product lines.

As a result, investments by users on network application products can easily be moved to other network transport environment as long as they support the NetBIOS interface.

In doing this, they have turned NetBIOS into a session layer interface that straddles multiple transport protocols. For example, a NetBIOS application can be executed over TCP/IP as well as SPX/IPX networks.

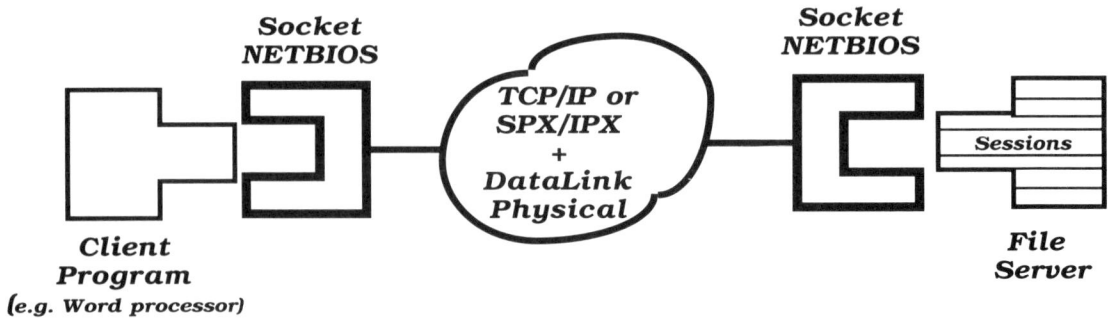

Figure 4–34. NetBIOS and other Transport Protocols

Peer-to-Peer

NetBIOS/NetBEUI is a peer-to-peer based protocol by which any computer on the network can initiate a communication session with other computers on the same network, provided that the destination computer recognizes the requests.

4.3.3 Network-Layer-Only Protocols

Why do we have network-layer-only protocols? For local area networks, it is feasible to control the message delivery from the physical layer to the application layer. However, if the message must be delivered to a computer in another continent, then the public data network comes into play since very few enterprises have the resources to own their own private transcontinental data network.

Network layer protocols are responsible for determining the route by which a message can be delivered from one computer to another computer, but it does not identify the exact destination program within individual computers. It expects other user programs to look after that.

The two popular types of public data networks are CCITT X.25 and Frame Relay.

4.3.3.1 CCITT X.25

Public data networks are digital networks that deliver messages from one computer to another. They are network layer protocols. Each data packet flowing through a transmission circuit carries within it the destination address. Electronic ears are placed in various points in the network to decide how it should be routed to the correct destinations. Hence, the term "packet switching" is used.

Most existing public data networks use CCITT X.25 packet switching technology. Examples are GTE's Telenet and AT&Ts Accunet in the United States, DataPac in Canada, Transpac in France, Euronet in Europe, PSS in the United Kingdom.

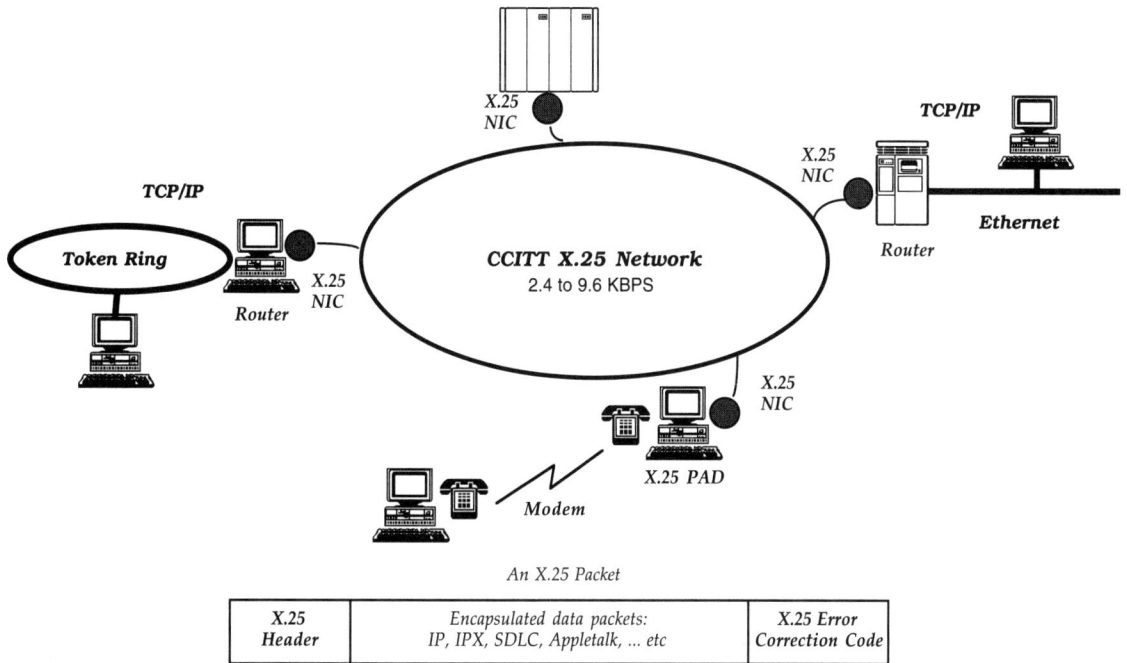

An X.25 Packet

X.25 Header	Encapsulated data packets: IP, IPX, SDLC, Appletalk, ... etc	X.25 Error Correction Code

Figure 4–35. CCITT X.25 Public Data Network

Standards

The OSI specification for X.25 has three tightly integrated levels. Level 1 addresses the physical layer level 2, the data link layer; and level 3, the network layer. Level 3 of X.25 directs the X.25 packets through multiple X.25 network nodes in the public data network. The data link protocol is responsible for packet transmission between two adjacent nodes. It uses either the Link Access Protocol (LAP) or the Link Access Protocol—Balanced (LAPB). Both are functional subset of the High Level Data Link Control (HDLC) bit-oriented protocol.

Most computer manufacturers now make X.25 network interface cards for their computers. They also supply software drivers for their own operating systems and hardware.

Vendors' Role

An X.25 line has to be ordered from, and installed by, the telephone company to put a computer onto their X.25 network. While the X.25 data network will deliver a message from one computer to another, it does not know how to deliver the same message to the appropriate program within the destination computer. The transport layer protocol must finish the final part of the delivery.

If, for example, the network-transport protocol is TCP/IP, the IP packets can be encapsulated in X.25 packets to be delivered through the X.25 public data network. Upon arrival, the TCP/IP software unwraps the data packet and treats it as though it were delivered by any other data link mechanisms (e.g. Ethernet, Token Ring, SDLC, or Start-stop).

Software drivers for your X.25 network interface card are available from the card manufacturer. The card is necessary to incorporate the encapsulation of your local network transport protocols.

Availability

Availability of X.25 lines are not yet as universal as the telephone lines. Many smaller cities in North America, for example, do not have X.25 services.

Telephone companies have extended the availability of X.25 through the establishment of packet assembling and de-assembling units (PADs) in major cities. Users can use the simple ASCII Start-Stop transmission via their modems in accessing this X.25 service.

Users can also write their own application using the X.25 software programming interface. They can send application messages from one computer to another computer connected on the same network. The computers can be from the same or different manufacturers.

4.3.3.2 Frame Relay

X.25 usage is limited by its slow speed caused by its overly conservative amount of error-checking such as numbering, acknowledging, monitoring, and retransmitting (if the transmission failed) every data packet as it travels to its destination.

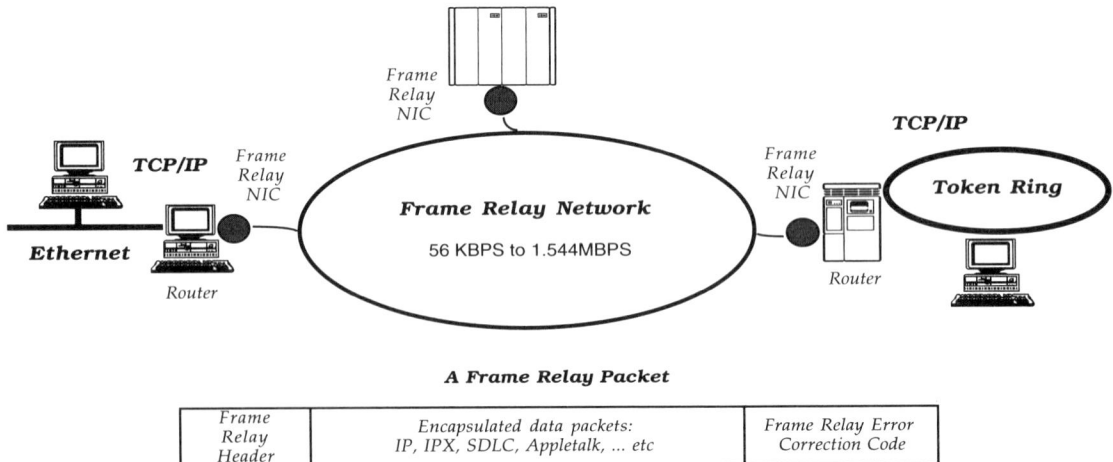

Figure 4–36. Frame Relay Network

A new technology known as frame relay is now being test-marketed by public data network vendors. Frame relay is a new interface and switching technology supported by both CCITT and ANSI. It is targeting both the LAN-interconnection market and the X.25 replacement market.

The frame relay technology reduces the overhead of the X.25 protocol to lower cost and increase throughput. It is based upon the assumption that modern transmission circuits are clean and quiet (today's all-digital networks routinely offer bit error rates of 1 in 1,000,000,000,000!), and it is better to put those error checking facilities inside the network interface card than to put them onto the switching gears of the public network to handle the infrequent network transmission error.

If there is a problem, the frame relay network simply discards the data and expects the network interface card or the terminal equipment to take corrective action. This approach makes a lot of sense because almost all commercial grade transport-network protocols have their own error checking and retransmission scheme.

In effect, frame relay networks—either public or private—are similar to LANs. They can be compared to LAN bridges, with the addition of network congestion control and guaranteed throughput. Providing peer-to-peer connectivity between remote LANs is the pre-eminent Frame Relay application. Multiple devices, handling different application and network protocols, could therefore attach to a frame relay network allowing the sharing of bandwidth and nodes.

4.3.3.3 *Private vs. Public WANs*

Computer users now have a choice between public data network and privately-leased lines. Many users like the public data network the way they like the public voice network. They do not want to be bothered with another activity that they do not deem part of their core business.

The telephone companies are no longer satisfied to be mere providers of the "copper." They are competing with manufacturers of data communication equipment such as IBM's 3745 communication controllers, which work only on privately-leased line networks. The battle will be intense and the stakes are extremely high.

In Europe, Japan, and Canada, the X.25 packet switching data networks have been well received. In the United States, the largest data processing market in the world, telecommunication deregulation has created intense competition from the leased line business. The price drops on the U.S. leased lines are such that the growth of the public data network has dampened somewhat.

Ultimately, the competition between private and public networks boils down to cost, availability, and performance. The cost of using X.25 to compete with privately leased, X.25 lines, are priced on usage (number of bytes sent), while leased lines are not. Both privately leased line networks and the local area network are more cost-effective and higher performing than public data networks in many application situations.

4.3.4 Dialup Access

One aspect of the wide area public network that we have not covered is the circuit switched networks—the public telephone lines. The unique characteristic of the telephone network is that its reach is worldwide. The device that makes dialed access feasible is the modem which is discussed in Section 4.1.2.5.

One aspect of the dialed access is to LAN severs and subsequently to the host applications on the network. To many business people, dialed access is their principal means of communication with their applications. Accessing LAN resources remotely means that a user with a PC can dial into the network from anywhere. This is particularly useful for field workers who do not actually have a PC of their own at the office but need access to the network.

There are four techniques by which this can be accomplished:

- remote client,
- modem remote control—single PC,
- access server, and
- modem server.

Remote Client

The remote PC uses network software similar to that of a client machine on a LAN. The remote client PC treats the modem as a slow network interface card and routes all of the network activity through the serial port. This technique's only advantage is that it gives the remote PC a full set of network drives, allowing application programs to use their standard paths for program and data files.

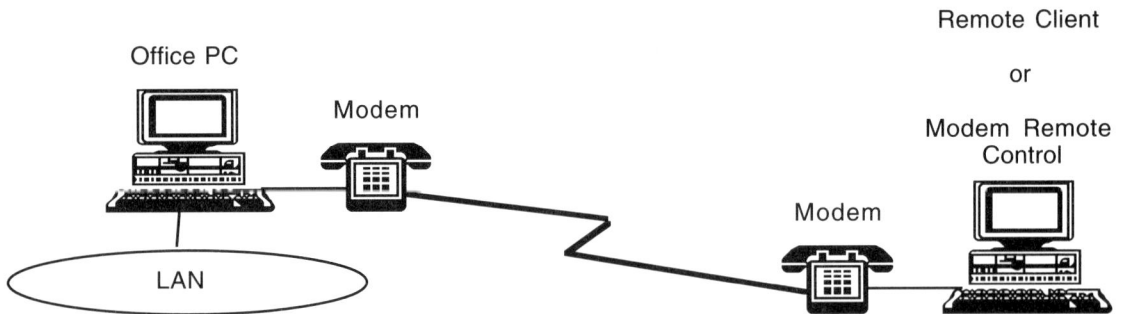

Figure 4–37. Dialed access to LAN: Remote Modem Control

Modem Remote Control

The second technique is known as modem remote control. It works by setting up the office PC with special remote control software. The remote PC, which dials in to the office PC, needs only to run the remote-control software. The keyboards and screens of the remote and LAN-connected PCs operate in parallel, allowing keystrokes from the remote PC to control the LAN-connected machine and allowing the screen displays of the LAN-connected machine to appear on the screen of the remote PC. Application programs run on the LAN-connected PC, where they get full access to the high-speed network connections and resources. Examples of commercial products are Norton's PC Windows and Carbon Copy.

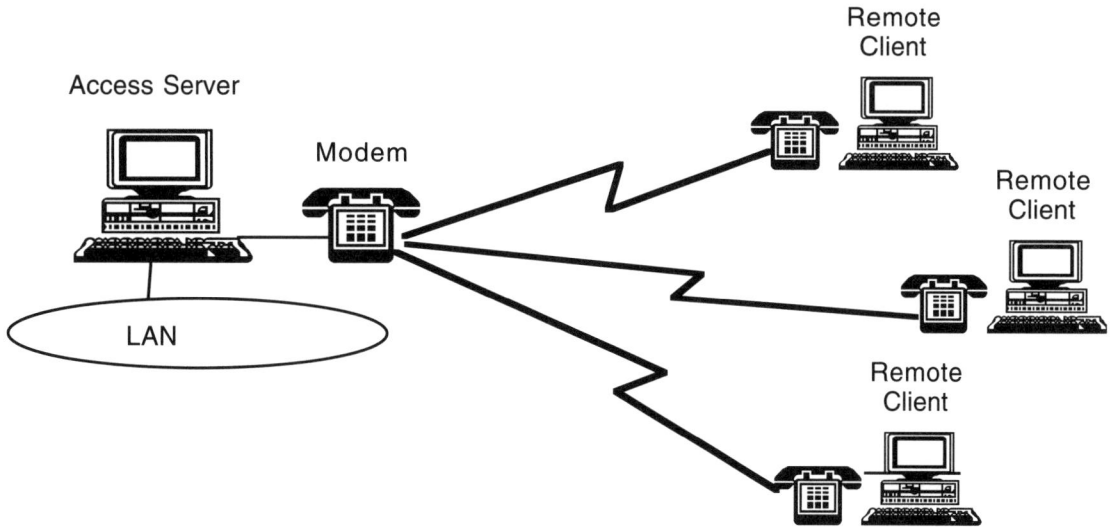

Figure 4–38. Access Server that handles multiple remote clients

Access Server

The third technique is known as access server. It is a dedicated PC on the LAN with special remote software that handles multiple calls from remote PCs. Access servers answer incoming calls and allow the caller to run networked applications from the answering PC.

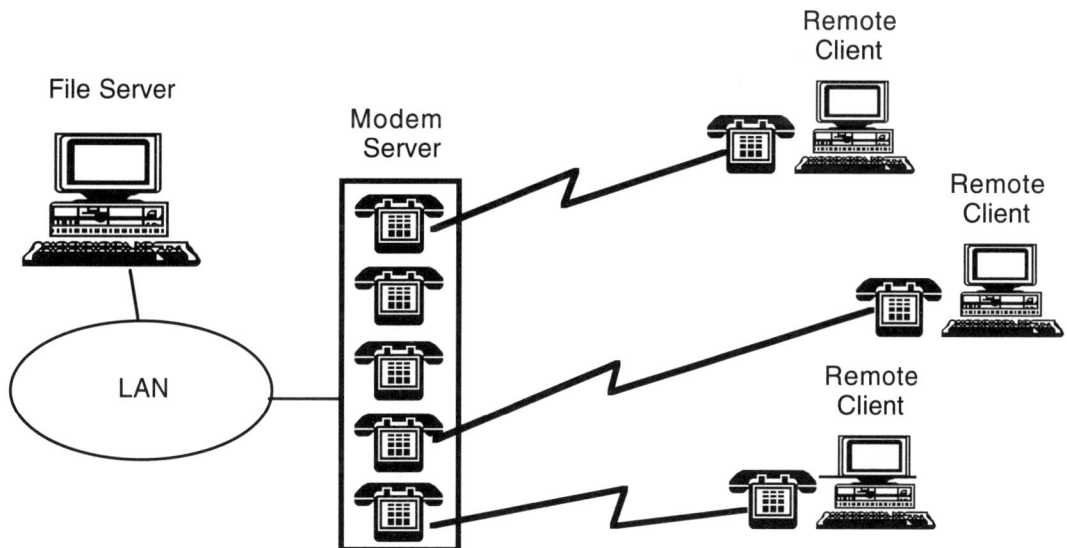

Figure 4–39. Modem Server that handles multiple remote clients

Any spare PC equipped with modem remote-control software, a serial port, and a modem, can be used as an access server, which can handle four or more simultaneous incoming sessions. With these products, each user dialing in has access to a CPU or a virtual CPU.

Modem Server

A modem server is a group of modems—as many as 16. Each modem is connected to a dedicated telephone number or line. They are made available to the remote client workstations on a first-come-first-served basis.

In the LAN-attached PCs the modem server must be provided with a redirector to send the serial communications traffic to that LAN server. Some redirectors are software-based and some combine hardware and software.

4.4 HETEROGENEOUS INTER-CONNECTIONS

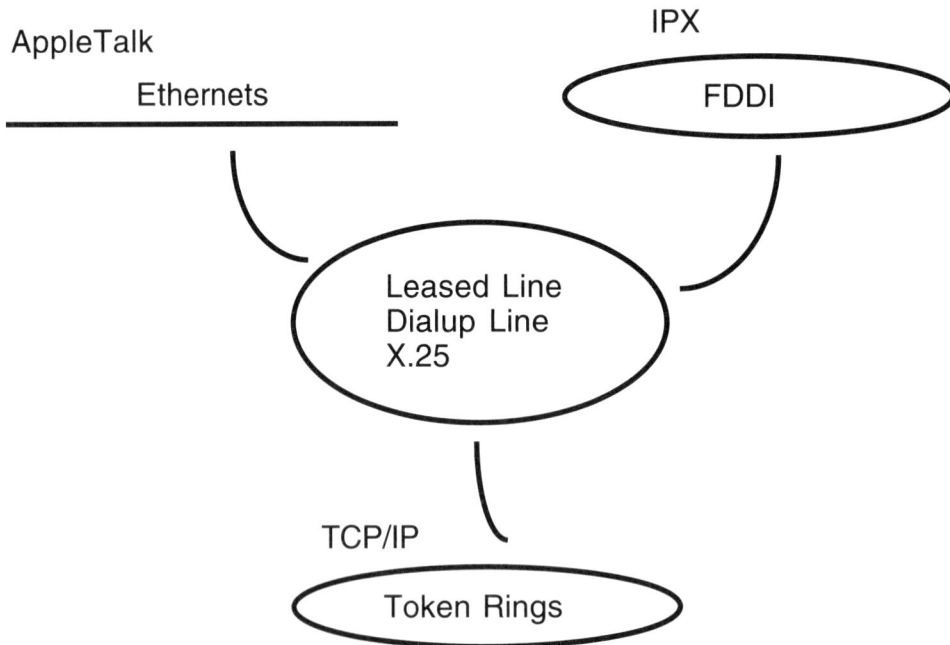

Figure 4–40. Typical heterogeneous network transports

Up to this point we have discussed how various data link, network, and transport layers protocols work individually. But in the real world, a homogeneous networking environment seldom exists. Figure 4–40 shows the typical situation of an organization which has a number of incompatible technology islands with a mix of physical transmission circuits and public data networks and different kinds of local area networks.

In this section, we review the technology and methods for heterogeneous systems interconnection. In Section 8.6, Design Network Transport Environment, we show how these islands can be tied together so that a user can access all the information resources from a single point: the workstation.

4.4.1 Interconnecting Devices

Our starting point will be the introduction of interconnecting devices. These devices are:

- Repeaters
- Bridges
- Routers
- Gateways

Repeaters are devices that connect the physical network segments. Bridges are devices that connect the datalink layers. Routers are devices that connect the network transport layers. Gateways are devices that connect all levels up to the application layers.

4.4.1.1 Repeaters

Physical layer entity—simply repeat the communication signal with no modification to extend the network segment for a short distance

Segment 1   **Segment 2**   **Segment 3**

Segment 1 = Segment 2 = Segment 3 = same data link protocol

Figure 4–41. Repeaters

Figure 3.40 shows the simplest inter-networking devices—repeaters, which regenerate, or repeat, the electronic signals over dispersed networks or between cable segments. Repeaters work at the OSI Model's physical layer. It does not add anything to the packet address or control logic.

4.4.1.2 Bridges

Bridges work at the media access control sublayer of the data link layer. Bridges regulate the traffic from one network segment to another strictly according to the destination address on each packet. Bridges extend a LAN to a wide area.

The main difference between a bridge and the repeater is in the ability of a bridge to recognize the packet address. Since the transmission circuit over the wide area at 56 KBPS is much slower than a LAN, it is not practical to broadcast all the packets across the wide area if a packet is destined to an address in the local area.

Data link layer entities called bridges have the capability to filter out the data packet that does not require going through the slower data link in Segment 2, typically a wide area circuit around 56 KB.

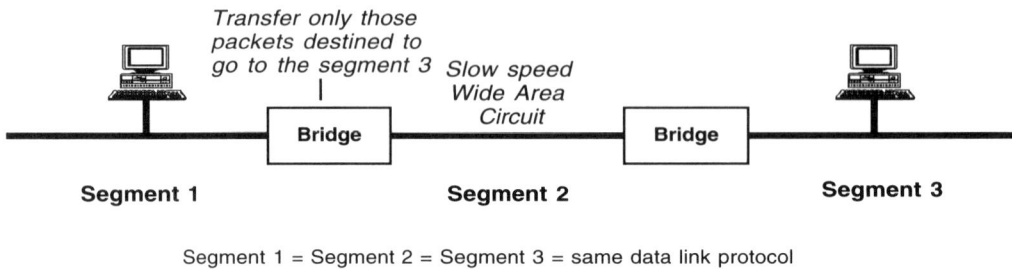

Segment 1 = Segment 2 = Segment 3 = same data link protocol

Figure 4–42. Bridges

Bridges can be used to filter out those packets that should be sent across to the other LAN. As a result, a bridge reduces the wide area network traffic and improves network performance for both LANs.

Routers are used to connect two different network segments that are using different data link protocol BUT sharing the SAME network transport protocol.

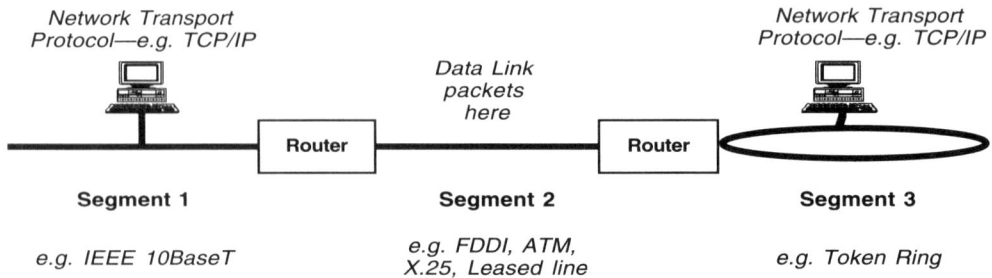

Segment 1, Segment 2, and Segment 3 do not share the same data link protocol

Figure 4–43. Routers

4.4.1.3 *Routers*

Routers are used to connect two networks that use the same network transport protocols but have different kinds of data link protocols. As shown in Figure 4.43, Segment #1 is a 10BaseT network, and Segment #3 is a Token Ring network. Both use TCP/IP as their network transport protocol.

To move the IP data packets from Segment #1 to Segment #3, two routers are needed. In between the two routers is network Segment #2, which can be a straight physical layer transmission circuit such as a leased line, an FDDI Segment, an ATM Segment, or an X.25 Segment.

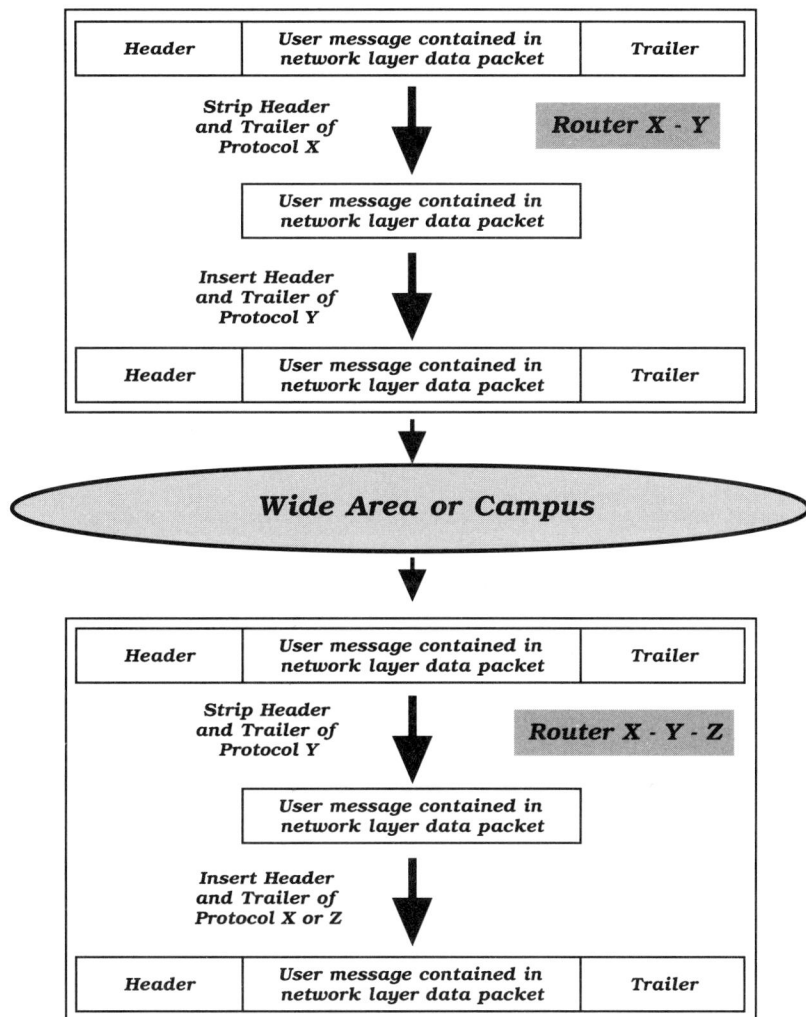

Figure 4–44. The working of a Router

A router is equipped with at least two network interface cards. For example, the router on the left in Figure 4.43 has a 10BaseT network interface card as well as a FDDI network interface card. It is a full member on the 10BaseT network. It keeps a table of the network transport protocol addresses of Segment #1 and Segment #3. In other words, the bridge knows the IP addresses of all devices on both segments.

The bridge examines every 10BaseT data packet appear in Segment #1. It strips the 10BaseT data packet header and trailer, exposing the IP packet. It then examines the address of the IP packet. If the IP packet is destined to a member on network Segment #3, it will encapsulate the IP packet with its own FDDI header and trailer. The FDDI data packet is destined to the router connecting Segment #3.

When the FDDI data packet is picked up by the correct router, it will strip off the FDDI header and trailer information, exposing once again the IP data packet. The router on Segment #3 knows the Token Ring hardware and IP address pairs there. The IP data packet will then be encapsulated in a Token Ring data packet and sent away to the receiving host computer on Segment #3.

Other Router Configurations

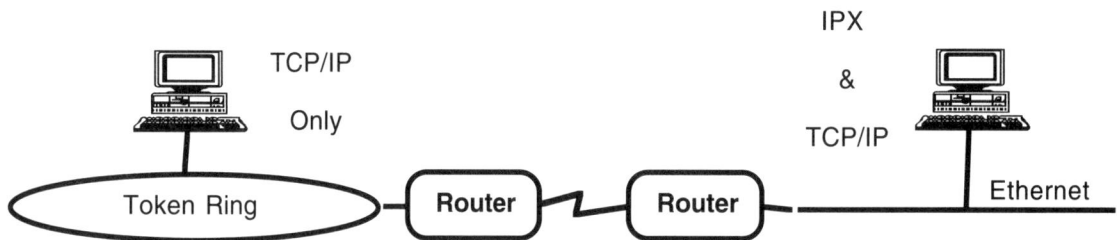

Figure 4–45. User routers to connect un-like transports and unlike datalinks

To connect two different data link protocols with different network transport protocols (e.g. one is Token Ring using TCP/IP, and the other is Ethernet using DecNet), one protocol MUST be adopted for both LANs or have at least one LAN running dual protocols.

To connect two segments with the same data link protocol but with different network transport protocols (e.g. both are 10BaseT networks, but one uses Novell's IPX, and the other uses TCP/IP), a network transport protocol or dual protocols on at least one side must be adopted.

In other words, the lower layers may different (e.g. Ethernet and Token), but the network transport layers must share the same protocol (i.e. network family) for heterogeneous interconnection.

4.4.1.4 Gateways

Unlike routers which work at the bottom four layers of the OSI Reference Model, and bridges which work at the bottom two layers, gateways work at all seven layers.

Gateways are used to connect different host based hierarchical network transports between themselves or to the LAN-based workstations

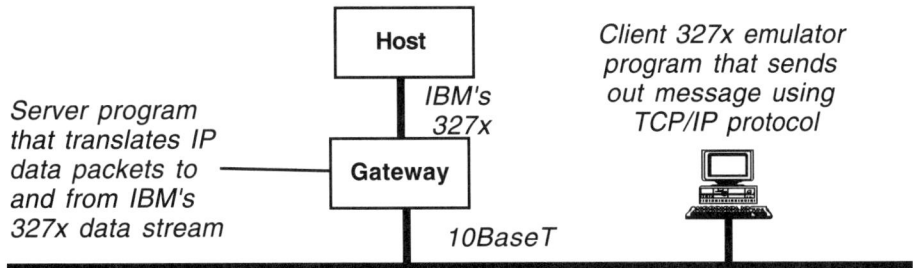

Server program that translates IP data packets to and from IBM's 327x data stream ——— **Gateway**

Host

IBM's 327x

10BaseT

Client 327x emulator program that sends out message using TCP/IP protocol

Figure 4–46. Gateway

Gateways translate messages between networks that use different network transport protocols. For example, a gateway is used to bridge between DecNet and IBM's SNA DG's Xodiac and IBM's SNA TCP/IP and IBM's SNA. Gateways are used to connect the hierarchical and proprietary host based network such as IBM's SNA to another network. Since these older networks do not follow the OSI layers as closely as the modern local area network protocols, gateway is the only way to connect them to the outside world.

Figure 4–46 illustrates a typical gateway design. A gateway in the form of a PC, a minicomputer, or an intelligent wiring hub runs a server program. This server program works with two network interface cards. One card uses IBM's SDLC. The other card uses 10BaseT. The server program "talks" to its client programs in the workstations on the 10BaseT network segment, as well as to the IBM mainframe host computer. It gets data packets from either side and translates them to the correct format before forwarding it to the receiver.

A Gateway Example

Since gateways are very important in terms of interconnecting host based application islands, we will use an example to show exactly how it works.

Let us take an on-line IBM IMS on-line ticket reservation system as an example. It is a host-based application. The application has a number of 327x screens (or panels) that a user must use. The physical screen is connected to the host via the SNA network.

Therefore, by our definition, the on-line application is a server or a software object. The server interface is the set of 327x panels peculiar to that application. The server protocol is IBM's logical unit type 2, the screen driver for a 327x terminal.

To put a host-based application on the network as an accessible object, we are building an equivalent infrastructure for another program that needs to communicate with the host based application. The host-based application plays the role of a server. Figure 4–46 shows this equivalence.

Dumb Terminal Access

On the left, the user is accessing an application through its input output screen panels. These panels are specific to this online ticket reservation application. Since applications are servers, these panels can be viewed as the server interface.

These server interfaces are carried throughout the network by the network transport environment. The server protocol is IBM's SNA Logical Unit Type 2.

The same server protocol may be used by other server interfaces of other servers. But a server interface is restricted to a server.

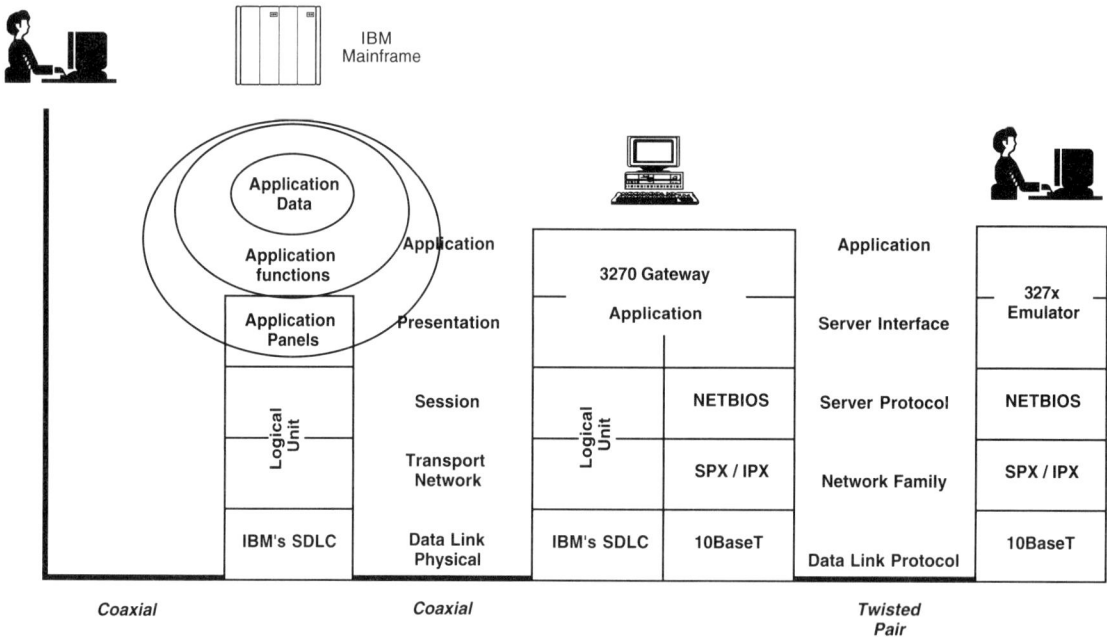

Figure 4–47. Host-based application as an object on the network

Workstation Access

On the right hand side of Figure 4–47, the same application is being put onto a network computing platform.

In between the client workstation and the mainframe is a gateway. The gateway has a gateway program that translates the server interface to a format that can be used by the terminal emulator program in the client workstation. In the gateway, two server protocols are needed. On one side, it is IBM's Logical Unit Type 2 protocol. On the other side, the server protocol is NetBIOS.

A client program running in a workstation that emulates a dumb terminal makes contact with the application through the exported server interface from the gateway. The server interface is composed of the client panels as they would have appeared on the dumb terminal screen. Users interact with the emulator program as though it was a terminal. In essence, gateways are translate-and-forward agents between two server protocols.

In Section 8.8, we will explore the opportunities in using the emulators' programming interfaces as a way to put the old applications on the network so that other client programs can access them for data.

4.4.2 Summary Of Interconnections

To connect two different network families, a gateway is required.

To connect the same network family over two different data link protocols, a router is required.

To connect the same network family over the same data link protocol but separated by a wide area network, a bridge is required.

To connect the same network family and the same data link protocols within the same local area, a repeater is required.

More examples:

1. To connect two like data link protocols with the same network transport protocol, use bridges for wide area network or repeaters for local areas (e.g. both are Token Ring networks, and both use TCP/IP).

2. To connect two like data link protocols with different network transport protocols, use routers (e.g. both are 10BaseT networks, but one uses Novell's IPX, and the other uses TCP/IP).

3. To connect two unlike data link protocols with the same network transport protocol, use routers (e.g. one network is Token Ring, and the other is Ethernet both use IPX as its transport).

4. To connect two unlike data link protocols with different network transport protocols, use routers (e.g. one is Token Ring using TCP/IP, and the other is Ethernet using DecNet).

5. To connect a LAN to a host-based network, use gateways (e.g. an Ethernet LAN to IBM's SNA network).

5

Network Operating System

Network transport environment provides a virtual communication circuit for two programs to exchange messages on the network. Client server applications can be built using the transport layer APIs as demonstrated by the popular TCP/IP applications such as NFS and FTP.

However, application developers still have to worry about starting and terminating a communication circuit, reconciling the differences in data formats between different computers, and learning to use different operating system utilities. These are extra tasks unique to network computing. They infringe on the increasingly precious time of an application developer. The intent of the top three layers of the OSI Reference Model, the network operating system, is to provide an environment that will free application developers from worrying about the extra work referred to above.

For many users, choosing a network operating system is the most important decision in migrating from a host-based environment to client server network based platform. A good understanding of the three top layers is essential in making an intelligent decision on a network operating system.

In this chapter, HP's Network Computing System (NCS), which has now been adopted by OSF as its Distributed Computing System (DCS) will be reviewed in detail similar to the review of TCP/IP in the last chapter. We will also discuss, in lesser detail, Novell's Netware and Microsoft's LAN Manager.

Common server functions in the application layer, such as database management, directory service, and electronic mail service, are also reviewed in this chapter. The relational database technology is discussed in greater detail because of its central role in commercial client server application.

5.1 AN OVERVIEW

Unlike the four bottom layers, which are independent of user processes, the three top layers of the OSI Reference Model deal with user processes rather than with the transport processes. Since there are many more types of user processes than there are transport processes, setting standards for these layers is not a simple task. In fact, OSI Standards for these three layers are still partial and incomplete.

5.1.1 Main Components

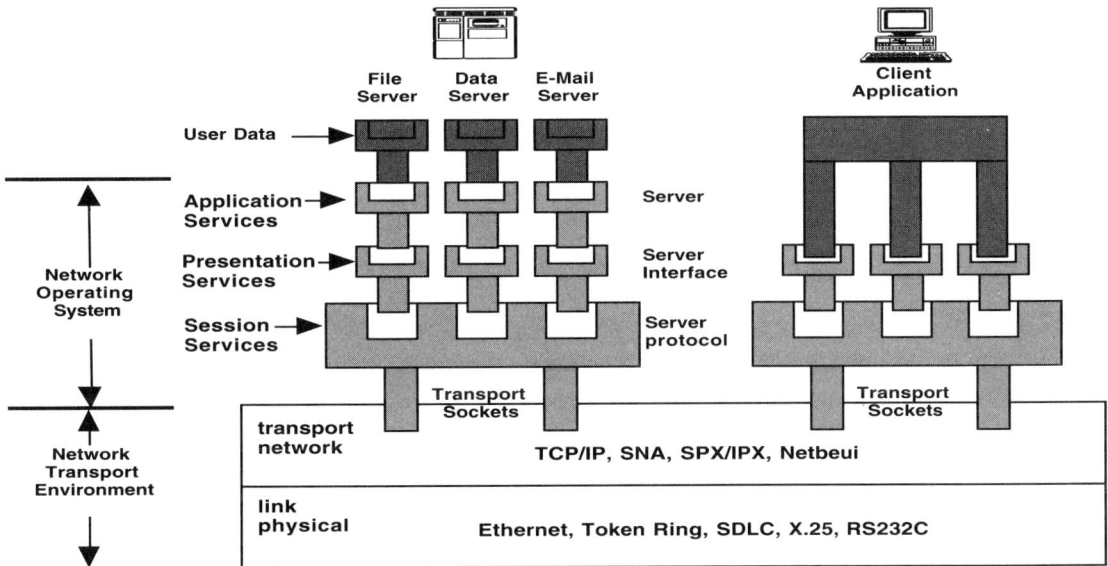

Figure 5–1. Network Operating System Components

Figure 5–1 shows the major components of a network operating system. The application layer consists of servers that provide various types of application services, and user applications that make use of them. The presentation layer presents the servers to the outside world through pre-defined server interfaces. The session layer establishes and maintains a communication session between a client and a server program using a virtual communication circuit provided by the network transport environment.

5.1.1.1   NOS Definition

The definition of a network operating system has never been straightforward because it depends on who is talking about it. A vast array of terms used by hardware vendors, database vendors, and network software vendors to describe various aspects of a network operating system further confuses the situation.

In this book, the term a network operating system is defined as an application environment in which all application shares the same session layer protocol, and all user applications use a common set of application services. Each application has its own presentation layer protocol, for interacting with the outside world. These interfaces are known as the server interfaces.

As a minimum, the application services of a network operating system should include file management, directory management, and device management. Though not absolutely necessary, finding an application environment without a database management system is difficult.

To avoid confusion, this book has adopted the following terms to describe network operating system functions. Similar terms used to describe similar functions used by others are also listed for reader's reference.

OSI Layer	Terms used in this book	Terms used by others for comparable functions
Application + Presentation + Session	**Network operating systems**	Distributed computing, Open network computing, network computing system, middleware, ...
Application	**Servers, Clients**	Applications, object classes, objects, network resources, network applications, common servers, workstation hardware, ...
Presentation	**Server interfaces Exported server interfaces**	Server stubs, client stubs, application panels, application user interfaces
Session	**Server protocols**	Network libraries, RPC runtime libraries, Network APIs, server communication protocol, ...
Transport + Network	**Network family**	Transport sockets, Transport APIs. TCP/IP, SPX/IPX, SNA, ...

Data Link	**Data Link**	Topology, Link, Ethernet, Token Ring,
Physical	**Physical**	Transmission circuits

5.1.1.2 Servers and Clients

In a network operating system, the application layer consists of a number of common utility functions such as file management, printer management, communication management, electronic mail management, database management, and directory management that are needed by all user applications on the network. These functions are provided by the common servers of the network operating system.

User applications are custom applications, such as payroll, credit cards, and order processing. They use the application services provided by the network operating system similar to a host-based application using the host operating system facilities.

Common vs. Application Servers

Server is a concept not limited to common services as defined by the software vendors. User applications such as the employee directory can also be viewed as a server even though the employee directory is in fact a user application based on a common database server.

This employee directory is a common server from the user's point of view rather than from the software vendors point of view. Within the user organization, many client programs (e.g. payroll, human resources records) make use of the employee directory through its server interface.

The fact that user application servers use the services of the common servers do not make them secondary in the overall architecture of network computing.

The concept of application server can also be applied to host based online applications with a programming interface (server interface) such as IBM's 3270 format through which other programs or users direct their requests for data or services.

File and Directory Servers

A file server is a special server since it must be present in any network operating system. Its presence defines the brand of the NOS. Filing services, such as copy, delete, edit, and catalog, are required by all types of servers. In traditional host operating systems such as DOS, MVS, VMS, and UNIX file servers, are known as the filing systems.

There are two types of file servers. The first type uses the local host operating system's own filing system such as Sun Microsystem's Network File Services (NFS). The second type of file server uses its own filing system such as Novell's Netware File Servers.

5.1.1.3 Server Interfaces

Presentation layer is an interface through which the server interacts with the outside world. All servers have their own set of operations. For example, an RDBMS has specific instructions for data base update, read, and deletions. An e-mail server has specific instructions for storing and forwarding mail. For other programs (clients) to make use of the services, the server must have a way by which these services can be advertised on the network.

Exported Server Interface

A server interface is like a storefront for the server. It tells the outside world the server's available services, resources, and operations. On the interface are indicated function names and calling syntax. This interface, in the form of software modules, is exported or placed in another computer. Programs in that computer can interact with the server interface as though the server was inside the same computer. Of course, in reality, such interactions are sent back to the real server via a physical network.

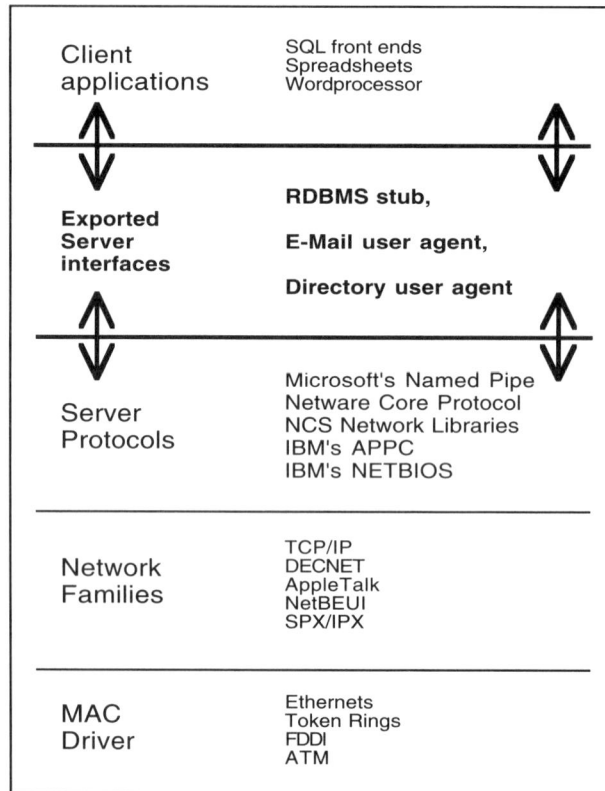

Figure 5–2. Exported server interface in a client computer

For example, when a client program in a UNIX workstation accesses data on the MVS mainframe, it makes database calls as though the database manager was inside a UNIX machine.

As shown in Figure 5–2, a server interface has two sides. On one side, it interacts with server protocols. On the other side, it provides the APIs for a user's application programs.

Each server has its own set of APIs. When a user purchases a server such as the Microsoft's SQL server, the server interfaces for various client workstation environments (e.g. DOS, UNIX, OS/2, Macintosh) are part of the software package. They are to be loaded onto the client computers. The server interface is sometimes called a stub.

5.1.1.4 Server Protocols

A session layer provides the transmission control on behalf of a server or a client program. It does this by controlling the underlying transport environment through which a virtual circuit is established, maintained, and terminated for the client server pair.

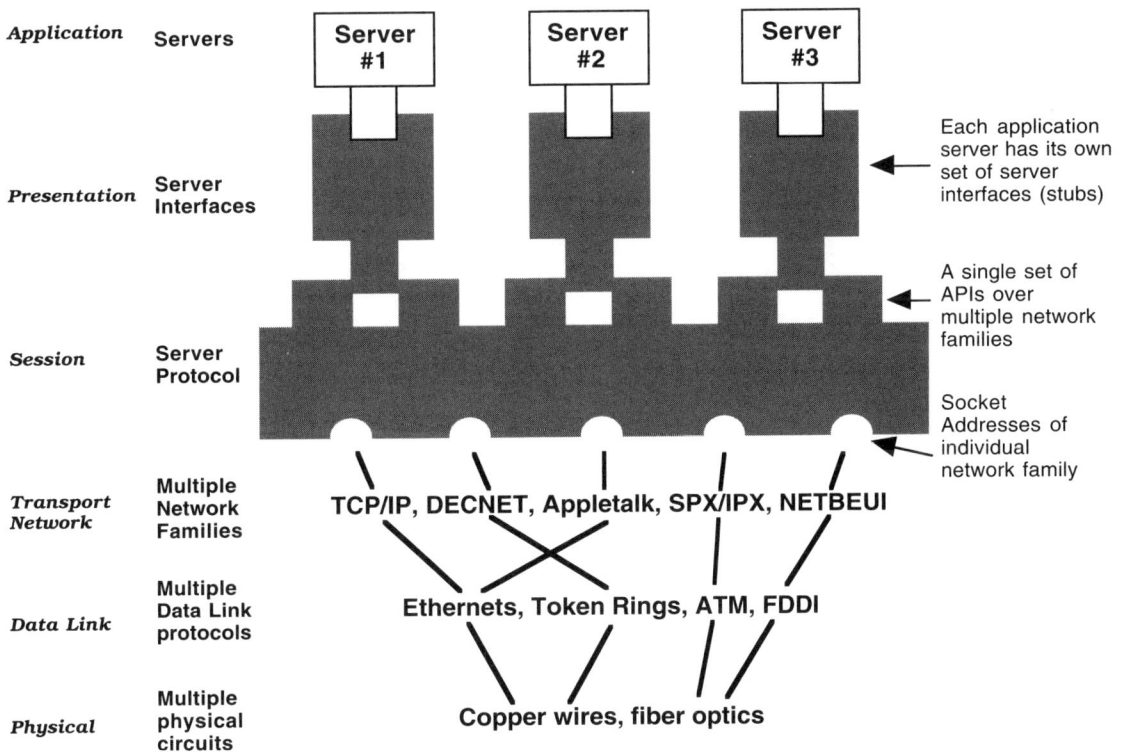

Figure 5–3. A server computer with three servers, three server interfaces, and one server protocol

Server protocols are also known as remote procedure calls RPC. RPC runtime libraries, network libraries, and network APIs interact with transport layer programming interfaces (Transport APIs or socket API) of various transport protocols such as SPX/IPX, TCP/IP, and DecNet.

Main Functions

A server protocol is a session layer entity. A server depends on a server protocol, not on the network transport environment, to communicate with its clients. The server protocols perform two main functions in a network operating system:

- to ensure delivery of the application message to the presentation layer of the receiving computer; as a delivery function
- to help to shield the complexity of underlying multiple transports by providing a common programming interface for user programs; as an interconnecting function

As shown in Figure 5–3, there are two sides to the server protocol. On the upper side, the APIs are for the application interfaces or stubs. On the lower side are the transport APIs. In this case, five network families are using four types of data link protocols and two types of physical layer transmission circuits.

The discussion in socket programming in Section 4.3.1.6 stated that a set of TCP commands must be used to establish a TCP connection. Similar commands would be required of other network families such as Digital's DecNet, IBM's SNA, and Apple's AppleTalk. This is like having different dialing sequences for different telephone networks: AT&T, Sprint, MCI, etc.

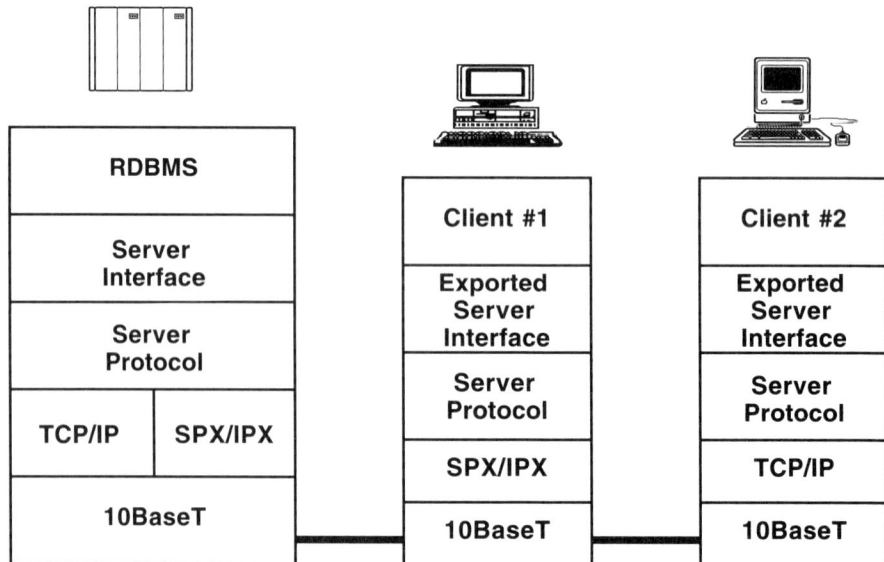

Figure 5–4. A server protocol over multiple network families

A server protocol such as Named Pipe will shield the application developers from the need to learn a new socket API every time a new network family is added. Instead, the upper side of the server protocol APIs will remain constant. As a result, not only do the programmers not have to learn new socket APIs, the application programs do not have to be changed since they will still be dealing with the same APIs.

Multiple Network Families

Figure 5–4 shows a situation in which a data server must serve two types of clients that use two different network families, TCP/IP and SPX/IPX.

Client #1 uses TCP/IP while Client #2 uses SPX/IPX. Although they use different socket addresses, the RDBMS server interface sees only a single interface, the upper side of the server protocol.

Thus, any change in the network families requires changes to the lower side of the server protocol. No change is required in the application. Server protocols make a network operating system independent of the network families.

Server protocols are developed and maintained by software vendors, who can spread the cost of development to many users. All users need will be a new set of server protocols when a new network family is introduced to their environment.

For example, Microsoft's Named Pipes can be used over TCP/IP, NetBIOS/Net-BEUI, and DecNet. With them, a developer can build a Named Pipe application (e.g. a data server) using all Named Pipe calls. The product should then be able to work in any network family supported by Named Pipe. Any new addition or changes in the network families require modification to the server protocols only but not the user application.

NetBIOS

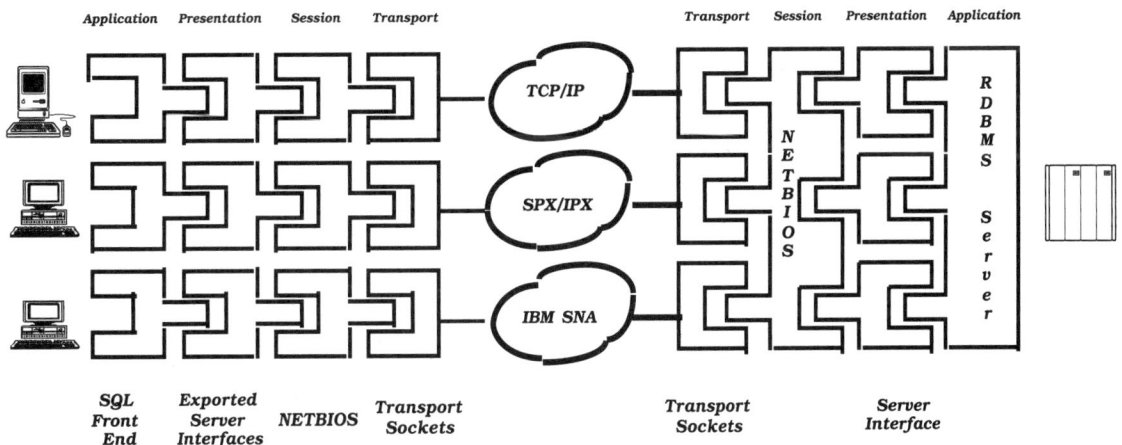

Figure 5–5. Single Session Layer Interface (e.g. NetBIOS) over Multiple Transports for three different clients

Figure 5–5 shows NetBIOS, a popular server protocol used by many network applications. It shows how client workstations from different network transports can be connected to the same data server.

5.1.1.5 A Network of Objects

Clients, common servers, and application servers are all **objects** on the network. Application results are achieved by their cooperating with one another on a peer basis.

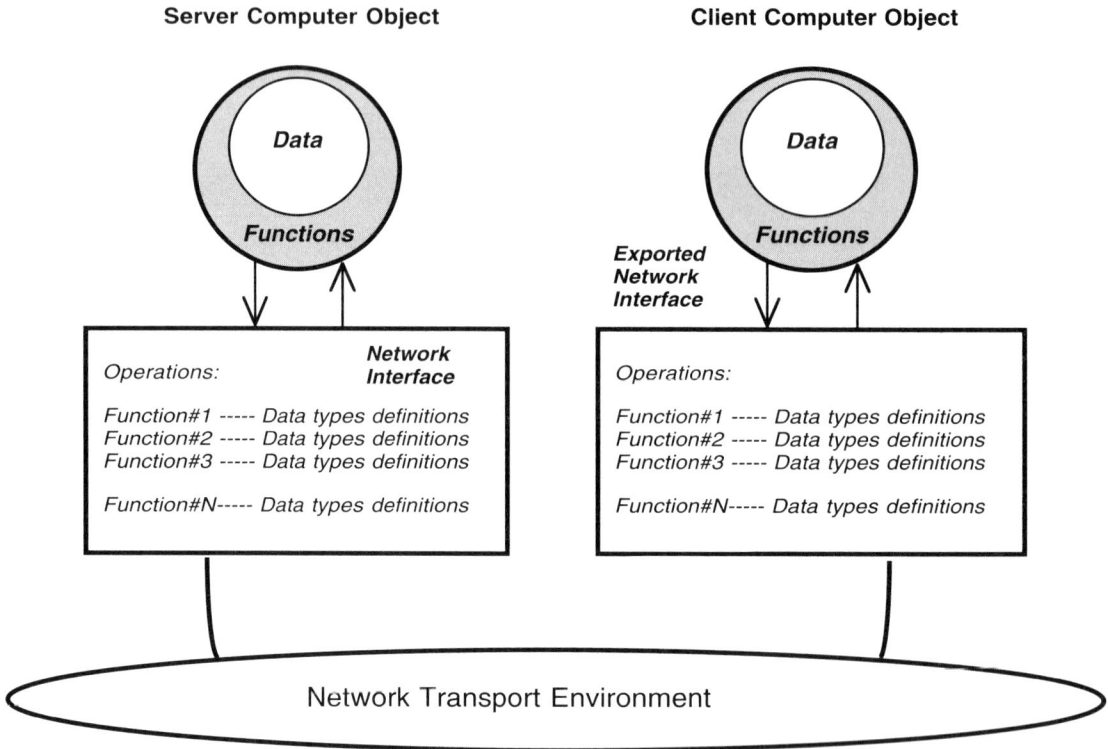

Server Computer Object   **Client Computer Object**

Data

Functions

Exported
Network
Interface

Data

Functions

Operations: **Network
Interface**

Function#1 ----- Data types definitions
Function#2 ----- Data types definitions
Function#3 ----- Data types definitions

Function#N----- Data types definitions

Operations:

Function#1 ----- Data types definitions
Function#2 ----- Data types definitions
Function#3 ----- Data types definitions

Function#N----- Data types definitions

Network Transport Environment

Figure 5–6. Putting an object on the network

Figure 5–6 shows the concept of a network of objects in which the application layer has both common application and user application servers. Each server has its own server interface. Exported server interfaces are resident in the client workstations. Every object uses the same session layer protocol, the server protocol. These objects are all tied together by a heterogeneous network transport environment.

5.1.2. General Characteristics

In this chapter, we review the fundamental characteristics of a NOS. In Section 8.7, we will review the criteria for choosing the right NOS for your organization.

5.1.2.1 NOS Essential Features

Two main goals of a network operating system are: computer system independence, and network independence. The following is a list of functions normally expected of a network operating system.

NOS Transport Transparency

Network transparency simply means that the transport, network, link, and physical layers should appear as though they do not exist. Access to remote resources by a program should look and feel as though they were local resources. Server interfaces and the server protocols provide this transparency. All RPCs from the local programs should be intercepted by the server interfaces, which then handle the required communication to send the request and to receive the response on behalf of the local program.

With server interfaces, a DOS program always makes a DOS call, a UNIX program always makes a UNIX call, a MVS program always makes an MVS call, and so on. A network application must be faithful to the local call semantics. Server protocols shield server interfaces from different transports.

When a new transport is introduced, the only module that needs to be changed is the server protocol, which should be provided by the network developers. Application developers need only to re-compile and to re-link the source programs with the new libraries.

NOS Reliability

Network application reliability should be independent of the network transport reliability. The network application may sit on top of a reliable or connection-oriented transport such as the transmission control protocol (TCP/IP) and unreliable or connectionless transport such as the User Datagram Protocol (UDP).

The NOS, or more specifically the server protocol, must implement its own virtual circuit, regardless of the underlying network transport environment. This function is important since users often do not have a choice on the transport types. For instance, low end print or plotter services may not support a connection-oriented protocol since the devices are slow speed.

NOS Performance

Like host operating system, a key concern for network operating system is performance. Not only do layers of network protocols introduce overhead, the need for an intermediate data representation for data exchange will impose a penalty on general performance, especially in bulk data transfers. Some server interfaces have the intelligence to bypass data translation when they recognize that a particular transaction is between two similar types of computers. Some will always enforce an intermediate data representation, such as ASN.1 or the XDR, despite the computer systems.

NOS Data Size

Since local procedures may pass unlimited amounts of data to other local procedures, should be no limit placed on arguments within the calling parameters to the remote resource. If reading one million rows out of a DB2 table within the mainframe is possible, then the network operating system must be capable of doing the same.

NOS Security

Security is a major concern for users who are accustomed to the security features of a centralized mainframe. Any network operating system must prove it has the same level of security as its mainframe predecessor. Security measures such as encrypting and password can be implemented at the application, the transport, the network, data link, and the physical layers of the Reference Model. The issue is a tradeoff between the cost and the risks.

Application Servers

The availability of a wide range of servers for a particular network operating system will ultimately determine its viability. In other words, a NOS is only as good as the application services are useful to the users.

Ultimately users buy application functions, not network infrastructure, which they cannot afford to support on their own.

5.1.2.2   NOS Peer vs. Server Based

According to the OSI Reference Model, all computers on the network are peers. In other words, every computer enjoys equal status—no master nor slaves. However, there is a subtle difference in interpretation of the term peer in a network transport environment and in a network operating system.

"Peer-to-Peer" is true for most network transport environments (the bottom four layers) where every computer on the network can initiate a conversation with another computer. The notable exception to this is IBM's SNA, which we will review in Chapter Six.

However, the peer-to-peer property diminishes in the top three layers, where the real units of work are accomplished. Division of labor is the most efficient way to organize resources to get a job done. While it is possible to let everyone talk at the same time in a peer-to-peer manner, it is far more efficient to get a job done by organizing them into units of work.

Here, the model is a client server relationship in which a client requests for services from a set of servers on the network. The client is the initiator of a request-response dialogue. The roles are no longer peer-to-peer. They are client-server.

NOS Peer-to-Peer Based

The term peer-to-peer loosely means that if the design of the client and server pair is such that both can exist in the same computer, then the network operating system is said to be a peer-to-peer NOS.

In a peer-to-peer network operating system, every workstation on the network can contribute disk drives, printers, and other resources to other client workstations on the network. Many DOS-based networks such as IBM's PC LAN, Microsoft's LAN Manager, LANtastic, 10NET, TCP/IP and other NetBIOS based networks are peer-to-peer. Each workstation on the network can function either as client or server at the same time.

For example, the File Transfer Program (FTP) of TCP/IP can be configured as a FTP client or a FTP server on the same workstation without any 'special' programming effort. This approach is quite appealing to smaller installations where the cost of a dedicated server machine can be avoided.

NOS Server-Based

In a server-based network operating system, client workstations cannot easily be made to communicate or share resources with other client workstations. A client workstation remains to be a client workstation, and a server is always a server.

Servers provide all the remote resources for the client workstations. Client workstations can only access these resources from the servers. For example, using a DOS Netware workstation to be both a client and the file server is quite difficult. Other examples of server based networks are Banyan's VINES, and to a certain extent IBM's SNA.

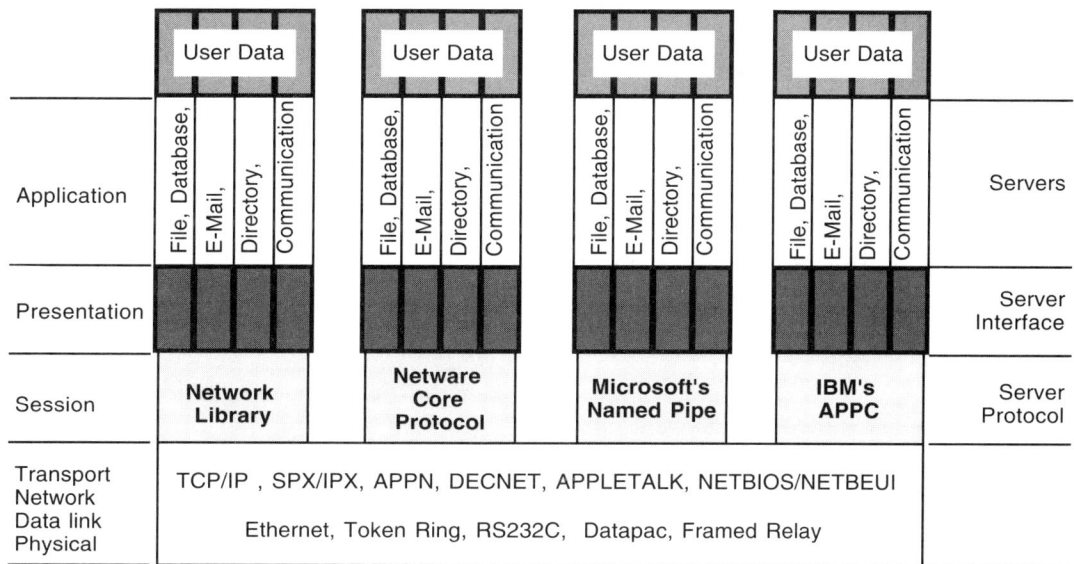

	User Data	User Data	User Data	User Data	
Application	File, Database, / E-Mail, / Directory, / Communication	File, Database, / E-Mail, / Directory, / Communication	File, Database, / E-Mail, / Directory, / Communication	File, Database, / E-Mail, / Directory, / Communication	Servers
Presentation					Server Interface
Session	**Network Library**	**Netware Core Protocol**	**Microsoft's Named Pipe**	**IBM's APPC**	Server Protocol
Transport Network Data link Physical	TCP/IP , SPX/IPX, APPN, DECNET, APPLETALK, NETBIOS/NETBEUI Ethernet, Token Ring, RS232C, Datapac, Framed Relay				

Figure 5–7. Commercial Network Operating Systems

5.1.2.3   NOS Commercial Products

Figure 5–7 shows four popular network operating systems. They are largely defined by its native server protocol.

- IBM's APPC, which we will describe in detail in the Chapter Six on IBM's SNA
- HP's NCS, which has been adopted as the OSF's chosen server protocol product
- Novell's Netware Loadable Modules (NLM)
- Microsoft's LAN Manager

Although all of the above have similar common servers, their server protocols are different and are not interoperable. Microsoft's LAN Manager for example uses Named Pipe as its server protocol. Netware uses Netware Core Protocol. NCS uses its own Network Library. IBM uses APPC or LU6.2. In this chapter, we have chosen to describe in greater detail HP's Network Computing System (NCS) because of its textbook-like features and its recent adoption by OSF members. Other network operating systems that will also be described in this chapter, though in lesser detail, are Novell's Netware and Microsoft's LAN Manager.

5.2   HP'S NETWORK COMPUTING SYSTEM

NCS is a network operating system that is equipped with a set of common servers which enable users to develop their applications. Such applications consist of mainly client programs that interact with the exported server interfaces in their computers. This should be sufficient for most users' application requirements. But for some applications, users need to develop their own network client servers. NCS has a set of tools that allows them to do that.

5.2.1   NCS Background

NCS was originally from Apollo Computer, Inc. In the late 1980s, Apollo was acquired by Hewlett Packard. Since then, NCS has been enhanced jointly by HP and Digital Equipment Corporation (DEC). The new NCS Version 2 has a variety of new features, including transport independence, name service independence, support for ISO standards, and support for large data processing applications.

Another big boost to NCS is the fact that it has been officially adopted by the Open Software Foundation as the standard server protocol for its Distributed Computing System (DCS) for its members, which include IBM, DEC, and HP. In this book the term NCS will be used although it is likely that OSF's DCS will be widely used also.

5.2.2 NCS Operation

In this section, we describe the major components in the NCS system and how they work together.

5.2.2.1 NCS Objects

NCS adopts an object-oriented and a client-server model. NCS does not stop at providing a network transport environment by which two programs can exchange messages with one another. Instead, NCS pushes the message exchanges to a higher level: the software object level.

Objects vs. Programs

The difference between an object and a program is that an object has both a program and data. An object has clearly defined interface or declared operations for outside agents to make use of its service.

On the other hand, a program requires an external agent, a person or another program, to bring the data and the program together. In an object, data is encapsulated within its programs.

In NCS, communication always takes place between objects instead of between programs. It is no longer sufficient to identify a program on the network. NCS also identifies an operation within a program.

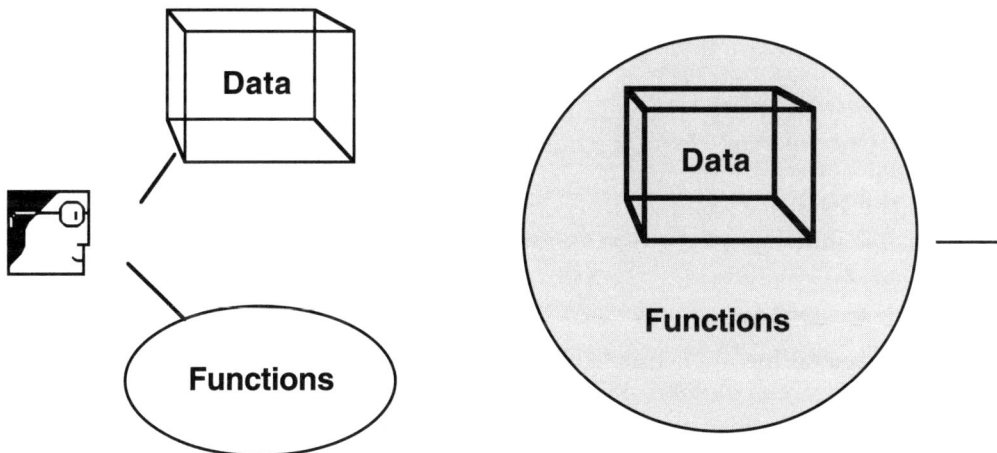

A user is responsible for matching the data to the functions.

A user deals only with functions which shield the data formats from the users.

Figure 5–8. An object-oriented approach—Data Encapsulation

Objects' Data Encapsulation

Objects are software entities that model a physical or an administrative process. Software objects possess both data and functions. As shown in Figure 5–8, external agents cannot directly access the data. The data in an object is meaningful only to an external agent through the object's associated functions or operations. This characteristic of data hiding behind the function is known as data encapsulation.

Encapsulation is an important feature of object-oriented programming. With it, the traditional concept of separation of data and program are gone. In an object-oriented world, data and function are glued together. One cannot exist without the other. A more detailed discussion on objects is found in Chapter Three.

Objects as Servers

Data inside an object is stored as instances. Each instance object responds to the same set of functions. The object is referred to as the object class.

Each object class may contain thousands of instance objects. For example, a document is an instance of a word processor object. The word processor is an object class, and the document is an instance of the object class. A data table is an instance in a relational database management system which is the object class. A record is an instance of an order processing system, which is the object class.

The object class of unstructured ASCII files may contain thousands of ASCII files. Each ASCII file is an object instance. Many familiar functions may act on the instance objects: open file, close file, delete file, print file, and append file.

In NCS, database managers, communication managers, file managers, and location managers are servers on the network. They are treated as software objects containing both data and function.

In this book, the term "server" means an object class. It contains specific callable functions that will act on its encapsulated data. To manipulate such data, an external agent (a user or another program) must do so through the available functions of the object class (i.e. the server).

Objects as Online Applications

Host-based online applications only update their data via the application's user interfaces (screen panels). These screen panels are equivalent to the server interfaces that we have just described.

Any of today's host based online applications can be viewed as an object, a concept that is key to integrating them to the new network computing environment. More on this will be presented in Section 8.8.

Objects' Granularity

In fact, the concept of an object is a matter of granularity of data encapsulation. An object ranges from a host-based online application to an software entity (such as an order or a customer).

What has made for much finer granularity in the object-oriented approach (at the data element level) is the availability of the object-oriented programming languages, the relational database technology, and the data modeling technique. We discuss all of the above in subsequent chapters of this book.

5.2.2.2 NCS Object Identifications

How can the operations available from a server be invoked? To put a server program on a network and to make it available for calling by client programs, the following information must be specified:

- What network family is used by the computer in which the server program is located?
- What is the network address of the computer?
- What is the server program identification within the computer?
- Which operations of the server are to be executed?

The first three questions can be condensed into one: Where is the server program? The last question is: Which operation on the server is to be executed?

Question #1: Where is the Server?

Since NCS is meant for a heterogeneous environment, its address design must work with multiple network families. NCS address must identify the location of a computer on a network, and the location of an object inside the computer.

NCS uses the Berkeley UNIX socket address. Each socket address is identified uniquely by the following three components:

- Address family, also called the protocol family (TCP/IP, SNA, DecNet, AppleTalk . . .), which determines the communications protocol.
- Network address, a value that uniquely identify a host computer on a network family
- Port number, also known as the program ID or the program address within a host computer. The program is either a server or a client.

Officials of Berkeley UNIX assigned socket identifiers in the form of a 16-bit integer to the major network address families. For example, CCITT X.25 has an identifier '10', for IBM's SNA an '11', for Xerox Network Systems (XNS) a '6'.

Protocol Family	Port Number	Host Computer Network Address
16-bit Integer	16-bit Integer	Number of bits varies with protocol families

Figure 5–9. Berkeley Socket Address

For host computer addresses, different network families have different schemes. For example, TCP/IP has 32-bit addressing, whereas Apollo's Domain uses 64 bits. Berkeley UNIX uses a 16-bit integer to designate a program or a server process within a host computer.

NCS Network Library

The NCS addressing scheme is independent of the network transport environment. This is made possible by the Network Library or Remote Procedure Call runtime library (RPC Runtime Library) or Server protocol which translates an NCS address to suit different network transport protocols. The NCS Network Library is the server protocol used by NCS based applications.

Question #2: Which Operation Within the Server?

Finding the server is not enough; we must also know which operation within the server has been selected for execution.

NCS's UUID

In NCS, a unique way of identifying operations on an object is provided by an identifier known as the Universal Unique Identifier, UUID.

The UUID is a 16-byte (128-bit) word. It specifies the host (Berkeley Socket Addressing Scheme) and the time at which an operation or an object is created. Six bytes identify the time, two are reserved, and eight bytes identify the host.

UUID's uniqueness comes from the 48-bits time stamp. The high 32 bits is the number of 4-microsecond intervals that have passed between 1/1/1980 0:0 GMT and the time of the UUID creation. Unless two operations are created within 4 microseconds, each UUID is unique.

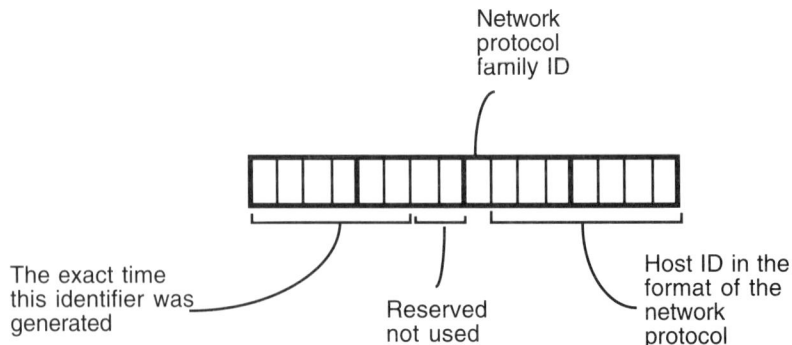

Figure 5-10. Universal Unique Identifier, UUID

Each available operation on the network has a unique identifier. The small size of UUID makes it easier to be embedded in application data structures. More importantly, UUID can be generated anywhere without the need for a network administrator who hands out identifiers.

NCS has a program utility known as uuid_gen that can be used to generate an UUID for any given object on the network. This utility generates UUIDs as ASCII character strings. These UUIDs can then be used as part of the compilation of the network program modules.

In the UNIX environment, a UUID can be generated by entering the command: /etc/ncs/uuid_gen, a unique string of 37 hexadecimal digits will be returned in the form:

```
cccccccccccc.ff.h1.h2.h3.h4.h5.h6.h7
where,
cccccccccccc = time stamp in hex digits
ff = address family (e.g. SNA, IP, CCITT, . . .).
h1 to h7 = 7-byte host ID in hexadecimal.
```

An UUID Example

```
3a2f883c4000.0d.00.00.fb.40.00.00.004.2.1.3
```

NCS Handles

With UUID, we can identify any operation on the network. The next question is: How does NCS make use of the Berkeley UNIX Socket Address and the UUID to locate services on the network? The answer is in another NCS facility known as Handles.

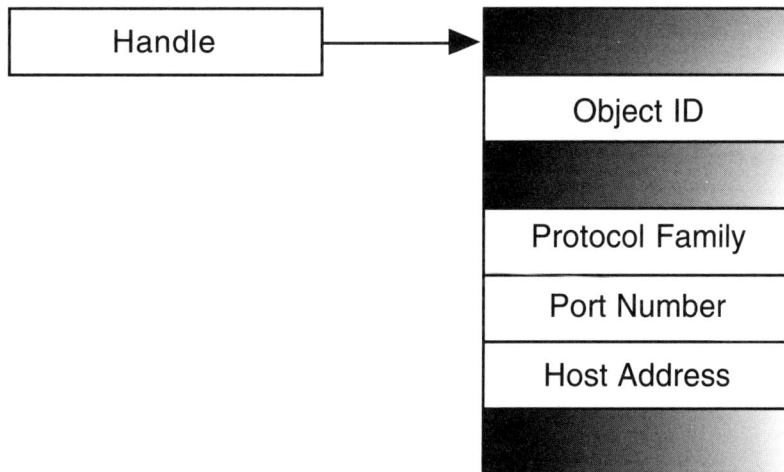

Figure 5–11. NCS Handle

When a network client wants to call the service of an operation, it must first establish a connection (also known as a bind or a virtual circuit) with the server in which the operation is going to be executed.

The client program does this via a software handle. The handle is a pointer to an opaque data structure used by the server protocol (NCS calls it the Network Library or RPC Runtime Library) to initiate the session between a server and a client. The server protocol needs the handle to establish a virtual circuit.

A handle is like a ticket with which a client program must hold to access services. The client gives the handle to the server protocol which must then figure out the best way to locate the operation based on the information on the ticket.

Once again, this is analogous to an auto-dialer (the server protocol) trying to establish a connection, including mundane things, such as re-trying on failures and using the cheapest connection. User needs only to tell the auto-dialer something like: "Call my mother."

Its intent is to help application programmers to concentrate their efforts on delivering application functions rather than utility-type functions. A handle contains two pieces of information:

- the name of the operation (i.e. the UUID), and
- the location of a server that can perform the specified operation.

A handle is always associated with an operation on an object. But the socket address in a handle may change at different times, or may not exist at all. When a handle contains the full specification of the socket address: 16-bit network family, 16-bit port number, and the host network address, then the handle is said to have a bind.

NCS Binding

The three types of binding for a handle are:

- unbound, (when the requester has no clue as to where the requested operation can be found on the network)
- bound to host, (when the requester knows the location of the computer in which the operation resides, but it does not know the port number for the server object)
- fully bound, (the requester knows the computer location, the object class identification, and the operation number (UUID))

A client program may request an operation on the network, but the program may not know where it resides. For example, requesting the telephone number of a person when the client program does not know where the directory server is located or even existed.

In this circumstance, the server protocol must broadcast the request to all hosts on the network. Any server that exports the requested interface and supports the requested object can respond. The client accepts the first response it receives.

This is, of course, a rather inefficient way to achieve the goal. The handle that contains the object ID but not the socket address is known as an unbound handle.

NCS Location Broker

Another client program may request operations of an object by specifying host address but not the port number. The host, upon receipt of this request will pass it on to the local location broker to pin point the port number of the server.

The handle that contains the object ID and the host address, but not the port number, is known as the bound-to-host handle.

When a client program requests an object by specifying the full socket address, the handle is known as a fully bound handle.

In all three cases, a fully bound state becomes reality when the server responds positively. The virtual circuit thus established can now be used between the client and the server programs as though two people were talking over a telephone line.

The termination of the virtual circuit can be initiated by either the server or the client.

5.2.2.3 NCS Network Libraries

NCS's Network Library or RPC Runtime Library is equivalent to what this book calls a server protocol. The library contains software routines that provide a consistent interface to a server interface even though the server must support a multiple network families environment.

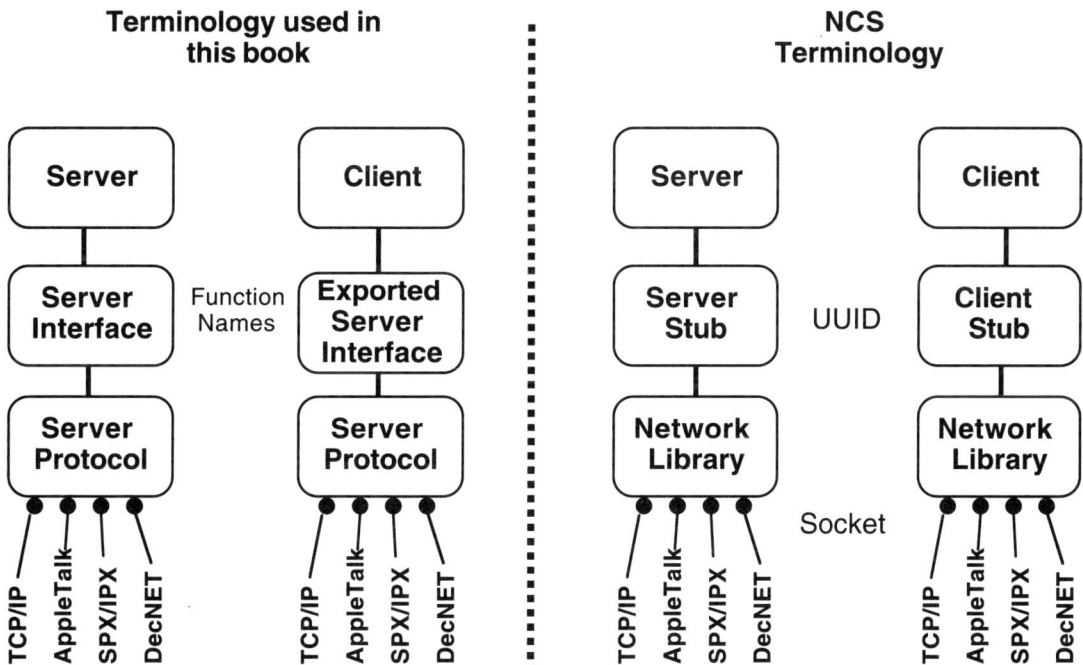

Figure 5–12. Terms used in this book vs. those used in NCS

The UNIX socket address scheme is designed to handle multiple network families. (see Figure 5–9) When a new network family is needed, users simply obtain the new Network Library from an NCS vendor. Without changing a single line of an application's code, the server is now accessible through the new network family. Figure 5–12 shows the terms used by this book and the equivalent NCS terms.

5.2.2.4 NCS Client Server Exchanges

Up to this point, we reviewed the concepts of object, object class, client-server, functions, procedures, socket address, handle, server interface, server protocol, and network transports. We also know how a virtual circuit is established by the use of handles.

But who generates the handles? How do they all pull together to enable message exchanges between two programs on the network? How does a client request find its way to the server? The following example shows the key steps involve in a message exchange, NCS Style.

From Client to Server

When a client calls a remote operation, it invokes a routine in the exported server interface. The exported server interface packs the input parameters (message) into an NCS data packet. (Remember: Each protocol layer has its own data packet design. See Section 3.2.2)

The exported server interface calls rpc_$sar, a server protocol (Network Library) routine which is called only by server interfaces to send the requesting NCS packet and await a reply. The server protocol interacting with the underlying network transport layer sends the NCS packet to the server.

Upon receipt of the NCS packet, the server protocol in the server host calls the server interface, which unpacks the input parameters from the NCS packet into data types expected by the server. (e.g. integers, strings, ...)

If the client's native representation is different then the server interface converts the input data to the server's native representation (for example: ASCII to EBCDIC).

Finally, the server interface calls the server manager procedure that implements the required operation. The operation thus called upon will act on the input parameters.

From Server to Client

The result of the operation passes to the server interface, which represents the calling client. The server interface packs the result into an NCS packet. It passes the data packet to the server protocol routine rpc_$sar. The rpc_$sar, interacting with the underlying network transport layers, sends the NCS packet to the client computer.

The client computer network transport layer picks up the NCS packet and passes it onto the client's server protocol module, which in turns passes the NCS

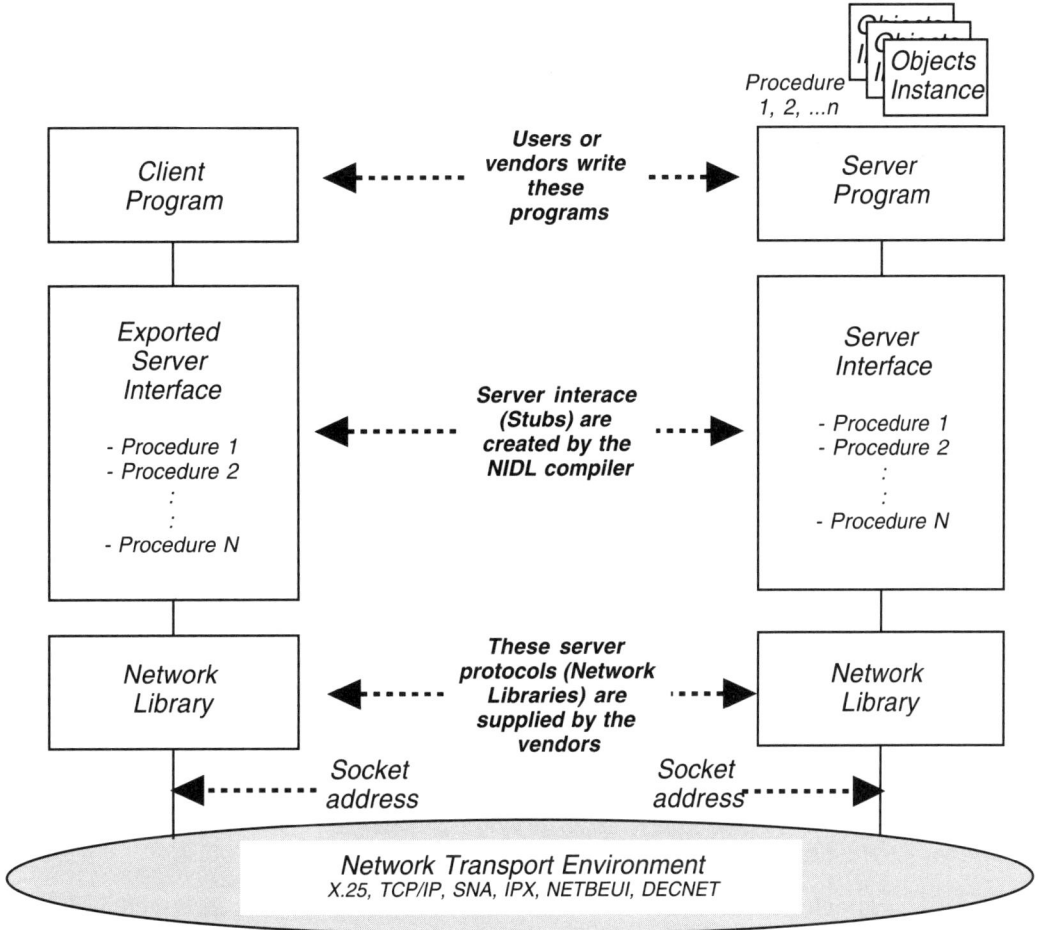

Figure 5–13. NCS Communication Flow

packet to the exported server interface. The exported server interface takes apart the reply packet into data types expected by the client program. The exported server interface converts the output data to the client's native representation, if the server's native representation is different. The exported server interface passes the results back to the client program.

5.2.3 NCS Application Development

In this section, we discuss the steps required to create a network application using NCS. We also discuss a unique tool for network application development which is known as the Network Interface Definition Language or NIDL.

5.2.3.1 NCSs NIDL Compiler

The two main components in an NCS package are the network library (server protocol) which supports multiple network transports and the Network Interface Definition Language or NIDL compiler.

NIDL is a C-like declaration language with no executable constructs. It allows users to define a server interface for a server. Without NIDL, generating server interfaces would be extremely difficult.

Where Does NIDL Fit In?

NIDL provides a consistent syntax for users to describe an interface. Such description is used by the NIDL compiler to generate the server interfaces. There are server interfaces for the client program and for the server program.

Server interfaces generated by the NIDL compiler are uncompiled source code files either in C or in Pascal. They are the programming representations of the interface. They handle the packing and unpacking of data, perform all communications needed to handle the server protocol, and contain special error-handling codes to detect and report errors. These source code modules are included through the include statements as part of the client or the server source programs. All source code is then compiled and linked to form executable modules.

When a client program makes a RPC, it simply calls the procedure identified by the exported server interface as though it were a local procedure call. The server interfaces also perform data conversion, assemble and disassemble packets, and interacts with the server protocol. The results of the procedure will also be presented back to the calling program as if the results were given back from a local procedure.

How Does NIDL Work?

The server interface definition specifies both the way in which a client application sees a remote service and the way in which a remote server sees requests for its service. It consists of the following:

- Heading
- Import, Constant, Type, Operation declarations

From this definition, the NIDL compiler generates client and server interfaces source code and header files. NIDL can be written in C or Pascal. NIDL compiler takes the declarative statements, the definition of an interface object, and converts them into:

- Insert files   —header file
- Client server interfaces files   —C source code file
- Server's server interfaces files—C source code file

These three files fully describe a server interface. **Any client or server programs that need to access this interface will have to include these three files in the programs source code to be compiled and linked together.**
Writing in NIDL is much easier than writing the server interface code directly.

Data Types

The NIDL compiler accepts all of standard types such as integers, floating point numbers, structure, union, enum, etc. Furthermore, it supports the use of complex data structures, such as linked lists, dynamically sized arrays, trees, etc. In essence, if a data structure can be described using C types, the NIDL compiler can be used to produce the code needed to move data structures between the pieces of your distributed application. Examples:

```
int size ();
double log10 (double x);
int find (char c, char str[20]);
struct link_type { int data1 int data2 struct link_type
*ptr };
int send_list(struct link_type *head);
double vector_add ( int num, double v[num][20] );
int sort () { extern int num extern int values[1024]};
```

To make the remote procedures to appear as local procedures, NIDL generates code to support the use of external variables. As a result, data structures appearing within external variables can be passed to a remote procedure, modified, and returned as if the remote procedure was a local procedure.

Flow Control

Besides describing whatever data structures are needed to support applications, the NIDL compiler provides a mechanism for controlling the way the data structures are passed between the pieces of your distributed applications.

```
in      —passed only to the remote procedure
out     —returned only by the remote procedure
in/out—passed both to and returned from the remote
         procedure
```

Example

```
int add_complex
      { struct complex [in] a,
      struct complex [in] b,
      struct complex [out] *rtrn };
```

Bindings

When two parties communicate with each other and the circuit is severed, one party must initiate the conversation again or the system will automatically reconnect without either party's action.

The first binding is known as non-persistent binding, while the second one is known as persistent binding. NIDL supports persistent and non-persistent connections.

Binding can occur by identifying the UUID string, which may represent procedure or interface.

Examples

```
extern connection_id [bind in out] conn
int open ( )
{extern connection_id [bind out] conn;}
int read ( char [out] data [80] );
int write ( char [in] data [80] );
```

5.2.3.2 NCS Programming Steps

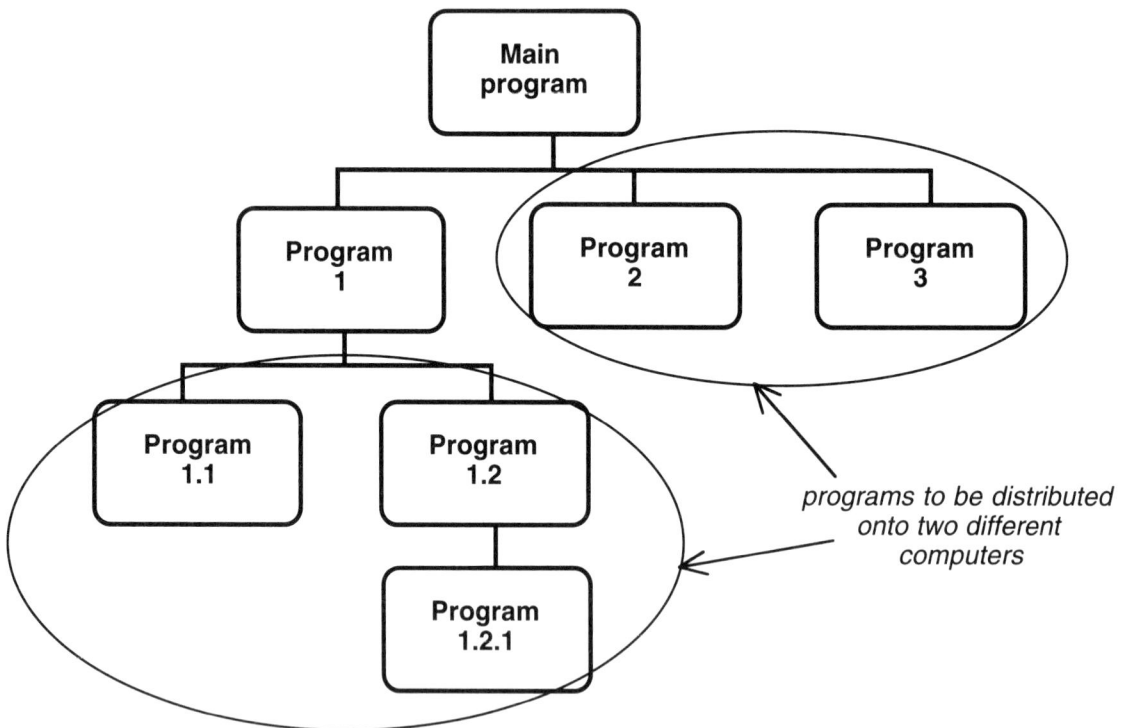

Figure 5–14. From single processor to multi-processors

Figure 5–14 shows a classical approach to application design. Network application development methodology is fundamentally the same as that of a non-network application. The big difference is deciding which part of the application belongs to a client or to a server.

The following are brief descriptions of steps involved in building network applications using RPC technology. Readers should refer to Figure 5–15 for the following description:

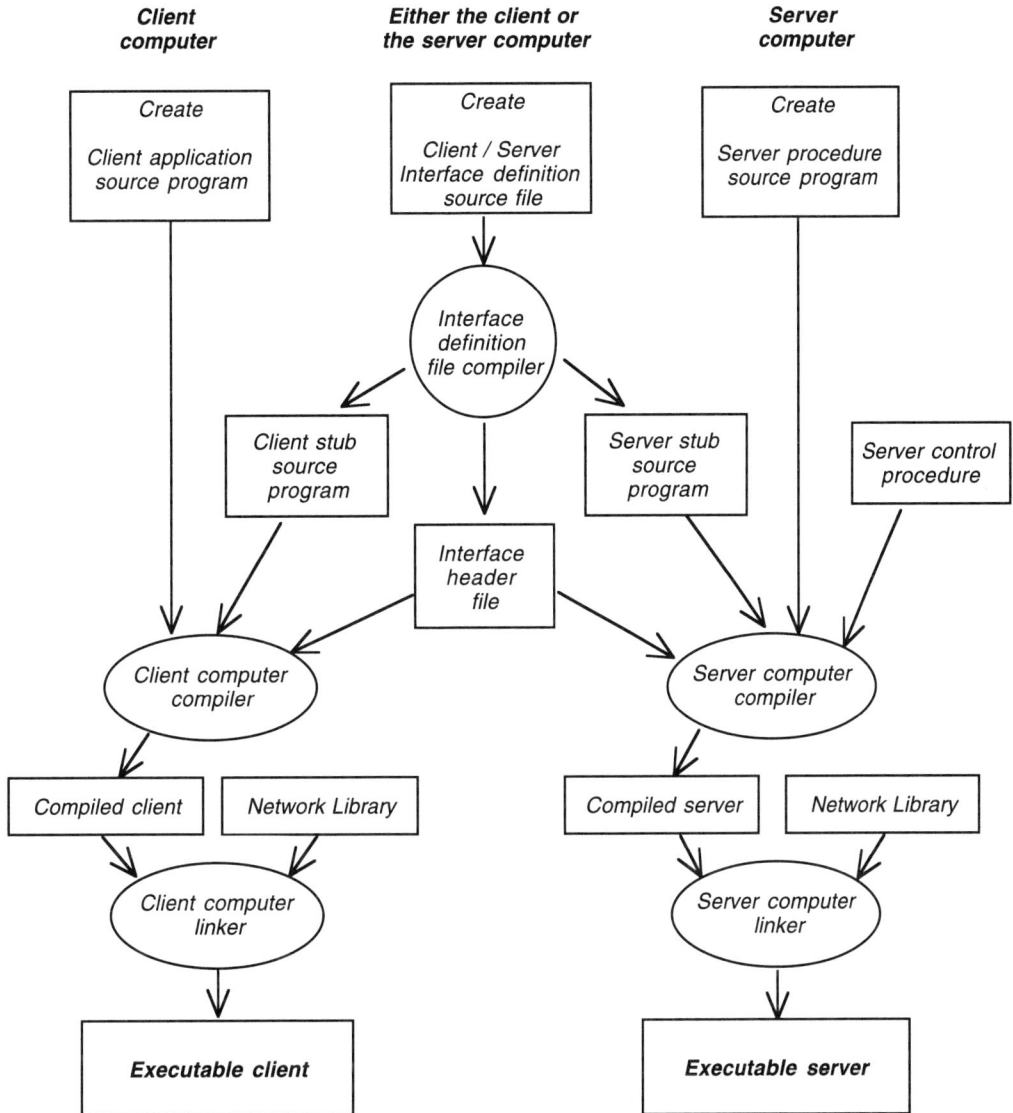

Figure 5-15. Network Application Development—General approach

1. Design the application using the standard structured analysis.
2. Decide which functions should be executed on what computers.
3. Decide where the clients and the servers should run
4. Decide which network operating system to use (e.g. HP's NCS, Sun's RPC, Netwise, Novell's NLM, etc.)
5. Define the interface characteristics in a text file using the data definition syntax in the chosen programming language for the network operating system

6. Write the source programs for the client application
7. Write the source programs for the server application
8. Write the source programs for the server control, which specifies the server operation characteristics such as ability to handle multi clients at a time or just one client at a time. Generally speaking, these source programs are supplied by the network operating system vendors as a component of the whole package.
9. On either the client or the server computer, compile the input file in step 5 with the server interface definition compiler. The results are a server interface (server stub), an exported server interface (the client stub), and a header file.
10. On the client computer, compile the client application program, the exported server interface, and the header file to produce the compiled client.
11. On the server computer, compile the server application program, the server interface, the header file, and the server control file to produce the compiled server.
12. On the client computer, link the compiled client in step 10 with the server protocol to produce the client executable.
13. On the server computer, link the compiled server in step 11 with the server protocol routines to produce the server executable.
14. Test.

5.3   OTHER NOSs

OSF's NCS is just one of many ways to develop network applications. There are other network operating systems on which network applications can be built. Next, we will review Novell's Netware and Microsoft's LAN Manger. Not to be overlooked is IBM's Advanced Program to Program Communication (APPC), which we discuss in more detail in Chapter Six.

5.3.1   Novell's Netware

Novell's Netware was introduced as a file and printer server in the early days of local area networks. Since then, it has been upgraded with other common services including the directory services, network management services, security services, remote dial, electronic mail, multi platforms support, and other user administration services. Netware is now a full function network operating system. It is the market leader in local area network services.

5.3.1.1   Netware File Server

Like other file servers, the Novell File Server is an integral part of the Novell Network Operating System. Unlike other file servers, Netware is designed to function as a network file server capable of storing information from many different host computing platforms. Unlike Sun Microsystems' Network File Service which uses the local file system format, Netware File Servers uses its own file storage format. Netware file format are converted to the local host system format by the Netware File Server.

Netware's file server and print server programs were originally designed to run on Intel 286 microprocessors. They have since been extended to the 386, 486, and other platforms. Netware 2.X has a 16 bit architecture. Netware 3.11 is based on the Intel 386+ chip has true 32-bit architecture.

Netware OS and the Bindery

Netware servers are neither DOS nor OS/2 applications. Netware has its own operating system. The file server, in particular, uses a database to control and manage access to the file server. Novell calls this database the bindery. The bindery contains control information that allows the administrator to organize users, user groups, work groups, file servers, print servers, and other network resources.

Netware file server has proven to be quite reliable and responsive. Its reliability is due to a design known as the System Fault Tolerant (SFT). To ensure data integrity, Netware file server adopts techniques such as disk mirroring, and disk duplexing. To boost performance, it adopts techniques such as elevator seeking, disk caching, and I/O queuing.

Netware 3.X supports file size as big as 4 gigabytes, and disk space of 32 terabytes, exceeding the storage requirement of most large business organizations.

Netware File Server also supports multiple client name spaces including DOS (the *.* file names), OS/2, Andrew File Protocol (AFP), Network File System (NFS), and Macintosh. This function enables Netware to be the integrating LAN for other LANs.

Portable Netware

To quell users' concerns about the single Intel platform for which the file server was originally designed, Novell licenses the Netware C-code to other computer manufacturers so that the Netware file server can run under operating systems such as VMS and OS/2. Novell calls this portable Netware as opposed to the native Netware on Intel platforms. Many minicomputer vendors have announced Portable Netware for their machines, essentially turning them into Netware file and print servers while also supporting other applications, including their own DBMS products.

5.3.1.2 Netware Loadable Modules

The fact that Netware is the dominant vendor in the file/print server market is not lost on the minds of the DBMS and the e-mail developers. They know that users would much prefer incremental functional enrichment on their existing Novell LANs than to go wholesale changes to another LAN configuration. That is

the main reason that Netware is supported by many third-party data server vendors. Novell is now teamed up with many database vendors including Gupta, Oracle, Informix, Progress, and Sybase.

Novell's Netware Transports Licensing Program encourages third parties to
develop distributed applications, intelligent peripherals, and Netware products
with pre-linked drivers. The process of network application development is similar to what we discussed before. The final products are a set of software modules
that include:

- the server itself
- server interface
- server protocol
- exported server interface

These applications are known as Netware Loadable Modules (NLM). NLM is a
program that can be loaded and unloaded from the file server memory while the
file server is running. The NLM programs need the file server because the program receives its memory allocation from the file server.

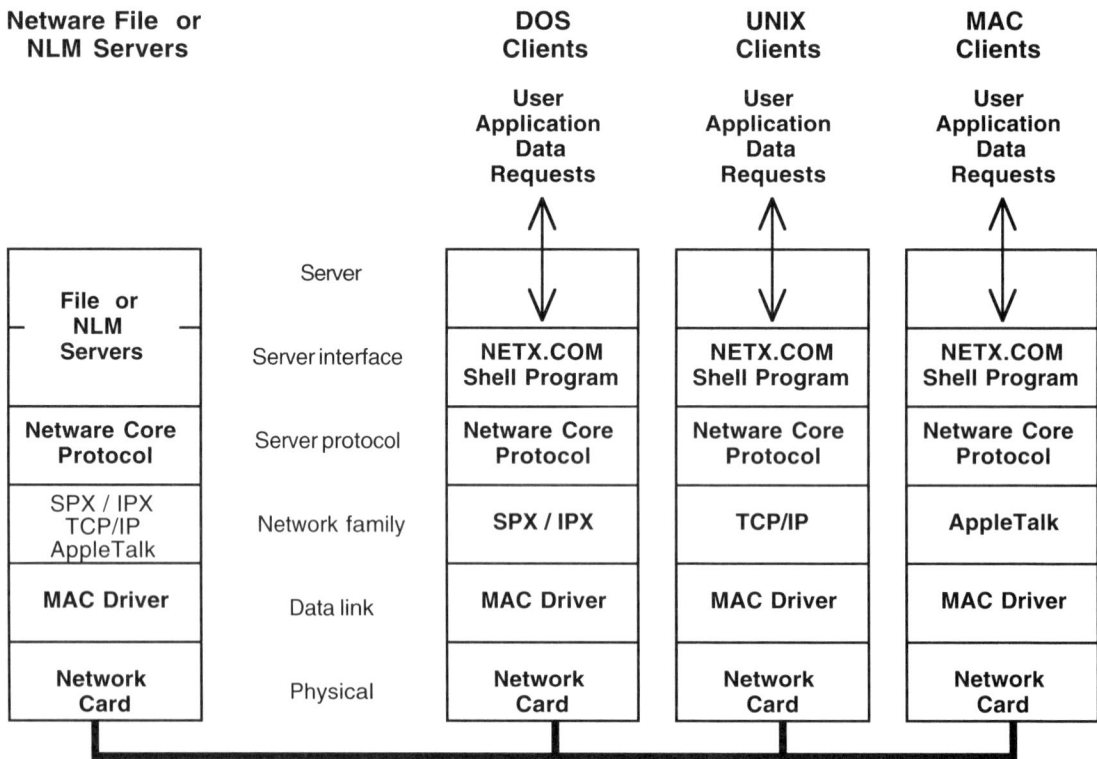

Netware File or NLM Servers		DOS Clients	UNIX Clients	MAC Clients
		User Application Data Requests	**User Application Data Requests**	**User Application Data Requests**
		↑↓	↑↓	↑↓
File or NLM Servers	Server			
	Server interface	**NETX.COM Shell Program**	**NETX.COM Shell Program**	**NETX.COM Shell Program**
Netware Core Protocol	Server protocol	**Netware Core Protocol**	**Netware Core Protocol**	**Netware Core Protocol**
SPX / IPX TCP/IP AppleTalk	Network family	**SPX / IPX**	**TCP/IP**	**AppleTalk**
MAC Driver	Data link	**MAC Driver**	**MAC Driver**	**MAC Driver**
Network Card	Physical	**Network Card**	**Network Card**	**Network Card**

Figure 5–16. Netware Client Server Configurations

Netware Core Protocols

The file server uses the Netware Core Protocol, which is Netware's session layer protocol. Common requests handled by the NCP service protocols include creating or destroying a service connection, manipulating directories and files, and printing.

Netware V3.11 NCP supports transport protocols of SPX/IPX, TCP/IP, and AppleTalk. Client stations that are loaded with one of three transport protocols, the Netware server interface and server protocol will be able to access the file server or any other NLM server.

5.3.1.3 Netware Shells

Netware File Server comes with the DOS server interfaces for the DOS workstations, Mac server interfaces for a Mac, and UNIX server interfaces for UNIX workstation. Users simply load them into their networked workstations to talk to the Netware server.

Netware calls these programs the shell programs. In the Novell DOS clients, the server interface program labeled as NETX.COM intercepts all the software interrupts related to any data requests and which normally would have gone directly to the operating system DOS. The Netware shell program will decide whether a particular call is for local data or remote data. If the call is for remote data, the server interface passes the request to the DOS operating system as though the request came directly from the user application. If the request is for data in the file server, the request will be taken over by the Netware Core Protocol, which converts the requests compatible to the file server's own protocol.

When the conversion is done, the request is passed to the transport environment of SPX /IPX, MAC Drivers, server interface card, and the physical wire of the network.

5.3.1.4 Novell's Strategy

The fact that Netware has its own operating system instead of a mainstream system, such as DOS, OS/2, or UNIX, was an aspect that worried some users in its early days. Notwithstanding the cynicism, Netware is today's market leader in local area networking. Its success can be attributed to a high quality product, excellent timing on the introduction of new features, and an astute business alliance with third party developers.

For example, Novell acquired the Message Handling System (MHS) technology from Action Technology Inc. The MHS engine will be included as part of new Netware releases. Novell is betting that this feature will bind customer loyalty as there will be no escape that the electronic mail is the next big network application. MHS already has the support of many E-mail application developers. More on this in the Electronic Mail section in this chapter.

LAN applications when needed in a wide area network typically have to compromise their performance because of slower transmission speed. To improve wide area network performance, Novell came up with a new feature for its server known as Burstmode IPX, an enhanced version of its IPX local area network (LAN) transport protocol that will increase the speed of file transfers across wide area networks. Burstmode IPX operates at a speed comparable to that of a 4 MBPS Token Ring across a T1 line, and lets users connect their LANs over wide areas to utilize WAN bandwidth with many IPX packets of varying length.

Another strategic move by Novell is its recent alliance with IBM. Today, one can purchase Netware directly from IBM. The only difference in the product is in the color of the box it comes in: blue! To many, this alliance legitimize Novell's place in the industry. No longer will it be regarded as a lightweight by some IS people.

5.3.2 Microsoft's LAN Manager

LAN Manager was originally developed by Microsoft and 3Com. 3Com dropped out in 1989 to concentrate on her other network products. For a while, IBM joined in the LAN Manager development efforts. That did not last long when the 1992 dispute between Microsoft and IBM over Windows and OS/2 put the IBM's commitment to LAN Manager in a no man's land. The battle is far from over, and the result is uncertain at best.

The LAN Manager is an OS/2 application which used to hold a special appeal to the user community, that want sto put the data server, communication server, mail server, and other servers under the same OS/2 roof. The affinity towards OS/2 is its true multi-tasking 32-bit architecture, which DOS cannot match.

A similar product developed jointly by Microsoft, Hewlett-Packard, and 3Com, called LAN Manager/X, is available from a number of vendors including Santa Cruz Operation (SCO), DEC, HP, AT&T, and Unisys. In the same way that LAN Manager is an OS/2 application, LAN Manager/X is an UNIX application.

5.3.2.1 LAN Manager Servers

Four basic servers are available with the LAN Manager product. It manages four types of resources:

- file (or disks and directories),
- printers,
- communication devices (modems), and
- named pipes

The LAN Manager file server uses the OS/2's High Performance Filing System (HPFS) to store its files. The communication server enables a number of client programs to share a single communication device, such as a modem and image scanner. The communication device queues manage user's requests until the device is available for use. While the user is waiting to use a device, he or she can switch to another program and work on a different task.

5.3.2.2 LAN Manager Server Protocols

The LAN manager's native session layer protocol (i.e., the server protocol) is called "Named Pipe." It also supports the NetBIOS server protocol. In transport protocol, it supports TCP/IP, NetBEUI, and AppleTalk.

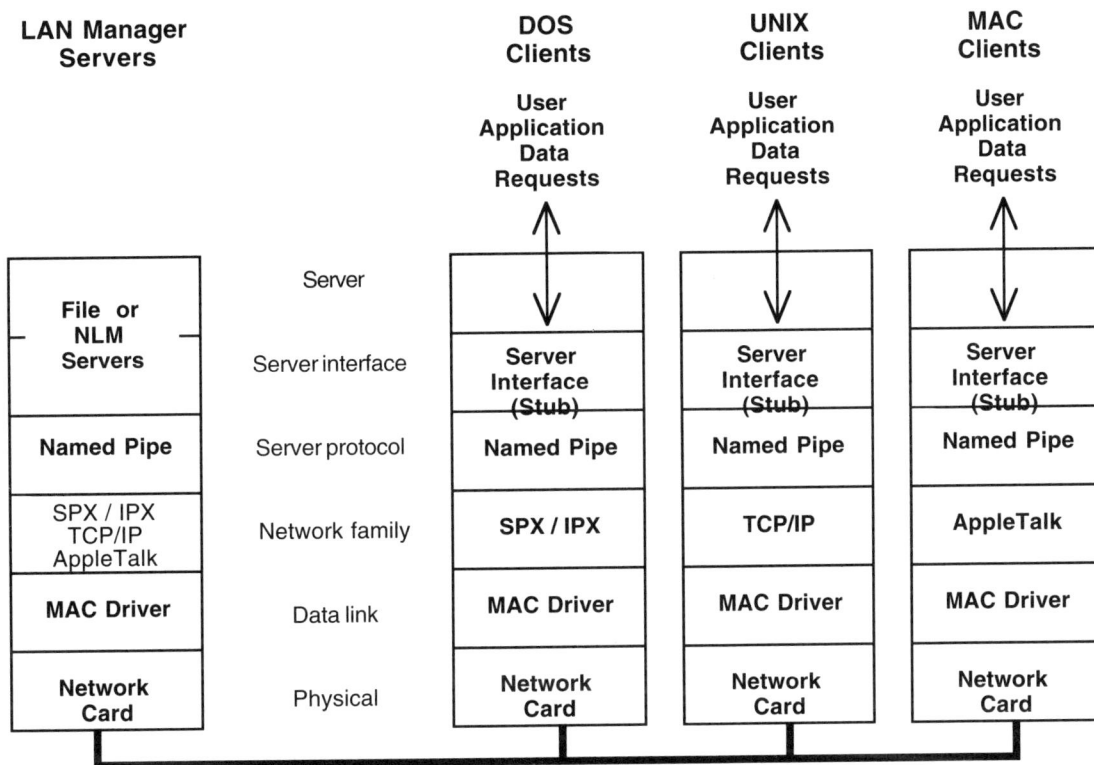

LAN Manager Servers		DOS Clients	UNIX Clients	MAC Clients
		User Application Data Requests	User Application Data Requests	User Application Data Requests
	Server			
File or NLM Servers	Server interface	Server Interface (Stub)	Server Interface (Stub)	Server Interface (Stub)
Named Pipe	Server protocol	Named Pipe	Named Pipe	Named Pipe
SPX / IPX TCP/IP AppleTalk	Network family	SPX / IPX	TCP/IP	AppleTalk
MAC Driver	Data link	MAC Driver	MAC Driver	MAC Driver
Network Card	Physical	Network Card	Network Card	Network Card

Figure 5–17. LAN Manager's Client Server Configurations

NetBIOS

NetBIOS was described as a transport layer socket entity in last chapter. It can also be viewed as a session layer entity. Many network applications for PC have been written using the NetBIOS programming interface. And many network families, including Novell, have a NetBIOS emulator sitting on top their own protocol stacks!

From a technical point of view, NetBIOS contains application programming interfaces similar to those found in a server protocol or RPC Runtime library. User programs can be written using specific NetBIOS commands to start and stop server or client processes.

Named Pipe

Named pipe is a more advanced version of NetBIOS. Overall, named pipe is easier to use than NetBIOS commands. Named pipes are the LAN Manager's virtual circuits through which client and server programs communicate with one another over multiple network families. Like NetBIOS and others, named pipe is a session layer entity.

Named pipes are treated like any other physical resources, such as disks and printers, by LAN Manager. A named pipe is generated by the server application during its start up. A server application must have a named pipe registered with the LAN Manager. This is sort of like asking for a 1-800 number for your phone. Any client program that needs to "talk" to this server must do so via the named pipe as though it were writing to a disk or printer device.

For example, if the named pipe for an SQL server is XYZ, then any client workstations making SQL calls must be addressed to XYZ. In the initialization file: LANMAN.INI, the user must specify the maximum number of connections that any given named pipe can have.

5.3.2.3   LAN Manager's Peer Architecture

Unlike Novell's Netware, a LAN Manager client workstation can choose to run the so called Peer service function as an equal to servers on the network. With it, the workstation can share its disks and printers with other client workstations.

The difference in running peer service on a client workstation and in a real server is the ability to serve multiple clients. For example, running the SQL server using Peer service in a client workstation can only serve one client at a time.

6

IBM's Network Computing

In its early form, SNA could hardly be identified with what we now call network computing. It was a network architecture designed to support host computers that are connected to thousands of non-programmable (dumb) terminals and printers.

IBM's determination and strategy to evolve SNA to a new form to satisfy customer demand for a client server computing platform was made known in its April 1992 announcement of future networking direction for IBM.

Since the majority (over 90%) of today's mission-critical commercial applications of the top Fortune 1000 companies are based on IBM mainframes, it would be unrealistic to talk about client server computing without a good understanding of the IBM mainframe environment.

Ironically, IBM's past successes are also its greatest barriers to its aggressively seeking new technology for fear of eroding its existing installed base. SNA is an excellent example of this: Its built-in, hierarchical structure makes it a non-starter in client server peer computing methods. Yet IBM held on to it until its customers started using competitors' products.

In 1994, the new IBM chairman publicly stated that the single largest mistake that IBM made in the 1980s was its failure to recognize client server technology.

IBM, the most powerful and vertically integrated computer manufacturer, is struggling to remain a dominant player in a fast-changing, global market. IBM still has the financial and technical resources to greatly influence the data processing industry.

6.1   SNA BACKGROUND

IBM's SNA was designed in an era without personal computers and local area networks. It was designed for a host computer with thousands of non-programmable display terminals and printers. It has a master-slave architecture in which the IBM mainframe computer is the master.

It can be argued that SNA (minus the new Logical Unit Type 6.2, which we will discuss in detail later) was not network computing. It was host-based computing.

The 1970s

SNA was introduced by IBM in 1974 as a technical solution to help IBM customers to change from a batch to an online environment. This change resulted in IBM SNA products such as: Time Shared Option (TSO), Information Management System/Data Communication (IMS/DC), and Communication Interactive Control System (CICS). A more detailed description of CICS can be found in Section 7.4.3.1.

Through IBM's technology leadership, large scale online applications such as the airline ticket reservation system, credit card, automatic teller machines, and points of sale started a revolution in business operation automation. By all measures, SNA was a huge success.

The 1980s

The 1980s ushered in the age of the large scale integrated (LSI) technology. Mainframes and minis were no longer the only places where computing could occur. Personal computers and local area networks were beginning to provide credible alternatives to solve new business problems.

Prior to the advent of personal computing, IBM's leadership had never been challenged. IBM was evidently blinded by the healthy profit margin generated from the mainframe products up to late 1980s. Its less-than-aggressive position on client server technology during the 1980s destroyed IBM's preeminent leadership in the industry.

Upstarts, such as Microsoft, Novell, 3Com, Apple, Banyan, and Sun Microsystems, have established themselves as worthy competitors. The belated effort to turn SNA from a hierarchical host-centric model to a more distributed model is not a simple undertaking because every change must be considered in relation to its impact on current users' application investments.

The 1990s

A number of false starts in the early 1990s have given IBM's most loyal customers legitimate concerns about its ability to produce a true client server computing platform.

In this chapter we review in some detail the latest announcement from IBM with respect to its future SNA direction.

6.2 SNA Fundamentals

In this section, we first discuss the basic concepts and terminology of SNA. We then go into some detail about SNA's data link layer, known as the Synchronous Data Link Control, which is the common thread linking all SNA network nodes. After SDLC, we will discuss the concepts and software products related to SNA network nodes, physical units, and logical units.

6.2.1 SNA vs. OSI

OSI	SNA
Application	Application
Presentation	Function Management
Session	Data Flow Control
Transport	Transmission Control
Network	Path Control
Link	Datalink Control
Physical	Physical

Logical Units span these three layers ← (Function Management, Data Flow Control, Transmission Control)

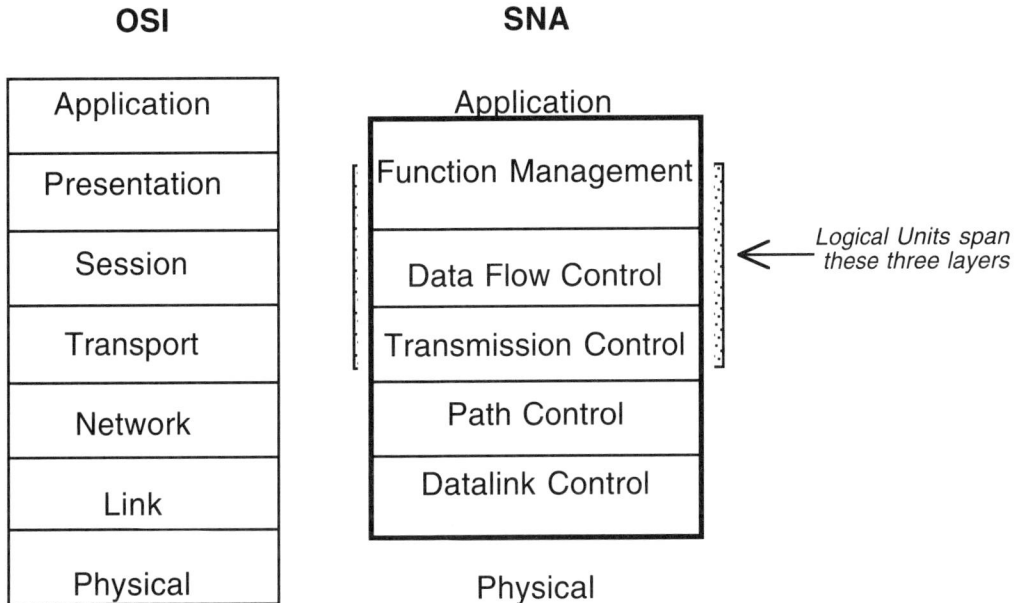

Figure 6–1. Approximate Equivalent Functional Layers of OSI vs. SNA

Like the OSI reference model, SNA is a layered protocol, even though its functions are not separated by the same OSI layers. The names for the SNA layers are also different.

The data link and the path control layers of SNA can be approximated by the data link and the network layers of the OSI Reference Model. The transmission control is similar to the transport layer. The data flow control, and function management layers are equivalent to some combination of the session, the presentation, and application layers.

In OSI, a set of application management services is defined for the application layer. No common and explicit application management services exist in SNA. They come as part of the SNA applications known as online monitors such as the Time Sharing Option (TSO), the CICS (Computer Interaction Control System), and the Communication Monitor System (CMS). Each has its own set of application management services.

If one must look for parallels with what we discussed in the last two chapters, then TSO, CMS, and CICS are equivalent to individual network operating systems that share the same network transport environment of SNA.

6.2.2 SNA Components

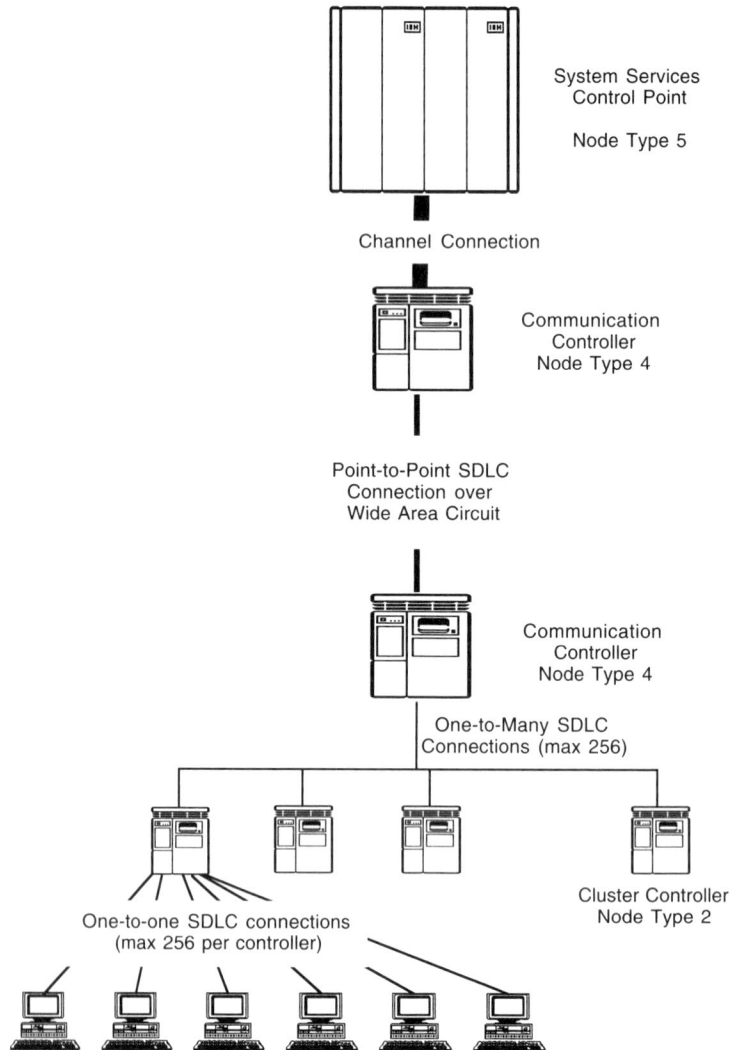

Figure 6-2. A Typical SNA Hierarchy of Nodes and Devices

Figure 6–2 shows the building blocks of an SNA network. SNA is designed around a hierarchy of hardware devices of varying degree of programmability and network control importance.

At the top are the mainframe computers. They are followed by the network communication controllers, the equipment cluster controllers, and then non-programmable screens, and printers. SNA terminology is both cryptic and often quite redundant. But users becomed accustomed to it.

A Type 5 network node is a Type 5 Physical Unit, and it is a mainframe computer. A Type 4 network node is a Type 4 Physical Unit, and it is a communication controller just as an IBM 3745. A Type 2 network node is a Type 2 Physical Unit, and is a cluster controller such as an IBM 3174!

6.2.3   Synchronous Data Link Control (SDLC)

In the following sections, we review in some detail the structure and the operation of SDLC and show that it is a data link layer protocol unlike the Ethernet and Token Ring.

The following section also shows that the SDLC hierarchical design is inimical to client server computing. However, the large installed base of SDLC makes any change to it very difficult.

Like other data link protocols, SDLC is implemented through a combination of hardware and software. The hardware are network adapters inserted into the input-output slots of a computer. Typically, they have a thin coaxial cables RG62 connector.

A De Facto Standard

Because of IBM's dominance in the marketplace, other computer manufacturers have no choice but to make SDLC connection hardware to allow their products to be connected to IBM computers. Therefore, for most of 1970s and 1980s IBM's SDLC was the de-facto industry standard for computers interconnection. In fact, many non-IBM computers can only communicate with one another using IBM SDLC protocols.

6.2.3.1   SDLC Hierarchy

Figure 6–3. IBM's Synchronous Data Link Control (SDLC) Frame

Within the SDLC protocol, a network device can either be a primary station or a secondary station. The primary station initiates a data transfer and is in control during the exchange of messages. In other words, a primary station is always the master.

The secondary station is contacted by the primary station and is controlled by the primary station during the exchange of message frames. It is the slave. Secondary stations cannot communicate among themselves.

For each message exchange, one station must be designated as primary and the others as secondary. For example, the communication controller, IBM 3745, is a secondary station to the mainframe, but a primary station to the cluster controller IBM 3174. In turn, the cluster controller 3174 is a secondary station to the IBM 3745, but a primary station to the 327x terminal or printers.

6.2.3.2 SDLC Data Packet

There are three types of SDLC data packet. The first type is known as the I-data packets, the information data packets. They carry user data. The second type is known as the S-data packets, the supervisory data packets. They carry supervisory information such as requesting transmission, requesting suspension of transmission, requesting polls, acknowledging the receipt of I-data packets, and reporting status. The S-data packets have no data field. The third type is known as the U-data packets, the unnumbered data packets. They are used for special functions such as initialization and diagnostic procedures.

As shown in Figure 6–4, a data packet consists of three parts: the header, the data, and the trailer. The header consists of the flag, the address, and the control fields. The trailer consists of the Data packet Check Sequence and the Ending Flag field.

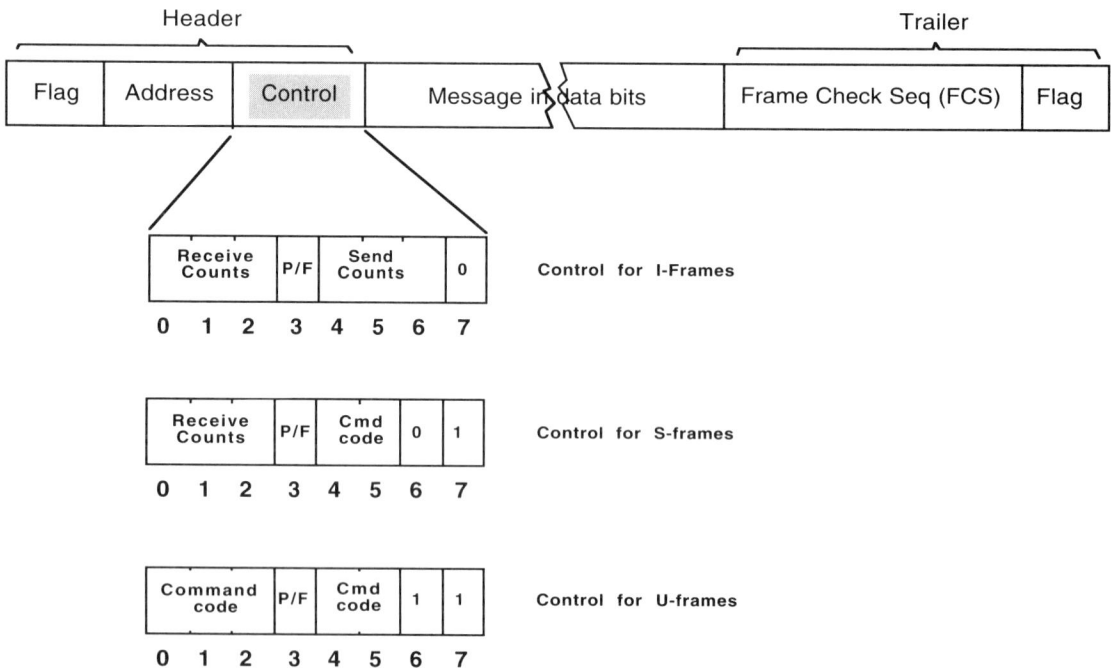

Figure 6–4. SDLC Control Frames

The beginning flag field is a single byte (8 bits) that always has the following pattern: 0111 1110. In other words, any 6 consecutive ones tells the software that this is the beginning of a data packet.

Bit-stuffing techniques such as the **non-return-to-zero encoding (NRZI)** ensures that six consecutive ones will not occur in any other fields of the data packet, including the data field.

The address field is 8 bits wide. It contains the address of the secondary station. Because of the 8-bit field, the maximum number of secondary stations a primary station could have is 256. Multiple byte address fields can expand this number to a much larger value, but it is seldom used. In other words, 256 slaves for one master is quite sufficient for most application situations.

An important but subtle point on addressing must not be overlooked here. Each secondary station can have multiple receive addresses, and one send address. The send address is always that of the primary station since it can exchange data with its master but not with anyone else.

However, many secondary stations on the same data link (under the same master) belong to different groups of users or applications. Thus, each secondary station may have a group address and its unique address on the link. When the primary station sends out a data packet with the group address, all secondary stations with the same group address will respond.

The control field is normally 8 bits in length, but it can be 16 bits in length. The 16–bit length control field is defined in the hardware, meaning that both the primary and secondary stations must have the compatible hardware. The control field defines what type of information is carried by the data packet.

The send and receive counters are three bits in length. Up to seven data packets can be sent or received between acknowledgments. For a 2-byte control field, up to 127 data packets can be transmitted between acknowledgments.

To ensure that no data packets are lost and that all data packets are properly acknowledged during a transmission, the transmitting station always tracks how many data packets it has sent via the Send Counter, and the receiver station always keeps track of how many data packets it has received in the Receive Counter.

The command code for the S-data packet is a 2-bit field. It identifies the type of command or response the data packet represents. The command code for the U-data packet is a 5-bit code.

6.2.3.3 SDLC Addressing

SNA addresses are quite different from that of TCP/IP and others. Every SNA node must be a member of the hierarchy. Each SNA primary station can only have a maximum of 256 secondary stations, a limit imposed by a single byte address field in the SDLC frame.

In SNA two levels of addressing are necessary. The high level address name is used by network and above layers. The low level address is used by the data link layer. The 2-byte address in a SDLC frame is the low level address. This means for one VTAM host, the software limit of SNA devices under its control is 65,535.

The high level address designates the network node names. Each node must have a name with characters. IBM does not have a global naming convention for

SNA networks like TCP/IP. Rather, each organization establishes its own network naming conventions appropriate for its business.

System Services Control Point (SSCP)

The System Services Control Point (SSCP), which is the master program of the domain (as explained in the next section), is responsible for translating them to the corresponding network addresses through a facility known as the network directory service. Separation of names and addresses shields users from making changes to their LU, PU, or SSCP names even though their physical addresses may have been altered.

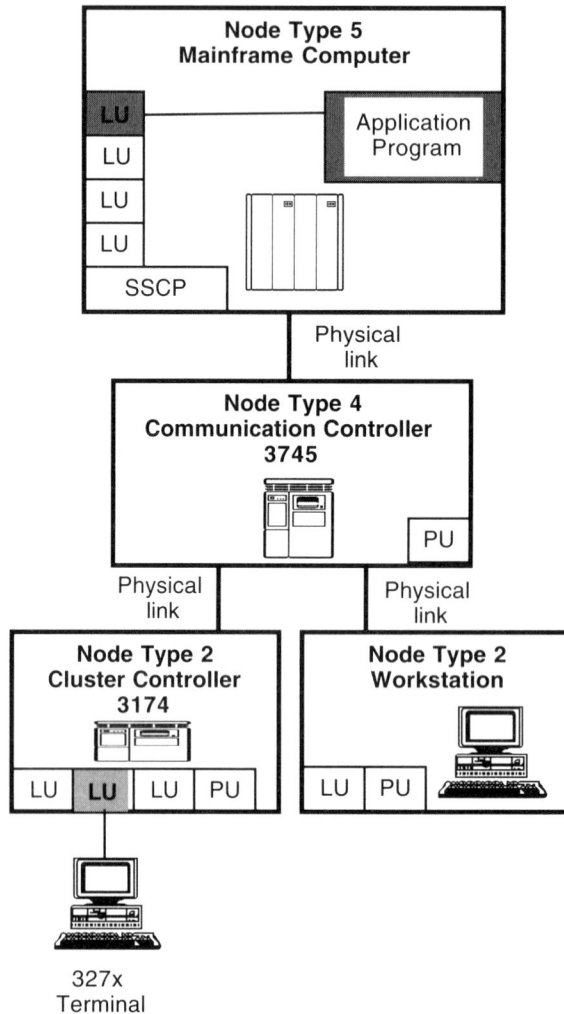

Figure 6–5. SNA Nodes and Hierarchy

For example, Company XYZ names its IBM 3745 communication controller in New York City as XNYC. The names for the three IBM 3174 cluster controllers connected to it could be XNYC78, XNYC79, and XNYC80. The last two characters represent the secondary station numbers with respect to the primary station, the IBM 3745 communication controller.

If one goes another hierarchy level down to the 327x devices level, or the logical units level, then the name for logical unit address 15 in the cluster controller XNYC78 would be XNYC-78-0F, or simply XNYC780F.

The SNA low level addresses can only take on the value from 00 to FF in hexadecimal. As noted earlier in the SDLC discussion, secondary stations may have multiple receive addresses for the purposes of receiving broadcast messages or group messages. This again must be resolved at the higher level in the SSCP. By convention, the address 00 is always reserved and no station can be assigned that number. The address FF is reserved as the broadcast address.

6.2.4 SNA Network Nodes

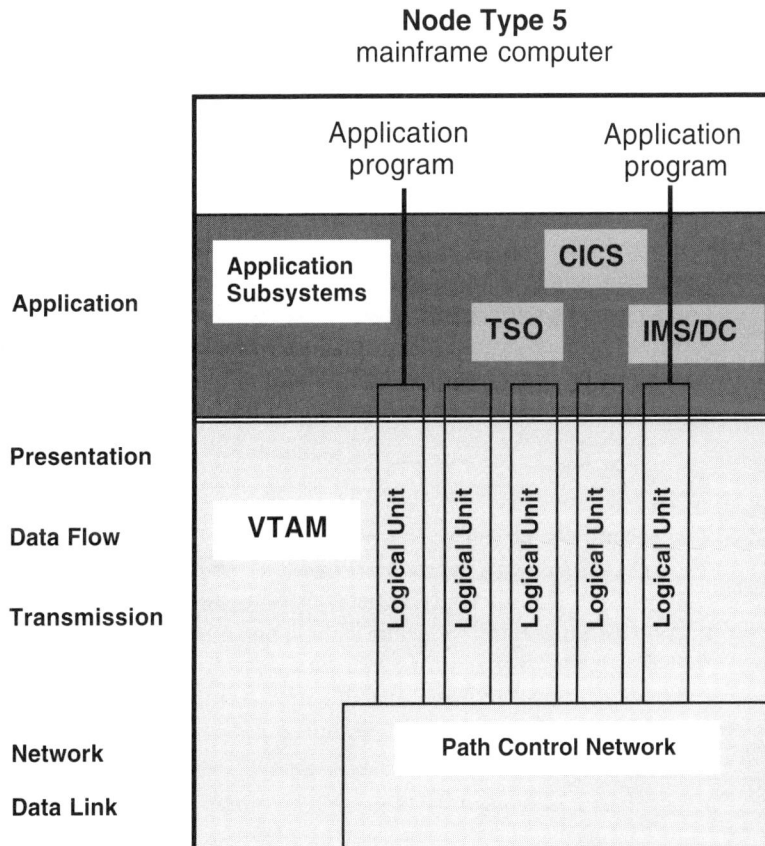

Figure 6–6. SNA Layers and IBM mainframe network software products

SNA defines network nodes as physical points on a network through which messages are stopped, examined, and forwarded to their next stop on the network. SNA nodes are joined to the other nodes through the physical link.

An SNA node can be a mainframe computer, minicomputer, communication controller, cluster controller, and personal computer. There are three principal types of network nodes: Type 5, Type 4, and Type 2. Each network node serves a different network function.

6.2.4.1 SNA Type 5 Node

The Type 5 Node is the master and the central nervous system of an SNA domain, which consists of one Type 5 node connected to a number of Type 4 Nodes and Type 2 Nodes. Multiple Type 5 nodes form multiple domains network. Type 5 is known as a System Services Control Point (SSCP). The Type 5 node always is a mainframe computer inside which other data processing activities such as batch processing, and on-line database applications also reside.

For this most powerful SNA network node, two sets of software products create the SNA environment shown as two different shades in Figure 6–6.

Virtual Telecommunication Access Method (VTAM)

The first set of software products relates to the telecommunication access method known as the Virtual Telecommunication Access Method (VTAM), available in both the Multiple Virtual Storage (MVS) and the Virtual Machines (VM) operating systems, two major operating systems for IBM's mainframe computers.

VTAM contains logic spanning from the transport layer up to the presentation layer of the Reference Model. Its major function is to manage software components known as logical units, the virtual circuit sockets through which a mainframe program can "talk" to a dumb terminal. More on this in the section on Logical Units.

SNA Online Monitors

The second set of software products belongs to the application layer, and they are known as the online monitors. For MVS, the on-line monitors are Time Shared Option or TSO, Computer Interactive Communication System or CICS, and the Information Management System/Data Communication Monitor or IMS/DC. For VM, the on-line monitor is called Communication Monitor Subsystem or CMS.

These online monitors are the hierarchical equivalent version of the network operating system discussed earlier.

6.2.4.2 SNA Type 4 Node

Type 4 node is an intermediate node. It is implemented on the IBM 3745 communication controller. The program that runs in it is the Network Control Program.

Node Type 4
Communication Controller 3745

Application

Presentation

Data Flow

Transmission

Network Control Program

Network

Path Control Network

Data Link

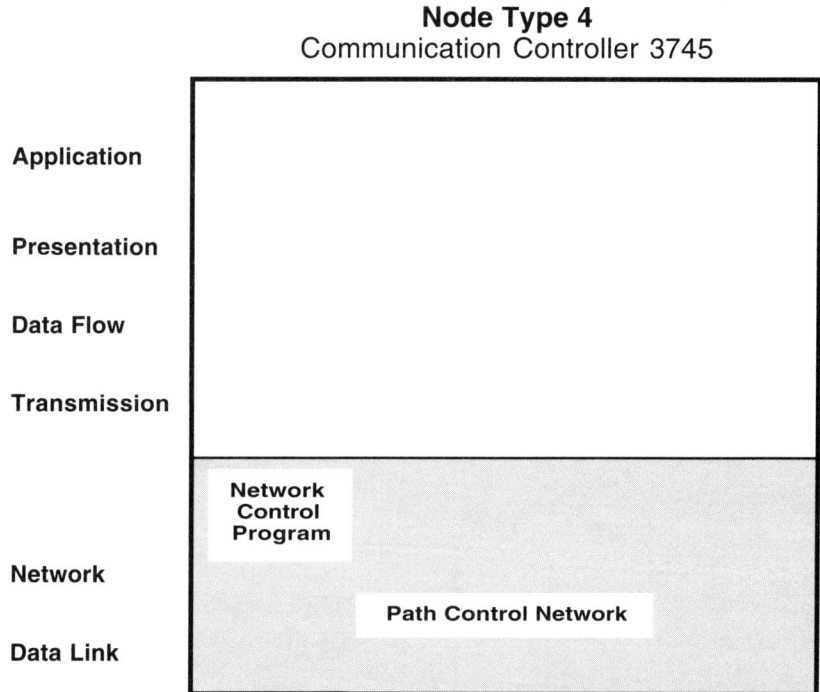

Figure 6–7. SNA Layers and IBM 3745 network control program

SNA Network Control Program (NCP)

The NCP serves two main functions. It provides a connection for all the local cluster controllers to communicate with application programs in a mainframe. As noted in Figure 6–7, NCP controls both the data link and the network layers.

At the network layer, the NCP is responsible for connecting the local cluster controllers to the rest of the network. Through it, the cluster controllers can also be connected to other network domains.

A second function of the NCP is to provide a cross domain connection for multiple Type 5 nodes (mainframes). IBM calls these network layer activity SNA subarea routing.

6.2.4.3 SNA Type 2 Node

Type 2 nodes are known as 3270 cluster controllers such as the IBM 3174s. The program running inside them is the 3174 Control Program or CP. As shown in Figure 6–8, the control program has no network layer functions which are handled by the Type 5 communication controller described previously. The Type 5 controller simply passes whatever comes in from the mainframe to the terminal or printer, and whatever comes in from the peripherals back to the mainframe to the next higher node.

The logical units are software modules that emulate various peripheral devices such as a terminal or a printer.

6.2.4.4 SNA 327x Devices

The IBM 327x series of terminals and printers is designed specifically for the SNA software. They are so widely used that many clone manufacturers appear in the marketplace to satisfy demands that IBM alone cannot fulfill.

A 327x terminal is a buffered, but not user programmable terminal. It is not as dumb a terminal as the old teletype machines, where all processing features must be executed by programs in the controlling computer.

327x devices have limited processing capability, designed specifically to interface with the software sockets of LUs Type 2 and Type 3.

Node Type 2
Cluster Controller 3174

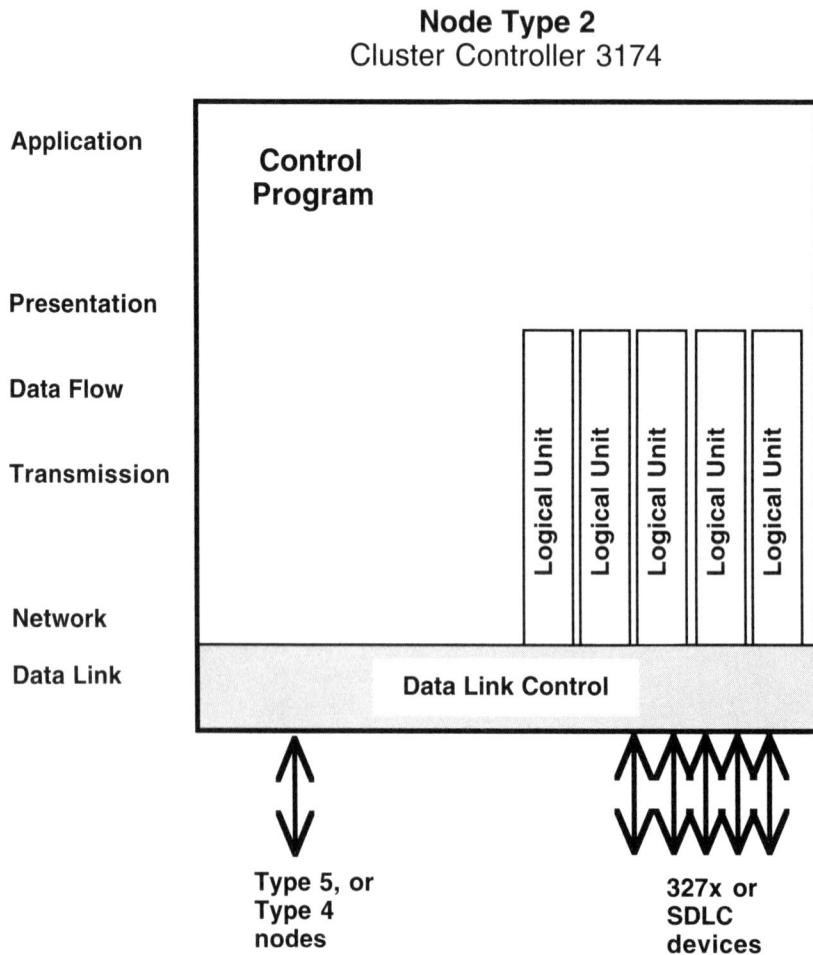

Figure 6–8. SNA Layers and IBM 3174 Cluster controller software products

For example, when an operator enters data at the keyboard, the data is stored in a buffer at the terminal until the "Enter" or other attention key is pressed. This action sends to the host computer, in a single SDLC data packet, selected fields from the screen buffer.

To save transmission time over slow wide area network circuits, IBM has specified with the design of the 327x terminals that only changed fields will be sent back.

There are special 327x devices with additional hardware and software making it into a Type 2 network node with one logical unit. These terminals can be directly attached to a Type 4 node without going through the cluster controller.

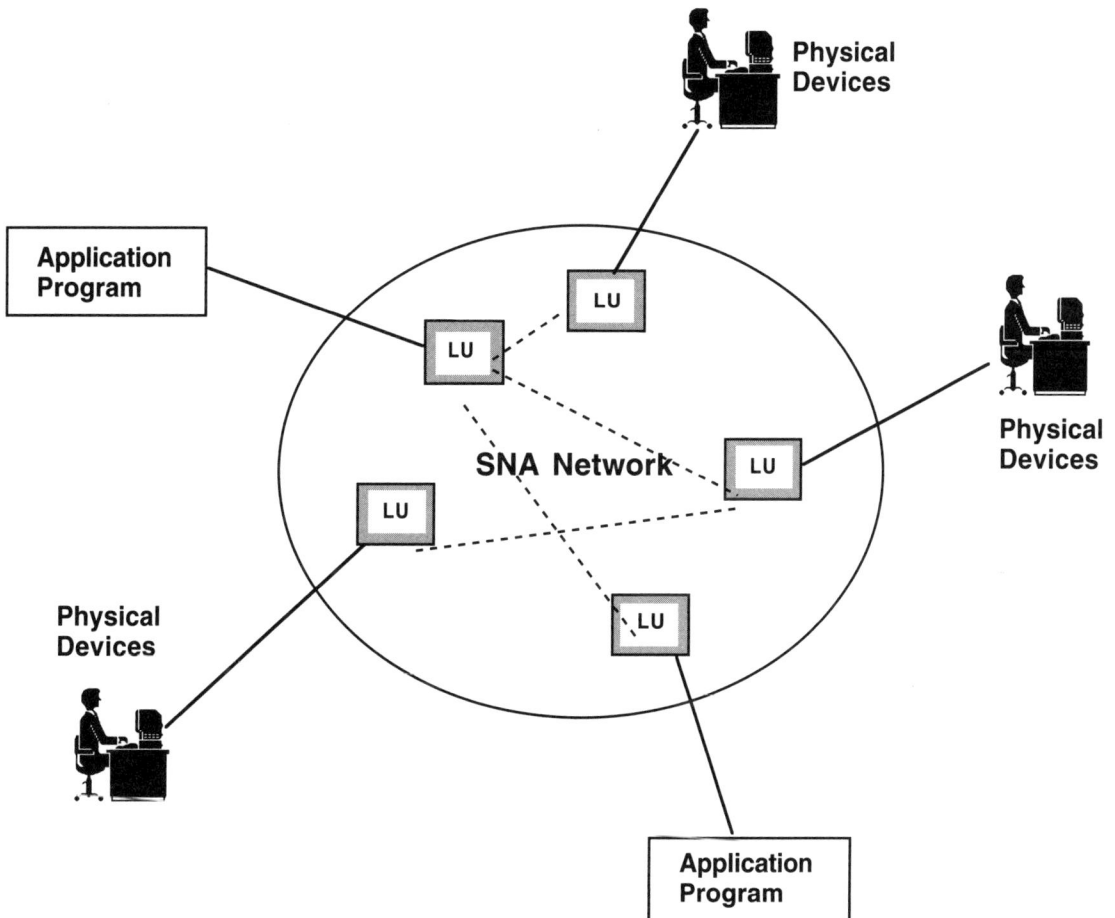

Figure 6–9. Logical Units: network sockets through which programs and physical devices can communicate with one another

6.2.4.5 SNA Peripherals

Many special terminals can be used for applications: the automatic teller machines, supermarket bar code readers and checkout stations, fast food computerized cash registers, stock quote terminals, factory floor process control equipment, credit card verification terminals, and so on.

The common protocol for this equipment is the SNA data link protocol—Synchronous Data Link Control (SDLC). The applications that interact with these devices are executing in IBM mainframes.

6.2.5 SNA Logical Units

Besides the three network node types, another important concept in SNA is the logical unit. Through logical units, users of the computing resources communicate with one another. Users are the application programs or human operators interacting through an input device such as the screen and keyboard. Logical units are software programs executing in two types of nodes: Type 5 and Type 2. There is no logical unit inside a Type 4 node.

SNA LUs are like telephone wall jacks. A user simply plugs in his or her telephone, dials the number of the other party, and the two exchange messages.

Similarly for logical units, a user can plug a terminal into the logical unit. Through it, the terminal user can dial into an application program on the mainframe. Once the circuit is established, the user and the application program can start talking to one another.

Logical units are end points of virtual circuits. The larger the network, the more logical units will be required. Like the telephone jacks, logical units are the entry points through which virtual circuits can be established for communicating parties. Like the telephone jacks, behind the logical units are immensely complex switching network software responsible for generating, and keeping track of thousands of virtual circuits.

Logical units belong to the session-transport layer of the Reference Model. Logical units exist only in Type 5 network node (mainframe) and in the Type 2 network node (cluster controller). Even for the same type of logical units, the one in the mainframe is more complex, but complementary to the one in the cluster controller.

6.2.5.1 SNA Logical Unit Types

There are seven types of logical units designed to handle different type of applications. They are simply identified as LU type 0 to Type 7.

    LU 0 applications' own non-SNA protocols
    LU 1 emulates a generic printer device
    LU 2 emulates a 3270 non-programmable display terminal
    LU 3 emulates a 3270 printer
    LU 4 supports terminal to terminal communication
    LU 5 does not exist

LU 6 supports program to program communication in a SNA
LU 7 emulates 5250 display terminals for System 38s or AS 400

The LUs in the mainframe computer are part of system resources generated during the system start up, specifically when VTAM is started. These LUs are then assigned to the various application subsystems.

For example, CICS may have been assigned 100 LUs. A CICS application thus can have a maximum of 100 virtual circuits into which users can dial for message exchanges. On the other hand, a user must have access to an LU of the same type through which it can form a virtual circuit with one of the 100 available LUs for CICS. The user LU is provide by the cluster controller IBM 3174.

6.2.5.2 SNA Logical Unit Communication

The LUs in the cluster controller are generated and defined when the 3174 is configured. A maximum of 256 LUs can be defined per controller. Most LUs are either 327x terminals or 327x printers.

Theoretically, 256 physical devices can be supported by one cluster controller although in practice the number of devices is limited to 32 because physically constrained by the fact that each terminal or printer coaxial cable will take up one port of the cluster controller. Each terminal or printer is assigned one specific LU defined in the controller.

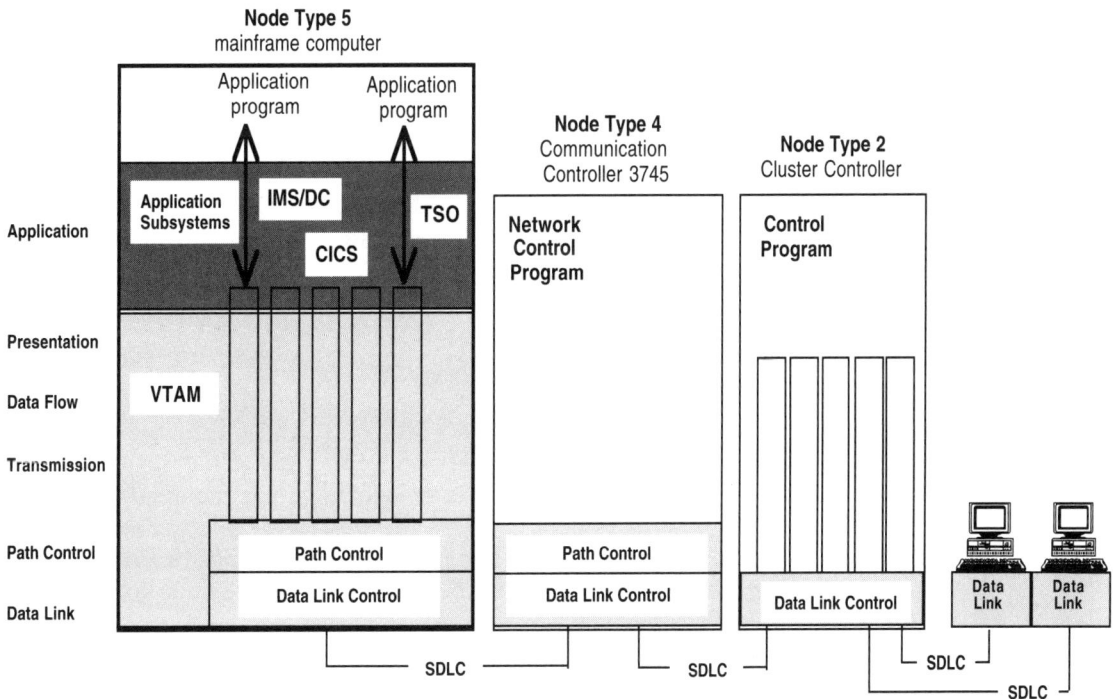

Figure 6–10. How Logical Units Communicate?

The LUs defined in the mainframe can be connected to the LUs defined in the cluster controller in two ways. The first is by attaching the 3174 directly to the mainframe. The second is by attaching the 3174 to a communication controller IBM 3745, attached to the mainframe.

The former is used when both the cluster controller and the mainframe computer are in the same building. The latter is more common when the cluster controller is located many miles away from the mainframe computer. In this case, the communication controller, the 3745, is a store-and-forward device. The reason that the Type 4 nodes do not contain any logical units is that they do not need any.

In either case, the mainframe, via the BIND command in VTAM, initiates and establishes the virtual circuit (a session) between the mainframe LU and the cluster controller LU. Once a virtual circuit is established, the mode of communication is quite typical of any other communication protocol.

For example, when a CICS application sends a message to an LU, VTAM will take it through the SNA layers inside the mainframe. In the end, the original message combined with layers of headers and controls added to it by VTAM will be transmitted across the physical network as an SDLC data packet.

When these SDLC data packets arrive at the 3745 controller, the Network Control Program (NCP) will reassemble and forward (store-and-forward) them to the correct 3174 cluster controller in a single SDLC data packet via the data link.

When this data packet arrives at the cluster controller, the logical unit inside the 3174 cluster controller forwards it to the buffer memory in the 327x terminal via a single SDLC data packet. The terminal in turn displays the data packet on the user terminal screen. When a user presses the "Enter" key, the full screen or the changes since the last screen are sent back to the main data packet via SDLC data packets.

The LU programs are the intelligence behind all peripheral massaging controls. Software products may support several LU types. For example, the application CICS supports all LUs except LU7 AIX supports APPC OS/400 supports LU7 OS/2 communication manager supports APPC.

6.3   ADVANCED PROGRAM-TO-PROGRAM COMMUNICATION (APPC)

Traditionally, IBM's products, such as AS400, AIX, and OS/2, and the mainframe have hardly anything in common. For example, AS400 has its own operating system and network architecture. Its user interfaces use non-3270 keyboards and terminals.

The inconsistency and incompatibility is not limited to mainframe and midrange computers; the same applies to personal computers and to UNIX environments.

For cost and performance reasons, these non-mainframe computer products compete in the mini computer markets and are favorite departmental machines.

6.3.1 System Application Architecture (SAA)

In the late 1980s, under great pressure from its customers to bring compatibility to its various product lines, IBM announced an ambitious product plan known as the System Application Architecture (SAA).

SAA's two main goals are to standardize the user interface (Common User Access (CUA)) for all IBM operating systems and to enable program-to-program communications (Advanced Program to Program Communication (APPC)) across all IBM's computer platforms.

Both CUA and APPC are independent of platforms as they apply to MVS, VM, AS400, OS/2, and AIX.

6.3.1.1 Common User Access (CUA)

With CUA, a user should see no difference in the touch and feel of applications on any of the platforms listed above because they all abide by the CUA standard.

This means that there are no longer 3270 or 5250 screens. There is only one CUA screen. The aim is to shield users from needing to know the computer platform on which their application is running.

In this book, our interest is in network computing. For those who are interested in the IBM CUA standard, many good reference materials are available from IBM.

6.3.2 APPC Verbs

To achieve the goal of CUA, it follows that there must be the ability for programs running on different IBM computers to communicate with one another in a seamless manner. This is the goal of the so called Advanced Program to Program Communication (APPC) architecture.

In APPC, IBM provides a set of APIs at the session layer known as the APPC verbs. They can be used as part of a user program written in standard programming languages such as C, COBOL, and others.

6.3.2.1 Logical Unit Type 6.2

The session layer socket through which these APPC verbs act is known as Logical Unit Type 6.2, or commonly known as LU6.2. The terms APPC and LU 6.2 are interchangeable, as in APPC verbs and LU6.2 verbs.

The term logical unit is a carryover from the old SNA tradition even though it is a foreign term for non-mainframe platforms. Lately, IBM has also been using the term "APPC" to give this technology a multiplatform image.

APPC verbs shield application programmers from the complexity of the underlying network transport environment. These verbs are identical across all IBM platforms.

Like other session layer protocols, the functions provided by a few key APPC verbs are quite simple. Although the exact spelling of the verbs may not be the same, they all do similar things. The following is a simplified explanation of these generic functions:

Open: To dial up a person
Close: To hang up the phone
Send: To speak to your partner
Receive: To listen to your partner
Status: A busy signal

From a programmer's point of view, the APPC verbs can be used to write an application for MVS, VM, OS/2, AIX, or OS/400 as though they were all connected in a homogeneous network transport environment.

6.3.3   APPC Application Services

There are two types of APPC programs: APPC Services Transaction Programs and APPC Application Transaction Programs. The former are application services written for utility functions such as operator functions and electronic document management. The latter are user application programs.

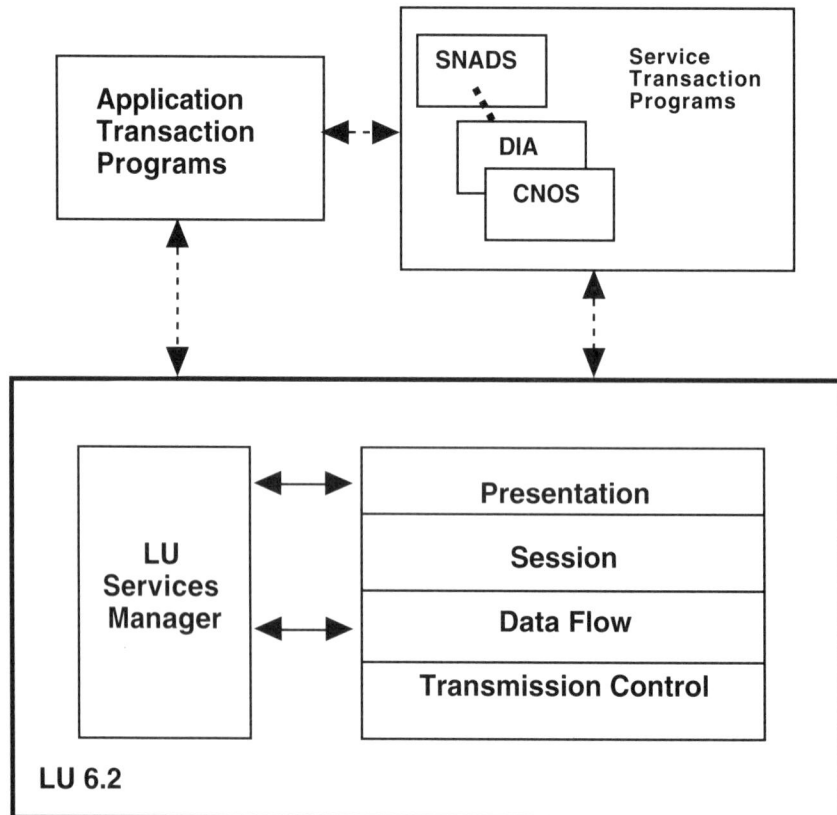

Figure 6–11. Components of Logical Unit Type 6.2

APPC is IBM's session layer protocol for its network operating system. Like any other network computing environment, its application layer must provide certain critical application services.

These application services are known as the Service Transaction Programs, as opposed to the Application Transaction Programs. Notable among them are the Document Interchange Architecture (DIA), SNA Distribution Services (SNADS), Distributed Data Management (DDM), and Change Number Of Sessions (CNOS). Unfortunately, these services are available on the mainframe only and as such are quite useless to non-mainframe installations.

Document Interchange Architecture (DIA) describes formats and protocols for document library and distribution services. It is implemented in office related products such as DISOSS for 370, System 36, and System 38.

SNA Distribution Services (SNADS) provides a general purpose store-and-forward capability for asynchronous transfer of data. It is used by DISOSS.

Distributed Data Management (DDM) provides transparent access to distributed data bases. Programs can reside and execute on one system (Source DDM) and have access to data files residing on other system (Target DDM) acting as a file server.

Change Number of Sessions (CNOS) performs control functions relating to parallel sessions of an LU6.2 application.

The readers are reminded that the above products are still evolving, and new features are being incorporated continuously. Users who want to use these products should check with IBM for their latest status.

6.3.4 APPC for Mainframes

APPC is supposed to solve IBM's problem of incompatibility between its different product lines. In the beginning, APPC had a slow start because it was available for program-to-program communication between mainframes only.

The problem is not in APPC, which is a session layer protocol. The problem lies in the SNA's implementation of the lower four layers (the network transport layers) of communication protocols. There are two problems.

The first is the incompatibility in the network transport protocols among IBM's own mainframes, AS400s, RS6000s, and PCs. The second is the hierarchical and complex nature of the SNA network transport protocol (SNA Data Flow and Transmission Control) implemented deep in the VTAM of the mainframe. This structure makes downsizing SNA to small computers such as DOS PCs an almost impossible task.

Also, the master-slave nature of the SDLC data link layer protocol makes spontaneous client server communication virtually impossible because of the number of store-and-forward nodes that a packet must go through to reach its destination.

Therefore, the early existence of APPC was quite useless for client server applications. The only practical application for APPC technology was to allow two programs running on two networked mainframes to communicate with one another. Other computer platforms were not able to participate.

Although the non-availability of APPC on non-mainframe platforms was a big blow to APPC being accepted as a client server protocol, one good thing about it is that the APPC verbs have been thoroughly tested for a number of years in the mainframe environment. The benefit is that APPC verbs have been proven to be industrial strength. More importantly, the extensive network monitoring facility of the mainframe is available for its operation.

To enable client server application, IBM must provide something that will allow program-to-program communication between mainframe and non-mainframe computers.

What is IBM's solution to the problem?

6.3.5   APPC for Non-Mainframes

APPC verbs for non-mainframe platform is the key to client server computing with mainframe. IBM has deployed a two-pronged approach: Physical Unit Type 2.1 (also known as PU2.1 or node type 2.1) and Advanced Peer-to-Peer Networking (APPN). In this section we will discuss PU2.1, and in the next, APPN.

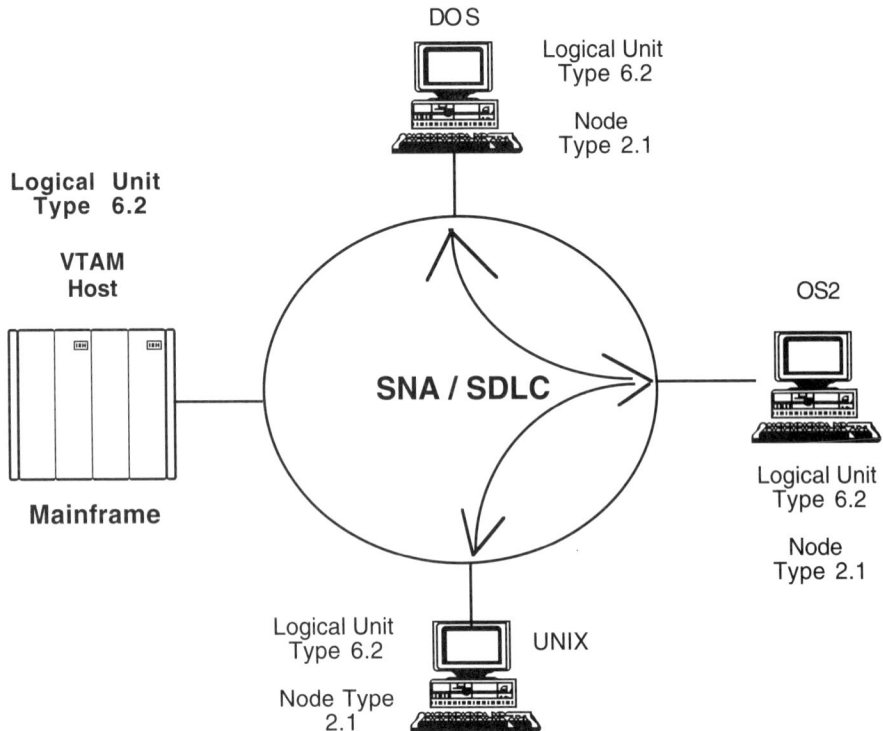

Figure 6–12. APPC based on VTAM/SDLC SNA

6.3.5.1 Low Entry Node, LEN

To enable network computing in the SNA/SDLC environment, IBM invented a new network node Type 2.1, also known as Physical Unit Type 2.1 (PU2.1), or the Low Entry Network Node (LEN).

Type 2.1 is different from the network node Type 2 cluster controllers (3274s), which are user configurable, but not programmable. Type 2.1 devices could be a personal computer, an AS400, or a RS6000. They must have the network Type 2.1 software as well as the Logical Unit Type 6.2 software designed exclusively for that OS environment.

A user program uses an LU6.2 socket to communicate with another program using an LU6.2 socket on another Type 2.1 device. These devices are connected via an SNA network that uses the SNA Data Flow and Transmission Control transport-network layers protocols.

6.3.5.2 APPC over Wide Area Network

When two Type 2.1 devices are separated by a wide area network, LU6.2 programs cannot directly communicate with one another without the help of a Type 4 (IBM 3745) communication controller or a VTAM host, which serves as a store-and-forward agent.

These two Type 2.1 devices must have IBM SDLC network cards. Both are secondary stations to the VTAM host, which will continuously poll them for activity.

6.3.5.3 APPC on Local Area Network

When two Type 2.1 devices are on the same segment of a local area network, no network transport layer protocol is needed because all data packets, being non-SDLC, are directly addressable within the same physical segment.

In this case, two LU6.2 programs can directly communicate with one another without the need for a store-and-forward agent such as the IBM 3745.

6.3.5.4 APPC on Non-IBM Platforms

The influence of IBM on other vendors' product directions is still evident in the evolution of the APPC verbs. Availability of APPC verbs on non-mainframe and non-IBM platforms has been steadily increasing after the introduction of the LEN.

For examples, third party APPC software such as Brixton Software is available for various UNIX platforms including Sun's Solaris, HP's UX, SCO's UNIX, and IBM's AIX 6000.

All major non-IBM computer manufacturers and third party software vendors now have LU6.2 products for non-IBM platforms since IBM has make the specification of LU6.2 a public domain. In fact, at one point in time, many industry experts sponsored LU6.2 as an OSI standard.

To obtain the latest list of non-IBM computer platforms that support LU6.2, readers who have access to CompuServe can join the "APPC Forum" there, or contact IBM directly.

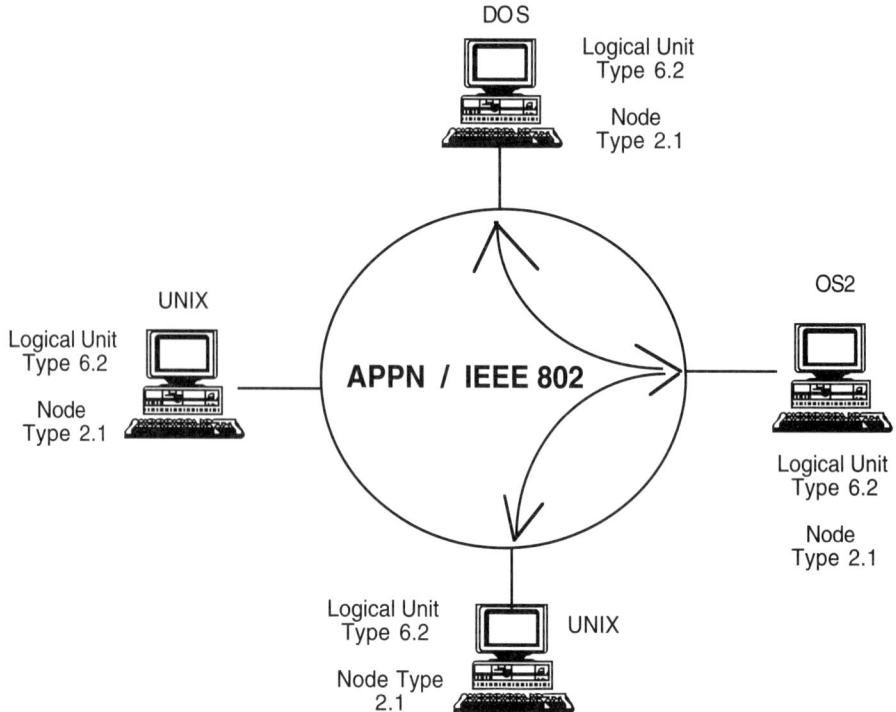

Figure 6–13. APPC based on APPN/LAN—VTAM host is NOT required

6.4 SNA's NEW TRANSPORT

Although the newly-created Node Type 2.1 enables client server application on non-mainframe computers, a VTAM host based SNA network would still be required for wide area network access.

This is obviously not acceptable because a growing number of IBM customers or non-IBM customers may not even have a mainframe in their shops. Does that mean that they have to look somewhere else for client server solutions? In order to participate more fully in the client server marketplace, and to ensure survival of its mainframe technology, IBM must replace or flatten SNA.

Outright replacement will not be acceptable to the existing customer base. The only sensible way for IBM to do is to gradually flatten SNA without jeopardizing billions of dollars of application investments by its customers. To flatten SNA, IBM must find another set of communication protocols for the transport, network, and datalink layers. By the late 1980s, the data link layer protocols were quite well defined and matured. For IBM to reinvent any new protocol is pointless. Besides, IMB's Token Ring protocol has already been widely recognized.

6.4.1 Advanced Peer-to-Peer Networking (APPN)

The same cannot be said of the transport network layers. Here IBM could have adopted other vendors' protocol or TCP/IP. Instead, IBM has decided to adopt the APPN protocol pioneered by AS400 as IBM's mainframe transport-network layer protocol that will co-exist with existing SNA VTAM.

6.4.1.1 APPN Nodes

APPN is a network and transport layer protocol similar to TCP/IP. As its name implies, it is a peer-to-peer transport protocol. Each networked computer can be directly connected to every other computer, or they can all connect through a single routing hub. All computers on an APPN network are called nodes.

APPN networks include three types of computers: low entry networking (LEN), which we described earlier, end nodes (ENs), and network nodes (NNs).

The LEN architecture allows computers in a hierachical SNA network to communicate with each other as peers. But as indicated previously, LEN nodes still need a pre-defined relationship with a VTAM host for network control purposes. LEN nodes do not have the ability to do APPN with others.

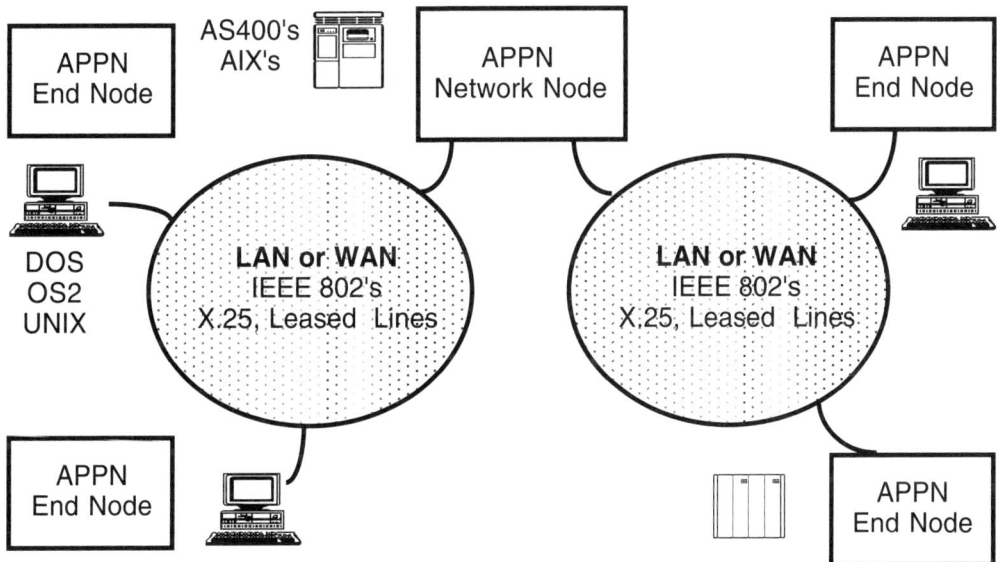

Figure 6–14. APPN Nodes

End Nodes

An APPN end node provides all of the functions of LEN nodes but also knows how to use the services offered by the APPN network. When an end node connects to an APPN network, they identify themselves, whereas a LEN node does not.

Also, at the start of an APPC application, the end node works with the APPN network to find the application's partner. This makes setting up a network using end nodes easier than with LEN nodes.

Network Nodes

An APPN network node provides all the functions of end nodes and adds two important services. First, network nodes work together to route information from one node to another. Network nodes providing this intermediate routing form the backbone of a network. The second service that network nodes provide is to assist LEN and end nodes in locating partner LUs in the network. By finding LUs directly, very little system definition is required at each node in the network.

6.4.2 VTAM and APPN

Things are also changing with the next two releases of VTAM. Now let us see how IBM proposes to allow VTAM and APPN to co-exist on the mainframe.

The answer lies in making changes to the mainframe VTAM. The trick is to put the mainframe directly on a local area network datalink protocol without going through the traditional SNA nodes, thus bypassing the need for SDLC, and then running the APPN transport protocol instead of the transmission control function of VTAM in the mainframe.

To make this happen, either a separate APPN should be run under MVS or VM, or VTAM should be modified to include APPN. The latter is the route that IBM has chosen. To merge VTAM and APPN, IBM has been modifying VTAM to allow a mainframe to take part in an APPN network.

6.4.2.1   VTAM Version 3.4

VTAM version 3.4 in 1991 allows devices such as an AS400 and a workstation on the APPN network full access to applications and resources of the VTAM mainframe. It also permits the use of the Type 4 communication controller's subarea backbone as the transport between two APPN sub-networks. In most other networks, this is done via a router or a bridge.

Using the SNA Type 4 communication controller such as the IBM 3745 as a bridge has the cost advantage of sharing the physical links with other SNA traffic.

Up until the VTAM version 3.4 making any change in the SNA network configuration for even simple things such as adding a new 3174 cluster controller has been very difficult. Every network device must be pre-defined in specific tables in VTAM and in NCP. The network had to be regularly shut down to refresh the new definitions.

VTAM version 3.4 permits addition to the network of intelligent workstations running APPC applications without requiring definitions to be added to VTAM or NCP as long as the workstation talks in APPN protocol. This "self-definition" enables a user to install a personal computer running the APPN, and use it to access host applications.

6.4.2.2 VTAM Version 4

IBM announced that VTAM version 4, when released, will evolve VTAM into a full APPN node instead of the current LEN (Low end network node) while maintaining the existing SNA hierarchical installed base.

While this APPN scenario has no parallel in the SNA architecture, it can be compared as though the mainframe would have to be changed from a Type 5 network node to a Type 2.1 network node in the SNA parlance. This gives the once mighty mainframe the same status on the network as a humble PC.

6.5   CLIENT SERVER WITH IBM's MVS

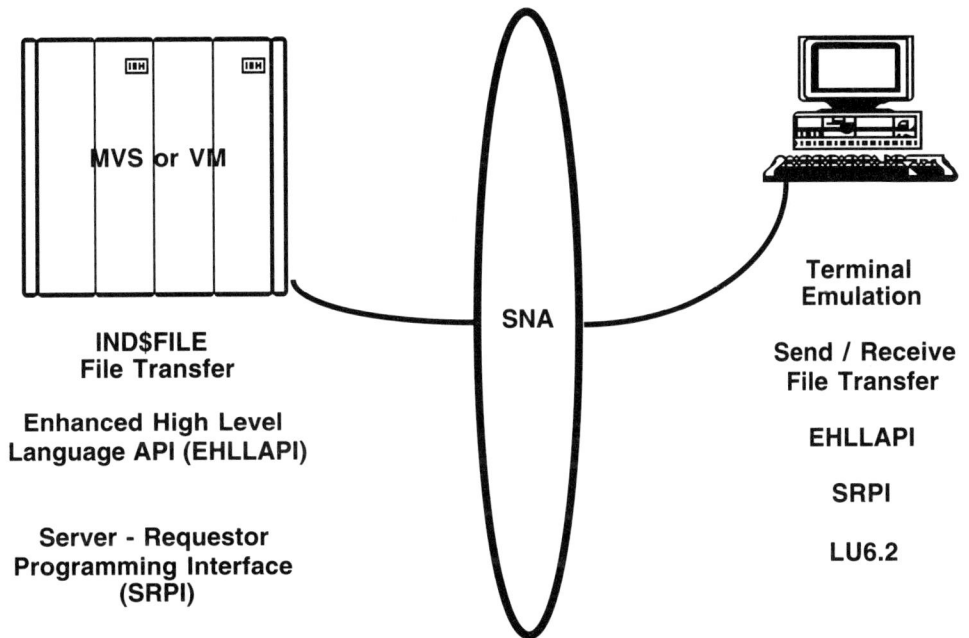

Figure 6–15. Workstation Mainframe Connectivity

Before APPC, IBM had provided three ways for program-to-program communication with the mainframe. All three are quite limiting and not as efficient as the APPC. Yet the industry has built many applications using them because they were the only tools available. Figure 6–15 shows the program modules:

- IND$FILE file transfer,
- Enhanced High Level Language API (EHALLAPI), and
- Server-Requester Programming Interface (SRPI).

They are the first generation of server interface and exported server interface that allow client server applications to be developed between a mainframe and

PCs. The server interface runs inside the mainframe while the exported server interface runs on the PCs.

6.5.1 IND$FILE

Using the PC as a dumb terminal is convient, but more benefits come from integrating the mainframe data with the workstation applications through file transfer and cooperative processing.

A large data base is best kept centralized in the mainframe. But for smaller files, providing the entire file or data base to the user is sometimes more cost effective, allowing the user to work with it on his or her workstation.

3270 emulators are like dumb terminals displaying data one screen at a time. The most one could do with a screen full of data is to cut and paste or to do dynamic data exchanges with other windows applications. A dumb terminal cannot store data or read from a file like a workstation can.

To solve this problem, IBM has created a batch program known as the IND$FILE file transfer program that cooperates with the 3270 terminal emulator on a workstation.

On the workstation side, the Send/Receive program is required. With this pair, files can be transferred back and forth between the mainframe and the workstation with an active 3270 session with the MVS/TSO or VM/CMS on-line monitor.

Electronic file transfer is like an electronic version of paper transfer. It does little in taking advantage of the processing power of the client server technology. On the other hand, information exchanges at the program level allow much finer control over the business processes and data. This is exactly what the next API will do.

6.5.2 EHLLAPI

Very often a file or a database is too big either for the network speed or for the size of the hard disk on a personal computer. A more flexible way should be available to facilitate workstation mainframe data exchanges.

For instance, if only three out of three million rows of data is needed, downloading the huge database to a workstation would be wasteful. A solution would be for the workstation to send a request to the data server on the mainframe where the extraction takes place. Then only three rows of data need to be actually downloaded to the workstation.

Enhanced Entry Level High Level Language Application Program Interface (EHLLAPI) is an IBM software product. EEHLLAPI lets the PC application appear to the host to be an operator at a 3270 terminal keyboard. Instead of an operator interacting with the host application, the application is doing so, using EEHLLAPI calls.

The application must determine what prompts are on the host screen, transmit data that makes appropriate responses to the prompts, look for a keyboard that indicates the host received the proper response, and extract the desired information and send it to the PC.

The application must also be able to anticipate host behavior. If, for example, the user misspells a keyword or specifies the wrong location, the application will not be able to find it. Thus the major challenge is to keep "in sync" with the host screens: knowing when the host is ready to receive keystrokes, and always knowing what screen the host is displaying. Many programmers call this type of server interface screen scrapper.

The normal way to perform this application is to search for an identifiable string using the Search Presentation Space function or the Search Field function of EEHLLAPI. Often the presence of the string does not ensure that the host screen has arrived in its entirety or that the presentation space is ready for input.

To find out whether the host screen is ready for input, the Wait function or the Pause function can be used. EEHLLAPI can be used with a number of programming languages including COBOL, BASIC, C, and PASCAL.

6.5.3 Server Requester Programming Interface (SRPI)

Server Requester Programming Interface (SRPI) is a more advanced programming interface than the EEHLLAPI. It is not screen driven. It requires writing the server program on the mainframe and the client program on the workstations.

A mainframe TSO session must be present for the client server program to work. It is not as widely adopted as the EEHLLAPI except in IBM's OS/2 environment.

OS/2 is not as widely adopted as DOS. For example, an option in the latest release of IBM's Application Systems (AS) in the mainframe MVS environment can interact cooperatively with the OS/2 version of the AS client programs.

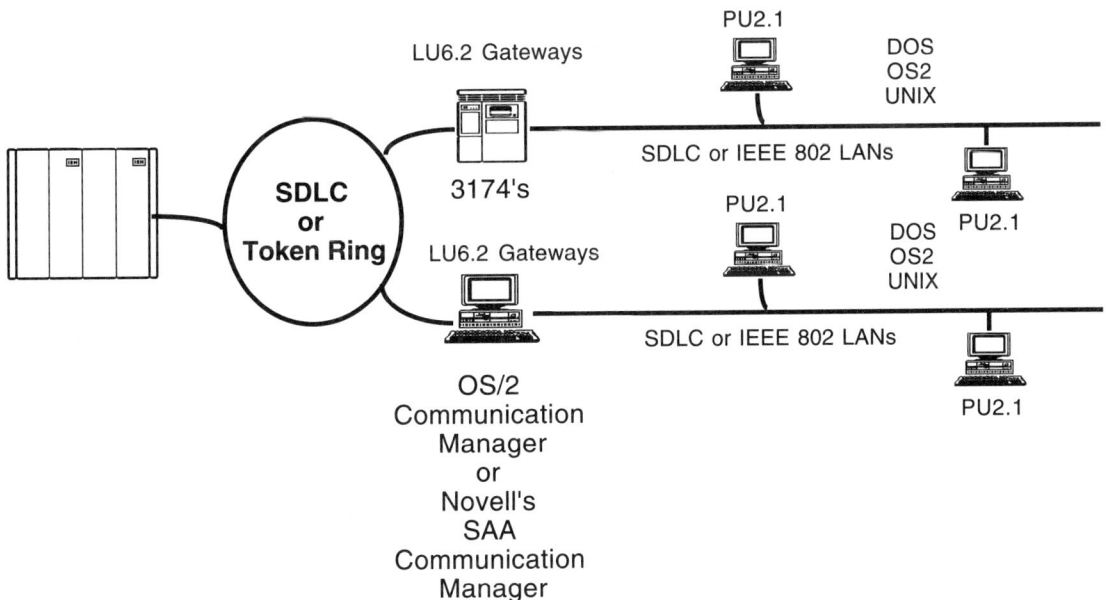

Figure 6–16. APPC gateway to mainframe

6.5.4 APPC for Workstation

In order to allow client server application to tap into the rich data banks on mainframe, APPC verbs must be made available to client applications running in the low end workstations such as DOS, Windows, and Macintosh. However, it would be hard to jam the functions of a Physical Unit 2.1 into them because of the memory requirement and other resource constraints.

An innovative way to get around this is to put a client stub into the low end workstation. This stub allows client applications in the workstation to invoke APPC verbs on a APPC server to which it is connected. The client application uses the APPC verbs as though they were located in the workstation whereas in fact they are executed by the server. The server in turn passes the client request to the mainframe as though a full PU2.1 program was making the request.

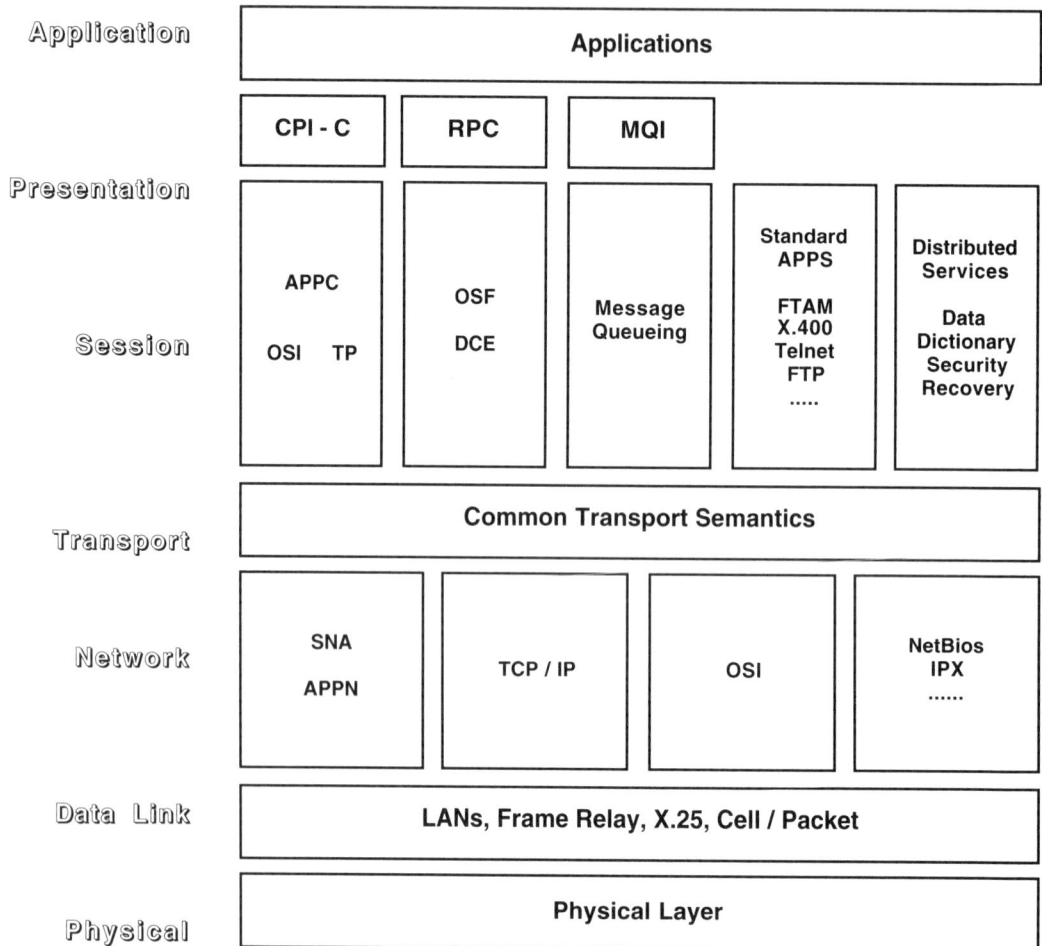

Figure 6–17. The IBM Networking Blueprint

Both Novell's Netware SAA communication controller and IBM's OS/2 Communication Manager provide this capability. The client workstation must have the necessary stubs. For example, IBM's software product for the DOS/Windows environment: Networking Services/DOS provides a full set of APPC verbs for client application development.

6.6 IBM'S NETWORK BLUEPRINT

In April 1992, IBM made public its future direction for network computing. True to IBM tradition, the announcement keeps the existing installed base compatible with future products.

Figure 6–17 is IBM's view of the main components of IBM's future network products.

This blueprint reveals a substantial change in IBM's product development philosophy. IBM has been the most integrated computer manufacturer. IBM sells only those products that are made by IBM.

However, this network blueprint says that IBM now accepts the existence of other network protocols and standards, and of a multi-vendor connectivity requirement.

IBM is designing the new system so that it can easily be part of other vendors' network, a step that previously was unheard of for IBM. The customers won.

6.6.1 IBM's New Network Operating System

IBM will support client server computing by providing two types of network operating system functions:

- Application Enabling Services, and
- Application Programming Interfaces (API).

The new Application Enabling Services are Messaging, Security, Directory, Transaction Processing, and Voice / Data.

The new application programming interfaces (API) for the new network operating system include a hodgepodge of old and new applications. In other words, IBM's product will allow network applications to be developed using any one of the following three categories of APIs. They are:

- APIs for the Common Programming Interface—Communication or CPIC which is an extension of the existing APPC verbs
- APIs for the Remote Procedure Call or RPC, which is an extension of the OSF's Distributed Computing Environment DCE
- APIs for the Message Queue Interface or MQI, which is a multiplatform extension of today's IMS/DC messaging capability on the mainframe.

6.6.1.1   Application Enabling Services

Like every network operating system, a minimal set of application services must be available for the developers. IBM's new network operating system is no different.

Messaging Services

IBM does not have a well-integrated messaging service. Instead, it has its own, as well as licensed products from others. The "home grown" ones include Profs, Office Vision, and DISOSS. All were eventually supposed to work seamlessly together under the banner of SAA.

IBM also supports non-IBM messaging services such as TCP/IP's Simple Mail Transfer Protocol (SMTP) and OSI's X.400. Bridges already exist between Profs, DISOSS, and X.400.

Security Services

IBM has and will continue to use the industry standard for cryptography known as Data Encryption Standard (DES) in most of its product. IBM will also support Kerberos, the industry standard security system. IBM believes that Kerberos will be implemented in SNA and OSI in addition to TCP/IP. Both DES, and Kerberos are now specified by the Open Software Foundation as part of the OSF standards.

Directory Services

Directory services locate and retrieve information about system resources on a network. IBM is committed to the OSI X.500 directory service standard.

Transaction Processing Services

Transaction processing is the online access to and update of shared data. Today, online monitors IMS/DC, and CICS are examples of host-based transaction processing environment. IBM labeled the support structure for distributed transaction processing as the Enterprise Transaction Management or ETM.

ETM allows the incorporation of an enterprise-wide framework based from which the best connectivity (multi-protocol), price performance (multi-vendor), availability, security, integrity, system management, application, and end user interfaces can be deployed.

At this point, ETM is a concept or a philosophy espoused by IBM. No software products have been announced in support of ETM. To quote IBM's announcement: "IBM will ensure that ETM considerations influence the evolution of transaction processing products on each of the platforms."

6.6.1.2 Application Programming Interfaces

In this strategy, IBM basically has all grounds covered. For those customers who are mainframe-centric, the client server application can be developed using the CPIC verbs. For those customers who are UNIX-oriented, IBM will support the use of DCE's Remote Procedure Calls.

Since a significant amount of the client server applications are event-driven and message based, IBM also provides the Message Queue Managers, which are supposed to be available on multiplatform.

CPI-C (APPC)

IBM now labels APPC as the Common Programming Interface for Communication (CPI-C). Unfortunately, IBM does not stop there. IBM penchant for product names have often led to unnecessary confusion.

IBM product names for APPC in the OS/2 environment as the Network Services/2, in the DOS/Windows environment as the Network Services/DOS, and in the AIX environment as the SNA Services.

The important point here, though, is that IBM's own brand of network computing environment will be based on APPC using the APPN transport protocol. VTAM will become a full APPN node, making it a peer participant on the network. In the meantime, VTAM will retain its previous incarnation of hierarchical SNA.

OSF's DCE

IBM has pledged to implement DCE on all the platforms including MVS, OS/2, AS400, and AIX. In effect, this is an alternative to the IBM's own brand of network computing, APPC.

Message Queue Interface (MQI)

In today's IBM's Information Management System Online Monitor IMS/DC, transaction messaging is available. Messaging is the transmission of data between applications via queues. The objective is to allow for the opening and closing of named queues, and for enqueueing and dequeueing messages to speed up the transaction rate. In essence, IBM is saying that the current IMS/DC function will be enhanced to work in environments other than the MVS environment.

The multiplatform product is known as Message Queue Manager (MQM), available in 1994. See Section 7.5.3 for more detailed description of this product.

6.6.2 IBM's New Network Transport Environment

IBM is evolving current subarea routing in VTAM to APPN. VTAM will continue to support host applications and will simultaneously support APPN. IBM will continue to enhance its existing supported transport protocols of TCP/IP, Net-BIOS, IPX, AppleTalk, and OSI.

6.6.2.1   Sub-Transport Protocols

In IBM terminology, sub-transport protocols refers to those between the network layer to the physical layer. In this layer, IBM is no longer solely dependent on its own SDLC and Type 4 communication controllers, which depend primarily upon leased line private networks.

Instead, IBM is embracing all the popular local area network protocols and public data network offerings such as frame relays, X.25, and ISDN.

While IBM is not yet a major player in LAN interconnections such as Wellfleet and 3Com, the IBM 6611 Network Processor is one IBM product that will provide bridging and routing for LAN interconnection.

7

Critical Network Servers

INTRODUCTION

Client server computing started when LANs were brought in to share two resources: files and printers. Now the push is to expand client server to all kinds of resources including the all important application data.

In this chapter, we review five types of servers that provide critical application services on a network: database server, transaction monitor, message server, electronic mail server, and directory server.

The success of a network operating system depends not upon the technical elegance of the network transport environment, but upon the availability of its application services to support the bread and butter commercial applications— accounting, order processing, payroll, process control, and the like.

Without industrial strength application services, network computing cannot be expected to take up the role as the new application delivery infrastructure.

7.1 RELATIONAL DATA SERVER

Choosing a data server is arguably the most important step in designing a network computing platform, since most commercial applications are dependent on some kind of data server.

The file server serves filing functions. It leaves the question of what to do with the content of the file up to the user application. In a data server, more functions are available to manipulate the data on behalf of a user application. These data management functions would otherwise have to be written by individual applications. For example, a data server will be able to respond to requests for names of employees with the last name Smith from the employee data base, whereas a file server will send you the complete employee file.

In this section, we will devote our discussion to the defacto standard data server for network computing: the relational database management systems, RDBMS. We will review the RDBMS characteristics that make it ideal for client server applications.

7.1.1   The Relational Advantages

Certain fundamental properties make the relational technology the premier choice for client server applications. They are:

- guaranteed data integrity
- simple mathematical foundation
- single data representation
- common data access language, SQL
- simple prototyping
- easy transition to objects

7.1.1.1   Terminology

First of all, we need to clarify and set some common ground on the terminology associated with RDBMS usage. They are tabulated as follow:

- A entity means a table with rows and columns.
- A tuple means a single record, or a row in a table.
- An attribute means a field in a record, or a column in a table.
- Atomicity refers to data elements in a table.
- A domain contains all the possible values for an attribute.
- The degree of an entity is the total number of attributes in it.
- The cardinality of an entity is the total number of tuples in it. Degree does not change with time. Cardinality does.

7.1.2   Data Integrity

An advantage to using entities to represent data is an RDBMS's ability to guarantee the correctness or the integrity of the data. One way to achieve integrity is through the concept of a key.

A key consists of one or more selected attributes whose values that are distinct for all rows in that entity. A key is required by the RDBMS to locate a row in an entity, which may have a number of unique keys.

The word key is analogous to a door key. In order to accurately access data stored in the entity, you must have the right combination of the entity attributes—the key. Without the key, the RDBMS will not be able to locate the exact row of data that the application would like to access.

Primary Keys

Every entity must have at least one key that is unique. This key is known as the primary key. Other keys that are unique for the same entity are known as the alternate keys.

Foreign Keys

A foreign key is an attribute combination of an entity whose values must agree with the primary key of another entity. A foreign key and a primary key should always share the same domain. The primary and the secondary keys are used to enforce the integrity of data in the tables.

Primary and foreign keys are features by which a RDBMS data integrity can be enforced.

7.1.2.1 Entity Integrity

At least two types of integrity checks are performed by an RDBMS. They are Entity Integrity and Referential Integrity. Entity integrity means that no attributes identified as part of a primary key can be null (i.e. empty). All entries in a primary key must have a value that is known. Null is an unknown identity. This means that no one will be able to locate that row in the table, which is not logical. The fact that a primary key cannot be null is a statement of the real world: We cannot have an unknown identity in a primary key.

When a user application tries to put a null in an attribute identified as the primary key, the RDBMS will raise an alert to the application.

7.1.2.2 Referential Integrity

Referential integrity means that the values of an attribute combination identified as a foreign key in an entity must equal the values of the same attribute combination identified as a primary key in another entity.

For example, the product name attribute is the primary key in the product master entity. Whereas in the sales entity, the product name attribute is identified as a foreign key. In a sales update, if the product name does not exist in the product entity, the sales transaction cannot be accepted because the product name in the sales entity is a foreign key. Something that has been taken out of the product master cannot be sold. As a result, the data integrity of the entity is protected.

7.1.3 Set Theory Foundation

Unlike earlier data management methodologies, the relational data management concept builds on a strong mathematical foundation. As a result, it has taken away much of the black magic and proprietary nature of the previous generations of hierarchical database management systems.

7.1.3.1   Dr. E.F. Codd

Discussing relational data model is not possible without mentioning Dr. E. F. Codd and his landmark 1970 paper titled: "A Relational Model of Data for Large Shared Data Banks." The basic theme of his paper is that the mathematically well known set theory can be applied to any data represented as sets. Codd proved that any fact can be extracted from a correctly designed relational database using logical expression instead of procedures. In other words, simple set operations such as intersections, unions, and others can be used to manipulate data to yield predictable results.

The fact that data, when represented as sets of tables, can be manipulated with mathematical clarity and certainty is a major revolution in computer programming. Before such revelation, each application has its own arbitrary way to manipulate its data based on a hierarchical or a networked relationship. As a result, different programmers may use vastly different models for an application.

7.1.3.2   Relational Operations

Codd also proposed that eight operations are needed to manipulate the tabular data. They are: Union, Intersection, Difference, Cartesian Product, Join, Divide, Select, and Projection. The first four are no different from the mathematical set operations. A useful aspect of relational databases is that any set operation on a table results in another table. Figure 7–1 shows the eight set operations.

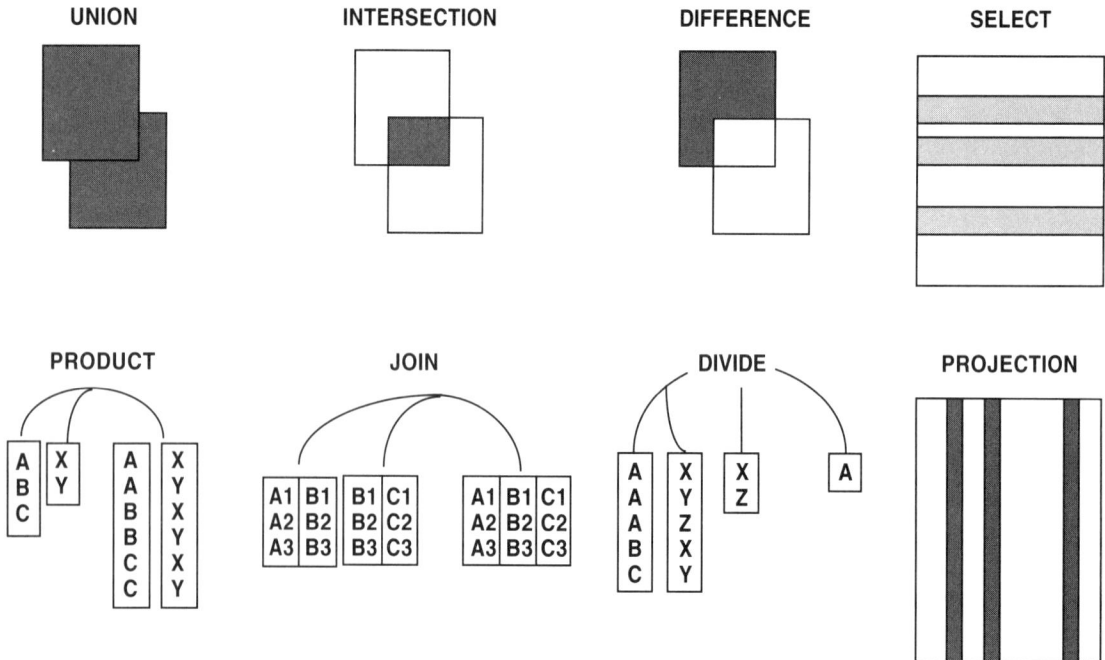

Figure 7–1. The eight basic relational operations

7.1.3.3 Tables

RDBMS uses a single format—tables—to represent application data. It greatly simplifies the number of operators required for data manipulation. There is only one operator required for each of the four basic manipulative functions: "retrieve," "change," "insert," and "delete."

Similarly, much fewer operators are required for other functions such as data definition, integrity controls, and security controls. For example, user security is administered not through flat file records, but through another table.

This single format, the table, is also applicable to the catalog data, which is data about data (metadata). There is no difference in operations on catalog data and user data. This makes the development of generic (metadata-driven) applications such as the data dictionary or repository a much easier task compared with a non-relational approach.

7.1.3.4 Metadata

Where the data values are kept, what system creates the data, and which systems can access the data are data about data or metadata. There are two types of metadata: logical and physical.

Examples of the logical metadata are entity type as in an employee or a customer, attributes as in the name of an employee or the type of customer, and entity relationships as in:

- An employee **works** in a department.
- A customer **places** an order.

Examples of physical metadata are data tables as in a DB2 table, elements in a data table, and the foreign key.

7.1.3.5 Data Dictionary

Data dictionary is a place where the metadata is stored. There are two types of data dictionary: active and passive. A passive dictionary acts as a catalog of information about the data but is not connected directly to the data in any physical way and is not used in the physical retrieval of the data.

The catalog in your neighborhood library is a passive dictionary. Users can use the catalog in a variety of ways, but someone has to get the books off the shelf. A passive dictionary does not need to be in the same medium or technology as the data it represents.

An active data dictionary plays a direct role in the retrieval of data. The dictionary must contain exact physical locations, of data that can be used by a retrieval program. An active dictionary must be in the same medium and in a technology that is the same as, or accessible by, the technology of the data it represents.

7.1.3.6 Repositories

The term "repository" is often used in conjunction with the term "data dictionary." A subtle distinction exists between a data dictionary and a repository.

A data dictionary deals with the metadata of data. A repository deals with the metadata of ALL aspects of an information environment, including data. The other aspects of information requirement are hardware, software, security, and people.

7.1.4 Structured Query Language (SQL)

Another advantage that RDBMS enjoys over other database management systems is an industry wide accepted data access language: Structured Query Language (SQL).

SQL was developed by IBM in the early 1970s along with its mainframe DB2 RDBMS. By the early 1980s, SQL was accepted as an industry standard.

However, SQL is still a weak standard because many "dialects" were implemented by vendors for marketing reasons. The ANSI SQL-86 and SQL-89 standards were behind commercial SQL products in terms of functions and features. As a result, ANSI SQL was viewed as the lowest common denominator by the vendors and is pretty useless for user application development.

SQL incompatibility posts a big problem in connecting different brands of RDBMS. Users cannot use the same SQL code with different brands of RDBMS and expect the same result. This issue is examined in more detail in the next two sections: SQL modes of operation and RDBMS interconnectivity.

All is not yet lost in the battle for SQL compatibility. The latest release of the ANSI SQL-92 standard has many features that are not available in many commercial products. Additionally, ANSI has indeed played the role of a standard-setting body rather than following the lead of commercial products.

7.1.4.1 4GL Productivity

SQL is known in the industry as a fourth-generation programming language, as opposed to C and COBOL which are regarded as third-generation programming languages. The difference lies in the level of data independence.

With SQL, the RDBMS removes the burden of locating data on physical storage from the users. RDBMS allows its users to concentrate on their data instead of worrying about the mechanics of getting the data. For example, a user does not have to worry about the length of an attribute when the program accesses the record.

This ability of users to deal at the set level greatly increases the productivity of the users of RDBMS compared with other types of database management systems.

For example, in the simple SQL query below, a user does not have to worry about the location of the table product_t, the format of the product data, and other columns of the table product_t. The RDBMS takes care of all that.

```
SELECT PRODUCT FROM PRODUCT_T
WHERE PRODUCT_CODE =  10
```

Even in situations where programming is required, the higher degree of data independence of a RDBMS means that a program is easier to write and requires less maintenance than it would in a non-relational system.

For example, one can imbed SQL query in a COBOL, PL/1, or C program, thereby reducing the amount of work that would have been spent in defining data types, in counting the text positions in a record, and so on.

Another saving is in user interface changes. Table changes do not automatically require corresponding changes in the user interface as would be in the case of non-relational database management systems.

7.1.4.2 SQL Front Ends

Because of the simplicity of relational operations, a large body of generic data access tools is available for the RDBMS. The fact that Structured Query Language (SQL) is now an industry standard increases the flurry of more user-friendly front ends.

A typical SQL Front End has some form of graphical user interface by which a user can navigate through the data tables in the RDBMS. A user who knows little or no SQL will be able to browse through the selected parts of the database and will be able to produce reports on the spot by pointing and clicking with the mouse. Examples of commercial SQL products are:

- Brio Tech's Data Prism
- Business Object's Business Objects
- Clear Access's ClearAccess
- Cognos' Impromptu
- Gupta's Quest
- Informix's Viewpoint
- Oracle's Data Browser
- Q+E's Database Editor

The front end tools have great impact on programmer's productivity. Functions that would have previously required a professional programmer to perform are now directly executable by the users.

7.1.4.3 Prototyping

The high degree of data independence of relational database also means that doing the entire application design all at once is no longer necessary. Prototyping an application with users is made easier with the RDBMS. By letting users participate fully in the design process, much re-working can be eliminated.

The overall application development process can be far less rigid than it used to be because of the simplicity of the relational operations, which makes design changes less costly than their non-relational counterparts.

7.1.4.4   Data Modeling

The relational technology also introduced a new method for application development known as data modeling. This modeling technique allows business data to be related to one another via tables. We review tables in more detail in Chapter Eight: A Network Of Objects.

7.1.5   SQL Modes of Operation

SQL by itself is a programming language. Like any other programming language, SQL code can be executed in a number of ways. In this section, we review SQL modes of execution in detail, as they are important in the heterogeneous RDBMS interconnectivity.

7.1.5.1   Parser, Optimizer, and Compiler

Inside every RDBMS are at least three components that deal with the transformation of SQL source code into machine executable code.

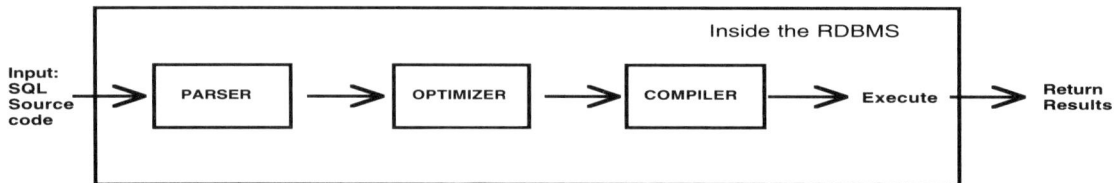

Figure 7–2. Parser, Optimizer, and Compiler Inside an RDMS

The first component is known as the Parser. Its main function is to parse the incoming SQL source code to ensure that the syntax and the semantic is correct. This includes validating identifiers for tables and columns, and checking access authority.

When everything is checked out, an Optimizer determines the best possible ways by which the RDBMS can "navigate" through the database to complete the request. Since a series of set operations can take place to arrive at the same resulting in many ways, the Optimizer will consider the database structure and performance statistics to decide on the best data access path.

Once the access data path within the RDBMS is determined, the Compiler will generate machine code that will perform the task following the specified optimum path.

Four Ways to Use SQL

Commercial RDBMSs are designed to process commands issued to them in SQL. Users or user applications pass SQL commands in text format to an RDBMS "engine." There they are processed and the results are passed back to the caller.

There are four modes of SQL usage. The first two modes, Online SQL and

Database Resident SQL Procedures deal with "pure" SQL commands. The second two modes, Embedded SQL and Call Level Interface (CLI) SQL deal with using the SQL languages along with another host programming language in a program.

7.1.5.2 Online Dynamic SQL

The first mode of SQL execution is known as online SQL. It is done through an online interactive facility in which users' SQL commands can be typed in text and directed towards the RDBMS.

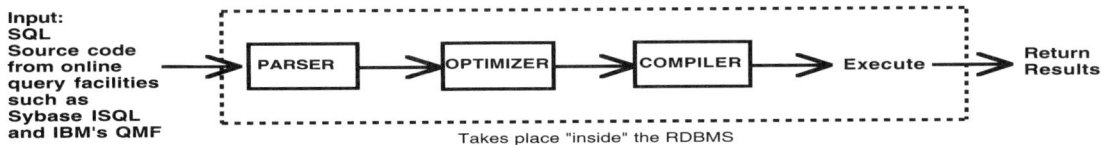

Figure 7–3. Online Ad Hoc SQL Execution

Upon receipt of the SQL text string, the RDBMS immediately parses, optimizes, compiles, and executes the user request. The result is then sent back to the user. This mode of execution is also known as Dynamic SQL.

Examples of this type of environment are online query management systems such as IBM's QMF Query Management Facilities, and Sybase ISQL Interactive SQL. Users typically type their SQL commands on a screen and ask that the commands be executed by the RDBMS. The results are returned to the user's screen.

7.1.5.3 Database Resident SQL

For those data activities (extract or update) that are frequently needed by users, programmers often pre-compile the SQL commands and store the compiled executable code as database-resident procedures.

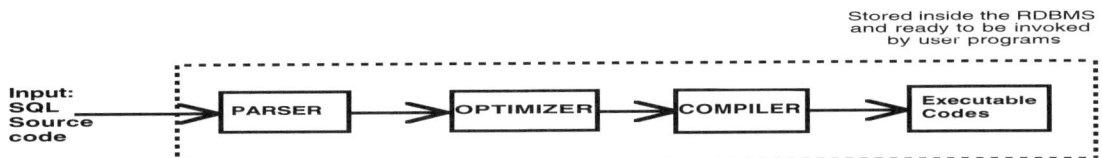

Figure 7–4. SQL Stored Procedures

For example, a company has a corporate policy on deleting a customer from the customer master: The customer's outstanding balance must be cleared, otherwise the supervisor in charge must be informed. Although a number of situations may lead to a customer deletion, all must follow the same process.

The set of SQL commands required to enforce the above policy can be pre-compiled. But it must not be tied to a single application. It should be tied to the customer master data table. Any application wanting to use this SQL procedure can simply invoke the procedure name "delete_customer." Recompiling for each execution is not necessary, as the SQLs are permanently bound to the database.

The action is shown in Figure 7–4. The advantage of database-resident stored procedures is the avoidance of parsing, optimizing, and compiling every time the same request is made. This means better use of computer hardware resources as well as much better performance (response time) to user requests.

7.1.5.4 Embedded Static SQL

In many ways, RDBMS is like an external device to an application. The application asks the RDBMS to do something. The RDBMS goes away and does it. The results are then fed back to the main application. What happens inside an RDBMS is strictly between the RDBMS and the SQL statements.

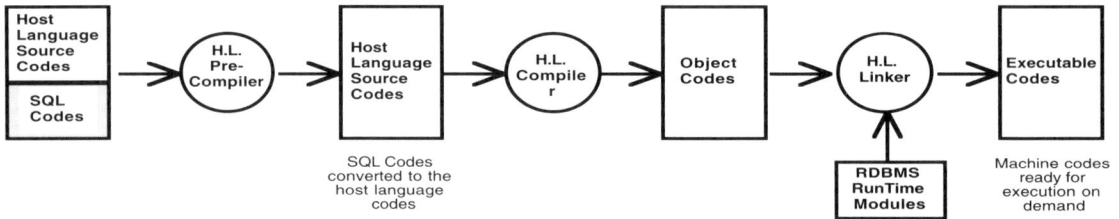

Figure 7–5. Embedded SQL or Static SQL: SQL used along with a host programming language

SQL requests deals only with data managed by an RDBMS. This alone will not satisfy all data processing needs, however. For example, finding the square root of a number, or optimizing linear programming algebraic matrices, are not functions that the SQL programming language can handle efficiently, if at all.

Therefore, SQL commands are often used along with a host programming language such as COBOL, PL/I, and C to deliver the appropriate application functions.

"Embedded" or "Static SQL" refers to SQL statements that are incorporated into programs written in another programming language such as COBOL or C. As shown in Figure 7–5, these statements are prepared in advance of execution. Compilers or interpreters for the other programming language usually do not understand SQL. The SQL statements are embedded into the source program between the standard delimiters "EXEC SQL" and "END SQL."

Before the program can be compiled or executed, a pre-compiler is used to locate the embedded SQL statements and expand them into commands and function calls written in the host programming language. The resulting programs are usually compiled and linked with special libraries of SQL functions that perform the actual database processing.

The advantage of using embedded SQL is that the SQL commands required to perform database processing are much more concise and easier to write and understand than the equivalent host language (such as COBOL and C) commands generated when the code goes through the pre-compiler.

Another advantage is that embedded SQL is more efficient on computer machine cycles. However, the executable program also assumes that there is a "connection" to a RDBMS, which may not be always true in the case of a distributed data and processing environment.

7.1.5.5 Call Level Dynamic SQL

Another way to connect an application to an RDBMS is through the Call Level Interface (CLI). In this mode of operation, an RDBMS is like an independent server. It has an address. This server may be residing in the same computer or in a separate computer.

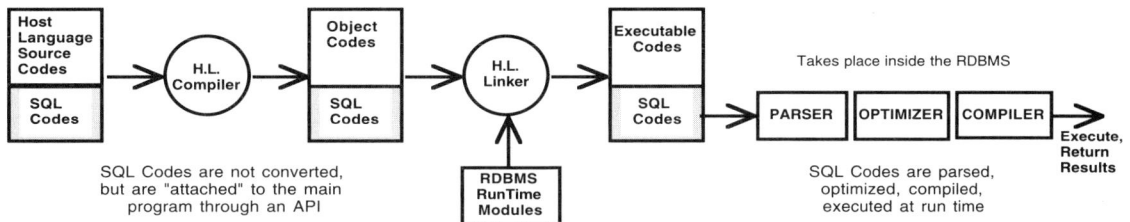

Figure 7–6. Call Level Interface or Dynamic SQL: SQL used along with a host programming language

The call level interface is a set of subroutine calls with which a main line program can use to connect itself to the RDBMS. Once connected, the main line program can pass the SQL commands to the RDBMS in text mode. The main line program may wait or go on to other tasks until it is interrupted by the RDBMS call level interface. Eventually the RDBMS returns the results to the main line program via the call level interface.

For example, a C program contains a set of SQL statements somewhere in the middle of its flow. Instead of pre-compiling the statement, they are served to the RDBMS during the program execution. The C program initiates the connection to RDBMS. Upon successful connection, the whole set of SQL statements is served to the RDBMS, which proceeds to compile them in a process similar to the one described in the last paragraph.

This method of compiling SQL statements is known as Dynamic SQL or late binding, as opposed to the in the Static SQL early binding approach, which was illustrated in the last section.

The advantage of late binding is flexibility. The parameters of the SQL statements could be changed during the program execution, for example, in an application in which the number of customers to be searched is dependent upon variables which are known only after mid-way into the program execution.

The main disadvantage of late binding is inefficiency. It uses up more machine cycles than the pre-compiled option. For example, when a particular set of SQL statements seldom changes, but the statements are required to be executed quite often, it is far better to have the statements pre-compiled instead of compiling them again and again for each execution.

Another disadvantage of this approach is the incompatibility of the call level APIs among the RDBMS vendors. This means that when you write a C program in which SQL statements are included, you must compile your program with the necessary library supplied by a particular brand of RDBMS.

This compiled code will not work with any other brands of RDBMS unless and until the source code is recompiled with the new call level APIs from the new RDBMS vendor. We discuss this in more detail in the section on RDBMS incompatibility.

7.2   RDBMS CONNECTIVITY

In many user organizations, different types of database management systems are used in their application portfolio. With re-engineered business processes, these previously disconnected islands must now start "talking" to one another.

In fact, a key benefit of client server technology is its capability to connect different application islands at the procedure level as opposed to the file transfer level. We discuss this aspect of client server technology in more detail in Chapter Eight.

In this section, we restrict our discussion to the challenges surrounding connectivity between different brands of relational database management systems. This is an important issue because RDBMS is the database technology in the 1990s, and "open architecture" means that management systems must be able to accommodate different brands of RDBMSs.

This requirement is indeed an extension of network computing inter-connectivity imperative for the lower communication layers that is discussed above. This is simply a higher level of interconnectivity.

7.2.1   The Three Barriers

Although a SQL program that is good for one brand of RDBMS should be good for other RDBMS, the situation is not quite that "black and white" in a heterogeneous RDBMS environment.

A client program typically contains all the SQL code for updating or browsing data tables in a RDBMS. The challenge is: how to enable a client program to access multiple brands of RDBMS on the network using the same SQL code. At least three hurdles must be overcome.

- **The Delivery Problem:** The SQL code must be "mechanically" delivered to the destination data server.
- **The SQL Problem:** The execution of the same SQL statements may elicit very different responses from different brands of RDBMS
- **The Call Level Problem:** The calling sequences to the destination data server must be compatible. Each RDBMS is a complicated machine. Its operation (initialize, connect, disconnect, . . .) requires a

complex sequence of commands. These commands are obviously very different among different brands of RDBMSs.

7.2.1.1 The Delivery Problem/Solution

The delivery problem can be overcome by adopting the same server protocol (i.e. the session layer) for both the client and the server. This means a NetBIOS client talks to a NetBIOS server a Netware client to a Netware server, a named-pipe client to a named-pipe server, an APPC client to an APPC server, a NCS client to a NCS server, and so on.

Even though an RDBMS can run in DOS, MVS, and UNIX, and through network transports of TCP/IP, and SPX/IPX, the RDBMS must be attached to compatible server interface (presentation layer) and server protocol (session layer) in various machines for them to "interoperate."

If a client workstation is not equipped with the Named Pipe server protocol, then users would not be able to access a Named Pipe data base server such as Microsoft's SQL Servers. Similarly, the same SQL Server configured to run as a Netware NLM data server cannot accept a client workstation equipped with Named Pipe server protocol because only the Netware Core Protocol equipped workstation can access this SQL Server.

7.2.1.2 The SQL Problem/Solution

Every vendor's implementation of SQL is unique. These SQL dialects are not compatible with one another although they may look the same. The same set of SQL code may elicit different results from different brands of RDBMS.

Looking at the procedural languages such as FORTRAN and COBOL, the portability of these codes are not universally guaranteed despite many years of standardization efforts. Different computers have different hardware structures that require modifications to the source code (though usually small) in order for the code to work properly.

The same can be said about SQL. Each RDBMS vendor has a slightly different implementation of its SQL compiler or interpreter for historical, technical, hardware, and marketing reasons. Today, the challenge is for application programmers to write their SQL code as server-neutral. This means simple SQLs. Programmers must avoid using complex SQL code such as "Group By. . . . Having." Simple SQL statements that will likely be interpreted the same by all brands of RDBMS should always be used.

Another obvious way to get around this problem is to standardize on a single RDBMS vendor. Users should avoid complicating their computing environment with multiple RDBMS vendors, if possible.

7.2.1.3 The Call Level Problem/Solutions

The third barrier to RDBMS interconnectivity is the call level problem. To understand the call level problem, one must understand how SQL commands work inside an RDBMS. Readers should refer to the subsection on dynamic SQL in the previous section.

The call level APIs link the non-SQL part of a user program to the SQL part. When a COBOL code segment has completed a task and is ready to invoke the RDBMS for services, it uses an RDBMS call level API to "open" the RDBMS. After a successful open, the user program sends the SQL code (in text mode) as though the code were dynamically typed in from an online facility.

The results of the RDBMS execution of the SQL code are returned to the user program as part of the call level APIs. Typically these APIs are a "behind-the-scene" activity involving dynamic linking between the user's C code and the RDBMS.

Although each data server vendor will supply its own call level APIs for various compiler environments, the API has the disadvantage that it only works with its own brand of RDBMS but not with others. The three basic approaches to solve this call level problem are:

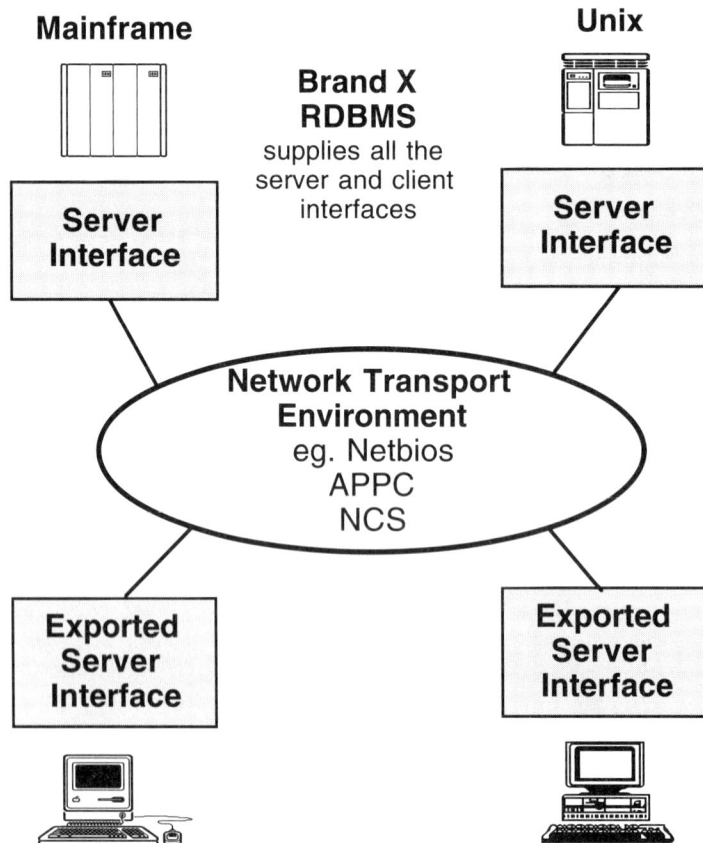

Figure 7-7. Single RDBMS vendor supporting multiple platforms

- Use of the same brand of RDBMS
- Use of the "middleware" APIs
- Use of database gateway

All three approaches are reviewed in the following sections.

Single RDBMS

One obvious way to bypass the call level problem is for a user organization to adopt a RDBMS from a single vendor whose products are available on multiple hardware platforms.

This means that multiple client environments can access the same brand of RDBMS on different hardware platforms. When something does not work, a user has a better chance of getting resolution from a single vendor. Many RDBMS vendors such as Oracle, Sybase, Ingres, Gupta, and Progress have ported their SQL engines to multiple machine types (UNIX, OS/2, Netware, MVS, VM, VMS), and multiple network transports (TCP/IP, IPX, DecNet, AppleTalk).

With this approach, the call level APIs are of the same brand, even though the underlying SQL engine of each platform is as proprietary as the vendor wants to make it. Application development and training costs can be drastically reduced. Users should avoid complicating their computing environment with multiple RDBMS vendors, if possible.

7.2.2 Middleware APIs

When multiple brands of RDBMS on the network are necessary, the help of "middleware" is required. Middleware consists of the software modules that lie somewhere between the application and the network transport layers.

Whenever a user application is ready to update or to query a RDBMS, it must first provide the details of the target RDBMS. Such details include the name of the target server, its network address, its activation sequence, and so on. Middleware APIs are those "calling" APIs that can be inserted in the middle of a C or COBOL program. These APIs allow the user program to control and direct its SQL requests to the target RDBMS.

Although the actual syntax to invoke these control functions is different for different brands of RDBMS, they all use similar commands to open the database, close the database, commit the transaction, and so on.

A middleware software vendor will provide you with a set of generic call APIs. It takes on the task of translating these calls into their brand specific equivalent. If an application requires access to two different brands of RDBMS, and if both brands support the same set of call level APIs, then the programmer needs only to specify the names of the target RDBMS using the same API call.

These APIs shield the application programmers from the need to learn the complexity of the calling sequence of individual brands of RDBMS as well as the network transport layers. They are better off concentrating on coding application functions while leaving the open, close, send, and receive processes between their program and the RDBMS completely to the middleware APIs.

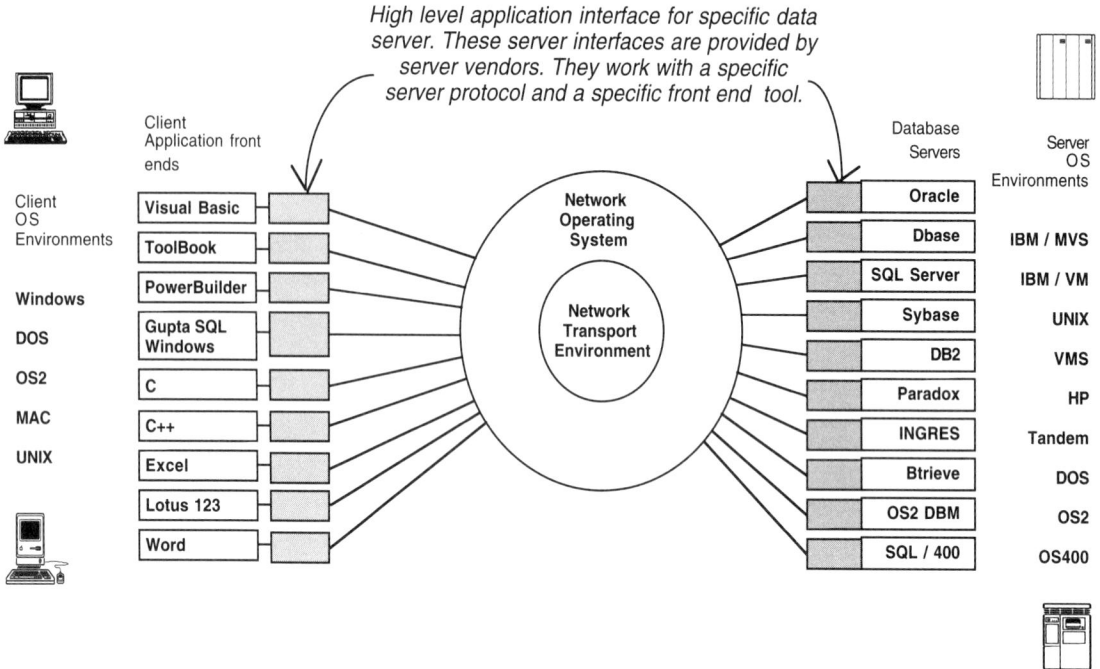

Figure 7–8. The problem to be solved by Middleware

The advantage of this approach is that users only need to learn one set of APIs. The disadvantage of this approach is that users will be dependent upon the middleware vendor for support on target RDBMS. If the programmer has written all his or her applications to a middleware vendor's API, and the programmer's customer wants to switch to an unsupported RDBMS, then the programmer must re-code all the applications to meet the programmer's customer's needs. Figure 7–9 shows these APIs can be located in quite a number of ways.

7.2.2.1 Middleware Commercial Products

Many middleware software products are available in the market today. Once again, major RDBMS vendors have come up with their own sets of APIs. They all would like others to adopt their own set of call level APIs as standard. As of this writing, no single vendor clearly stands out above the rest. The following is a partial list of RDBMS products:

- Apple's Data Access Language (DAL)
- Oracle's GLUE
- Sybase's DB-Library
- IBM's Distributed Relational Database Architecture (DRDA)
- ISO's Remote Database Architecture (RDA)
- Borland's Integrated Database Application Programming Interface (IDAPI)

- SQL Access Group, is an organization that aims to develop standards for interoperable SQL servers using ANSI SQL and ISO Remote Database Architecture (RDA) as a base.

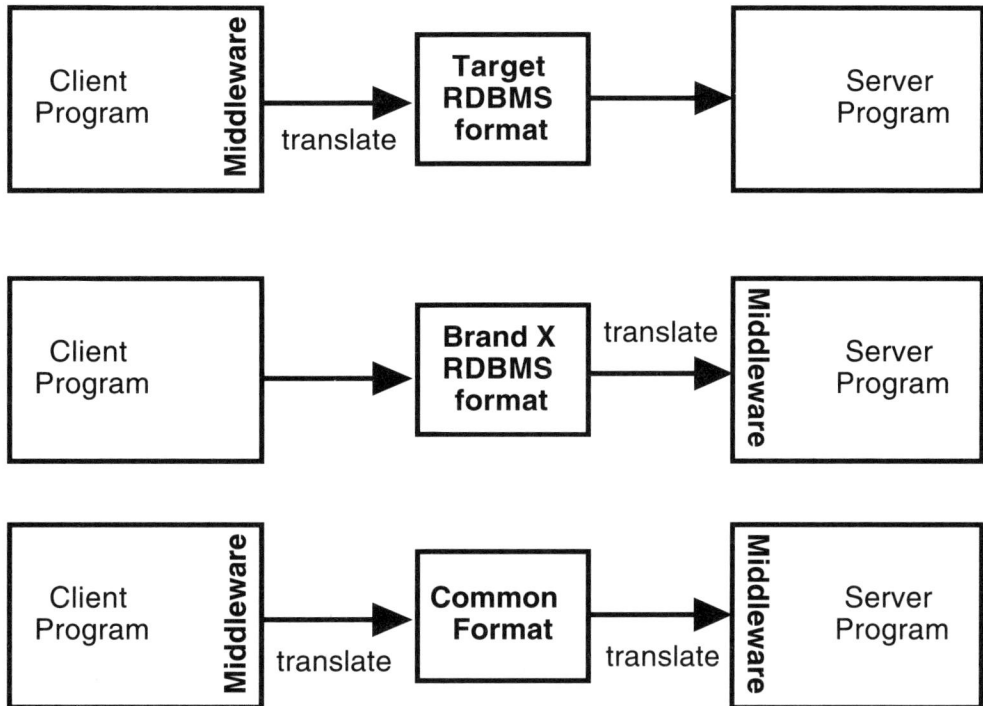

Figure 7–9. Potential locations of middleware

7.2.2.2 Open Database Connectivity (ODBC)

Perhaps the most talked about middleware standard is Microsoft's Open Database Connectivity (ODBC) API set. The product that contains the API set is known as the ODBC Driver Manager. ODBC Driver Manager is available on Windows and Windows NT platforms. Given the Windows-dominant market position as a client workstation, all major RDBMS vendors have already declared their support of ODBC.

As shown in Figure 7–10, the RDBMS vendor must supply the ODBC driver for its own brand of RDBMS. These ODBC drivers sit on the "outboard" side of the ODBC Driver Manager. User programs make calls to the APIs of the ODBC Driver Manager on the "inboard" side.

In theory, the ODBC Driver Manager acts like a switch. For example, if the user's incoming call is directed at a Oracle database server, then ODBC Driver Manager will simply direct the request to the Oracle's ODBC Driver, which translates the request to a call to the standard Oracle Call Interface.

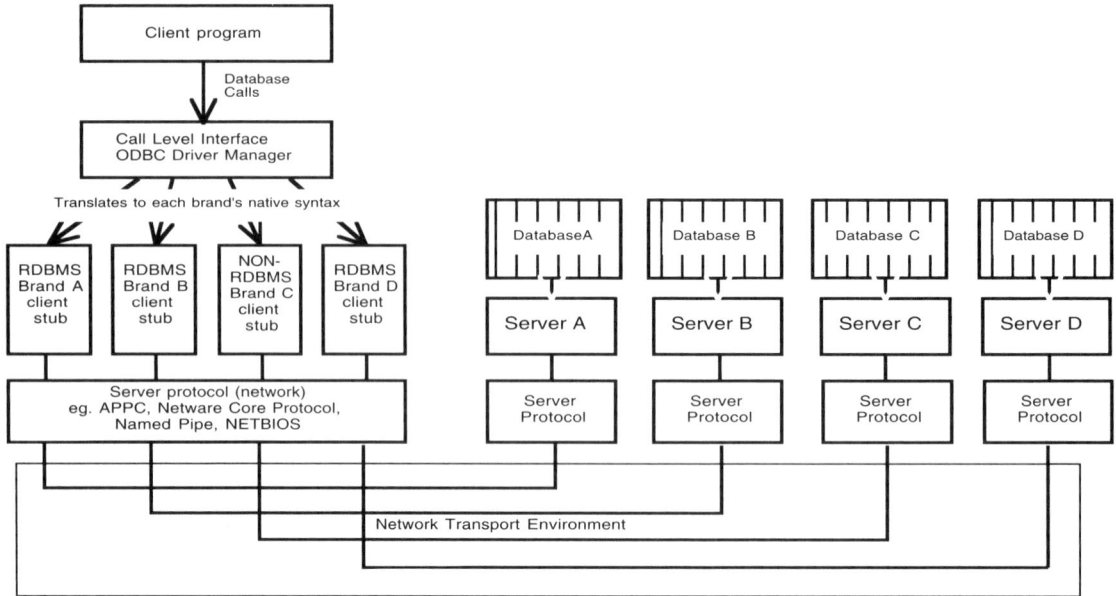

Figure 7–10. ODBC Driver Manager: A client side translator

7.2.3 Database Gateways

Another way to connect a client workstation to a host RDBMS such as IBM's
DB2 is via a third agent known as data gateway.

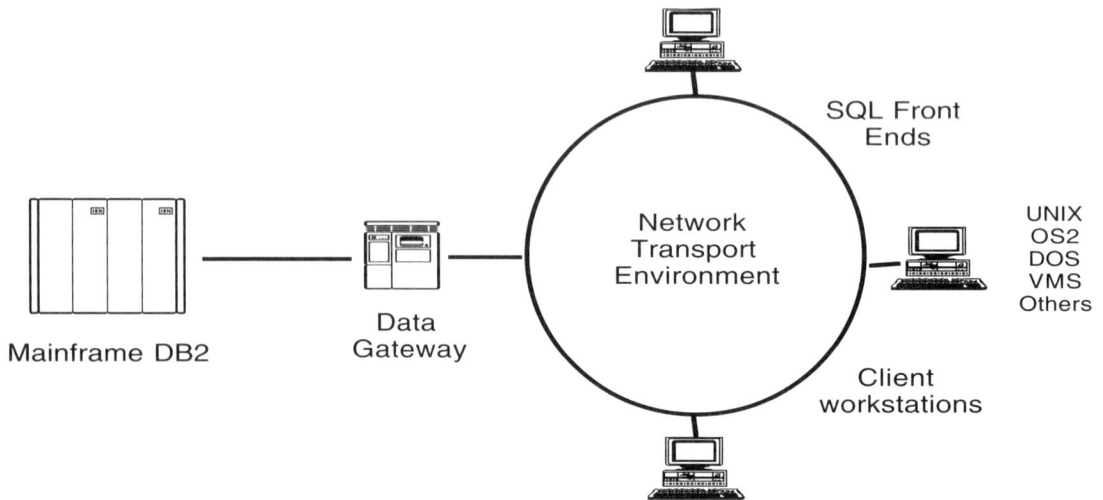

Figure 7–11. Database Gateways

A client program in a workstation is ready to update the mainframe RDBMS, DB2. The call level API intercepts this request and sends it from the workstation to the gateway. The gateway then translates such a request into a format compatible with the DB2 environment and sends the translated request to DB2 for execution.

Typically, the middleware vendor such as Micro Decisionware Inc. (MDI Gateway) sells three components to make this type of setup work properly. The first is the client stub in each of the workstations. The second is the database gateway itself, which typically runs on a personal computer. The third component, typically the most expensive one, is a server module on the mainframe.

7.3 RDBMS APPLICATIONS

This section discusses a new application architecture that is made possible by certain unique features of the RDBMS technology.

7.3.1 Components of An Application

A major advantage of the RDBMS technology is its ability to enforce data integrity according to the business rules, and to do it inside the database management system. This makes client server application development more efficient on a RDBMS than traditional data base management system.

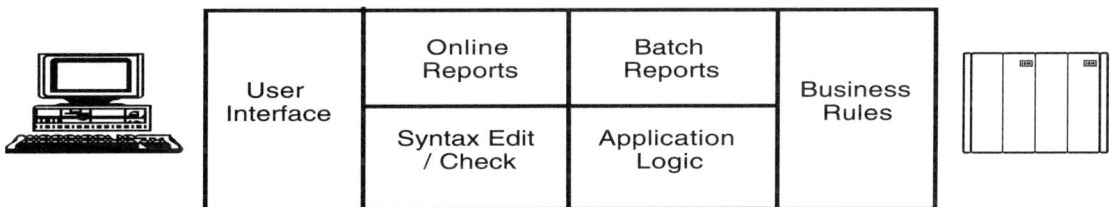

Figure 7–12. Typical components of an application

Figure 7–12 shows the components of a typical commercial application. Traditionally, an application development team spends a lot of time coding the business rules and syntax edits that are either company-wide or have been done by previous applications. They are simply re-coding, perhaps for the tenth times, what have already been done by others.

Other items in an application are various reports. As stated earlier, in today's market users have a wide-ranging choice of SQL Front End tools to extract data from a RDBMS. Even if some of these tools are too sophisticated for end users, they represent a substantial productivity gain for programmers.

If we could magically take away those duplicated business rules, the reporting efforts, the project team could deal with the real project-specific application logic. Tremendous productivity gains are made at this point.

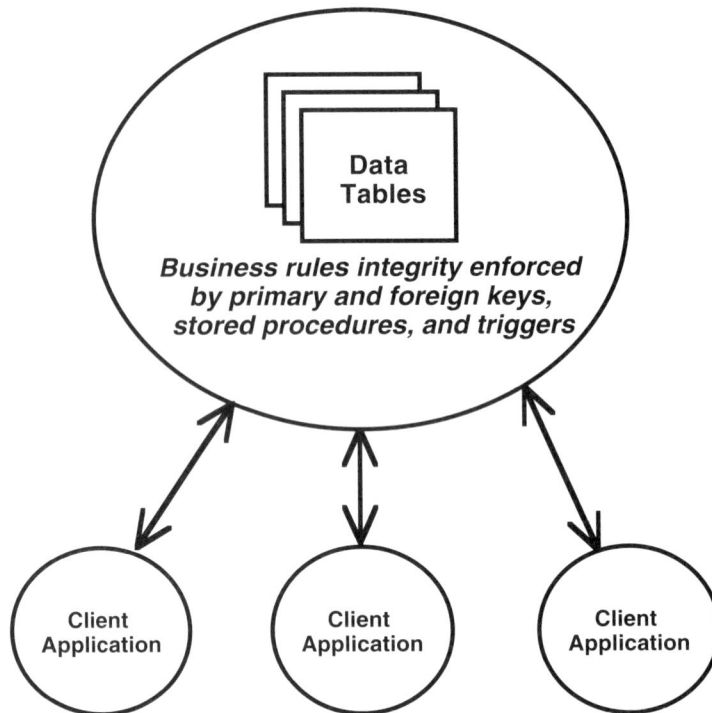

Figure 7–13. Centralized control with distributed functions

The ability to embed complicated rules to be triggered by events is a fundamental behavior of a software object. Although true object-oriented database management systems are still in their infancy and may take a number of years to mature, for now, RDBMS is the closest technology we have to use in the transition to a fully object-oriented environment. This is the topic of next section is how to implement database resident controls in a RDBMS.

7.3.2 Business Rules Enforcement

In every organization, administrative activities are governed by certain rules, without which there would be chaos.

7.3.2.1 Business Rules

What are business rules? Here are some examples:

- A checking account can be protected against overdraft only by a credit card account owned by the same customer.
- The shipping destination of an order with more than ten line items cannot be changed.

- All sales agreements for a given customer must have unique effective dates.
- The customer making a credit card application must have placed an order previously.

7.3.2.2 Types of Enforcement

In the past, business rules were enforced manually. This gave rise to the so-called "white collar" work force in the commercial world.

When computerization of commercial processes started in the 1960s, departmental business rules were encoded into computer applications to replace manual methods. Typically, this meant writing COBOL or PL/1 code to implement them against some kind of database. With this approach, unless the application makes a point of providing programming interfaces for others, its data tables should not be used by other applications since there is no data integrity control on them.

With the arrival of the RDBMS technology, a third method by which these business rules can be enforced became available. This method uses the special features available in RDBMS to implement database resident business rules enforcement. These special features are primary key, foreign keys, triggers, and stored procedures.

When a database server is embedded with stored procedures, it becomes the closest thing to a pure software object, which is defined as an entity that possess both data and functions. Instead of embedding the business rules as part of an application, the database can now be open to many other data-sharing applications. Any client application can access the data confidently because "someone" is always ensuring the data integrity in that database.

7.3.2.3 Foreign Keys

Primary and foreign keys are the declarative integrity rules that are part of the SQL Data Definition Language (DDL). The following is an example of the DDL usage.

There are three data tables: the SUPPLIER table, the PART table, and the SHIPMENT table. The primary key in the SUPPLIER table is the SUPPLIER_NO. The primary key in the PART table is the PART_NO. Both primary keys are referenced by two foreign keys in the third table: SHIPMENT.

In the notation used below, the arrow points from a foreign key to a primary key. The SUPPLIER table and the PART table are called the target tables. The supplier_PART table is called the referencing table.

Target Table	Referencing Table	Target Table
contains	contains	contains
primary key	foreign keys	primary key
SUPPLIER<———	SHIPMENT———>	PART

The following statements show how to create the third table SHIPMENT using SQL's Data Definition Language. Data Definition for the entity SHIPMENT.

```
CREATE TABLE SHIPMENT
(
QTY INTEGER, SUPPLIER_NO CHAR (5) NOT NULL,
PART_NO CHAR(8) NOT NULL,
PRIMARY KEY (SUPPLIER_NO, PART_NO),
FOREIGN KEY (SUPPLIER_NO)
REFERENCES SUPPLIER ON DELETE CASCADE,
FOREIGN KEY (PART_NO)
REFERENCES PART ON DELETE RESTRICT
)
```

"On Delete" Clauses

FOREIGN KEY (SUPPLIER_NO) REFERENCES SUPPLIER ON DELETE CASCADE means that if a delete is carried out on a SUPPLIER_NO in the target table SUPPLIER, then delete all matching SUPPLIER_NO records in the referencing table SHIPMENT.

By deleting an entry in a master table, all records with the matching entry in all other referencing tables (with the same foreign key) will also be deleted. This is a powerful feature for many application situations.

For example, when a person dies, all his or her driver's licenses should be deleted. By deleting the license at one place, the delete will be cascaded to all other referencing tables. As a result, when one views the drivers licenses table, one always can be assured that all the entries in that table refer to living people.

FOREIGN KEY (PART_NO) REFERENCES PART ON DELETE RESTRICT means that if a delete is to be carried out on a PART_NO in the target table PART, it must first check to see if a matching PART_NO is listed on the referenced table SHIPMENT. If the entry is found, then the PART_NO cannot be deleted (RESTRICT) from the target table PART.

For most RDBMS, "ON DELETE RESTRICT" is assumed if nothing is specified in the declaration of the foreign key. This means that records with matching keys cannot be deleted from the target table. This is indeed a powerful feature. For example, an employee number in the employee master table cannot be deleted if the same employee number exists in any other employee-related data table. The number can only be deleted when all records referencing that employee in all other data tables are deleted. This function is the opposite of ON DELETE CASCADE.

7.3.2.4   Trigger

A more sophisticated way to enforce complex data integrity is through the "Triggers." This RDBMS feature allows the execution of a custom SQL program upon pre-specified condition of the database status. The trigger could be activated before or after:

an insertion of an additional record

an update of an existing record

a deletion of an existing record

Typically, such conditions apply to the whole table. However, in the Oracle RDBMS implementation, the Trigger condition can be applied to the whole data table or to a specific row of the table. For example, in a customer data table, a trigger can be written to activate when a new entry (an insert) is to be created. Before the customer is added, the SQL program in the trigger must be executed.

One triggering scenario may be like this: The program will create the same new entry for other tables only if the same customer does not have a bankruptcy record.

7.3.2.5 Stored Procedure

Stored procedure is, at the time of this writing, a special feature of the Sybase SQL Server. Although the activation of a stored procedure can be triggered by database activities (update, insert, and delete), it can also be invoked directly by client programs as remote procedure calls.

A stored procedure is a server-resident program. It consists of pre-compiled program modules with an API through which client programs interact.

7.4 TRANSACTION SERVER

The concept of transaction management is very important in database applications in the host computing environment. It is equally if not more important in a network computing environment. Transaction management is arguably the weakest link in today's (circa 1994) client server technology. However, commercial products are now beginning to fill the void.

7.4.1 Transactions and Units of Work

A transaction is a "unit of work" performed by a single program in which "calls" are made to one or more databases, files, directory, or other servers. The unit of work is the smallest complete unit and cannot be half completed. This means that the transaction program must execute in its entirety or not at all.

The reason is to protect data stored in the servers from being corrupted by a program that is half completed. The program failure may be due to: hard disk failures, power outages, network malfunctions, program logic, and so on.

7.4.1.1 Commit and Rollback

Any industrial strength server must have the capability to "roll back" or to "recover" its database to the state prior to the execution of a failed transaction. Whatever was changed by the partially executed transaction must be restored to its original value.

In RDBMS, the SQL commands, COMMIT and ROLLBACK, allow an application to specify the termination for a transaction. The application determines when and if the current transaction is committed or aborted. By issuing either a COMMIT or ROLLBACK statement at the proper point in the application logic, the application terminates the current transaction.

If any failure occurs prior to the "commit" statement, the RDBMS database should not contain any changes made to it by a partially completed transaction program. This type of data integrity problem is not acceptable for mission-critical applications.

An overwhelming majority of today's application transactions take place against a single RDBMS. On a one-to-one client server exchange, individual servers protect themselves against being corrupted by user programs using the "rollback" feature.

7.4.2   Distributed Units of Work

More and more situations are beginning to arise where a transaction program may involve multiple sub-transactions, and these sub-transactions must take place in physically separated servers on a network such as RDBMS, file managers, directories, and application servers for performance or ownership reasons.

7.4.2.1   Two Phase Commit

The concept of a complete transaction still applies in a distributed environment. This time, a transaction program is considered to be successfully executed when all sub-transactions have been completed.

If one sub-transaction fails to complete while other sub-transactions have completed, the completed sub-transactions may have altered part of the database. This would leave the database to exist in a state that may not represent any "true life" situation. Therefore, when a transaction program requests the services of multiple numbers of servers, a final commit can only be issued when all sub-transaction commits have been successful. This two-step confirmation is known as a two-phase commit.

An Example

For example, let us say the network servers are a number of network-connected RDBMSs. What happens when a unit of work (A) consists of multiple sub-units of work (X,Y,Z) to be done separately by the RDBMS? See Figure 7–14.

By definition, a unit of work (A) must be completed or not carried out at all. This means that if any one of the units of work (X,Y,Z) cannot be completed for whatever reason, all units of work must be canceled, and all RDBMSs must be rolled back or recovered to their initial state. A transaction is required to ensure that all units or work are cancelled. Since the completion of a unit of work takes two phases, this type of transaction is known as two-phase commit transaction.

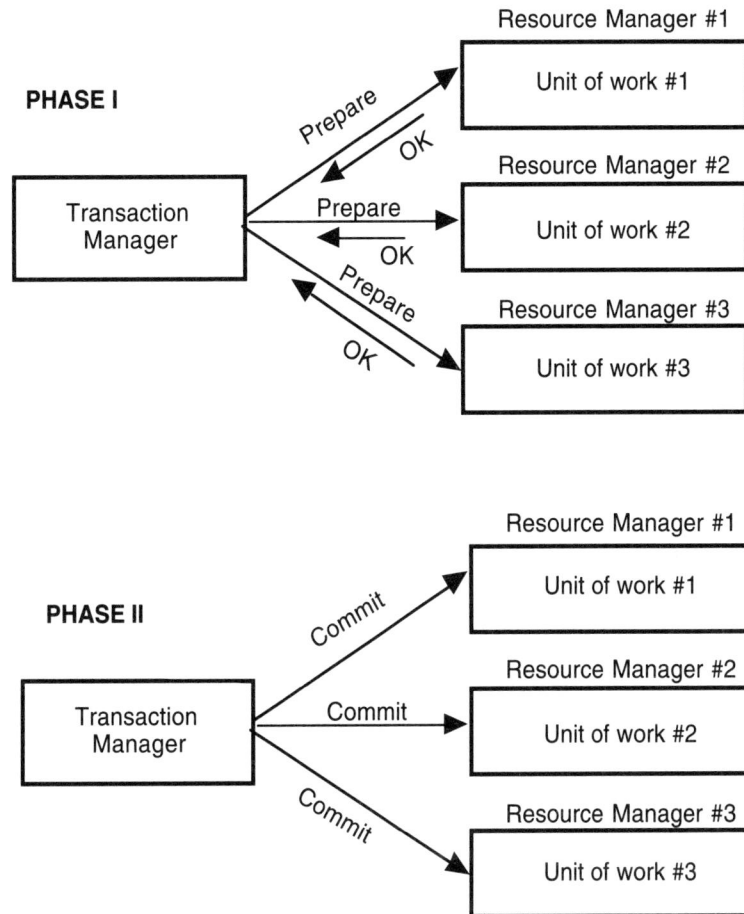

Figure 7–14. Two Phase Commit

Although a two-phase commit transaction may take place inside the same RDBMS, in this context, we are considering only the more generic cases where the transactions take place across physically separated RDBMS.

Another point worth noting is that the two phase commit may take place across multiple brands of RDBMS. The challenge here is to design an overseer of all these sub-transactions to ensure their successful completion prior to declaring the successful completion of the transaction program. This overseer is known as the transaction manager.

7.4.3 Transaction Manager

In the previous paragraph, we mention that a transaction manager watches over the completion of all the sub-units of work before committing a transaction. Briefly, the duties of a transaction monitor are:

- During Phase I, the monitor asks each RDBMS to prepare to commit and waits for responses. If each RDBMS votes OK, then Phase II commences and the transaction monitor tells all RDBMSs to commit.
- After the prepare to commit, if one of the RDBMS failed or timed out, then the transaction monitor instructs all the participants to abort in Phase II.

7.4.3.1 IBM's CICS

The most successful commercial transaction manager is IBM's Customer Information Control System (CICS). It is used by almost every IBM mainframe computer.

Over the years, CICS has developed a very rich set of functions. CICS guarantees that any data sources including databases or files that have been defined to CICS will be "recovered" to its original state if a CICS transaction program failed to complete for whatever reason.

CICS was originally designed as a teleprocessing (TP) monitor responsible for performing the rollback functions on behalf of user applications for IBM's mainframe database management systems. Over the years, however, CICS has also become a mainframe-to-mainframe transaction monitor responsible for accepting transaction requests from one mainframe application to another over IBM's SNA network.

Unfortunately, CICS is viewed by many as a mainframe tool, and the client server world has never paid too much attention to it. CICS would have been a natural transaction monitor for client server exchanges if it had not been so tied to the mainframe.

The new IBM strategy is to make CICS available on multiple platforms. As of 1994, CICS was available in many non-mainframe platforms including UNIX, OS/2, AS400, and others. Also, IBM is aggressively making CICS relevant to many C programmers in the client server world by providing C interfaces to CICS.

7.4.3.2 X/Open Transaction Manager

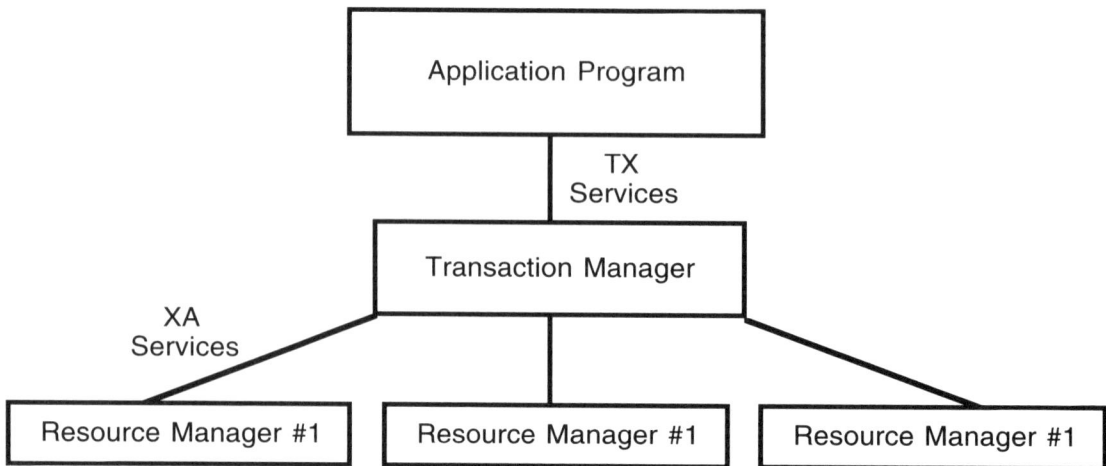

Figure 7–15. X/Open Transaction Manager

As shown in Figure 7–15, the X/Open DTP model consists of three components: application program, a resource manager, and a transaction manager.

As with CICS, the user application tells the transaction manager when a global transaction begins. The application program proceeds to call various resources managers (e.g. RDBMSs or File Managers) to perform the desired units of work. When the application transaction program determines (from its perspective) that the transaction is completed, it tells the transaction manager to complete the transaction across various resource managers using the "commit" or "rollback" commands.

Transarc's Encina

OSF's Distributed Computing Environment has adopted Transarc's Encina as its distributed transaction manager. In a way, Encina is UNIX's answer to IBM's CICS.

The Encina conforms to the X/Open Distributed Transaction Processing model and will coordinate transactions with any database or data storage product that supports the X/Open XA interface. Encina provides basic scheduling and load balancing, location and definition of servers being managed, configuration, and runtime definition and control. It monitors active clients, server availability, and server load. It also coordinates start-up and shutdown.

Database vendors can use the Encina transaction management services to build a recoverable database or a recoverable queue service. Encina Server provides logging that will enable the databases, managed by the Encina transaction manager, to be rolled back to their original state in the event that a transaction fails.

Encina allows two-phase commit transactions based on the DCE's Remote Procedure Call (RPC). All interfaces for the Encina products are provided in the C programming language. This allows workstations on a network to communicate as peers over TCP/IP. It supports IBM's CPIC interface, which has been adopted by X/Open for peer-to-peer communication.

7.4.4 Dates Rules on Distributed Computing

Although the architecture of distributed computing is a cornerstone of the client server technology, unfortunately, many improvements are still needed to "bulletproof" the ability to manage distributed transactions.

In 1993, Sybase released its System 10 which has features that help to break some of the barriers in distributed technology. For example, the replication server represents an excellent breakthrough in two-phase commit technology.

C.J. Dates, a pioneer in relational database technology, has laid out twelve characteristics of an ideal distributed computing environment. His twelve rules have been widely quoted. They represent a kind of "holy grail" for distributed computing database environment. Obviously, the ideal has not been achieved.

Each site in a distributed system must be able to continue local operations as though the distributed system did not exist.

This non-dependency reduces the vulnerability of the distributed system to disruption caused by an individual site.

Changes at a particular site, including adding or removing the site completely, should not affect any distributed applications that do not depend on data at the affected site.

Location independence allows users, programmers, and applications not to need to know the physical locations of data.

An enterprise user's view of a distributed relation will not be influenced by the actual structure of the underlying local tables. This allows a department to reorganize its local data independently of the enterprise-wide system.

The system must support data replication between sites without affecting application logic or requiring users to know where the data is located. Replication is important because it can improve performance and availability of systems by allowing local access to data that is "owned" by a remote site.

A distributed query system must support full access to enterprise data resources from any location in the enterprise.

A transaction management system for a distributed data environment must support multiple transaction processing simultaneously, without interference, and each transaction must be an all or nothing proposition. This means that a transaction must complete of fail as a single unit of work. In some literature this requirement is known as 2-phase commit.

Computing hardware independence.

Operating system independence.

Network independence.

DBMS independence.

7.5   MESSAGE SERVER

The previous section described one type of application in which useful results are delivered by transaction programs. Commercial transaction programs have a short execution time, varying from sub-second to a few seconds. An example is an automatic bank teller machine transaction. You do not want your customer to stand in front of an ATM for minutes before getting a response.

7.5.1   Message Based Applications

There is another important type of application in which useful results are achieved by message exchanges between two application islands also known as application servers or application objects.

Typically this type of transaction requires a much less stringent time constraint ranging from minutes to days. One example is a furniture warehouse application in which the turnaround time to ship the furniture ordered by a customer is typically a few days rather than a few seconds. Because electronic mail was the first popular message based application, many people call this type of application as e-mail-enabled application.

7.5.1.1 Application Objects

Figure 7–16 shows mainframe or mini computer application islands in a large organization. Each island has its own application program and database. They are application objects.

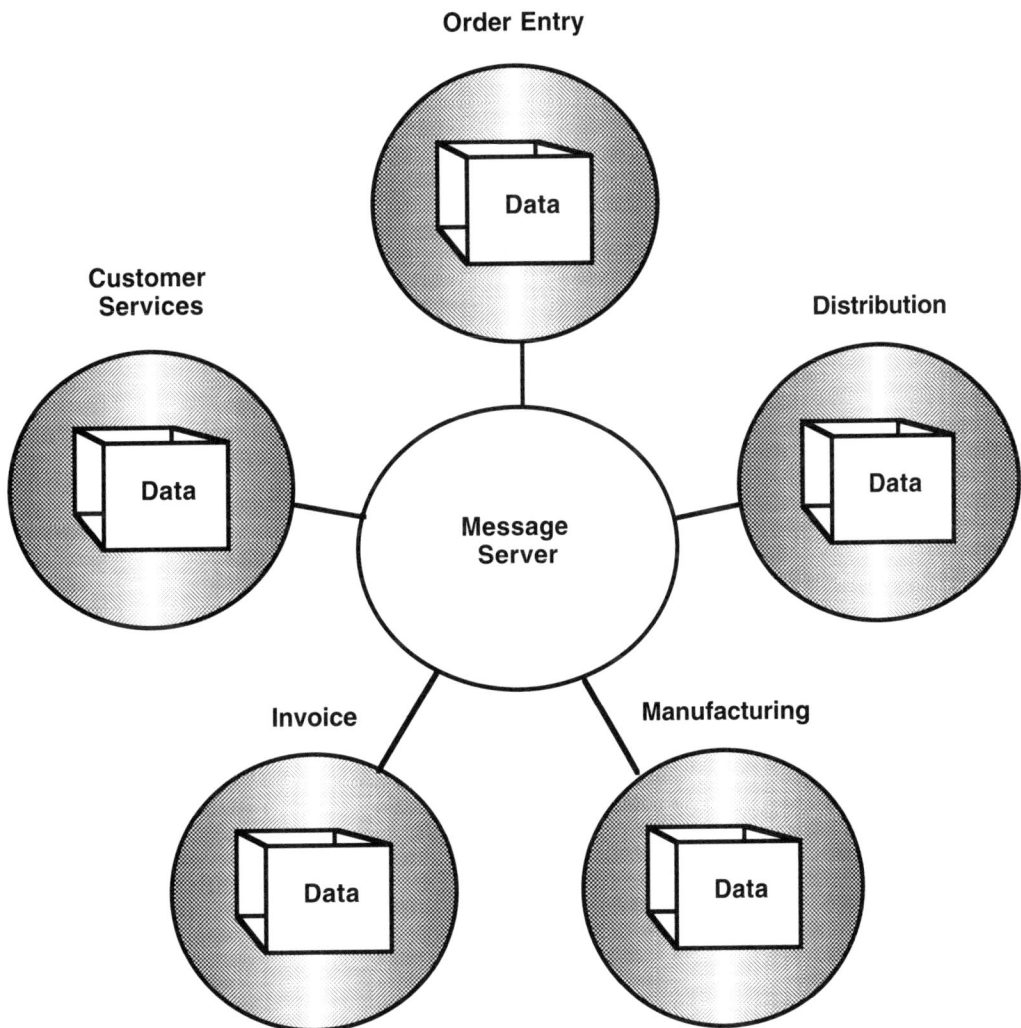

Figure 7–16. Application islands connected by a message server

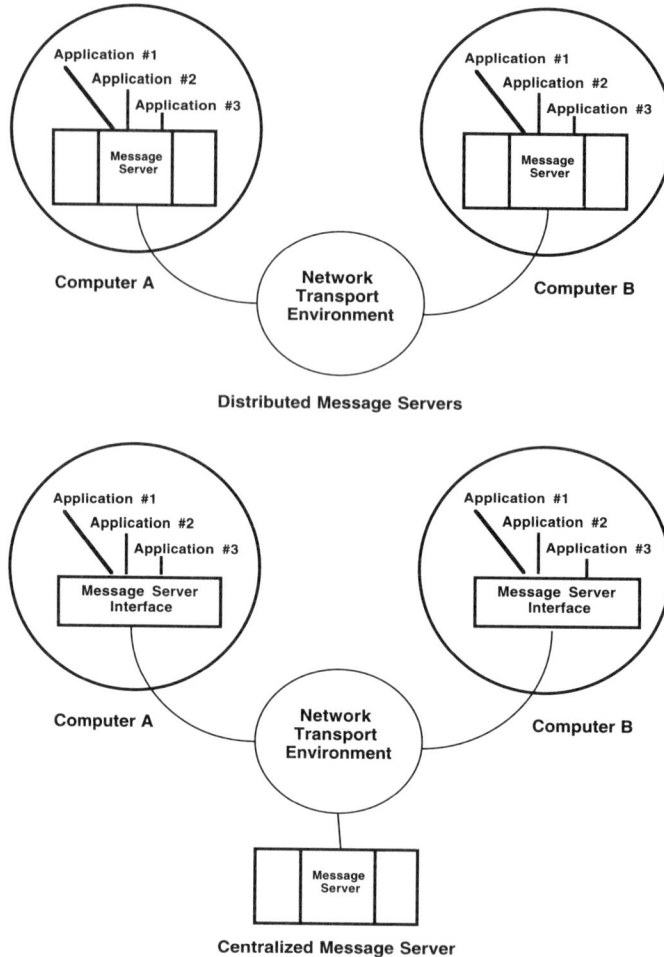

Figure 7-17. Two types of message servers

In our new business paradigm, these islands can also be business partners, suppliers, customers, and government agencies. These application objects are no longer isolated, but they communicate with each other using the services of a message server on the network. Units of work are performed by individual application objects in response to the requests from their neighboring objects.

Application islands are like the old divisions of an organization. Despite much computerization within their specific business areas, these divisions still communicate with one another using letters or memos.

With network computing, these application islands can now communicate effectively through the message server. As a result, much of the non-value adding administrative processes have become obsolete. Indeed, message based applications play a key role in many of business process re-engineering efforts in many large companies in North America.

7.5.2 Message Queues

A message server is a store-and-forward agent. Like all store-and-forward agents, message server uses queues to perform its duties. The queues in a message server are like a temporary holding tank to regulate and to protect the message traffic between application objects.

Once again, guaranteed delivery is the most critical feature of a message server. It will never lose any user message that it was asked to handle. This guaranteed delivery feature of a message server is as important as the guaranteed data integrity feature of a transaction manager described in the last section.

7.5.2.1 Distributed vs. Centralized

Message servers may exist as independent servers on the network accepting requests from application objects. The message queues are maintained within the message server. In this case, the message server communicates with all application objects on the network.

However, a message server may also be distributed and dedicated to a particular application object. Its message queue is dedicated to the services of that specific application object. In this architecture, every application object has its own message server with its own message queue. Application message exchanges through their respective message servers.

7.5.3 Commercial Products

Although electronic mail has been around for a few years, message based applications are just beginning to get the recognition that they deserve.

7.5.3.1 E-mail Message Servers

Most commercial message servers have been built for the purpose of one type of message based application—the electronic mail. The e-mail message servers are known as Message Transfer Agents (MTA).

Typically, users do not directly deal with a message server. Their programs invoke the message server services through a set of popular e-mail application programming interfaces, such as the X.400 API (XAPIA), and Microsoft's Mail API (MAPI). These APIs do not necessarily tie to just one message server because builders of the messaging engine can decide to support any e-mail API that they choose. The APIs and the messaging engine are not necessarily produced by the same vendor.

These are described in more detail in the next section on electronic mail servers.

7.5.3.2 IBM's Message Queue Manager

In the IBM's networking blueprint, the message server, which IBM calls the Message Queue Manager, is an important building block in client server computing.

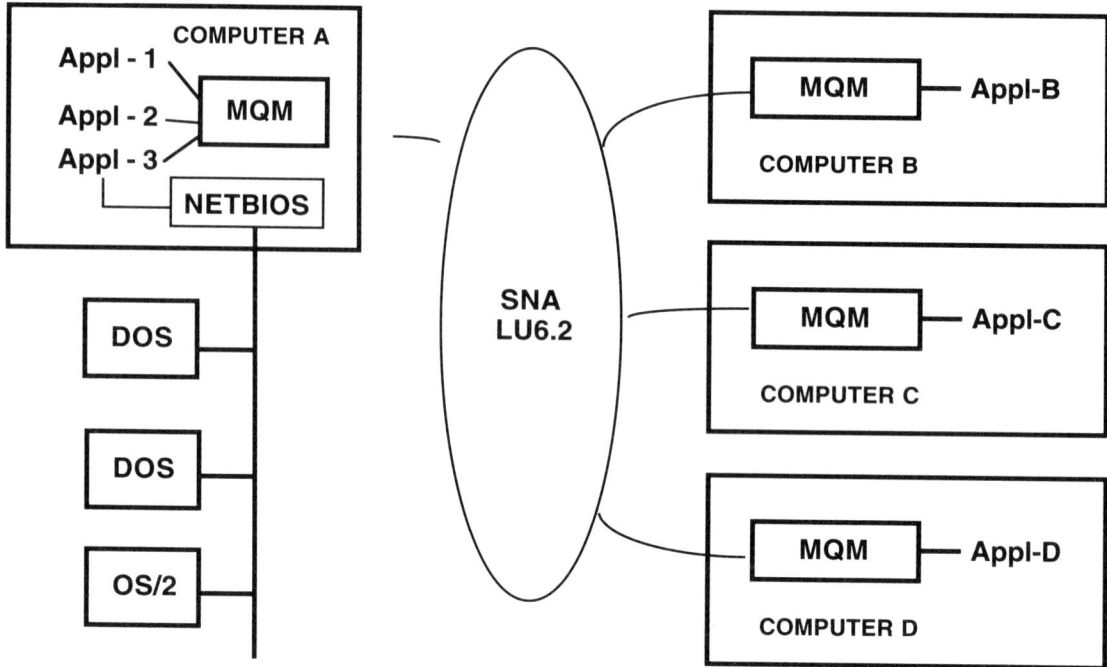

Figure 7–18. IBM's Message Queue Manager

The functions of MQM and its interface MQI can be implemented on IBM and non-IBM platforms. The current arrangement is that IBM will implement all mainframe (MVS and VM) versions of Message Queue Managers (MQMs), and another US company known as ezBridge Transact is responsible for all other platforms, which will include Digital's VMS, RS6000's AIX, AS400's OS/400, Tandem's Non-Stop, Stratus's System 88, and IBM's OS/2. The non-mainframe products will be available in 4th QTR 93.

As shown in Figure 7–18, in each computer, a copy of MQM is needed. MQM is designed for messaging between user applications running on the same or different computing platforms. Local programs in each platform can use MQM facilities to communicate with each other as well as with programs running on other platforms. For example, in the MVS/ESA environment, MQM provides a simple and straightforward way of transferring messages across MVS address spaces such as CICS/ESA*, IMS/ESA*, and Batch/TSO. Applications may operate in either the CICS/ESA, IMS/ESA, TSO, or Batch environments.

As another example, two applications (A and X) in computer A in the above figure can communicate with one another using the MQM. The MQM on computer A also interacts with other MQMs. Application A, for instance, can exchange messages with application Y in computer Y.

The advantage of MQM is that application A no longer has to "worry" about the network transport, or that the message might be lost due to system failures. MQM guarantees message delivery.

7.6   ELECTRONIC MAILER SERVER

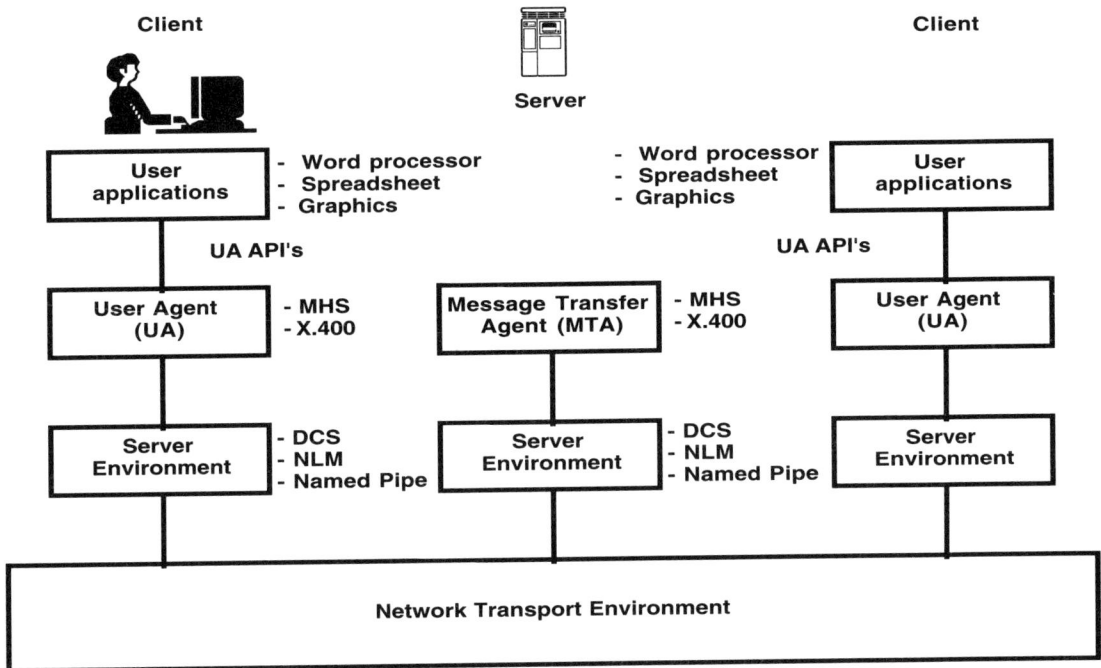

Figure 7–19. E-Mail Architecture

The client server based electronic mail system is the second generation network application, after the file and the data servers. E-mail is sweeping through users' communities. Most e-mail systems handle text and graphics. More advanced e-mail systems handle multimedia objects composed of text, pictures, graphics, voice, and video.

Figure 7–19 shows the architecture of an electronic mail network application. The e-mail server is known as the message transfer agent (MTA). The workstation client stubs are known as the user agents (UA).

The MTA and the UA forms a pair to perform the delivery functions only. Most end users do not deal with MTA or UA directly, Instead, they are using e-mail applications written to the UA's API. Examples of these e-mail applications are ccMail, DaVinci, and Microsoft Mail.

Like all other client server applications, both client and server must agree to the same server protocol. An X.400 user agent must use a X.400 message transfer agent but not a MHS message transfer agent.

Although many e-mail products have their own equivalent user agents and message transfer agents, two emerging standards are the Messaging Handling System (MHS) from Action Technology, and the International CCITT X.400.

7.6.1 Message Transfer Agent

MTAs are servers. They are designed to work with compatible client stubs known as user agents that share the same server protocol.

MTA functions like a post office. It is responsible for picking up and delivering messages between senders and receivers. When the receiver is on another network, it forwards the message to another MTA on the other network.

In high end MTA products, guaranteed delivery and message recovery capabilities are also built in to ensure no message will ever be lost by the system.

7.6.1.1 Message Handling System (MHS)

MHS is an MTA created by Action Technology. It has received wide support from all major LAN e-mail vendors. It is a low cost solution to linking e-mail systems in a smaller organization. MHS received a big boost when Novell decided to license and market it as an option in Novell's file servers.

MHS runs on a network-dedicated PC known as the MHS Server, which contains information about the system users: their names, their applications, and other network services (Profs, MCI Mail, and fax boards). MHS routes messages to and from a variety of client workstations with different operating systems on the same LAN (e.g. DOS, Windows, OS/2, UNIX).

7.6.1.2 CCITT X.400

X.400 is an international standard of a MTA. X.400 is used primarily as a high end system for larger corporations with an international network. Many value added network service providers sell this server service (e.g. MCI Mail, Softswitch).

7.6.2 User Agents

User agents (UAs) are the client stubs of the compatible MTAs. By themselves, UAs are useless. Their APIs, however, can be used by many standard workstation tools, such as word processors and spreadsheets, or as an e-mail application..

For example, a person can type a letter on his or her familiar word processor and send the letter to the recipient directly, from within the word processor. Similarly, the user can also view all his or her incoming mail from the same word processor.

7.6.2.1 User Agent APIs

Like the MTA-UA market, a number of User Agent APIs are being promoted by various vendors:

- Microsoft's Mail API (MAPI),
- Apple's Open Collaborative Environment (OCE),
- Vendor Independent Message (VIM), and
- X.400 API Associations (XAPIA).

Embedding mail functions with the current popular end user tools is an extremely powerful concept from an application point of view. Vendors are not going to see their market share challenged without a good fight. Ultimately, consumers win.

7.6.3 E-Mail Gateway

Different e-mail MTAs can be connected by e-mail gateways. Like other gateways, they are typically a PC on a network. The PC contains program that will transfer e-mail between two different E-mail systems.

For example, an MHS message will be transformed into an X.400 format message with its associated destination address. MHS will also route messages to remote LANs e-mail systems using the Gateway software in the same MHS Server PC.

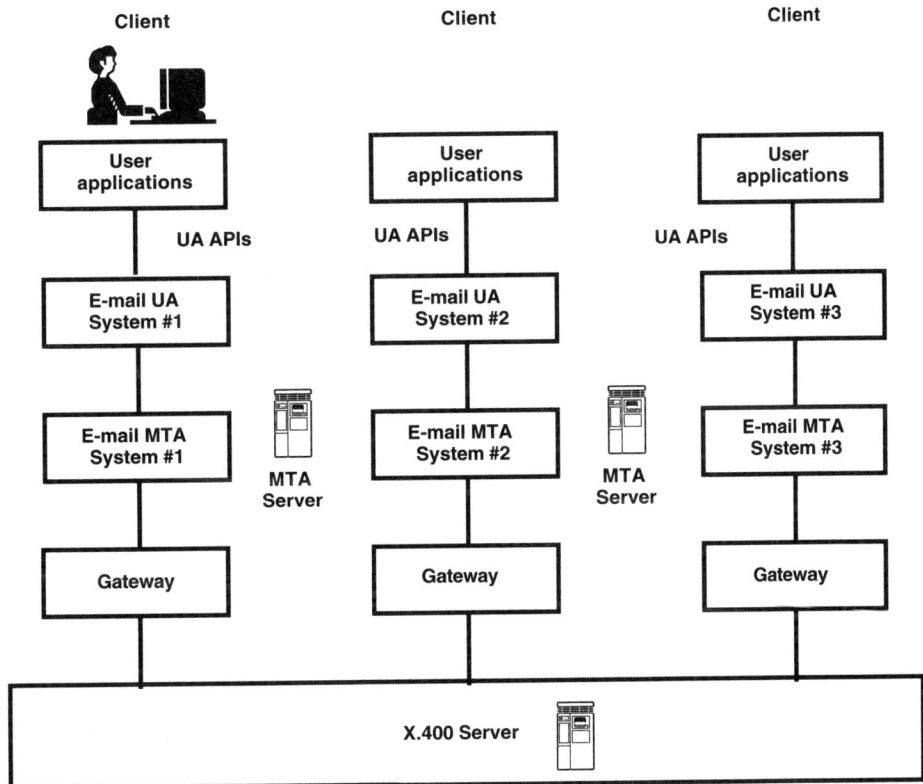

Figure 7–20. X.400 E-mail backbone

7.6.3.1 An X.400 Backbone Example

Typical large organizations have multiple types of electronic mailing system. Some are host based. Some are LAN based. They do not inter-operate with one another. These different e-mail systems can neither exchange messages nor calendars. This situation obvious are not desirable.

CCITT X.400 is an international standard, and global trade has enforced its legitimacy. It is no surprise therefore that almost all proprietary e-mail systems have a gateway to an X.400 MTA. For example, IBM's Profs system has an X.400 gateway and so has Novell's MHS, DG's CEO, DEC's All-in-One. The X.400 gateways are responsible for translating messages and addresses from the proprietary e-mail systems to and from the X.400 format.

The X.400 backbone is an X.400 MTA server which keeps track of all the user addresses in all the proprietary e-mail systems. It functions like any MTA that stores and forwards messages to and from the gateways, which in turn deliver the messages to the users.

7.7   DIRECTORY SERVER

One of the most important application services that can be provided by a network operating system is to help users to find out where things, servers, and people are located on the network—the directory service.

The more popular directory naming services are:

- Novell's Netware Name Service (NNS),
- Sun's Network Information Services (NIS),
- Banyan's StreetTalk directory service, and
- CCITT X.500 directory.

The following is an example of directory service. It happens to be the one adopted by the Open Software Foundation. It does not yet have widespread deployment, but its potential for being widely adopted is high because acceptance of the OSF recommendations by users and vendors is gathering momentum.

7.7.1   DCE Directory Server

OSF's DCE directory service is based on Digital Equipment Corporation's DECdns and Siemens DIR-X. The service was designed to support networks with up to 1,000,000 computers.

The DCE directory service meets these requirements by making use of partitioning, caching, replication, authentication, and authorization, and by complying with accepted naming standards, such as the X.500 worldwide directory service.

7.7.1.1   Multiple Directories

The DCE directory service distributes multiple copies of directories on many computers. This replication allows the name service to be available if one of the server computers fails. This can lead to inconsistency, when one copy is modified and others are unchanged. Therefore, DCE directory service provides an update mechanism.

The DCE directory also improves the performance for name lookups by allowing clients to make local copies of names. This caching improves performance by reducing the number of times a client must go to the network for naming information.

7.7.1.2   Access Control

Distributed services often require access to sensitive information about individuals. The name service must provide a security mechanism that protects the information, granting access only to authorized individuals.

DCE directory service uses Kerberos authentication, developed by the Massachusetts Institute of Technology's Project Athena, to prove that users and services are who they claim to be.

7.7.1.3   Partitioning

As computer networks grow larger, maintaining an entire name service on a single computer becomes difficult. Consequently, many organizations find it difficult to maintain large name databases. The solution is through a technique known as partitioning.

A partition under a single autonomous administrative authority is called an administrative domain. The DCE directory service provides the capabilities to operate a directory service administrative domain. Within that domain, the directory service administrator has control over the location of name partitions, the level of directory replication, and the level at which a user may participate in the directory service.

7.7.1.4   Global Directory Agent (GDA)

This DCE administrative domain is connected to other administrative domains by means of the X.500 worldwide directory service through the use of naming gateways called Global Directory Agents (GDAs).

It should be noted here that DCE Directory Services is not the X.500 Directory Server. However, it makes use of the X.500 Directory Services. We review X.500 Directory Server in the next section.

When a client in one administrative domain wishes to look up a name in another, it sends a name lookup request to its local GDA. The GDA then forwards this inter-domain name request to the worldwide X.500 directory service, which looks up the name and returns an entry to the GDA. The GDA in turn passes this entry back to the client.

7.7.1.5   Directory Agents

As with the X.400 specification, X.500 has two directory agents: the Directory Services Agent, DSA and the Directory User Agent, DUA.

With DSA and DUA, end users can add, modify, and remove directory entries. The DSA system can service directory requests from the DUAs on other OSI systems. The DSA maintains the name and address information about applications in its Directory Information Base.

7.7.2 X500 Directory Server

X.500 is an OSI specification for a global directory server with a strong tie to the electronic mail functions, especially those specified in the OSI's X.400 standard. X.500's current main objective is to let users and user programs to find out where people and organizations can be reached. Its architecture also allows it to be a location broker for other computer programs on the network.

X.500 is a huge undertaking on a global scale. It will take few years to materialize. In the meantime, many proprietary commercial directory servers will penetrate the user population. These commercial products all claim that they will support X.500 when it is available.

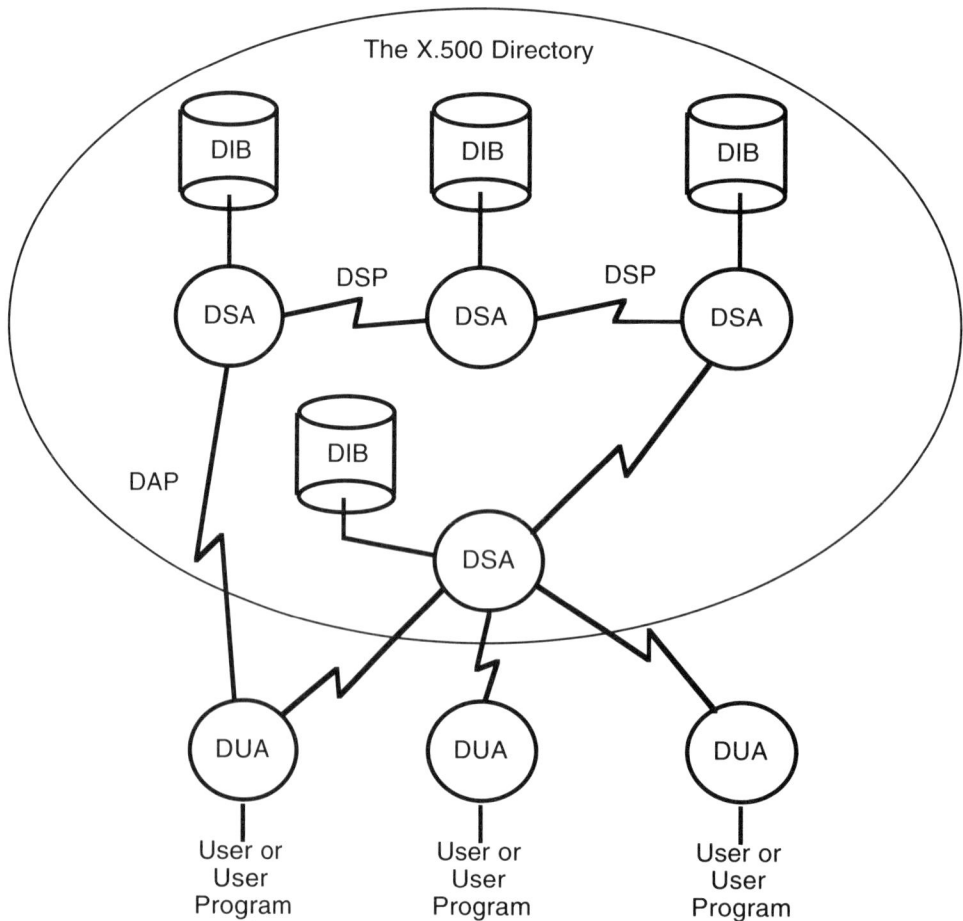

Figure 7–21. X.500 Directory Server

7.7.2.1 An Overview

X.500 Directory is an OSI Application Layer standard. Its objective is to provide a global electronic directory that contains information such as name, organization, address, telephone number, e-mail address, and facsimile number on all kinds of communication users and systems.

The Directory is accessible to both users and computer programs via modern database and communication technologies. Conceptually, there is only one global directory information base. In reality, the information is distributed among different computer systems based upon published X.500 recommendations.

7.7.2.2 Architecture

Figure 7–21 shows the X.500 architecture. X.500 is a distributed directory that is logically viewed as one global directory.

Directory Information Base (DIB)

DIB is a hierarchical, inverted tree structured database containing communication related information on objects. Typical objects are people, organizations, communicating devices, and computer applications.

Directory User Agent (DUA)

This could be a person or a computer program. It is a user of the X.500 Directory Server. It always goes through a Directory System Agent to get to the DIB.

Directory System Agent (DSA)

It is the server interface for the local access to the DIB. If a DUA request for access cannot be satisfied within the portion of the DIB managed by the DSA servicing the DUA, then the DSA routes the request for service to other appropriate DSAs on the network.

7.7.2.3 White and Yellow Pages

With access to the X.500 Directory, a user can find various attributes associated with a person's name similar to the white pages of today's telephone directories. Of course, other information is also available about the person that today' paper-based telephone directories does not provide.

In addition to the extended White Page capability, X.500 provides users with Yellow Page functions, including the capability to search the Directory for organizations or individuals that perform a certain function (such as government officials), or service (such as muffler replacements).

7.8   OBJECT SERVER

A directory server will tell you or your application where things are located on the network. But it does not take your request directly to the server. Your program must do the sending after obtaining the location from a directory server.

Location Brokers

In the paradigm of a network of objects, objects constantly need to exchange messages with one another. Therefore, instead of asking the objects to do a two-step sequence for every request (get the location, send the request), why not provide another network server which will "broker" the location for any request from an object? In other words, take the location dependence completely away from the objects and have them rely on a location broker.

7.8.1   OMG's Corba

The Object Management Group (OMG) in the U.S. is a consortium of vendors dedicated to advancing the use of object technology for distributed computing. In 1993, OMG produced the Common Object Request Broker Architecture (Corba), which is targeted at providing a platform-independent communication highway for distributed objects.

The stated goal of Corba is to provide the mechanisms by which objects transparently make requests and receive responses.

7.8.2   Directory/Message Server

Corba is a combination of a directory server and a message server. It is a directory server because it keeps tracks of where things are. It is a message server because it will store and forward message exchanges between objects on the network.

Using Corba-compliant object transaction server is similar to using other non-object-oriented directory service. Application programmers do not have to worry about where things are as long as they ask for it in a way that is understood by Corba.

Corba manages the identity and location of objects, transports requests to the target object (without knowing path names), and ensures that the intent of the request is carried out.

It should be noted that we are not talking about the application functions themselves. We are talking about the manner by which these application functions should be advertised, which is an interface issue.

7.8.3   Interoperability

Corba is necessary because as software vendors produce object-oriented applications, they must invent similar functions that are available from a directory and a message server as part of the application function.

In the name of interoperability, it is advantageous for both the users and the software vendors to follow a standard of exchange. Thus products such as IEEE LANs, TCP/IP, X.400, and ODBC have been developed. In this case, the standard is targeted at the level of message exchanges between objects on a network.

For example, if object-oriented application provider were to agree on a certain way to advertise its object's available operations, then application providers could easily produce software products to invoke those operations without worrying about interoperability with other products.

The function of Corba is to provide the type of interoperability among applications on different machines in heterogeneous distributed environments and to seamlessly interconnect multiple object systems.

For example, a document object whose origin was unknown other than the fact that it is a Corba compliant document could have been prepared with an unknown X-brand word processor or spreadsheet. When a user opens the unknown document object, Corba automatically finds out where the object comes from and how it can be opened in the user's environment.

7.8.4   Vendor Support

Support for Corba has been primarily in the North American market place. International standards are still based on the X.500 and X.400 standards for roughly equivalent functions. ISO has yet to advance to the Corba level of activity.

Among the first Corba-compliant computing environments are:

- DEC's Application Control Architecture
- NCR/AT&T's Cooperation
- SunSoft's ToolTalk
- Sun's Distributed Objects Environment

By 1993, the momentum of OMG's Corba was primarily with the UNIX centric vendors. Notable exceptions that have not completely signed on to Corba are Microsoft, IBM, and HP. Microsoft is supported by its Object Linking Embedding (OLE) Version 2.0. IBM and HP agreed to join HP's Distributed Object Management Facility (DOMF) with IBM's Distributed System Object Model (DSOM) to create a standard object management environment.

8

A Network of Objects

INTRODUCTION

In this concluding chapter, an eight-step planning process is presented for the readers' consideration in their evaluation of client server computing in their own situation.

In the opening chapter of this book we identified four barriers to the strategic use of information resources. They are barriers to data integration, data access, data presentation, and data analysis. We also said that network computing and object-oriented programming will help us to overcome these barriers.

To break down the barriers in data integration, a good understanding of the business organization's information needs and the data structure of its existing applications is essential.

To break down the barriers in data access, we need a network transport environment by which a workstation can access any application from anywhere on the network.

A network computing platform that is properly designed will not only integrate and extend the lives of the system's legacy applications, it will encourage the development of a new "breed" of client server applications that have far superior data presentation and data analysis capabilities.

8.1 AN OVERVIEW

The term "organization" in this chapter refers to an autonomous business unit ranging in size from a large division to a corporation that deploys multiple computer applications in its daily operations.

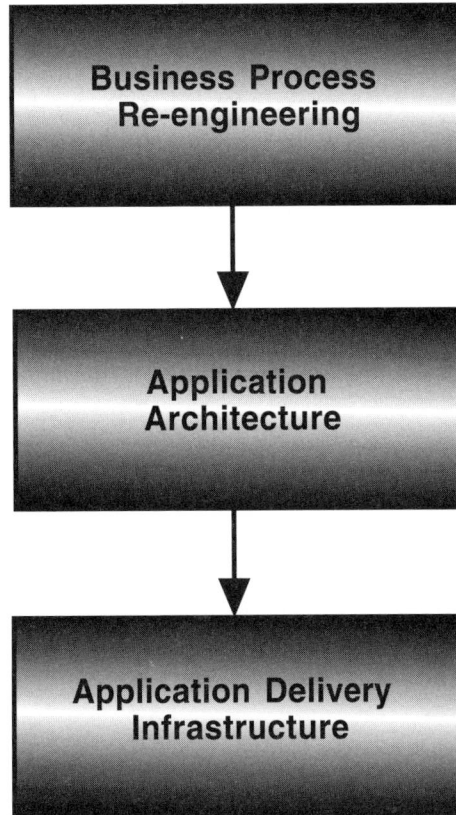

Figure 8–1. The right sequence to design a computing infrastructure

Before contemplating the transformation of an organization's host computing platforms to a single network computing platform, two activities must take place to make the transformation a meaningful enterprise.

The first activity is a complete, top-down review and redesign of the business processes of the organization. The second is the development of an application architecture to support the new business processes.

Although we do not need to know every minute detail of an application architecture, we must have a sense of what the application architecture is like before we can develop the new computing platform (technical infrastructure) to support the new application architecture. Figure 8–1 shows the correct relationship.

In this book, we assume the re-engineering stage of the business processes has been completed. We will outline an eight step planning process that will enable an organization to arrive at an application architecture and a computing infrastructure.

An undertaking of this process is understandably complex because of the scope and the number of people involved. The trick here is to get some quick hits by looking at issues from a higher level and by digging deeply only where it is absolutely necessary.

This broad approach will show the areas in which much of the transformation can start to take place immediately. It is not necessary, for example, to wait until the fine details of a network interface card are determined before the actual implementation can take place. If no such area can be found, the likelihood is that not much should be started.

Implementing client server with a "big-bang" approach is not possible in any large organization because the accompanying business processes transformations can only be carried out at a moderate rate. A learning period for both the IS professionals and the users to the new development processes must also be included. Therefore, instead of investing in today's technology as called for in the "big-bang" approach, an organization is better off implementing a client server architecture over a period of time.

8.1.1 Eight Steps to Client Server

The eight-step planning process will help an organization to develop its application architecture and the network computing infrastructure. The product of this planning process is a blueprint for making strategic use of information resources as a permanent part of an organization's daily operation. The eight steps are:

1. Develop an information architecture
2. Document existing applications
3. Decide on an application architecture
4. Design a data warehouse
5. Design the network transport
6. Choose a network operating system
7. Integrate legacy application islands
8. Roll out new applications

The first three steps help developers to arrive at an application architecture. The next three steps provide developers with a client server platform. The last two steps will enable the integration of the legacy systems and the implementation of new applications.

The four barriers to effective use of information resources are: data access, data integration, data presentation, and data analysis. The first three steps are aimed at breaking down the barriers to data integration. The next three steps are aimed at breaking down the barriers to data access. The last two steps are aimed at breaking down the barriers to data presentation and data analysis.

8.2 STEP 1: INFORMATION ARCHITECTURE

An information architecture is a specification of all necessary data elements (known variously as tables, entities, or object types) and their inter-relationships to support the business goals of an organization.

An information architecture is usually, though not necessarily, implemented on a relational database management system (RDBMS). Data modeling is an important technique to help users and IS professionals to arrive at an organization-wide information architecture.

The terms "data model" and "information architecture" are often confused. Are they the same? The answer is: not quite.

Any individual application area, such as payroll and warehouse, can have its own data model. But these models are not the information architecture. The term "information architecture" refers to a data model that crosses application and organization boundaries.

8.2.1 A Data Perspective

Traditional application development is based upon processes, sequences of events, or flows of data. Typically, developers first analyze the business flow of an application. Then they "create" various types of data records, databases, or files as by-products to support the business flow.

This approach reflects an intuitive simulation of the way we organize our business activities, which happens to fit the way computers work—a sequential machine executes commands one instruction at a time.

This application approach has been responsible for bringing us the many application islands used to computerize specific areas of business functions. Now the global economy is dictating that the totality of these islands must also be optimized. Like the former computerization of specific business areas, this global computerization requires corresponding changes in business processes.

In the course of making these changes, IS professionals have discovered that modification of today's commercial applications to fit the new business processes is expensive. Part of the reason is the outdated computing infrastructure. But the main barrier lies in the traditional application design that mixes processes and data relationships together in the same code module. As a result, changes in business processes cannot be made without corresponding changes in data design.

IS professionals found out that if the application design were based on the fundamental relationships among the data elements rather than on the processing of the data elements, making code changes to reflect new processes would have been much easier. In other words, by separating the data relationship design from the process design, an application is more modular. As a result, changes can be made more cleanly and easily. For example, changing business processes does not necessarily mean having to change the data relationship; and vice versa.

It is generally, though not always, true that changes in business processes do not lead to the same extent of changes in the relationships among data elements. Different processes can be implemented on a fixed data relationship more often than the other way around.

In other words, data relationships are more stable than business processes in an application. If we design our applications based on data relationships, then an application can be modified relatively easily without restructuring databases, records, or files.

This data independence is the key characteristic of the new breed of applications developed using the data modeling technique. These applications have been demonstrated to be more flexible towards business process changes.

8.2.2 Data Modeling

Data modeling is a technique born out of the mathematical relational set theory. It uses relational logic to describe the relationship between application data elements. As a result, a finished data model is best suited for implementation using the RDBMS technology.

In the next few sections, we briefly explore the fundamentals of data modeling. Once again, this book is not intended to be a textbook on data modeling. Readers are encouraged to read the relevant references recommended in the Reference Section of this book.

8.2.2.1 Data Views

Data has one interesting challenge to all of us. Data elements could easily mean different things to different people if we are not careful. In other words, the same data elements are viewed differently, depending on the role of the viewer.

The challenge for a data modeler is to translate the external view (business requirement) accurately into a physical view (database layout) in a manner that satisfies the needs of both the end users and the programmers. To facilitate a transformation from the external to the physical view, two intermediate data views are used, the logical and the conceptual views. The process of creating the conceptual/logical view is data modeling.

8.2.2.2 Data View—External

The view from which everyone can see the data is the external view. This view is independent of the underlying technology used to implement the database. It is natural and informal. For example, with the following table, a programmer could always have an intelligent conversation with the end user. The data is organized in a meaningful context.

Instrutor Number	First Name	Last Name	Dept	Course
100	Tom	Tsai	Computer Science	COBOL I
200	Mary	Brown	Mathematics	Algebra II
102	John	Smith	Physics	Quantum Mechanics I
105	Jane	Clinton	Law	Commercial Law 101
100	Tom	Tsai	Music	Piano 5

While the programmer and end users can discuss what they see in the external view, no one can know precisely what the other person is thinking. In fact, if both people were to write down their own thoughts, they might not reach the same conclusion.

Why? Because each sees only the resulting data, not the model that produced it. Without a data model, different people can interpret the same data differently.

For example, the user cannot tell if the instructor can be identified by more than one number, or whether he or she must be identified with any number at all. Also the data does not show whether an instructor can work for two different departments. Therefore, a clear and more formal way to represent the data must be found. That, in essence, is data modeling.

8.2.2.3   Data View—Conceptual

The conceptual view is one in which information about data is articulated in simple, natural concepts. It is people-oriented and implementation-independent. It is natural, expressive, and formal.

When people think about data and data relationships, they use language to form their ideas. Because language is a reflection of thought, it is the most direct approach to describing what one sees. For example:

- Instructor 100 **has** the first name Tom
- Instructor 100 **works for** the Computer Science Department
- Clinton **is qualified to teach** Commercial Law 101

The above expressions are clear, but they are not expressive or formal. The English may be formal, but the information in the sentences does not have a consistent structure. As a result, if an automating system such as a computer tried to process the sentences, it could not accurately determine the structure of the information presented.

This is why so many database design efforts fail: People write system specifications in English but use relational database nomenclature to design their database. This mismatch is a crucial problem; the database language does not originate from the language in which the design is specified (English).

To generate the conceptual view is data modeling. **Each data modeling methodology has its own unique way of expressing the conceptual views of the database.** Some use the entity relationship (ER) modeling technique while others use the object role (OR) modeling. Terms used by them vary slightly. For example, a relational table is called an "entity" in ER but an "object" in OR. The following are terms frequently used by the data modelers.

- *Facts:*

   A fact is a statement, or assertion, about some pieces of information within the application domain. Discovering facts is the key function in a data modeling process. For example: Instructor 100 works for the Computer Science Department.

- *Object types:*

   Object types are things such as "instructor," "course," "department," and "last name." All the facts in a model are built around object types which serve as the glue that holds the pieces of a data model.

- *Predicates:*

    Predicates are verbs. They are part of a fact that describes the roles the objects play. For example: "works for," "is qualified to teach," "has," and employs.

- *Constraints:*

    Constaints constrain over roles. They limit the values of a role so that data are not repeated. One constraint defines one-to-many, one-to-one, or many-to-one relationships: For example: Each department has at most one department name. Every building is on some campus. Every instructor has some last name.

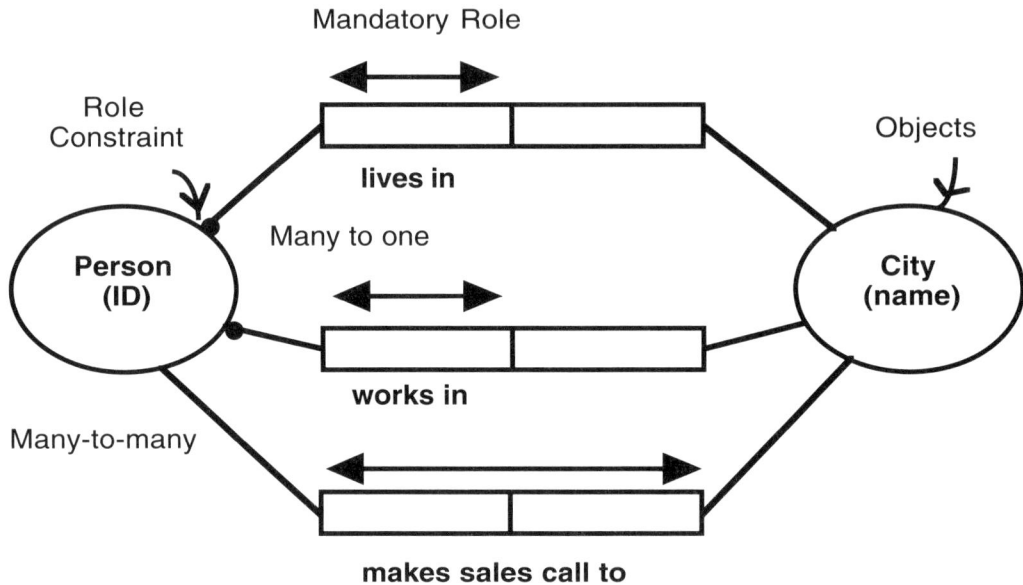

Figure 8–2. One way to symbolize a fact

An Example

Figure 8–2 shows a graphical representation of terms listed above. The figure shows one way to symbolize a fact, an object, the role, and other elements. In formal English, the conceptual view can be stated as follows:

- Person lives in City
- Every person lives in some City
- Each person lives in at most one City
- Person works in City
- Every person works in some City
- Each person works in at most one City

- Person makes sales call to City
- Each Person makes sales call to one or more City and vice versa

Once the conceptual view is symbolized in a manner that is clear and formal, we can proceed to the generation of the logical data view.

8.2.2.4 Data View—Logical

Many data modeling methodologies do not make a distinction between the conceptual view and the logical view. The logical view is one in which logical relationships are shown between entities (tables). It embodies the relational set theory to store data and data relationships in abstractions called entities and attributes.

These logical view terms have everything to do with generating the physical view of the database but very little to do with the basic concept behind the information the user is trying to convey. The logical view of the above example is shown in Figure 8–3.

8.2.2.5 Data View—Physical

The physical data view is a physical implementation in a particular database technology. For example, in RDBMS technology:

```
CREATE TABLE SHIPMENT
(
QTY INTEGER, SUPPLIER_NO CHAR (5) NOT NULL,
PART_NO CHAR(8) NOT NULL,
PRIMARY KEY (SUPPLIER_NO, PART_NO),
FOREIGN KEY (SUPPLIER_NO)
REFERENCES SUPPLIER ON DELETE CASCADE,
FOREIGN KEY (PART_NO)
REFERENCES PART ON DELETE RESTRICT
)
```

The above lines of code are the data definition language, or DDL, by which an RDBMS creates a physical table on the hard disk of a computer. These are discussed in the RDBMS section of Chapter Seven.

8.2.2.6 Data Model First

The data-centric approach places less emphasis on individual application boundaries and more emphasis on data integrity with an organization-wide perspective. It also means that data is defined before applications. Data ultimately determines the sequence of application implementation. This is an important change from traditional application development where "application areas" or "functions" are first defined.

A top-down view of information needs should be based upon the organization's mission, objectives, strategies, performance measurements, and other indicators that the organization deems as essential. This is the view that should be used for the building of an information architecture. Once the essential elements are established, a "virtual" application portfolio containing applications that are independent of the current organization boundaries and computer applications can be created. The portfolio is an ideal application architecture for an organization.

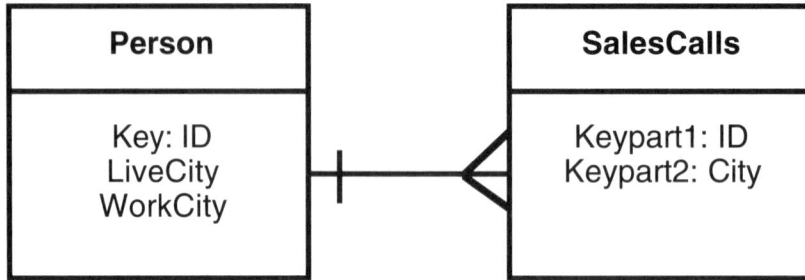

Figure 8–3. One way to express the logical view

8.2.3 Commercial Methodologies

Like its predecessors of structured analysis, the data modeling approach to application development has spawned a number of development methodologies. The translation of business objectives into data requirements is obviously not a straightforward exercise even with the help of development methodologies.

Users should not be tempted to fall into the trap of spending too much time seeking the ideal requirement. Rather, a prototyping approach of defining and re-defining the data requirement usually yields useful insights and results.

Every modeling methodology requires training before it can be effectively used by an organization. Consultants are available to teach and to lead their customers in the use of their own brand of methodology. Judging which methodology is better is difficult, since each must be adapted to suit an organization's structure and style. Establishing an information architecture is never an exact science. The success of the implementation is measured by its relevance to the business management.

The requirements of a 10-billion-dollar diversified company are quite different from those of a 10-million-dollar company with limited product lines. Users should shop around for those consultants who have good track records with businesses of a similar size and type.

Each modeling methodology provides a set of processes, guidelines, and templates to help the IS professionals and the users of an organization to translate real business requirements into a data model and an activity model (in other words, to convert the external data view to the conceptual/logical view). These development methodologies are known variously as:

- Strategic Information Planning
- Information Engineering
- Organization Information Planning
- Strategic Business Analysis

8.2.3.1   CASE Tools

Unlike their predecessors, data modeling methodologies have enjoyed a higher degree of automation because of the simplicity of the relational operation and availability of workstations.

Tools known as the Computer Assisted Software Engineering (CASE) tools are available to assist in the design of the entity relationship model as well as to generate automatically the application codes that are required to create those relationships in the target database management system. With this new breed of CASE tools, a developer no longer has to translate his or her business process analysis from a piece of paper into computer programs.

The high end CASE tools manage data models in terms of entity relationship, redundancy checks, normalization, consistency checks, and data dictionary maintenance for a development project.

8.2.3.2   Upper CASE and Lower CASE

The CASE tool that supports the design of the data model is known as an "Upper CASE" tool. The CASE tool that takes the output of an "Upper CASE" tool and turns it into executable code is known as the "Lower CASE" tool. Some industry examples are:

- Knowledgeware's ADW
- Texas Instruments' Information Engineering Facilities (IEF)
- Logic Works' ERWin
- Popkin Software's System Architect
- Bachman System Inc's Bachman / Analyst
- Visible Systems' Visible Analysts Workbench
- Evergreen CASE Tools' EasyCASE

Most CASE tools run on a workstation. Analysts can draw their conceptual view of data (entity relationship diagrams) on the screen. Once the data modeling is completed, the CASE tool will generate the database schema needed to create the database including all the necessary index and referential integrity controls.

Most CASE tools are available to run on multi-platform. The schema they produce can be implemented on multiple brands of RDBMSs. In a client server environment, once the database schema (with all the necessary index and referential controls) are created, a data server is formed.

Client programs running on a networked workstation can then be written to update, browse, insert, and delete with the data on the data server. The creation of client programs, though never trivial, has been greatly simplified because of the availability of a large number of SQL Front Ends as mentioned in Chapter Seven.

8.2.4 Architecture Documentation

An information architecture can be expressed in various types of entity relationship diagrams and matrices. They show the relationship between functions and data and between functions and data types. Each methodology has its own unique way of presenting an information architecture.

Terms such as Data Flow Diagram, Structure Charts, State Transition Diagrams, Entity Relationship Diagrams are all tools of the trade. Readers should consult their methodology vendors for specific details. The following is one example of documentation for an information architecture.

8.2.4.1 Entity Relationship Diagrams

Entity relationship diagrams (ERDs) are used to show the relationships among entities. In Figure 8–4, a simple diagram says a lot about the relationship among customer, customer order, order lines, and products.

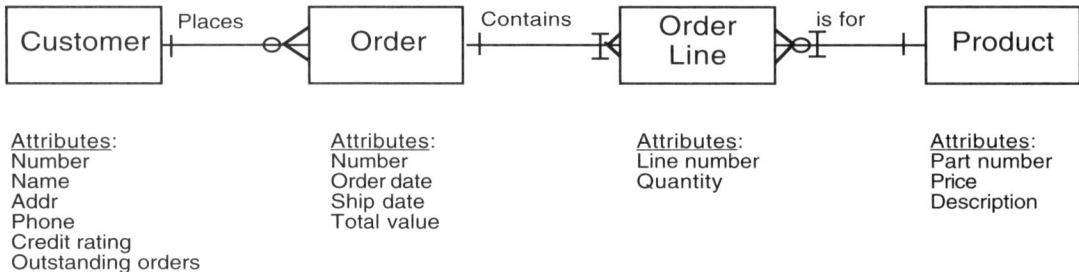

Attributes:
Number
Name
Addr
Phone
Credit rating
Outstanding orders

Attributes:
Number
Order date
Ship date
Total value

Attributes:
Line number
Quantity

Attributes:
Part number
Price
Description

Figure 8–4. One representation of data model: Entity Relationship Diagram

A customer can issue more than one order. This is known as an "one-to-many" relationship. Each order must belong to only one customer. This is known as an "one-to-one" relationship.

An order may contain many order lines. Each order line can only contain one product, which in turn means that for the same order, a product can only appear once in one of its many order lines.

An ERD defines the rules how the attributes of each entity can be updated, changed, created, and deleted. The lines that connect two entities are called relationships. For example, only a change in the customer entity can cause the creation of an order. No one else can.

When a database has to be shared by many users and applications, the best way to maintain these relationships is by programming them as database "resident" integrity controls.

These controls must be application-independent. Most modern relational database management systems provide features such as "stored procedures" or "triggers" to enforce the integrity rules or relationships.

Functions / Entities	Sales forecast	Prepare catalog	Procurement	Warehouse	Accounting	Prepare P/L	Order processing	Costing	Manufacturing	Design	Research	Recruiting	Payroll
Customer	R				U		C						
Product	U	C		U		R	R	U	U	C	C		
Purchase order				U			C	U	U				
Ledger					C	R							
Supplier invoice			C						U				
Employee												C	U
Job function												C	U

C = create, U = update, R = read only, D = delete

Figure 8–5. One representation of data model Entity vs. Function.

8.2.4.2 Entity vs. Function Matrices

In a business organization, the division of labor is inevitable for overall efficiency and effectiveness. Each organization is supposed to be responsible for specific functions: marketing, manufacturing, human resources, warehousing, and so on.

Functions use data that may or may not be common. For example, the entity "product" is shared by many Functions. Each Function is interested in specific attributes of the product entity. Some attributes will be updated by certain Functions but will be accessible as "read only" by others.

The matrix representation is important because it highlights shared data where much of the data "dis-integration" occur. It also shows the degree of sharing of data among different Functions. This type of diagram, sometimes referred to as the CRUD (Create, Read, Update, Delete) diagrams, will prove to be extremely useful for the implementation of a data warehouse.

8.2.4.3 Data Classification vs. Functions

Another documentation for an information architecture is a matrix that shows data classification by functions. Four types of application data serve four distinct business requirements:

- realtime data,
- routine operational data,
- decision support data, and
- personal data.

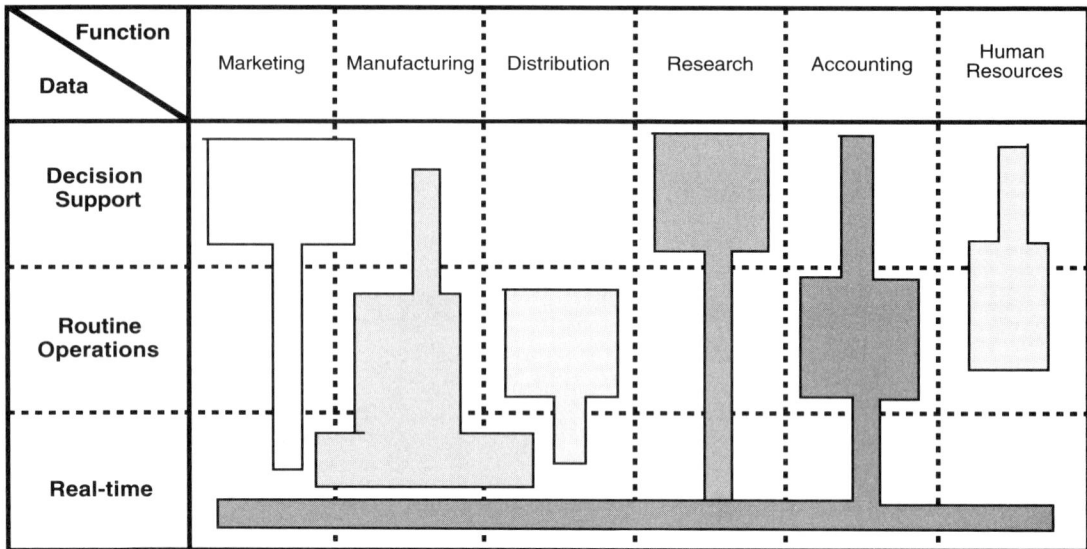

Figure 8–6. Data vs. Function

We review the definitions for these data types in the next section. For now, let us accept the statement that the definitions are based on their "urgency."

The realtime data must be available immediately and quickly on demand. Routine operational data are not needed immediately. They must be available within a day or a week. Decision support data are needed for trend and performance analysis on a monthly basis.

Figure 8–6 shows how different functions use different data. In manufacturing, where equipment operation is the prime function, realtime response is required. On the other hand, accounting people are more interested in routine operational data since they must balance the revenue and the expenses monthly or daily.

Marketing people formulate their sales strategy by analyzing customers' buying habits. They are not interested in single transactions of candy bar sales, but they are interested in the daily or monthly sales trends of candy bars.

Figure 8–6 also shows the nature of data requirement of each Function. This information will be very useful in the development of a data warehouse, a subject which we discuss later in this chapter.

8.3 STEP 2: DOCUMENT TODAY'S DATA

Unlike the top-down information architecture in Step 1, analyzing existing applications is a bottom up exercise. It is equally exhaustive, and absolutely essential.

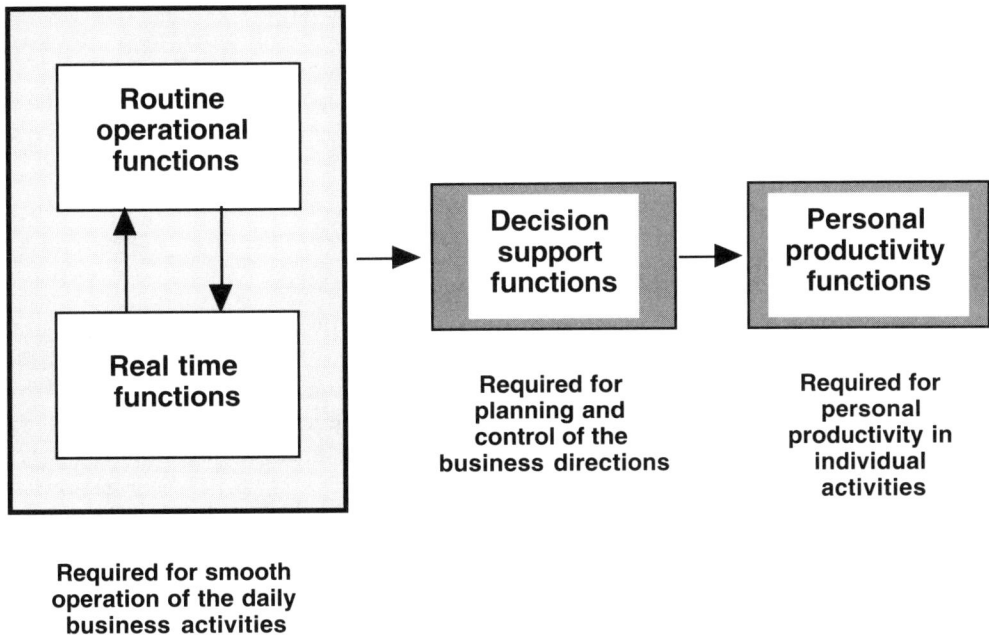

Figure 8–7. Application Function Types

8.3.1 Application Types

To know your applications, you must know the different application types and data. For most businesses, four types of application functions are needed: real-time functions, routine operational functions, decision-making functions, and personal productivity functions. See Figure 8–7.

8.3.1.1 Realtime and Routine Operational

Realtime functions deal with events that must be handled immediately. Real-time systems are also known by names such as online transaction processing systems (OLTP), process control systems, and point of sale systems (POS). Typically they deal with customer services, suppliers, and equipment operation.

For example, when a customer arrives at the check-out counter, the point-of-sale system must respond immediately because the customer is not likely to wait for an hour. When the stock broker takes an order from a customer over the phone, the system must respond immediately. Similarly, the control system for a nuclear reactor must act immediately if it detects an emergency.

Routine operational functions are those that handle events that must be executed regularly, though not immediately, to ensure the successful routine operation of the business. The nightly batch programs that tally up the daily transaction data and generate monitoring or exception reports are examples of this type of application. Operations such as totaling up daily sales, issuing paychecks, consolidating earnings, chalking up account receivable, and checking out bad checks are performed by these applications. They operate on data collected by the realtime systems.

While numerous operational opportunities are still waiting to be automated, the trend is to automate and to expedite the administrative type of analysis usually performed by white collar workers including clerks, planners, managers, and executives.

8.3.1.2 Decision Support

Realtime and routine operational systems produce a voluminous amount of data. However, questions asked by business analysts, managers, executives, and supervisors are of a higher granularity than individual transactions. These types of questions require a third category of functions known as decision support.

For example, every time a customer buys a candy bar, the system will generate a transaction in its database, and a receipt is printed for the customer right away. The customer has no need to see the daily total sales of the business.

However, the decision makers are more interested in aggregates (e.g. daily totals, monthly averages), trends, and the dynamics of the business. The following are typical questions raised by them:

- What are the year-to-date sales of a particular product or a line of products in a particular region?
- Which marketing channel provides the highest profit margin? Why?
- What is the buying pattern of large customers vs. small customers by regions, by product, and by channel? Why?
- What is the impact to the revenue by product, and by region if customers from a marketing channel are transferred to another?

Another characteristic of decision making is that the "next" question is not determinable in advance. Follow-up questions depend upon the answer to the current question, similar to the way human minds work—intuitive deduction—a series of exploratory questions and answers.

This, however, is not the way computers work. Computers can respond only to very specific requests. (Remember the last time you had to wait in line for a programmer to change a column of a report for you!) This conflict of working habits between human and computer is a major barrier to making good use of the immense raw data resources stored in computers. The decision making process is different from the straight automation of repetitive processes, the mainstay of many of today's application islands.

Today's global economy relentlessly forces companies to be quality, low cost producers. Fundamental adjustments are taking place in every corporation in order to stay competitive. The thinning out of layers of management has finally moved the age of automation from the sales counters and shop floors to the executive suites. This automation of the administrative level is what some people referred to as the decision support level where client server technologies will have the highest impact.

We review a special class of decision support application known as the Executive Information System (EIS) later in this chapter.

8.3.1.3 Personal Productivity

Personal productivity systems help individuals perform their job functions more productively.

Computer aided design systems (CAD) assist architects, process engineers, aircraft designers, and fashion designers to produce faster and better results in their respective fields. Word processors enable writers and reporters to edit their work much more easily than typewriters. Music programs help composers to compose. Spreadsheet systems enable analysts to perform "what if" exercises.

Personal productivity systems are not exclusively based on workstations. Many mainframe-based personal productivity tools simulate complex scientific and engineering problems. Unlike the three other application types, sharing data among personal productivity applications are minimal.

8.3.2 Application Data

Now you have an understanding of types of application. The next step is to examine and document the data files and databases of existing application islands. These findings are compared with the information architecture. Together they form the foundation for the design of the data warehouse and the client server platform.

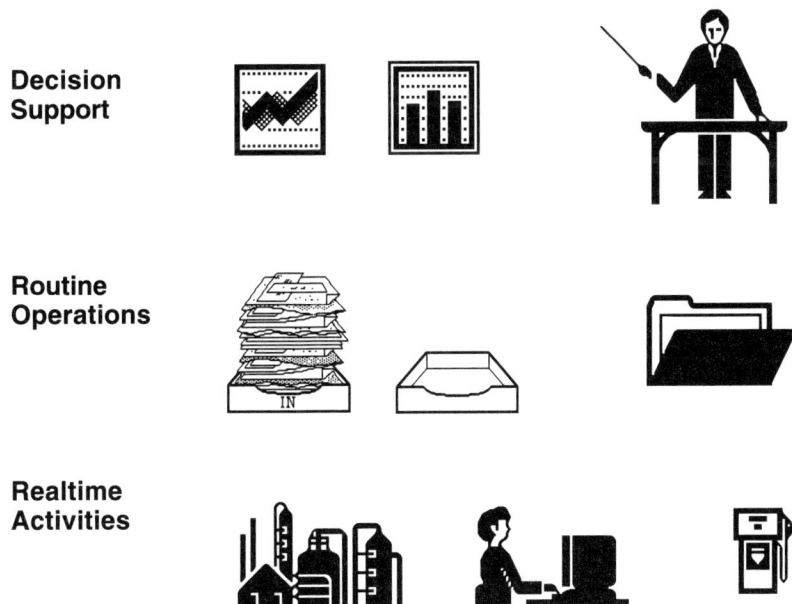

Figure 8–8. Application data classification

8.3.2.1 Data Classification

Application data should be classified by their primary function: realtime, routine operational, decision support, and personal productivity. For example, an order processing system is a realtime system with some routine operational functions and decision support functions. But the main purpose of its existence is to record customer orders, not to calculate the daily total sales or the average monthly sales for sales analysis.

Similarly, a general ledger application runs nightly to keep records of the day's financial activities. Its main purpose of existence is to balance the books so that correct amounts of funds are deposited to the banks at month-end to cover expenses. This type of application does not have to respond to a customer who suddenly shows up at the counter, but it must react within a day or a week. The same system may also generate reports on revenues or expenses by site, by region, and by customers to support decision making by management.

In a process control system, the internal pressure of a boiler is realtime data. It is critical to the boiler's second-by-second stability control. The daily average internal pressure of the boiler is important to the plant engineer who watches for any cumulative high pressure effect on the welding joints.

The former data element is for realtime routine operation, whereas the latter is for decision support function. The average value is generated, stored, and managed by the realtime system even though this is clearly a decision support function. This is done because there was no other cost effective alternative in the era of host based computing platforms. In the next section, we discuss the concept of the data warehouse which addresses this issue.

A realtime system should have more realtime data elements than decision support ones. Conversely, a decision support system should have more decision support data elements than realtime data elements.

Ironically, the best way to look for a badly-designed application is to look for one that has data elements evenly distributed among the four functions, as it tries to be all things to all users and usually satisfies no one.

8.3.2.2 Data Catalog

In Chapter Seven, we mention two types of data dictionaries: Active and Passive. In this analysis of current application, we also need a means to document what data elements are available today. A separate data dictionary can be used for this purpose.

Most large business users "live" in a multiple application environment that has evolved over a number of years. An exercise to document the application data using a central repository will help to assess the current situation of data integrity in their organization and to build a meaningful organization-wide information architecture.

Each application has its own data files. To determine what they are, one must comb through them, list them, classify them, and describe them in an orderly and consistent manner.

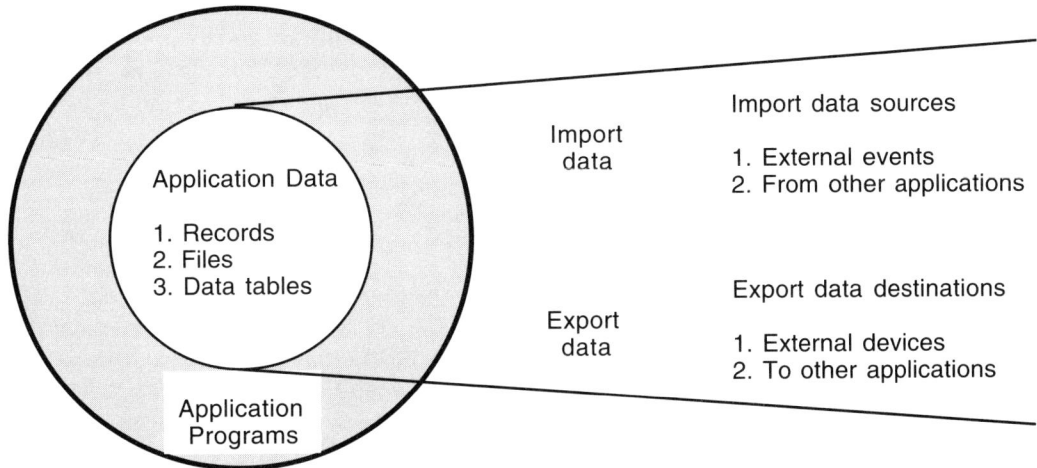

An application object   **Import / Export data**

Figure 8–9. Application data analysis

For example, the price of a yarn is 6 dollars per yard. Does this definition of price means the wholesale price? Discounted price? Retail price? Does it include tax? Is the discount based on some prior contractual agreement?

A cost effective way to document the findings is to build a simple form front end for analysts to enter information about the data elements of the various applications. The form should ask for things such as:

1. Identification for the data element
2. Application name (e.g. ORDER, stands for an order processing system)
3. Prime function of the application (e.g. real time, or routine operational)
4. Short name for the data element
5. Description (e.g. what is it? . . .)
6. Prime function of the data element (e.g. decision support, ...)
7. Data type of the data element (e.g. text, integers, decimals, date, . . . etc)
8. Updated by whom? (e.g. program name, manual process, import file, . . .)
9. Update frequency (e.g. hourly, monthly, . . .)
10. Historical updates kept online (e.g. one year)

This exercise is like creating a "data dictionary" for each existing application. The data dictionary will enable cross referencing of various data elements. It will help programmers or IS professionals to see the big picture of interplay among business activities in the organization.

To cover the wide spectrum of description for data elements, an organization should prototype a standard for itself. By documenting the application data, the organization is well on its way to building a client server platform that will lower its cost for future applications as well as ensuring that it can make best use of its current information.

8.4 STEP 3: APPLICATION ARCHITECTURE

Now you have in your possession two documents. The first document is about the information architecture to support the goals and strategies of your organization. The second document is about the data elements that exist in your current applications. What can you do with the results of the analysis? Comparison of these two documents will show the gaps, the overlaps, and inconsistencies of information needs of your organization.

Gaps are the missing entities that are needed but cannot be found in any of the existing application databases. Overlaps are those entities appearing in two or more application databases. Inconsistencies are entities that closely but not completely match the definitions in the information architecture.

After analysis of the collected data, an application portfolio should be created. The portfolio contains both existing and new applications islands that are needed to achieve the organization's goals and strategies. Now we must decide on an application architecture within which the portfolio applications can be developed.

Centralized Database Environment   **Distributed Application Environment**

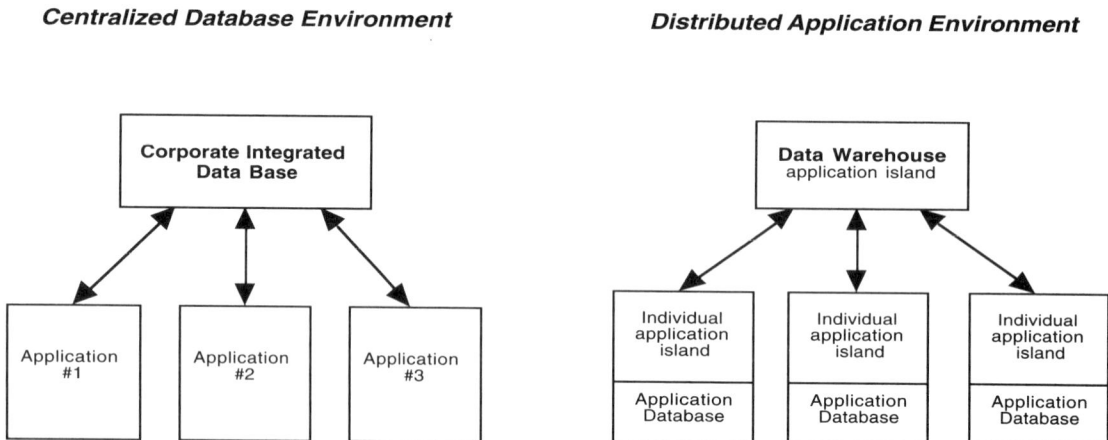

Figure 8–10. Two approaches to Data Integration

8.4.1 Centralized Database vs. Distributed Application

As shown in Figure 8–10, a large organization has a choice between two types of application architecture.

The first type of application architecture has all the entities in the information architecture implemented on a single RDBMS. ALL types of application programs: operational, routine, and decision support, will run against this centralized database. In this book this architecture is known as the centralized database architecture.

The second type of application architecture has the entities of the information architecture distributed to application islands. In this book this architecture is known as the distributed application architecture. It is inherent in such architecture that both data and processing logic are distributed.

Either application architecture can be implemented on a client server computing platform. Centralized database architecture does not necessarily mean mainframe computing. All the server procedures will be running against the same database in a server computer. However, client programs can be running on networked workstations.

8.4.1.1 Centralized Database Architecture

This architecture enables applications to interact with a centrally managed and typically voluminous data base. The data base design is derived directly from the information architecture.

The all encompassing data base contains realtime, operational, and decision support data. The intent is to capture data once and to share them with all applications.

Building an organization-wide integrated database environment has been a dream for many IS system professionals for many years. Until the arrival of mainframe relational data base management system (i.e. IBM's DB2) and the data modeling technique, there was no practical way to implement the concept.

Although this approach promotes data purity, it faces two major challenges: management style and technology cost effectiveness. A pure top-down information architecture across business lines requires a highly centralized management style. Entities must be very precise in their definitions, and they must be managed by data dictionaries. This, however, will not be simple to enforce in a large, diversified organization.

An Example

Company X sells locomotives and air conditioners to Company Y. The locomotive division and the air conditioner division of Company X are business lines managed autonomously, but reporting to the same CEO. Although both divisions sell to the Company Y, their view of Company Y as a customer may be quite different. Company X may be the sole supplier of locomotives to Company Y, which means a closer relationship between the customer and the supplier, whereas Company Y is only one out of one hundred thousand customers of air conditioners from Company X.

The attributes for a customer would be quite different for these two divisions. Forcing both operating divisions to use the same customer database and the same order processing system, while technically feasible, may cause undue data administration hardship for both.

From a central management point of view, however, it is "cleaner" to have the customer information all in one place so that analysis of customers' activities can be carried out accurately. Enforcement of such an approach is often done with great sacrifice to the efficiency and effectiveness of the business operation.

The Real Issues

The above problem is not in the top down analysis of information needs, an essential step in understanding the data needs of an organization. The challenge is in its implementation.

To solve the data integration problem, which is primarily a management planning and control problem, an organization should not build all its applications around a mammoth corporate data base.

The issue is not sharing data. It is sharing what data. The degree of sharing has a big impact on implementation cost and performance. The decision comes down to:

- Do we want to dismantle existing application islands to build the new top down architecture?
- Can we use both approaches to build something that fits the corporate and the business line's needs and will cost less than doing it in either existing way?
- Is an integrated application environment the only way to solve the problem of data integration?

A compromise must and can be made between the top-down and the bottom-up approaches to keep the balance of the corporate need for better data for decision making, and business lines' need for operational efficiency. Data warehouse is one such compromise.

8.4.1.2 Distributed Application Architecture

This architecture adopts an intermediate agent known as the data warehouse. A data warehouse is a data repository and clearing house for all shared data among different business functions and application islands. It is the place where data integrity as defined by the information architecture will be enforced.

This approach is more flexible than the "one and all" approach of the previous centralized database environment. This architecture allows the existence of application islands to serve the operational needs of the organization. Also, the existence of a data warehouse will ensure that the overall organization data integrity is protected.

The data warehouse is a network database application that implements the information architecture. The key difference between it and the centralized database environment is that data warehouse only keeps those data elements that are shared. This approach will not require the replacement of any of today's application islands. Users can keep their investments of the past.

A distributed application environment will encourage additions of new application islands as long as they fit into the new client server platform and work cooperatively with the data warehouse. This approach is discussed in greater detail in Section 8.5.

8.4.1.3 Decision Point

The decision on the application architecture is a choice between the centralized and the distributed environment.

The centralized version of every application sharing the same database is never much of an alternative in a large organization with multiple divisions because it is too inflexible. If an organization has divisions of sales, manufacturing, warehousing, accounting, and research, it is likely that this approach will not work. In fact, it is fair to say it has never worked.

On the other hand, a distributed application environment with a data warehouse is a comprise between control and flexibility. It is capable of expediently responding to changes in business processes and technology. Also, today's application islands can continue to operate while being gradually replaced.

No one approach has been established to help an organization to decide which application architecture is best for it. The organization's activity, size, information architecture, application portfolio, and management style are all factors which must be taken into consideration before a final choice is made.

8.5 STEP 4: DESIGN THE DATA WAREHOUSE

Up to this point, you have an information architecture, a good understanding of today's application data, and a desired application architecture. We now need to design the computing infrastructure that can best implement your application architecture.

Client server computing technology can be deployed in both the centralized database architecture as well as the distributed applications architecture. A centralized database architecture, though inflexible, can also be implemented using today's host computing technology.

Since this book is about client server technology, we will design a client server computing infrastructure to support the more generic distributed application island architecture. This computing infrastructure can also serve the simpler centralized database application architecture.

An application architecture may or may not include a data warehouse as a separate application island; however, it still can exist, as an architected entity in a centralized database.

A data warehouse is a network database application that manages a repository of shared data and report-only data for the organization. The center piece of any client server strategic plan has to be the data warehouse.

There is not much point in pursuing organization-wide client server if the organization derives no cost benefit in integrating the existing application islands. In this case it would be wise to leave the application islands alone.

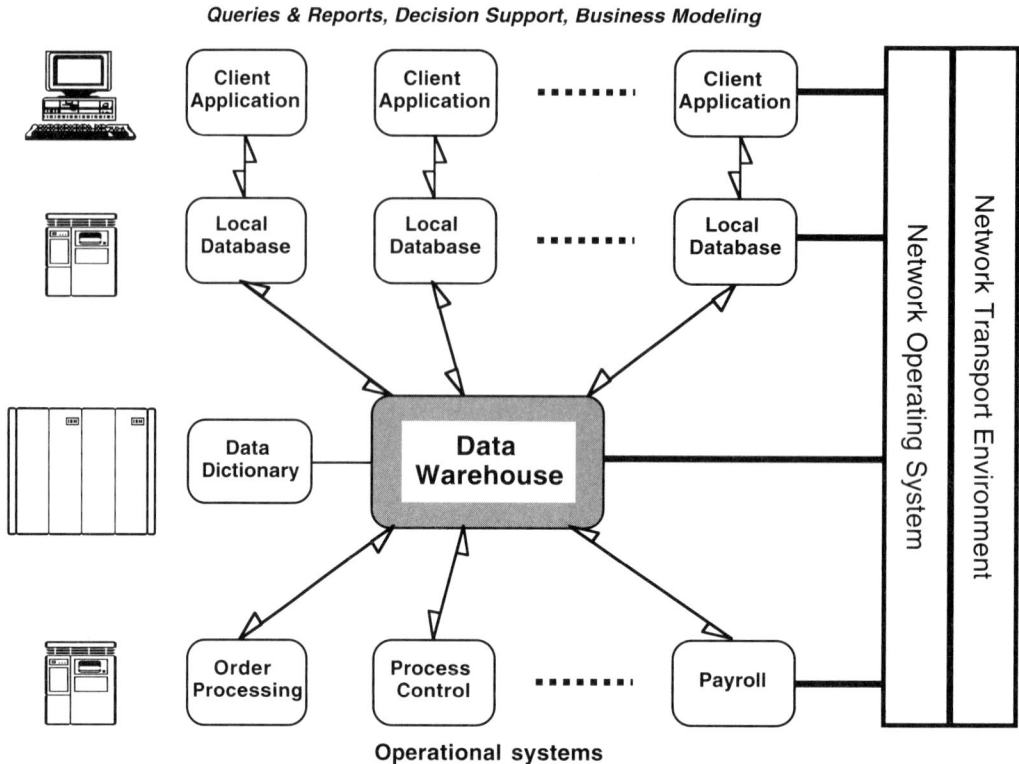

Figure 8–11. Data Warehouse Architecture

8.5.1 Data Warehouse Architecture

Data warehouse is an inclusive concept. It accepts all existing and future application islands. Once established, the addition of new application islands will be a relatively simple exercise. We discuss this in more detail later in this chapter.

A data warehouse architecture is shown in Figure 8–11. It consists of a four-layered structure tied together by the client server environment shown on the right hand side of the diagram.

8.5.1.1 The Four-Tiered Structure

Operational Systems

At the bottom are the business operational systems running on mainframes and mini computers. They are the "bread and butter" system for the business communities. They cannot be easily be replaced.

The main idea for a data warehouse is to solve the organization-wide data integration problem without dismantling existing systems. These systems feed data to the second layer component, the warehouse itself. They can also obtain any shared or required data from the warehouse on a scheduled or ad-hoc basis.

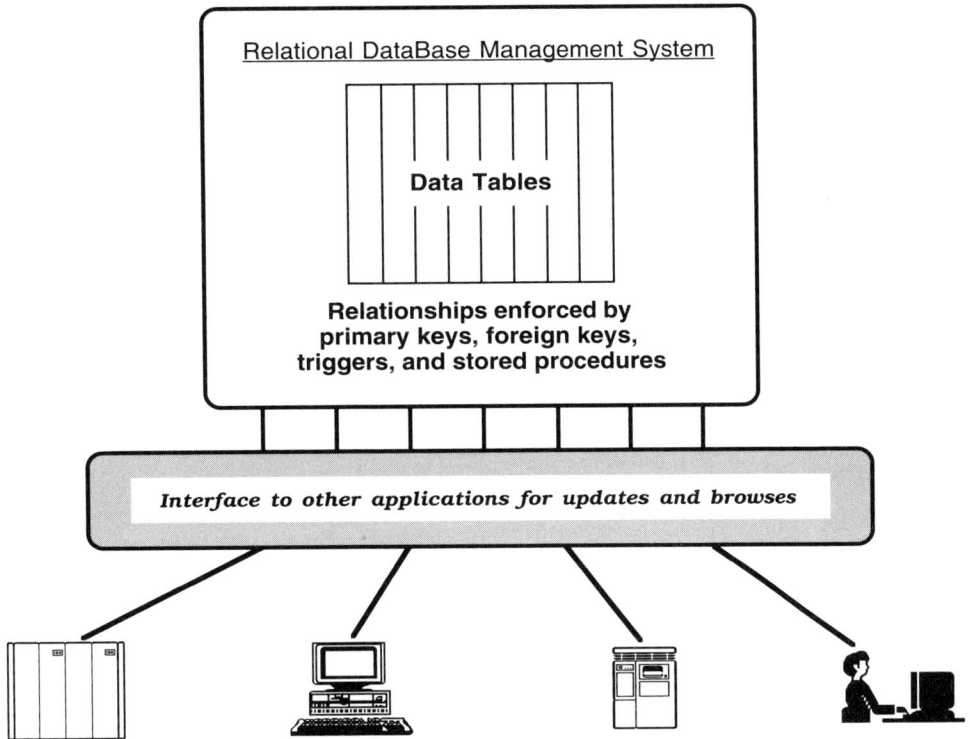

Figure 8–12. Data Warehouse for *shared* entities in the enterprise information architecture

Data Warehouse

Data warehouse is an application island by itself. As shown in Figure 8–12, the database schema of the warehouse should be guided by the data models of an information architecture, which determines who should update what, when, and how.

The data warehouse is an image of an organization's information architecture. In fact, CASE tools are ideal for generating the schema for the data warehouse. By using the database resident control facilities, such as stored procedures, triggers, and foreign keys available in most high end RDBMSs, data integrity as defined by the information architecture will be guaranteed. Users should always feel confident about the data they obtain from a data warehouse.

Data elements managed by data warehouses are not essential to the realtime or routine operation of the business. In other words, if the data warehouse "crashed," the business operation should not experience any effect for at least for one or two days. This is a very important concept because it separates the decision support function from other functions and affirms the legitimacy and critical nature of efficient application islands for realtime and routine operational functions.

Three essential steps should be considered in the design of a data warehouse:

- determine the data warehouse contents with respect to what entities and attributes should be in and what should be out,
- decide on a relational database management system to manage the
  warehouse, and
- design interfacing standards to the data warehouse.

Local Servers

Since accessing mainframe computer over a wide area network often means poor performance, it is necessary to distribute selected parts of it to local servers, which form the third layer of the architecture. The warehouse data in these local servers can be refreshed on a regular basis: daily, weekly, or monthly.

Client Workstations

The fourth layer belongs to the various client programs running on the worksta-tions, which are equipped to access any data and applications on the network. These client applications are for queries, reports, business models, and decision support functions.

Network Computing Environment

On the right hand side of Figure 8–12 is the network computing environment that ties the four tiered computing platforms. It should be designed to allow a user to ac-cess all applications, data warehouse data, and local server data from his or her workstation. We describe how this can be achieved later in the chapter.

8.5.1.2   Determine the contents

The documented analysis of the top down and bottom up analysis should help the programmer to decide which data elements should be in the warehouse and which should be left in the application islands. As a rule of thumb, data ware-houses should contain:

- decision support data elements,
- shared data elements, and
- report-only data elements

The data warehouse should not duplicate every data element of the application islands, even though some duplications will be unavoidable. The programmer or IS professional should also decide what is needed but is not being provided by the current crop of applications—the information gap.

For example, the daily average temperature of a boiler is calculated by a real-time application based on hourly samples. The information architecture shows that the difference between the weekly average temperature of the boiler and the ambient is required. Today, an engineer determines this by hand calculation based on a deck of paper reports from two different application islands.

Application Island #1

| Decision Support |
| Routine Operational |
| Real Time |

Application Island #2

| Decision Support |
| Routine Operational |
| Real Time |

Application Island #N

| Decision Support |
| Routine Operational |
| Real Time |

| Data Dictionary |

| Data Warehouse |

| Client Front Ends |

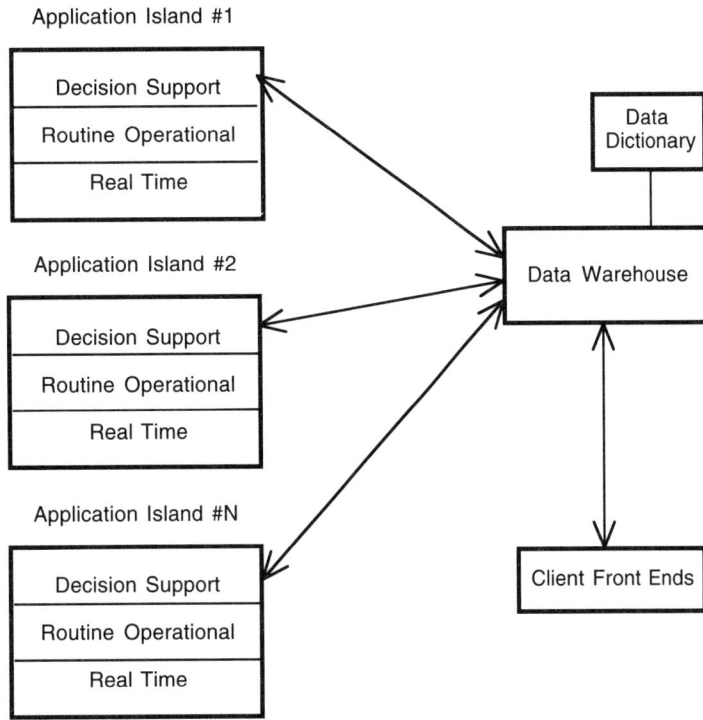

Figure 8–13. Off Loading Decision Support Data and Function using Data Warehouse

With a data warehouse, the daily average temperature of the boiler and ambient can be polled from the two realtime application islands. An internal procedure within the data warehouse can be invoked every time update occurs to calculate the average weekly difference. Or, the client applications that query the daily averages will take the two average values and calculate the difference dynamically.

Whether to calculate a data element as a data warehouse internal procedure or as a procedure within the client application depends upon the frequency of access and the complexity of a calculation. There can be no hard and fast rules. Each calculation must be reviewed individually.

8.5.2 Choose an RDBMS

A full function RDBMS should have all the commercial grade DBMS features such as data logging, data recovery, data archiving, stored procedures, triggers, and so on. A handful of products satisfy most of these criteria. Notable ones are IBM's DB2, Oracle, Sybase, Ingres, Informix, and DEC's RDB.

Find One That Fits

The choice of RDBMS for your data warehouse is critical. A multi-billion dollar diversified company is likely to require huge storage and a flexible polling capacity. The smaller organization should be looking for a mainframe or mini computer based RDBMS.

On the other hand, those who want to try the concept of data warehouse on a smaller scale—a good idea—may want to start with a micro computer version of Sybase, Oracle, or the like.

Another critical factor in choosing an RDBMS is to make sure that it supports the chosen network operating system. Many of today's RDBMSs support multiple network operating systems, but do not support all network operating systems. We discuss the choice of network operating system in Section 7.6.

8.5.2.1 Interface Standard

As part of the data warehouse design, establishing some form of interface standard is mandatory. This standard dictates how the data warehouse communicates with the application islands. The standards covers naming conventions, update frequencies, procedures, retrieval security, recovery procedures, data types, and others. For example:

- How does an application island put data into the warehouse?
- How does an application island request data from the warehouse?
- How does the warehouse request data from an application island?
- How does the warehouse export data to an application island?

Warehouse Updates and Browses

Since warehouse data are not essential for realtime or routine business activities the warehouse can also perform simpler schemes, such as making the warehouse as the "master" to poll data from application islands regularly. When the warehouse "knocks" on the door, an application island serves up the requested data.

Since a single source (the data warehouse application itself) is capable of updating the database, data integrity is assured partly because of the database resident referential control features described in Chapter Seven.

Copy or browse accesses to the warehouse by end users and application islands should be made available around the clock.

Data Conditioning

Apart from polling protocols, data in the warehouse must be stored in a format compatible with its environment. Three types of transformation with imported data are possible.

The first transformation is no transformation, just straight copying.

The second transformation is syntax transformation. For example, if a number is expressed in ASCII in one system but EBCDIC in the local system, the network interfaces should automatically handle such translation.

The third type of transformation is complete transformation. For example, the volume quota from marketing is in gallons while the process control system deals with temperature compensated volume in liters. The network automatically "transforms" the gallons to liters.

In many systems, such conversions are carried out by stored procedures by which any update to a specific data element will cause the procedure to be executed. Once a standard is established, any application sending data to, or retrieving data from, the data warehouse will know exactly what is required of them—an important step to guarantee data integrity.

8.5.2.2 Data Resources Management

Apart from the technical challenge in building the data warehouse application, appointing an owner of the data to ensure its objectives are met is equally important. Like any database application, the data warehouse should have an administrator.

The administrator is the guardian of the data. He or she manages the data dictionary. He or she ensures the definitions of the data elements are understood by his or her users. He or she monitors the daily activities and performance of the warehouse application.

The success of a data warehouse, and hence the overall transformation of an organization computing platform, is dependent upon the degree of acceptance and cooperation by the owners of today's application islands. In some organizations, this activity of administering data is the mandate of a central group known as the data resources management (DRM) group. This group is like a "data police" whose goal is to provide quality data to support everyone in an organization.

Data warehouse design should be an evolutionary process since the information architecture is dynamic. Its maturity will require adjustments to existing business methods and to application development methods. It will influence the way users interact with various applications resulting in new usage patterns and, inevitably, demands for higher functions.

Data warehouse design will also influence the ways by which new applications are developed. Buying, versus in-house development, will be a real choice rather than an bureaucratic paper exercise. In Section 8.8, we will explore ways in which the data warehouse can make use of the information resources stored in it.

8.6 STEP 5: DESIGN NETWORK TRANSPORT

By now, hopefully, you have analyzed your information needs, classified your application data, and designed the data warehouse. You have done as much as you could, at least for the planning stage, in finding a solution to your data integration problem. In this section, we concentrate on solving the problem of data access. We will show the techniques to tie all your disparate technology islands to-gether so that they can be accessed from a single workstation on the network.

In Chapter Four, we introduce various techniques by which different technology islands can be connected. This section shows how we can apply them in designing the network transport platform.

Multiple hosts access via the workstation terminal
emulator programs

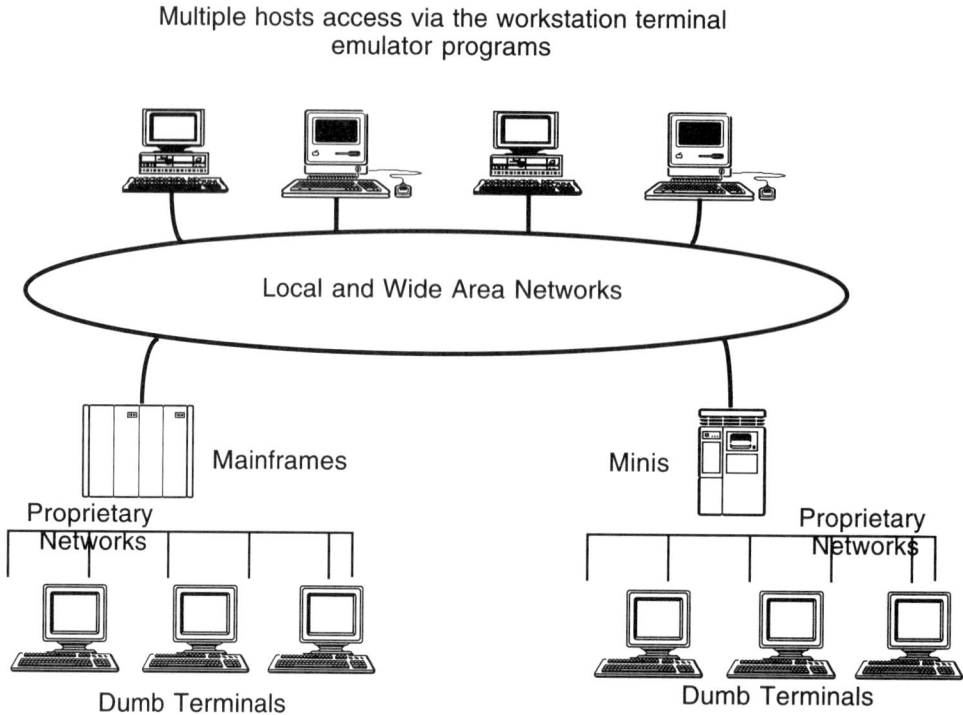

Figure 8–14. Using workstations and LAN/WAN to interconnect heterogeneous environments—A first step toward integration

8.6.1 Network Transport Choices

An important criteria in making the right choices for the network transport is openness. In other words, standards and practices that are widely adopted by the industry and the user communities should be selected. Such choices will produce a computing platform receptive to the widest choices of commercial hardware/software products for your application delivery.

Another important criteria is that users must be able to access any informa-tion resources on the network from their workstation connected to anywhere on the network. Figure 8–14 shows how a workstation can be configured to access all available applications of an organization. More on this next.

Technology management

Network transport technology is still far from having one set of standards. Standardization within an organization can be considered a great success if an organization can achieve an 80% compliance on its own self-imposed standards. The other 20% non-standard technologies should be viewed as a necessary compromise for business efficiency and effectiveness. Nevertheless, technology management processes must be in place to oversee the granting of technology exceptions.

In many information services organizations, the position of technology manager is created to oversee the introduction and the elimination of information technologies. This manager plays an important role in the evolution of network client/server computing by ensuring that all new investments in system technologies are directed toward the goal of universal connectivity at the application layer.

8.6.1.1 *Physical and Data Link Layers*

Physical Wiring

A review of the physical wiring of the organization's buildings is a good place to start. The existing wiring should be used as much as possible. Keep the twisted pairs, the shielded twisted pairs, and the coax. Consider using a wiring hub for bridging, if required. Rewiring should only be a last resort since this is more expensive than installing some wiring concentrators. If new applications must be brought in or if the organization must move to new buildings, then Fiber should be considered in addition to twisted pairs. Two good reasons not to pre-invest in Fiber-to-desktop are:

- Most commercial applications do not need 100 MBPS to the desktop. For high traffic areas, a switching hub might be a cheaper solution than laying fibers. (Also do not forget that you may have to throw away your whole investment in existing network interface cards.)
- The cost of Fiber is dropping as the technology matures. The money is better off staying in the bank until such time as the organization's requirements really call for it.

Although most commercial applications can be satisfied with the bandwidths of Ethernets and Token Rings, installing Fiber as the vertical transmission backbone for a building, or a cluster of buildings (campus) is still wise. FDDI-to-the-desktops (or Fiber wiring to the desktop) is required only for high traffic areas with special application needs.

IEEE LANs

Today, almost without exception, computer manufacturers support the IEEE local area network data link protocols of Ethernet and or Token Ring varieties. Their computers can always be accessed through the IEEE LANs. Gateways are usually available for the rare systems that do not support the IEEE LAN protocols.

The question of choosing between Ethernet and Token Ring is next. If we look at market share, Ethernet is still the predominant topology adopted by computer manufacturers other than IBM. Lately, with IBM's new emphasis on openness, Ethernet has gained acceptance there too. Today, IBM would probably not put out a computer product that supports only Token Ring and not Ethernet.

The vast installed base of Ethernets will guarantee its longevity and commodity pricing. For an organization wishing to keep its computer platform open, it would be wise to adopt Ethernet in particular IEEE 10BaseT as a standard. The organization should also allow other standards (e.g. Token Ring, Token Bus, FDDI, ATM) as exceptions.

Interconnecting Devices

The interconnecting market is an extremely fast growing field with new products coming out frequently. A good start to planning a network transport environment is to contact your suppliers of intelligent wiring hubs, bridges, routers, and gateways. Suppliers are experts in their own product lines, and they can spot connectivity alternatives that a programmer or IS professional may miss. Although their prime objective is to sell their products, they are helpful with technical solutions and assistance.

8.6.1.2 Network and Transport Layers

Only a handful of commercial grade transport protocols are available. Notable ones are those reviewed in Chapter Four: TCP/IP, Novell's SPX / IPX, Microsoft's Net-BIOS / NetBEUI, Apple's AppleTalk, IBM's Advanced Peer-to-peer Networking protocol (APPN), and DEC's DecNet.

At the network transport layer, the choice of an organization-wide standard network transport protocol is not as important as the choice of the multiple protocol support interfaces of IEEE 802.2, Microsoft's NDIS, or Novell's ODI. The network protocols must be compatible with the choice of the logical link control sublayer protocol. A client workstation equipped with one of these three Logical Link Sublayer interfaces has the capability to "talk" to multiple hosts simultaneously.

8.6.1.3 Access From A Workstation—An Example

Figure 8–15 shows how a single workstation on a network can be configured to access multiple hosts. Normal access to an IBM mainframe, an IBM AS400, and a DEC VAX would require three different terminals:

- IBM 3278 terminal,
- IBM 52XX terminal, and
- a VT100 terminal.

With a properly designed computing platform, all three applications can be accessed simultaneously from the workstation. The following three steps are required to make this happen.

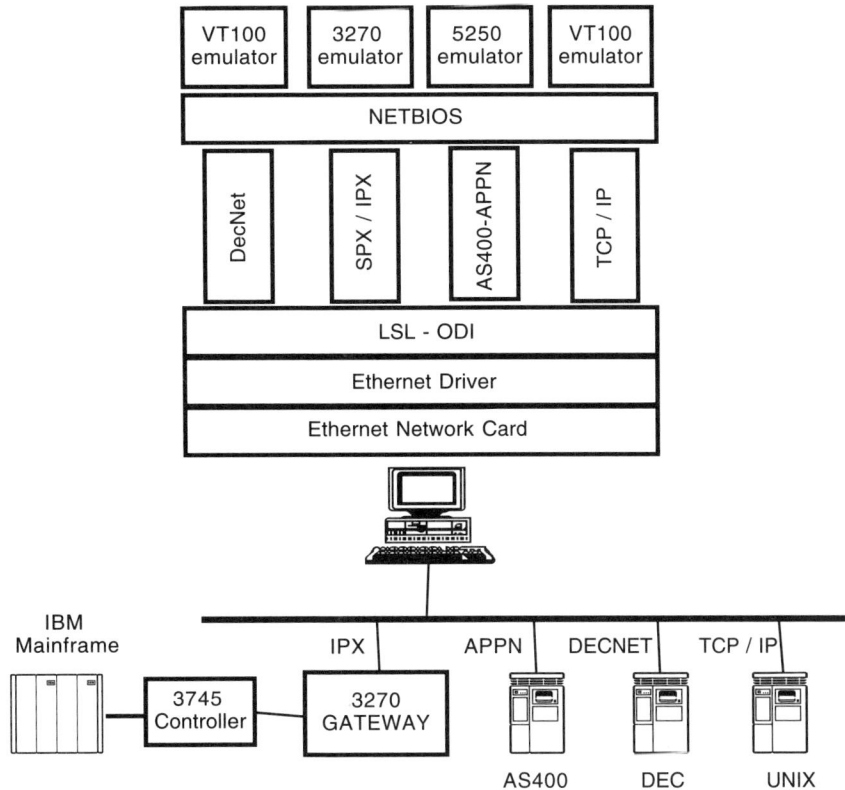

Figure 8–15. Protocol stacks in a client workstation for accesses to different hosts

Step One

The first step is to put in all necessary physical layer components such as wiring, wiring connectors, and wiring hubs. This is to be followed by the appropriate network interface card. In this example, the UNIX host, the DEC host, the AS400, and the 3270 Gateway must each have a 10BaseT card. (For those mainframe installations that use TCP/IP software, a channel attached device, IBM 8232, will join the mainframe directly to a local area network.)

Step Two

In the host computers, the following software modules must be activated:
- The 10BaseT drivers for the DEC, AS400, UNIX host, and the Gateway
- The transport protocol drivers (DecNet for the DEC, APPN or PCS for the AS400, TCP/IP for the UNIX host, and SPX/IPX for the Gateway)
- The session protocol drivers of NetBIOS for all individual host computers interface between NetBIOS and its application environments.

(VMS for DEC, OS/400 for AS400, DOS for the Gateway, UNIX for the UNIX host)

In the client workstation, the following software modules would be required:

- The 10BaseT driver
- The logical link sublayer driver, Novell's LSL-ODI
- The transport stacks: TCP/IP, SPX/IPX, APPN or PCS, DecNet
- All of the above stacks should have a NetBIOS interface.
- All of the above work under a multi-tasking environment such as MS- Windows.

Note that multiple transport protocols can exist over a single segment of 10BaseT or similar data link protocols. This enables the same workstation to have simultaneous accesses to all types of hosts that use different transport protocols. The only condition is that these transport protocols and the media access control sublayer (MAC) drivers must be either:

- IEEE 802.2 compliant,
- Novell's ODI compliant, or
- Microsoft's NDIS compliant.

Step Three

The third step is to install appropriate terminal emulator programs in the client workstations. These emulators must either plug into a server protocol such as NetBIOS or a transport socket such as TCP/IP. Their counterparts in the hosts should also be set up in the previous step. Once all the software is loaded, the emulator program should be able to make contact with selected host. Once contacted, the host will respond by sending its "log on" screen to the workstation.

Simultaneous Access to All Applications

The multi-tasking ability of workstation software such as Microsoft's Windows, IBM's OS/2, Apple's MAC, and UNIX X-Windows has opened an opportunity for simple and easy integration of applications within a user's workstation. For instance, many of today's host emulator programs are available in DOS-Windows or Apple's MAC.

For the workstation shown in Figure 8–15, the emulator programs use the NEBBISH programming interface to "talk" to their hosts. Host application screens will appear as multiple windows on the screen of the user's workstation. Information in each window can be "cut" and "paste" to one another or even to a third application such as a word processor.

This concentration of information resources in one spot and the ability of performing picking and choosing in the same spot is a very powerful change for many users. They no longer need to wait, to search, or to scream for paper reports from their programmers.

If users are provided with equally powerful data presentation and data analysis tools in their workstations, and if the information is stored in a manner that is easy for retrieval, then worker productivity will increase.

8.7 STEP 6: CHOOSE A NOS

In a host operating system, certain utility functions are deemed to be essential for application development and application execution. These functions are for management of files, databases, catalogues, messages, and input output devices. In a network operating system, similar functions are required for network applications. The main difference is that the network functions are running on a number of computers on a network.

From an overall computing platform point of view, individual NOSs are treated like host-based application islands. Users do not care whether their workstation are using IBM's APPC or Apple's AppleTalk as long as they can get to their applications.

A properly designed network platform would not exclude any type of host based environments or network operating systems (NOS) as will be shown below.

8.7.1 Basic Criteria

As far as possible, though not absolutely necessary, an organization should adopt one network operating system as an organization-wide standard. While technically speaking, NOSs can always be interconnected, the down side is the high cost of supporting NOSs.

The four principle criteria in choosing a NOS are market presence of the software, management style of the organization, consideration of the organization's existing system, and the projected future needs of the organization.

Market Presence

Because of the competitive nature of the software market, functional advantages of a particular NOS product last for couple of versions when others will catch up or even supersede. Once again, the prudent action for a user organization to take is to choose those vendors that have:

1. a significant market share,
2. consistently demonstrated technical innovations,
3. financial stability, and
4. a good "fit" to the organization's needs.

Prospective vendors should be interviewed so that the organization can fully understand the issues of capability, compatibility, performance, and support of their respective products. It never hurts to shop around.

A product should adopted that will be widely used by others, which typically means that the organization will have wider choice of available programmers, commodity price hardware, and software.

As a user of technology, an MIS manager's job is to deliver user functions. Choosing products that might not last and would eventually be very expensive to support is not be worth the risk. Organizations should stay away from the "bleeding edge" technology if possible.

Management Style

Choosing a network operating system is like choosing a host operating environment. From a user's perspective, the importance of such a choice depends very much on the business environment. If an organization is committed to developing its own in-house applications instead of buying application packages, it would be worthwhile to set an organization standard on NOS. The prime reason is to lower the training requirement for the future programming staff.

If an organization has a more decentralized management style, then it is likely to seek ready-made application packages. In this case, a standard NOS may not be a consistent or enforceable practice for that organization.

For Starters

Choosing a network operating system that fits the application needs of an organization starts with an assessment of what the organization already has in terms of hardware and software. If the organization has disconnected, host-based application islands with a minimal penetration of departmental local area networks, then it should start with a "clean sheet."

Such organizations should do an extensive review of what do they need short term and longer term and try to apply the criteria set out in the next section.

For the Front Runners

On the other hand, if the organization already has extensive penetration of local area networks, then the task of choosing a network operating system is quite different.

If an organization is already accustomed to, and its staff is already well trained for, any one of the more popular network operating systems, the choice often has already been made. For instance, changing the direction of the organization does not make sense if 70% of the installation is either Novell or IBM's APPC. Both are likely to do well in the future in terms of support and software application availability.

8.7.1.1 Potential NOS Survivors

While a number of commercial network operating systems are available today, the good news for users is that only a handful will survive in the long term. The reason is that the market simply does not need too many network operating systems. Today, these systems are all proprietary and do not fully comply with OSI standards. What are the real choices of NOS for today?

As mentioned earlier, an organization should pick the systems that are likely to survive the "rumble and tumble" of the market place. The four likely survivors—based on their current market share and the respective vendors' track record in technology innovation and financial stability—are: OSF's Distributed Computing System, IBM's Advanced Program to Program Communication (APPC), Novell's Netware, and Microsoft's Windows NT/AS.

OSF's DCS

Open Software Foundation's DCS will be a strong competitor because of the wide support it has with the major computer manufacturers and major user organizations. The stated goal and the initial momentum of OSF shows good promise.

OSF's DCS has adopted the best architected features of network products and functions available in the market today. The installed base is not substantial except in the UNIX world, which has small presence in the "big buck" commercial data processing arena. OSF Vendors commitment will be severely tested when their allies become competitors in other product areas that may have nothing to do with any OSF products.

IBM's APPC

IBM's APPC will also be a survivor simply because the installed base of mainframes will not disappear overnight, and IBM has both the financial and technical clout to make APPC a success.

IBM is very strong in the large RDBMS market. The majority of the Fortune 500 companies are storing their operational information in these huge DB2 databases. Mainframe applications are still the "bread and butter" of commercial data processing.

APPC, in its present form, may not look like the most elegant technical solution because of the need to accommodate the current installed base of hierarchical network platforms. But IBM's latest announcement does point to its strong commitment to a peer-to-peer network computing structure. Like most things IBM does, APPC is solid, stable, but expensive. It is not something that a small firm with no installed mainframe should consider.

Novell's Netware

Novell's current 75% LAN market share assures Netware to be a contender in the network operating system market. Novell has proven its critics wrong many times. High quality and efficient software products have kept Netware a leader, and there is no indication that such phenomena will slow down. On the other hand, Novell chooses to deliver solutions rather than standards. Novell does not appear to believe in standards or in participation in any OSF type of alliance. This may hurt it in the long run.

Microsoft Windows NT/AS

Microsoft's strong hold on the workstation software and its financial clout will ensure that windows NT will have its day in the market. For Microsoft, the session layer protocol—Named Pipe—provides a strategic differentiation in its push for network applications such as electronic mail and RDBMS. Windows NT/AS will survive. The question is how much market share it can take away from Netware.

IBM's NetBIOS

IBM's NetBIOS is today's leading server protocol. NetBIOS is not a network operating system. Many E-Mail and data server network applications are written using the NetBIOS protocol. If no commitment to enhancement is made by either IBM or Microsoft, NetBIOS will be eclipsed by Named Pipe. However, NetBIOS will be around for a while.

8.7.1.2 Common Servers

For a client server network based computing platform to be of use to commercial data processing, it must have, at a minimum, a file server, a data server, a directory server, an electronic mail server, and a network management server.

The four network operating systems described above have a full slate of servers that will fulfill those functions. User organizations build their applications using commercial servers. Many argue that the choice of common servers, the data server in particular, should dictate the choice of a network operating system.

File Servers

The choice of file servers for any given network operating system is quite limited because each network operating system has adopted at least one native file server. For example, OSF adopted the Andrew File System for DCS.

IBM has a number of file systems for APPC depending on the host platform (e.g. TSO, AIX, VM/CMS). Novell has its Netware File Server. Microsoft has LAN Manager. The file server provides access methods that are required for any kind of application development.

Data Servers

Organizations have more choices on network data servers because the market is dominated by software vendors instead of by computer manufacturers.

Sybase, Oracle, Ingres, Progress, and Gupta build their RDBMSs for different network operating systems. Once the network operating system is decided, users can pick the server interface and server protocol software modules supplied by the respective vendors.

The above database products support the major network operating systems.

Users should always contact their sales staff for their latest offering. Client programs in computers with the appropriate server protocol and server interface can access the data base management systems services as though they are local to their computers. All users have to do is to develop database applications for client workstations and implement procedures on the data servers. This approach is not much different from traditional host-based database application implementation.

NOS Compatibility

Not only are NOSs proprietary, they are also incompatible in the same sense as IBM's MVS is not compatible with DEC's VMS. Today, a LAN Manager client cannot access a Novell NLM data server and vice versa. Incompatibility is caused by the difference in the server protocol: Named Pipe and the Netware Core Protocol.

The same incompatibility exists between IBM's APPC, OSF's DCS, and others. But this is not an access barrier because a workstation can be loaded with multiple stacks of protocol separately. The only hindrance is that only one can be active at a time. (Contrast this with the link layer control sublayer concept in which multiple transport protocols can co-exist side by side!)

Nor is this a technical issue because a gateway can always be designed to bridge these systems. Ultimately, it is a marketing issue among the vendors.

8.8   STEP 7: INTEGRATE LEGACY APPLICATIONS

When all application islands are accessible from a workstation, half of the battle over data access is won. With a multi-tasking operating system such as Microsoft's Windows, users are now able to do electronic "cut" and "paste" functions across applications—an elementary form of application integration.

Indeed, for many users, a major data access barrier has been broken down with this elementary capability. The next step is to fully integrate host-based applications so that access to them can be done under programmed control (automatically) by another program.

The three reasons for connecting old application islands are:

1. Populating the data warehouse for decision support functions, which means off loading the host computers.
2. Using the data warehouse as an agent for data exchanges between application islands.
3. Re-using specific functions of an old application as part of a new application.

First, the basic properties of an application need to be reviewed, and the question of how an object-oriented view can turn a host based application island into an application object on the network must be considered.

8.8.1   Application Objects

An important step toward putting host-based applications on a network as an object is to analyze their essential components. These components are then paired with the equivalent components of a client server platform. The understanding of these equivalencies are critical to effective reuse of existing applications.

Servers, Server Interface, and Server Protocols

Host-based applications are software objects. They are servers. Users access application data through a set of application panels. These panels are an application's interface to the outside world. They are equivalent to the server interface which we discussed earlier.

These server interfaces are "delivered" by dumb terminals such as the VT100, and IBM's 3270. Each type of dumb terminal uses its own set of protocols for communication. These protocols, the screen drivers, are in fact our server protocols.

Applications as Objects on the Network

To turn a host-based application as an object on the network, users have three choices:

- using the emulator program APIs
- programming through server protocol APIs
- using the RPC technology

The first is simple to implement but is limited in performance and in flexibility. The last two are more flexible and powerful, but they require more programming efforts.

8.8.1.1   Using Emulators as Relays

Host-based applications are still the applications that keep the commercial world running smoothly. Although they may have an awkward user interface, they do manage functions and data very well. An important objective in building a client server platform is to integrate these stable, matured, and still very useful functions with the new ones.

Terminal emulators are the readily available relays for bridging the old applications to the new ones. In this section, we examine in detail how this can be done. Users may want to refer to some of the related discussions on emulators in Section 8.6.1.

Emulating a Relay Program

An on-line application's user interface (server interface) is done through some kind of interactive CRT terminals. This is the way applications have been built in the last quarter century. Terminal emulator programs combine the functions of the application layer and the presentation layer.

The application layer is the emulation of the physical dumb terminal. The presentation layer represents the server interface, which is the set of application panels that appear on the screen for a specific server.

When a user interacts with an emulator, he or she sees not only a blank terminal but also a terminal with application information on it. The application information is the server interface. The intent here is to use the emulator APIs as a relay to create new applications. This way, money in producing new functions can be saved, and the life of past application investments can be extended.

Terminal emulators as relays between application islands

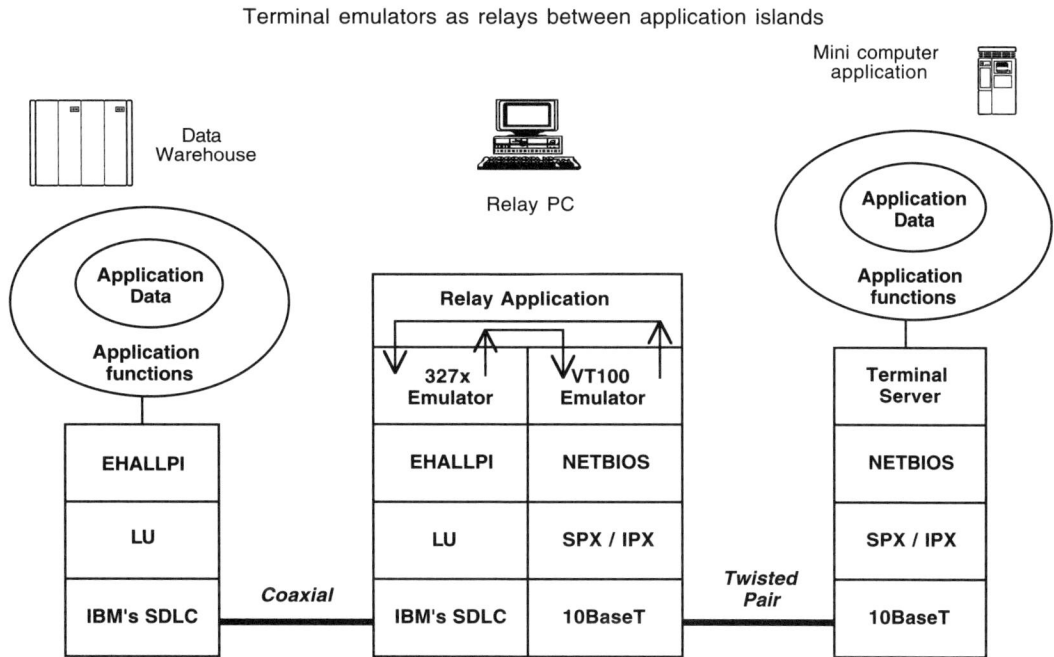

Figure 8–16. Integrate Legacy Applications

An Example

In Figure 8–16, we show a DEC mini tied to an IBM Mainframe by the relay application in the middle. The relay application uses the APIs of the respective emulators to do whatever is required. While this appears to be not a very elegant way to access data, it is too inexpensive to implement. And the application does not have to modified.

A popular way to interact with the IBM mainframe application is through IBM's High Level Application Programming Interface (EHLLAPI). EHLLAPI has two parts. One resides on the mainframe MVS or VM system, and the other resides on the workstation—a typical client server relationship.

EHLLAPI is a workstation program that contains programming interfaces with which other workstation programs, such as a terminal emulator program, can use to intercept the 3270 data stream from the mainframe that would have gone onto the display screen.

The workstation user program can then do something with the content of the display as though the actions were from a user working on the keyboard. All the while, the host application does not realize that it is interacting with a program rather than with a human. The relay program knows all the behaviors of the application panels as though it were a user of the application.

Scenarios

For instance, a data warehouse must track the daily average temperature of a boiler in a processing plant. The temperature is a data element generated by a realtime process control application.

Normally, an operator would have to call up some application screens and type in some specific commands to display the result. Now, we can write a program using the APIs of the terminal emulator program to simulate the command keystrokes and to intercept and forward the returning display data stream which contains the desired data element—the daily average temperature to either another application island or to the data warehouse.

Another example is a daily refresh of a database from the mini to the mainframe or vice versa. A simply relay program that is activated at precisely 12 midnight every day by a timer utility (e.g. Norton utilities on the PC) logs on to the mini and transfers the file to its own hard disk. Then it logs on to the mainframe computer to transfer what it receives to the mainframe database.

8.8.1.2 Using Server or Transport Protocol

If you find the relay concept to be less than robust, then you may try programming with the sockets of the session layer protocol—the server protocol. To do that, you need to find or adopt a common server protocol that is supported by the host computer that you are interested in. That may not be easy. Alternatively, you can also use any transport APIs of your choice. The only restriction is that you are limited to use a particular network family.

For both situations, you will find that programming expertise will not be easy to find. Socket programmers are technical resources that are typically hired away by software vendors.

Server Protocol Sockets

In the LAN world, the most widely adopted server protocol is NetBIOS. It is supported by almost all network operating systems as one of their server protocols (also known as network APIs). NetBIOS can also be used over a variety of network families.

However, NetBIOS is NOT supported in most hosts. Gateways are needed to translate the application contents and then forward them to other programs via the NetBIOS protocol. Other LAN-based server protocols are Named Pipe from

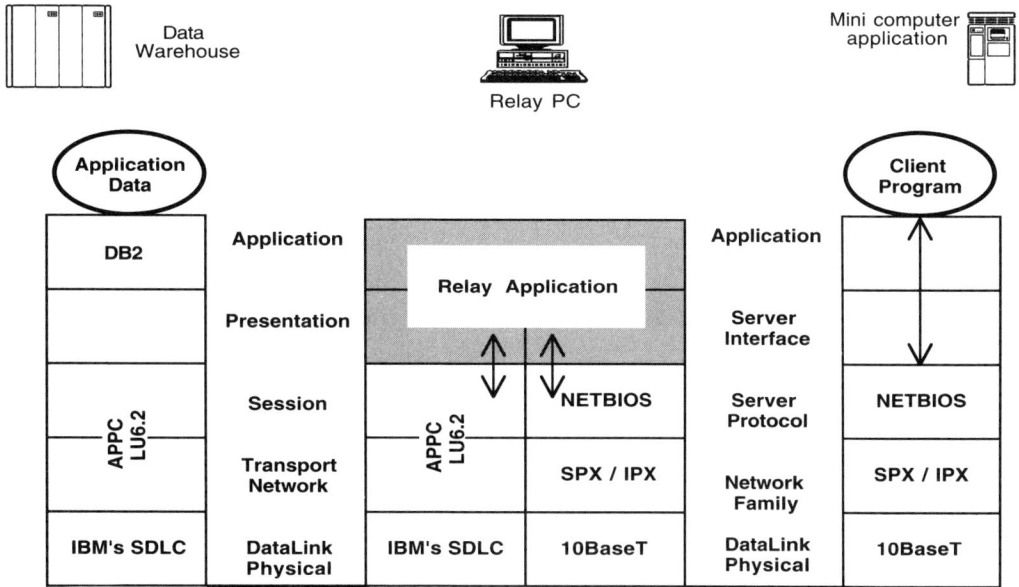

Figure 8–17. Relay application bridges host-based applications of unlike kind

Microsoft, and Netware Core Protocol from Novell. There is no host environment support for them.

The topic here is host computer applications, and the above server protocols will need a relay or gateway of some kind to work with the host environment. Figure 8–17 shows how it is done.

On the other hand, a pure IBM shop, may use IBM's Advanced Program to Program Communication, APPC or Logical Unit Type 6.2. With LU6.2, users can "talk" to practically all major IBM platforms including MVS, VM, AIX, AS400, and OS/2.

Many non-IBM host computers also directly support LU6.2. Some support it through a relay workstation, similar to that of the previous example. You can write programs that "talk" to a LU6.2 socket which in turn is connected to another LU6.2 socket in another host.

Transport Protocol Sockets

The most widely supported transport protocol is TCP/IP. Almost all host computers support TCP/IP—a definite advantage to adopting TCP/IP as the main network family interconnection for an organization. TCP/IP is the only protocol that is worth mentioning in the context of interconnecting host-based applications. IBM's APPC is a distant second.

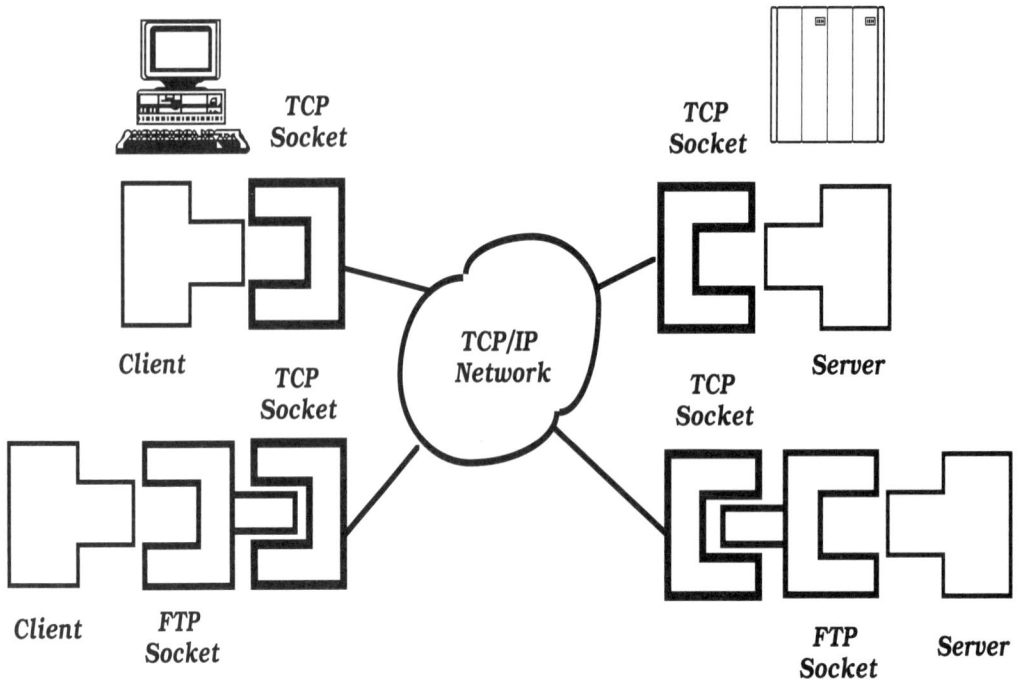

Figure 8–18. TCP socket and FTP socket programming

Two Useful TCP/IP Applications

As shown in Figure 8–18, you can write applications directly through the TCP sockets or through the APIs of some of the TCP/IP based server applications. The most important ones are the File Transfer Protocol and the Network File Services.

Both FTP and NFS have application programming interfaces through which a user program can invoke to transfer information among all members of a network. The only requirement is that the network must be a TCP/IP network. The APIs are quite "friendly," and they are far less technical than the socket programming of either APPC or TCP.

8.8.1.3 Using RPC Technology

File transfer is just one aspect of re-using application functions. There are other situations where the use of today's server interface (an application's input output panels) is not sufficient.

For instance, if a user needs a small piece of information when a certain event happens, he or she does not want to transfer a large file every time you need only 1 out of three million rows in a table.

A client program is needed to invoke a procedure within the host. Only the results will be sent back to your client program. This can be done in two ways. The old application's panel design can be modified as though the emulator did not exist, then the emulator relay application can be re-programmed to make use of the new functions.

Another way is to go directly to the subroutine level of an existing application. A server interface will have to be built using RPC technology.

Choose the Right RPC Tool

Today, OSF's DCS is the most promising RPC technology because of the wide support it receives from major computer manufacturers and major users. Other RPCs are Sun Microsystems Open Network Computing (ONC) and Netwise's RPC Tools.

To determine the right RPC tool for an organization the host systems and the network transport protocols the host supports must be determined. The RPC tool's network library should be consulted, and the programming languages supported by the tool's network interface definition compiler (RPC Compiler or NIDL compiler). If your environment is not supported by any of the RPC tools that are surveyed, then there really is not much point to pursue this alternative further.

Essential Steps

This is a brief review of the steps required to put a simple procedure accessible from any workstation onto a network.

1. Write the procedure as though it were being written for the same host. For example, write a simple C-program with imbedded SQL calls to your VMS RDB (Digital's relational database manager) to select one row out of a 2-million-row table.
2. Write an RPC network interface definition file which describes the type of machine for the procedure, the arguments it will receive, and several other settings.
3. Let the RPC compiler or the NIDL compiler generate source code that handles the network communications and differences in machine type.
4. Finally, link the generated source code and compile it along with the original code and the network library.

An Illustration

Figure 8–19 shows the interaction between a mainframe computer client program and a mini computer data server. This configuration is likely to occur when an organization decides to let the mainframe to be its data warehouse. Then nightly, the data warehouse application willl be required to poll data from individual application islands.

Figure 8–19 also shows the server interfaces (server and client stubs), the server protocol (network library), and the network transport environment. Note the fact that a gateway would still be required for the network transport environment.

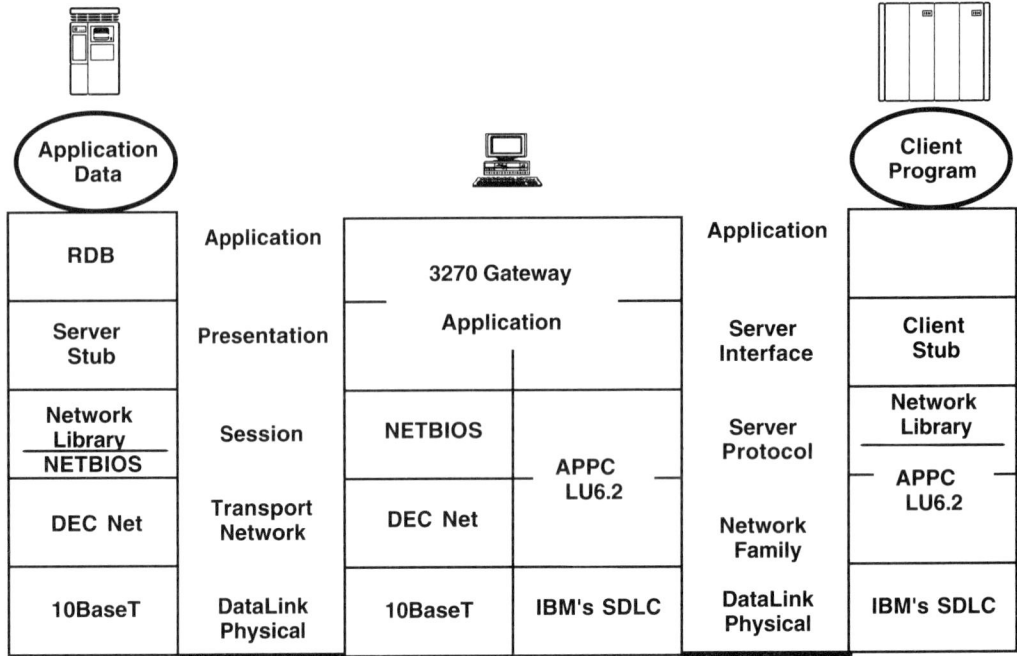

Figure 8–19. Example of an RPC between mainframe and a mini

8.9   STEP 8: ROLL OUT NEW APPLICATIONS

The establishment of a data warehouse will significantly alter the ways by which your new applications will be introduced. This influence will be felt when new application functions are required. It will also change your reporting and off load your host computer.

Many people call this movement as "downsizing" or "rightsizing." These activities are all related. The breaking down of the four barriers requires a gradual but fundamental change in the way we develop our applications, as well as in our use of applications.

Up to this point, we have reviewed the top down and bottom up analysis of data, the data warehouse concept, the network computing platform design, and the integration of the host-based applications. Together, they should help you overcome the barriers that exist for your data integration and data access. However, we still have two more barriers to overcome: data presentation and data analysis.

Data Presentation Barriers

Most host-based application user interfaces are limited by their inability to display graphics and multi-media data. Although many engineering applications have good graphics capability, commercial applications cannot make such a claim.

With client server and workstation technology, commercial data can now be presented in a more intuitive and graphical manner. Workstation technology allows powerful data presentation applications to be most gainfully deployed.

However, this alone is not enough unless these presentation applications can access the vast database on the host and do so in a seamless manner—as though all the host data were right inside the workstation.

Data Analysis Barriers

The barriers on data analysis are twofold. The first is data access. Unless the information can be accessed easily, there is really not much to be analyzed. Client server has a key role in this, as explained in the previous sections.

The second barrier is lack of good modeling tool for commercial business users. In recent years, a new breed of application, known as the executive information system (EIS) or decision support system, is appearing on the market. We review them later in this chapter.

8.9.1 New Development Approach

The significance of the data warehouse lies not only in integrating existing data, but in making data more accessible. It also is an agent of change for future application design.

8.9.1.1 Object-Oriented View

With an established data warehouse, an organization will no longer be tied to a single hardware or software platform in its search for application solutions. You will notice immediately that your system development approach will be data and object-oriented instead of procedural.

When a new application opportunity is identified, the opportunity should be analyzed and positioned properly within the information architecture established earlier. For example, users should first determine the data requirements of an application using their own adopted form of data modeling technique. Then they should match these requirements with that of their information architecture. The result should indicate several things:

- data that are needed by the new application are already captured by an existing application,
- data that are needed by the new application must be captured or generated by the new application, and
- new data that are to be shared by others must be kept in the data warehouse.

Once the net data requirement is determined, functions can be identified around each data entity whether it is a new entity or one that already exists in the data warehouse. Once these functions are identified, an organization can make a decision as to whether it should buy an off-the-shelf package, or develop its own.

With a client server platform and a data warehouse, the organization will have a wide variety of choices. Compatibility will the last consideration in the process. Data and functions should be the focus of any application development. The following is an example to illustrate this point.

8.9.1.2 New Application Islands

A well-designed client server platform frees an organization from the stranglehold of any technology. A platform is truly open when it can pick and choose application packages with little concern about its computer hardware.

For example, the new focus on customer service by senior management requires the organization to keep a better record of its customers' service history. When a customer makes a service call, the organization would like to immediately record when the call was made, what it was about, how it was handled, who it was delegated to, where it was repaired, and so on. The next time the customer calls, the staff will know exactly what has been done with this particular service request.

Senior management wants not only to keep customers happy for individual service calls, it also wants to track various aspects and trends of the service calls to decide on new product design and services—a good example of strategic use of information resources. It happens that there is one such software package available on an IBM AS400 computer.

In the past, organizations might have been hesitant to accept it especially if they are committed to the IBM mainframe or to the DEC mini technologies. They would have recommended forming an application project team to implement the new customer service record management system on the existing host system.

The Technical Side

With a client server platform, users should, however, have no qualm in accepting a ready-made application solution which is more economical than a customized solution.

All users need to do is to "plug" the AS400 into their network (IBM AS400 supports both Ethernet and Token Ring and it as the protocol stack designed for PC known as PC Support protocol—PCS).

Users' workstations need only to be reconfigured to work with a new protocol stack and then they can access this new application through the IBM 5152 emulator program. An application cannot be built any faster and cheaper than that.

The Data Side

The operational requirements of the application have been satisfied. But what about the data? If the information architecture dictates that the customer number must correspond to the number registered with his or her credit card, the customer master must be refreshed daily with the latest data from the data warehouse. This, in turn, gets its data from the credit card online system.

Once again, the client server platform allows easy and automatic file transfers between the AS400 and the mainframe data warehouse using configurations discussed in the previous section.

The above scenario is not unusual. Users' organizations are constantly finding that buying an existing application package is much cheaper than building one internally.

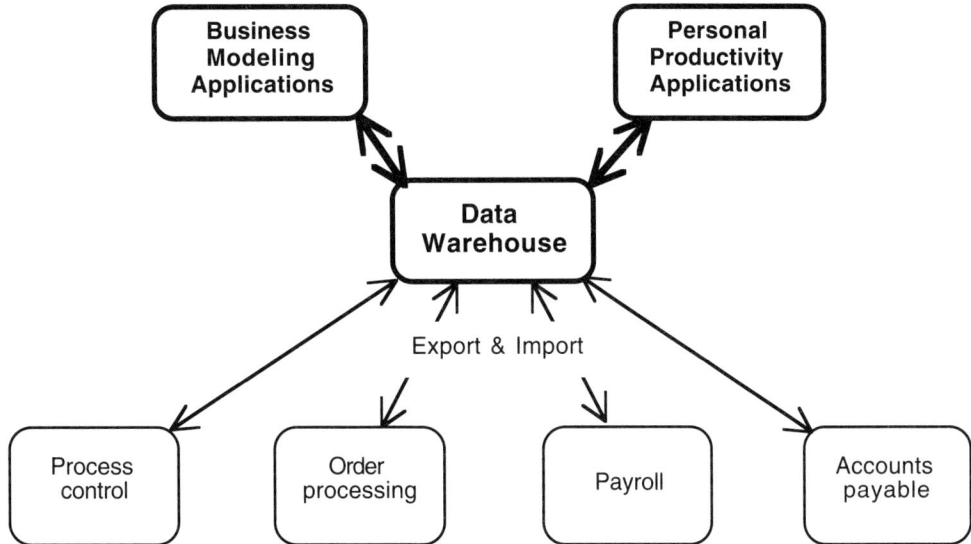

Figure 8–20. Data warehouse as the data hub for decision support and personal productivity applications

8.9.2 Data Warehouse Applications

Once a data warehouse and a complementary client server platform are well established, an organization-wide reporting infrastructure is in place. Most users' information needs should be satisfied by contents of the data warehouse.

If an application island deals with realtime activities, then it should concentrate on those activities. It should not be extended or to perform other non-realtime functions, such as reporting for decision support. A realtime online system should not spend half of its CPU resources generating reports!

Figure 8–20 shows that data warehouses tend to spawn two types of applications: the business modeling applications and the personal productivity applications. A combination of the two is known as the "executive information system" (EIS) or the "decision support systems" (DSS).

For commercial application users, a "true" EIS or DSS application will render better data access, better data presentation, better data analysis, as well as higher data integrity. The word "true" is in quotes because an EIS is not well-defined. Users interested in this technology should ask themselves the questions:

- Does it provide better data access?
- Does it provide better data presentation?
- Does it provide better data analysis?
- Does it provide higher quality data?

The above are the objectives of an EIS. They are not specifications of any particular EIS product. A major difficulty in defining an EIS is that most people are confused with exactly what it is supposed to do (the objectives). The marketing hype from software vendors is not helping either.

No single product can satisfy all the objectives. We should know by now that users must commit to a certain approach of managing their system activities to arrive at those objectives. No single software or hardware product will ever satisfy all of the above objectives.

8.9.2.1 Graphical User Interface

We discussed data integrity and data access in great detail in the last few sections. In this section, we concentrate on the last two barriers to the strategic use of information resources: data presentation and data analysis.

The graphical user interface (GUI) is a product of the microprocessor revolution. It eliminates the need for character-based display terminals. Also gone are reams of paper reports that help to cut down our forests. With it, data can now be made to come alive. Users can be more involved in the exploration of the potential of information resources. Presenting business trends in various types of charts is another advantage a GUI has over dumb terminals.

For those who have worked with the host-based full screen application or application development environment and have had to suffer the endless flipping from one screen to another screen in order to get at the information or to execute a required function, the GUI is a pleasant change.

Multi-Dimensional View

A significant feature that a graphical user interface provides is the multi-dimensional view of business data. In paper reports or in most host based dumb terminal applications, the best that can be done is to present a two-dimensional table. With GUI, through the context-sensitive drill down (or hyper access) method, business data can be presented in a "stereo" manner.

Paper Free World

Today, numerous paper reports generated by customized programs and based on routine operational data are supporting decision support functions. They are not viewed as separate systems, however, because in reality they are extensions of the routine operational systems.

It is easier to simply extend a realtime application than to move it to a data warehouse because there is no client server platform that ties every application island together. The combination of SQL front end and a well-organized data warehouse should reduce the dependence on existing application islands for paper reports and various cut-and-paste paper activities.

The advantages are obvious. The quality of the data will be much better than before. The data can be retrieved much faster than before. The reports will be immensely improved in terms of flexibility and quality of presentation. Also, this is an opportunity to reduce the use of paper, which is good for the environment.

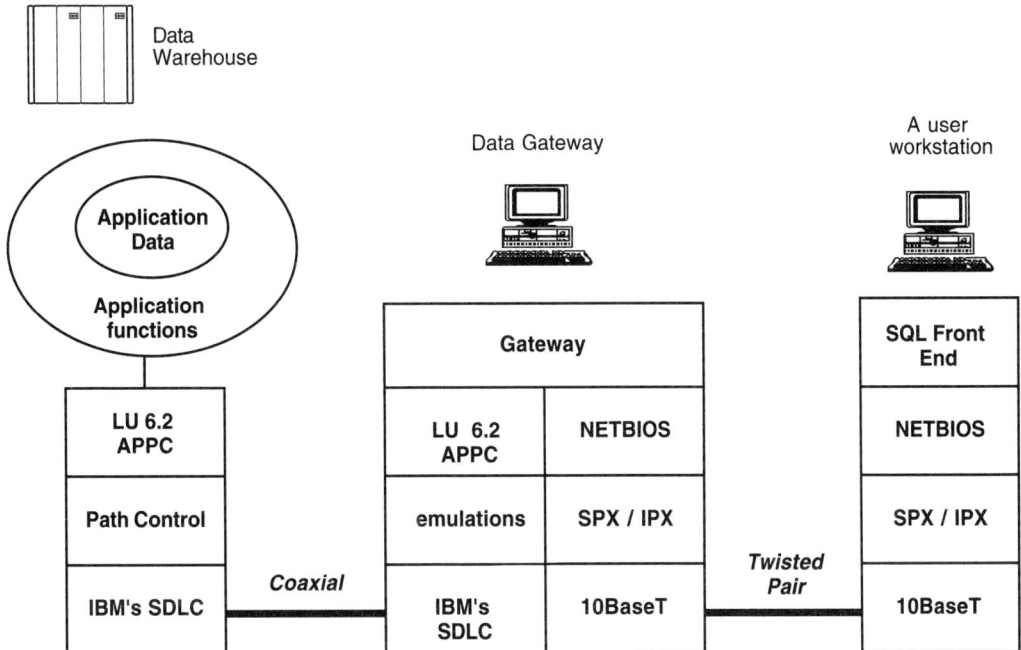

Figure 8-21. Warehouse data presentation

8.9.2.2 SQL Front Ends

Each RDBMS has its own proprietary access language—for example: Borland's Paradox, dBase, Novell's Btreive, or FoxPro, among others. However, a common characteristic among them is their additional support of SQL.

As briefly mentioned in Chapter Seven, a new breed of workstation-based and graphical user interface products known as SQL front ends or Database Editor have emerged. They provide varying degrees of capability for end user to navigate (or some would say "point and click") through data tables in the relational database management systems.

Not only do these front ends provide the navigating capability (which many in the industry calls "slice and dice"), it is also capable of creating SQL programs, designing reports, and even allowing customized user panels.

For example, users can put a map of their country on the screen and point and click on various cities where sales figures will pop up. Further clicking may show the revenue generated by sales persons, projected sales for those cities, or other data.

These tools (e.g. Q+E Database Editor) are easy to use. A good business analyst who is not computer phobic should be able to explore their capability within a few days.

The greatest impact this technology has is in the reduction of programming effort to produce paper reports. Whether it is classified as a programmer's productivity tool or a power end user tool is not important. What is important is that this technology helps both types of user to do their job better.

Examples of the current crop of data presentation applications are Pioneer's Q+E, Borland's Forest and Trees, Channel Computing's Forest and Trees, Omni, Lotus's Monarch, Gupta's SQL Windows, IBM's QMF, IBM's Personal AS, and many others.

From a user's workstation, data in the warehouse can be accessed via the SQL front ends. The front ends can access data in spreadsheets such as Lotus 1-2-3, and Microsoft's Excel database files such as dBase, Novell's Btreive, and ASCII flat files data servers such as Sybase SQL Server, Oracle, Gupta, and Netware SQL and host system such as IBM's DB2, and AS400.

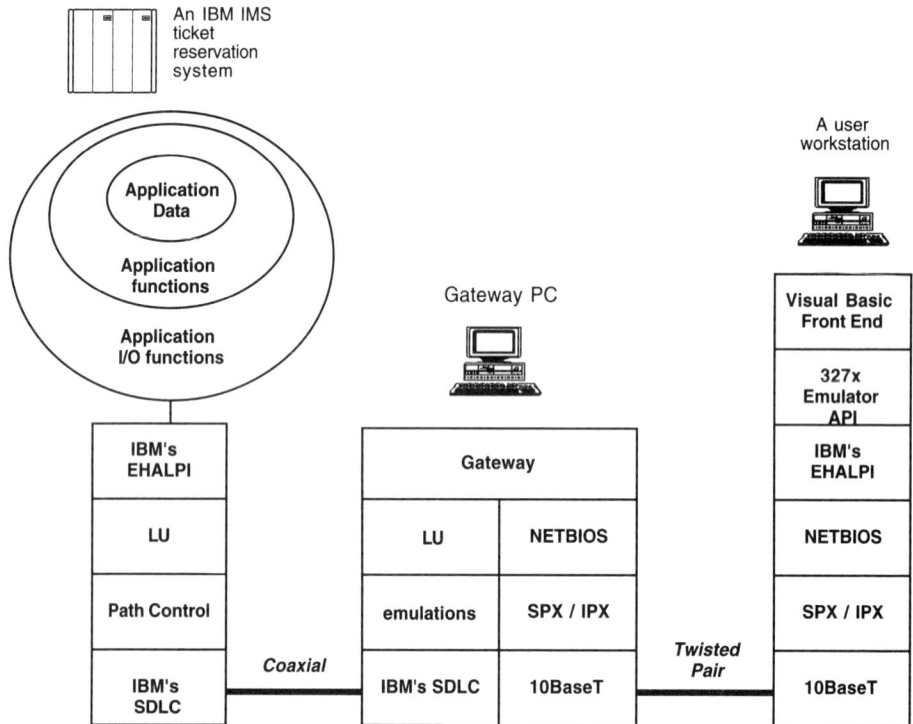

Figure 8–22. Face lift for an old application

8.9.2.3 Face-Lifts

Another favorite data presentation improvement to existing commercial applications is to present their character-based interactive screens using a GUI—in essence, a face-lift.

Figure 8–22 shows one way that this can be done. On the host side, nothing really needs to be changed. As far as the host application is concerned, it thinks that it is still "talking" to a person in front of a 327x screen.

On the client side, the workstation is equipped with a 327x emulator program with IBM's Enhanced Entry Level High Level Language Application Program Interface (EHALLAPI).

In the IBM host, there is also the same EHALLAPI. EHALLAPI is a session layer protocol. The 327x emulator is a Windows-based product capable of Dynamic Data Exchanges (DDE) with a Visual Basic based front end application.

As mentioned in the last chapter on object-oriented programming, Visual Basic is an object-oriented programming environment for Microsoft's Windows application. It is not difficult to put together a simple Visual Basic front end, using its array of buttons, menus, and drill down facilities to turn a dull character-based interface to a user-friendly graphical user interface.

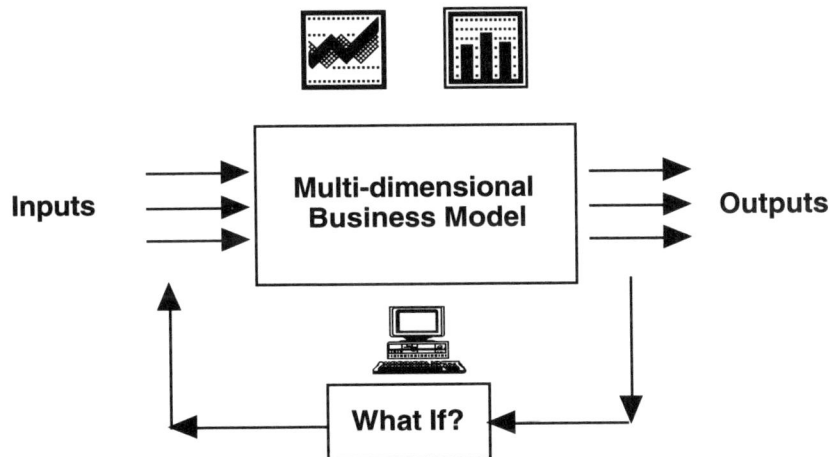

Figure 8–23. EIS Business Simulator

8.9.2.4 Executive Information System

A data warehouse also encourages another type of application known as decision support or executive information systems. These systems simulate commercial business transaction activities allowing the decision makers to ask "what if" questions.

What the decision makers need is a business "model" or a "simulator" through which they can estimate and understand the impact on their business under various scenarios—the dynamics of the business.

Multi-Dimension and Multi-Hierarchy

Commercial processes are multi-dimensional and hierarchical. A typical process is characterized by somebody who sold something to some customer through some distribution channels in some geographic locations to make money.

The model has at least six dimensions: customer, product, distribution channel, geographic location, money, and time. Within each dimension, a hierarchy of groupings usually exists.

For example, in the customer dimension, one can have the individual customers at the bottom of the hierarchy. The next rung represents groupings of these customers by their classes-of-trade. The highest rung represents the total of the classes-of-trade groupings.

Customer	Organization	Product	Geography	Time	Revenue
all	Corporate	all	country		
income groups	Divisions	types	states		
	Department	classes	cities		
customers	Sales	products	areas	mm / yy	dollars

Figure 8–24. Multi-dimensional model

In the Sales dimension, one could have different sales persons at the bottom of the hierarchy. Each sales person belong to a sales department. Each department is managed by a division. A number of divisions form the corporate headquarters.

In the Products dimension, one could have each product belong to a certain class of product. Each class of product belongs to a type of product. At the top of the hierarchy is the total of all products sold.

In the Geographic dimension, one can have cities rolling into states or provinces, states into regions, and regions into countries.

Model Size

The size of a business model is based upon the number of dimensions and the hierarchy groupings of each dimension. The number of possible combinations is the product of all of them—an astronomical number indeed.

For example, in the Customer dimension, if 1000 customers are at the base level, and if these customers can be rolled up to 10 income groups, then that dimension has a total of 1011 elements. In the Corporate Dimension, if 50 sales people are at the bottom, and if these sales people can be "rolled up" to 4 departments and 2 divisions, then the Corporate dimension contains a total of 57 elements. In the Product Dimension, if 30 products are at the bottom of the hierarchy, and if these products can be rolled up to 4 different classes and 2 types, then the Product Dimension contains 37 elements. In the Geographic Dimension, if 10 areas are at the bottom of the hierarchy, and if these areas can be rolled up to 4 different cities and 2 different states, then the Geographic Dimension contains 17 elements.

Now if we consider that two years of monthly data are needed to track the business performance, and we add another 24 elements to the Time Dimension. When we multiply these numbers ($1011 \times 57 \times 37 \times 17 \times 24 = 870$ million), the result represents the total possible number of combinations of the five dimensions that the business model could have with respect to the dynamic of the business.

Theoretically speaking, a marketing planner cannot ask a question about his or her business that is outside of this boundary. This all encompassing model helps the decision support process immensely in many business organizations. This is a very important feature in any so called Executive Information System (EIS). In fact, without such a hierarchical consolidation feature, a product can hardly called itself an EIS. Buyers beware!

EIS and DSS

In engineering, geological, and scientific computing, simulators are not new. Computerized simulators for aircraft, nuclear power plants and the like have been available for many years for the purposes of design testing and training.

Accessing and analyzing timely and reliable data is an important aspect in commercial business analysis. Because of the disjointed nature of most operational systems (application islands), analysts have to chase after seas of report from ten different systems, cut and paste them together, translate them, double checking their accuracy, and so on. It is not a very productive way to quickly spot trends and breakthroughs.

In large companies, the problems are so complex that executives often make decisions based on scanty and inaccurate data because they do not have the right tools. Today, except for some not so easy-to-use ad hoc query facilities attached to the real-time and routine operational systems, practically every new question from management requires a programmer to extract the information from the databases—a time-consuming and always frustrating experience.

Essential Features of EIS

Application programs, known generically as the decision support system or executive information system (EIS), are modeling tools for commercial transactional processes. The term EIS is often used so vaguely that it could mean anything from a SQL front end to a spreadsheet.

In this book, EIS means a modeling tool for commercial business applications. These tools should provide a multi-dimensional database to store the multi-dimensional data as explained earlier.

The multidimensional database is not a relational database. It has its own access language. And of course, these multi-dimensional databases are all proprietary. Most of them, however, do provide bridges to relational databases.

Navigational Front Ends

EIS comes with a powerful navigating front end for an executive to use to explore all aspects of his or her business. These front ends are always GUI: They should have the capability to convert numeric data into charts through the press of a button.

In a decision making process, many questions must be asked and answered. Typically, the next question is not determinable in advance since it will depend on the answer to the current question. The power of these tools lies in its inclusiveness.

The "consolidated" multi-dimensional model contains all the information that an executive could ever ask about his or her business. He can analyze the performance of his business in any way through pointing and clicking. Previously an executive would have required a programmer to extract special views of the database in paper reports for him or her.

The more powerful of these EIS systems also give users the ability to ask "what if" questions about their business model. For example, what is the impact on total revenue of a nationwide chain if a store in Los Angeles is closed? What is the right size of the inventory to produce a rate of return of 12%?

These types of commercial business simulations show that EIS is an ideal tool for executives to use to explore business opportunities. The success of EIS depends on accurate information and easy access to them. A client server platform and a data warehouse are essential for EIS success.

8.10   A NETWORK OF OBJECTS

Figure 8–24 summarizes the meaning of a network of objects. The innermost circle consists of the physical layer circuits. The next circle represents the data link layer that controls the signal flow in those physical circuits. The next circle represents the network and the transport layers that form the network families.

With the three circles, individual computer programs on the network can be identified. Together they provide a foundation for the establishment of a virtual communication circuit for two programs on the network. In the past, this would have been all that is needed for client server to occur. For a network of objects, however, joining two programs is not sufficient. A way must be provided to pinpoint an "operation" within a program.

By elevating network communication to the level of specific operations of a program instead of just a program, we now have, in effect, the true implementation of a network of objects: two software *objects* in communication, instead of two programs. One of the two software objects functions as a server and the other as a client. A server with published operations is an object.

The operation of a server is presented on the network by a server interface, a presentation layer function. A server is accessible by clients through the server communication protocol, or server protocol for short. Any client object can access any server function on the network when it has access within its own computer (the client computer), the "exported" server interface, and the same server protocol.

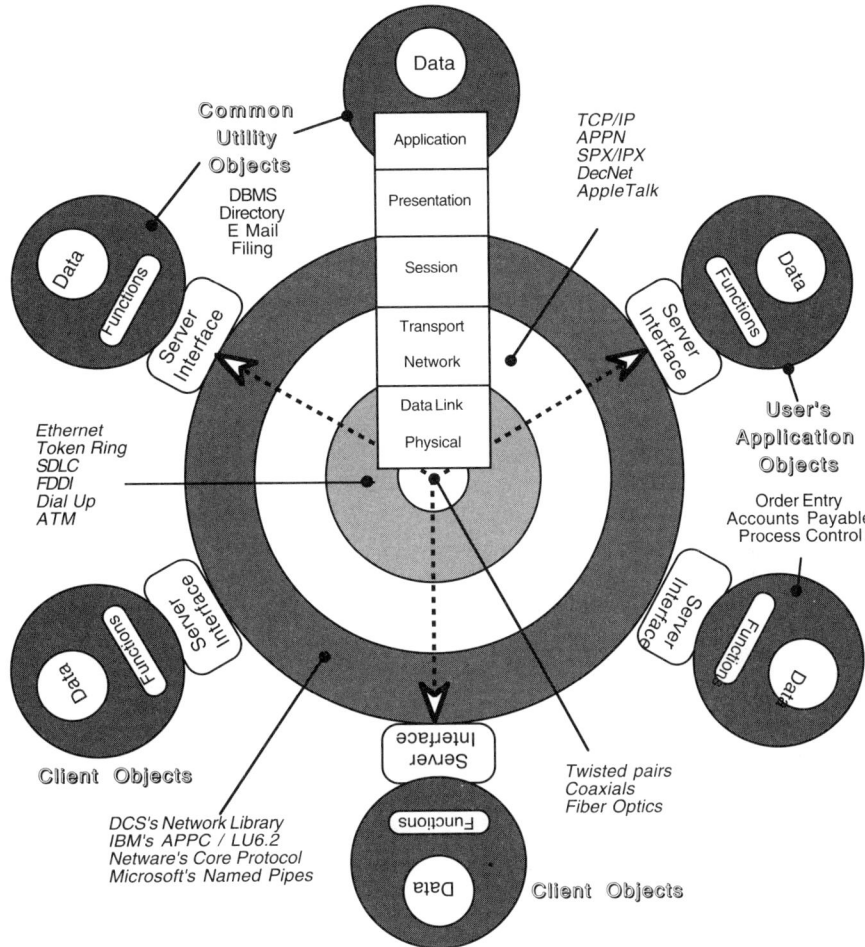

Data

Common
Utility
Objects

DBMS
Directory
E Mail
Filing

Application

Presentation

Session

Transport

Network

Data Link

Physical

TCP/IP
APPN
SPX/IPX
DecNet
AppleTalk

Data

Functions

Server Interface

User's
Application
Objects

Order Entry
Accounts Payable
Process Control

Ethernet
Token Ring
SDLC
FDDI
Dial Up
ATM

Data

Functions

Server Interface

Data

Functions

Server Interface

Client Objects

DCS's Network Library
IBM's APPC / LU6.2
Netware's Core Protocol
Microsoft's Named Pipes

Functions

Data

Client Objects

Server Interface

Functions

Data

Twisted pairs
Coaxials
Fiber Optics

Figure 8–25. A network of objects

If communication throughput and connectivity are sufficient, an application can be distributed to separate buildings, cities, and even continents. As long as the flow of messages continues, and each object performs its task and maintains its information, the application will continue to run smoothly. The advantage of such a system is that an organization can design an application without having to know whether it will be localized or distributed.

A network of objects architecture will allow the easy addition of new application islands, and the integration of the old ones. It helps to preserve yesterday's investment as well as to lower the cost of the new applications.

For many commercial organizations, the barriers of data access, data integration, data presentation, and data analysis can only be overcome with the establishment of a data warehouse built according to the organization's information architecture and with a properly-designed client server platform.

REFERENCES

Atkinson, L. 1990. *Using C.* Carmel, IN: QUE Corp

Booch, G. 1991. *Object-Oriented Design with Applications.* Menlo Park, CA: Benjamin/ Cummings

Chen, P.P. March 1976. *The Entity-Relationship Model - Toward a Unified View of Data.* ACM Transactions on Database Systems

Coad, P and E. Yourdon. 1990. *Object-Oriented Analysis.* Englewood Cliffs, NJ: Prentice Hall

Codd, E.F. 1970. "A Relational Model of Data for Large Shared Data Banks." Communications of the ACM, Vol.13, No.6 (June)

Date, C.J. 1986. *An Introduction to Database System.* Reading, MA. Addison Wesley Publishing Company

Date, C.J. 1986. *Relational Database: Selected Writings.* Reading, MA: Addison Wesley Publishing Company

Druck, P.F. 1991. "The New Productivity Challenge." Harvard Business Review (November-December), pp. 69-79

IBM. 1985. Systems Network Architecture: Transaction Programmers Reference Manual for LU Type 6.2, Document Number GC30-3084-2

IBM. July 1991. APPC and CPIC Product Implementation, Document Number CC24-3520-01

IBM. June 1990. TCP/IP Tutorial and Technical Overview, Document Number CC24-3376-01

IBM. October 1992. DataHub: General Information. IBM Document number GC26-4874

IBM. September 1991. An Introduction to Information Warehousing. IBM Document number GC26-4876

Jamsa, C. 1993. *Rescued by C++.* Las Vegas, NV: Jamsa Press

Martin, J. 1988. *Data Communication Technology.* Englewood Cliffs, NJ: Prentice Hall

Martin, J. 1989. *Information Engineering: A Trilogy.* Englewood Cliffs, NJ: Prentice Hall

McClain, G.R. 1990. *Open Systems Interconnection Handbook*. New York, NY: McGraw Hill

Meilir, P.J. 1988. *Practical Guide to Structured System Design*. Englewood Cliffs, NJ: Prentice Hall

Microsoft. 1992. Microsoft Open Database Connectivity Software Development Programmer's Guide

Mullen, M. 1989. *Object-Oriented Program Design with Examples in C++*. Reading, MA: Addison Wesley

Novell, 1991. *Netware TCP/IP Transport Supervisor's Guide*. Provo, UT: Novell Inc.

Novell. June 1987. Advanced Netware, Theory of Operations (version 2.1) Technical Document

Pierce, J.R. 1990. *Toolbook Companion*. Redmond, WA: Microsoft Press

Rumbaugh, J. 1991. *Object-Oriented Modeling and Design*. Englewood Cliffs, NJ: Prentice Hall

Schatt, S. 1990. *Understanding Local Area Networks*. Carmel, IN: SAMS

Sybase. 1989. Sybase SQL Server (Release 4.0) Product Documentation

Yourdon, E.N. 1979. *Classics in Software Engineering*. Englewood Cliffs, NJ: Prentice Hall

Yourdon, E.N. 1987. *Managing the System Lifecycle: A Software Development Methodology*. Englewood Cliffs, NJ: Prentice Hall

Zdonik, S. 1986. *Language and Methodology for Object Oriented Database Environments*. Proceedings of the 19th International Conference on System Sciences

INDEX